The Intelligent En. ʒ-am

The
INTELLIGENT
ENNEAGRAM

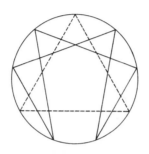

A. G. E. BLAKE

SHAMBHALA
Boston & London
1996

Shambhala Publications, Inc.
Horticultural Hall
300 Massachusetts Avenue
Boston, Massachusetts 02115

9 8 7 6 5 4 3 2 1

First Edition
Printed in the United States of America
⊗ This edition is printed on acid-free paper that meets
the American National Standards Institute Z39.48 Standard.
Distributed in the United States by Random House, Inc.,
and in Canada by Random House of Canada Ltd

Library of Congress Cataloging-in-Publication Data
Blake, A. G. E. (Anthony George Edward)
The intelligent enneagram / A.G.E. Blake.—1st ed.
p.   cm.
Includes bibliographical references and index.
ISBN 1-57062-213-2 (pbk.: alk. paper)
1. Enneagram   I. Title.
BF698.35.E54B57   1996   96-14474
155.2′6—dc20   CIP

No learning can substitute for intelligence, which is a sense of what is real: a sense of one's own being and the presence of the world. The wise imagine what they can see, feel what they can touch and reason about what they experience.

—Stephen Vizinczey, *The Rules of Chaos*

In expressing the laws of the unity of endless diversity a symbol itself possesses an endless number of aspects from which it can be examined and it demands from the man approaching it the ability to see simultaneously from different points of view. Symbols which are transposed into the words of ordinary language become rigid—then, they grow dim and very easily become "their own opposites" confining the meaning within narrow dogmatic frames, without giving it even the very relative freedom of a *logical* examination of a subject.

—Gurdjieff speaking in
In Search of the Miraculous by P. D. Ouspensky

Contents

Part Two: The Hazard of Transformation

Part Three: The Purpose of Transformation

List of Figures

Preface

THE ENNEAGRAM SYMBOL introduced by Gurdjieff near the turn of the century has captivated minds for generations. Some have spent considerable energy in researching its possible origins, while others have turned it to advantage in the expression of their own ideas. As one of many forms of thought that Gurdjieff experimented with, it remains the most powerful and evocative. It is a masterpiece of symbolic art.

Few realize that symbols are more than codifications of profound and ancient understanding; that they are, in their essence, starting points for action in the moment. They make no sense if they are taken as static configurations, residing in an eternity outside of the present moment. When Gurdjieff said that something had been left out of his presentation, without which the symbol of the enneagram could not be understood, I believe he was referring to the action that can initiate uniquely in a human being. Symbols are about the creative work that can unfold in us. Without this action, symbols become part of enculturation, a contribution to sleep.

The enneagram is the tip of an iceberg, the iceberg in its greater mass being the unspoken thoughts of humankind, which are sometimes called the noosphere. It is not a terminus but a starting point. As we enter into it, the enneagram dissolves into an intensity of thought that we can hardly sustain. It is then no different from the Kabbalistic Tree of Life or the Nexus of the *I Ching*. Only, to see this, we have to be able to create our own forms.

It is striking that very few of the reporters and commentators on the enneagram ever remark on the astonishing hypothesis it contains of the interweaving of three octaves or worlds or kinds of action. The result has been a mechanical approach and a defeat of the enneagram's purpose. In its picture of transformation, the enneagram shows how differently natured processes have to build into a perfection. In its picture of discovery, it shows how different kinds of veil have to be progressively removed in order to come to what is essential and true. This relates to the enneagram's foundation in the irreducible idea of cosmoses: of the supersystem, and the subsystem, which form a quantum whole of action.

The quantum whole is number 9 on the enneagram. This divides into the complementarities of 3 and 6. Points 3 and 6 form interfaces dividing and connecting three domains of action. The inner lines express an internal dialogue between the three domains that comes with understanding.

It is easiest to grasp the workings of the enneagram in terms of human enterprise, because we can more easily accept ideas of purpose and intelligence in that realm than we can in the realm of natural processes. For this reason, I have tended to concentrate on human endeavor. However, it remains essentially true that the human being is an exemplar of the whole universe and that what we can find in ourselves is also true of the natural order.

As far as possible, I have related my interpretations of the enneagram to the statements reported of Gurdjieff by his pupil Ouspensky. I believe we have to remain true to the initiatives of such a great pioneer, especially when we depart from them in our own journeys of discovery. I see Gurdjieff as part of an extraordinary incursion of a new order of perception into human life, an incursion that involved art, music, philosophy, science, and literature, as well as the occult. The world in general reacted violently to this influx, and we have suffered wars and chaos as a consequence.

One of the most important emergent ideas of this century has been that of information. This promises to enable us to see the sameness of different phenomena, especially the sameness between human and nonhuman processes. Gurdjieff did not have a concept of information, through it is to be found in his deep intuitions about the significance of impressions. For this reason, his teachings have been relegated to the domain of the occult, when they offered important insights needed for understanding our place in the world. I have taken the three categories of matter, energy, and information as my reference frame. This is to emphasize that Gurdjieff's approach was thoroughly physical, based on the unfolding of real events. His objective science was no arrogant ploy of self-aggrandizement. This science integrates into one whole all that we can gain from looking within with all that we can gain from seeing far into the world "out there." Without the knowing of oneself in the moment, one's understanding is incomplete and misleading. It leads to the absurdities of a Stephen Weinberg seeking the one to explain everything in a world that is meaningless.

In this book, I explore a variety of situations, hoping that one or another of them may evoke some corresponding experience and knowledge in the reader. As I am at pains to point out, the enneagram cannot give us any additional knowledge than what we have already. However, it is capable of changing what this knowledge means. Because of the variety of subjects, my treatment of any one of them is necessarily brief, a mere sketch of the possibilities. I hope the reader who knows a given subject well can fill in the gaps and take the exploration further.

The interpretations used in this book begin from the work of John Bennett. Consequently, there are innumerable references to his ideas that, in many cases, I do not have the space to explain at length. However, I do believe that I have written the book in such a way that the reader can find out what these ideas mean through their appearance in several places. Part of my motive for writing the book, one which is inextricably bound up in my desire to see these ideas laid out so that they can be thought about logically, is to provide a point of access for Bennett's remarkable and creative rendering of what he received primarily from Gurdjieff.

Arnold Keyserling once remarked to me about Gurdjieff: "He invented a different theory every day!" The demonstrative flow of creative imagination which Gurdjieff displayed could only have been turned into a set of dogmas by some determined perversity. When Gurdjieff spoke of people meeting and drawing enneagrams in the sand, an essential part of the picture is that these diagrams will soon be erased, just as in the sand-painting traditions. I hope that my own efforts are not lacking in the humorous spark of inspired invention. What is harder is to convey in a written text is the sense of an ongoing movement of insight in which everything is constantly reevaluated. The only point of this book is to stimulate others to think for themselves and keep on thinking through active dialogue.

This book is written on many levels and from many viewpoints. My personal advice in reading it is to find something that sparks you off and go from there. Otherwise, take the phone off the hook, lay in a store of decent coffee, and plow right through. It is only after you have become reasonably familiar with the book that its form and sequence can be understood.

There are three main parts. The first lays out the background and theory. The second delves into various examples of transformation as enneagrams and the third focuses on the intentional method that it implies. Lines of connection do not follow the outer sequence of the chapters. The whole thing is far too organized and complex for that. So you have to allow yourself to be working through two different kinds of order at the same time. It is the more obscure, relatively hidden order that is important.

The most succinct pieces in the book are: the "Overview," chapter 2; chapter 7, "Four Paradigms of the Enneagram," and the section "Reading the Enneagram" in chapter 19. The reader in a hurry can concentrate on these pieces, but they may not make much sense to you without all the rest.

I use music a great deal in my own studies. Readers might experiment with selecting particular pieces of music for each chapter and see which helps.

The essential features of the enneagram are really universal. I have found them in science, business, myth, and movies. They are locked up in the ancient liturgies. Please remember, however, that the enneagram is not just a model for what we do or study, but an *intent*. It is a stubborn human cry of desire for meaning.

It may well be that there are superenneagrams of even more universal intent. I believe it is so. I feel the very air vibrant with forms of thought which we can hardly begin to draw on. These are the angels of yore who are being transposed into the communities of dialogue in which we may hope to participate.

NOTE: in the text ISM stands for *In Search of the Miraculous* and BT for *Beelzebub's Tales to His Grandson* (*All and Everything:* First Series).

Acknowledgments

The people involved in producing the material of this book are many and various. Foremost among the contributors is the late John Bennett, who taught me that everything is uncertain and that the old absolutes are dead. I acknowledge the inspiration of the science fiction writer Philip K. Dick, representative of a new era of inquiry. The conception of the book is due to Bruno Martin, a friend and my German publisher. Without his stimulus and support, this book would not have been written. I also acknowledge the great debt I owe my wife, Eivor, for providing the conditions in which this work could go forward. And I thank my children for their interruptions!

None of the people listed below, who provided material, criticism, opportunities, support, etc., should be blamed for my shortcomings and mistakes.

In alphabetical order: John Allen, Eivor Blake, David Bohm, Henri Bortoft, Martin Carroll, Charles Clasen, Richard and Susanne Clemens, Simon and Luisa Coxon, Philip K. Dick, David Foster, Robert Fripp, Bob Gerber, Brian Hartshorn, Richard Heath, Anthony Judge, Arnold Keyserling, Vivien Koroghlian, Saul Kuchinsky, Peter Lipson, Peter Marcer, Bruno Martin, Ted Matchett, Steve Mitchell, Bob Ochs, Helen Palmer, Ken Pledge, Ivor Prince, Lynn Quirolo, Carol Roth, Allen Roth, Leslie Schwing, Carolyn Shaffer, Jack and Karen Stefano, Chris Thompson, Jerry Toporowsky, Dr. Edith Wallace, Simon Weightman, John Wilkinson.

The Intelligent Enneagram

Introduction

A PLACE IN TIME

It is useful to look at the enneagram in the historical context in which it appeared. Though it was presented as emblematic of ancient learning, Gurdjieff used it to point his students toward the future. The enneagram emerged as concerned with the organization of complexity—in such guises as goal-seeking, autonomous behavior, and discrete changes of order—and there is a curious sense in which it appears centered on information-processing. This is curious because Gurdjieff did not have the concept of information, especially as it began to develop fifty years later. The enneagram is a very subtle tool, capable of being used at many different levels. We need not remain within the confines of Gurdjieff's own cosmological and anthropological ideas to understand it, but we will use these ideas as powerful illustrations.

Preamble

IT WAS SOMETIME during the years 1915–1916 that G. I. Gurdjieff first spoke to his Russian pupils about the enneagram. But it was not until 1949, with the publication of *In Search of the Miraculous*, P. D. Ouspensky's record of Gurdjieff's teaching, that the symbol and its description were made available to the general public. Other books followed, too numerous to mention, which included some repetition of this original description. Among them were Maurice Nicoll's seminal *Psychological Commentaries on the Teaching of Gurdjieff and Ouspensky* (5 vols., 1952–1956) and Kenneth Walker's popularization *A Study of Gurdjieff's Teaching* (1957). Of even greater importance was the publication in 1950 of Gurdjieff's own masterwork, *Beelzebub's Tales to His Grandson* (*All and Everything:* First Series). This is a truly mythic creation, in which the ideas

1

he first taught to Ouspensky and others in those early days are transformed into new heights.

One of Gurdjieff and Ouspensky's pupils, John G. Bennett, also set himself to clarify and communicate, in a new and more scientific form, the essence of Gurdjieff's ideas. The result was another monumental work, *The Dramatic Universe* (4 vols., 1956–1966). When Bennett told Gurdjieff of his enterprise, Gurdjieff replied that it might help draw attention to his own book. Bennett immediately accepted this. He sometimes said that *The Dramatic Universe* should be seen merely as a set of footnotes to *Beelzebub's Tales* (just as the present book should be seen merely as a set of footnotes to *The Dramatic Universe*). It is a "study of everything," covering natural and moral philosophy, human nature, and history. In it, the enneagram hardly appears; but Bennett said that he used it in the writing and construction of the four volumes. In this book, by contrast, the enneagram is the prominent feature. I use it to explore the "dramatic universe" and how this cosmic drama can inform our lives.

Belief in linear progress has been shattered after a century of terrors. Many of Gurdjieff's once startling and revolutionary ideas—such as "Man has many I's"—have become commonplace and have blended with contributions from psychoanalysis, neurophysiology, and literature. The vision he had of the biosphere as a cosmic entity, and of our place in it, is beginning to find a place within the world of science, mainly because of the emergence of the new sciences of biospherics and complexity. Gurdjieff's ideas are no longer restricted to a narrow "esoteric" culture but have come to coexist and blend with other ideas in the global, though fragmented, consciousness of our information age.

Carrier of a Teaching

Gurdjieff pictured two intelligent strangers meeting in the wilderness and squatting down to draw enneagram symbols in the sand to compare their understanding. Today, all over the world, a surprising number of people are doing something comparable. In the early days, before the material was written up into books, the people who were familiar with the enneagram were relatively few. We can imagine Ouspensky and a few of his colleagues earnestly trying to make sense of the anomalies, drawing the diagram over and over again, and discussing it among themselves. As the ideas of "the Work" were spread, so there were increasing numbers of people who would find themselves having to get up and expound the meaning of the figure to others, discovering, as they did so, new insights coming to the surface. This has made for a very important component in what we might call the chain of transmission of the corpus of Gurdjieff's ideas.[1]

Gurdjieff's scared gymnastics or "movements" were, perhaps, even more important to him than the "ideas." Those who see or take part in these movements are often seized by a sense of a burgeoning insight in their hearts. The movements, in their specific way, can transmit a living image of Gurdjieff's vision of man and his existence in the cosmos. Right up to his death, Gurdjieff continued to work on the movements, so that they were continually in a process of being created.

Gurdjieff completely abandoned the language he used in the Russian period and recast everything into a new mythological form in his own series of writings, begun in the 1920s. if we try to find the "Russian enneagram" in *All and Everything* we have a difficult task, though not an impossible one. The teaching of the enneagram contains all kinds of anomalies, many of which are heightened in the treatment of the laws to be found in *Beelzebub's Tales*. It is working with these that opens the mind in a specific way. The "shadow side" of the enneagram, the aspects in which it does not appear to make sense, are the very places in which insight is possible. In this respect, the enneagram itself is an example of what was called by Gurdjieff a *legominism*: a device created by intelligent people to transmit an insight to future generations by means of deliberate "errors" in its construction.

The "scribbling" of enneagrams that goes on the world today is still connected with Gurdjieff's mission, even when thousands of people doing this may have no idea of the origin of the symbol with Gurdjieff, nor any acquaintance with his teachings as they are written in various books. Many simply have the diagram up on their walls and look at it from time to time. Meanwhile, a kind of research goes on, questioning and investigating the properties of this symbol. This, Gurdjieff himself advised us to do. The enneagram is not something to be taken passively. It is there to be wrestled with much as Jacob wrestled with his angel. Because the enneagram is not personified as many have personified, for example, the Archangel Michael, this does not mean that it does not belong to that level of being. The beauty of Gurdjieff's teaching is that it gets us onto the ground floor of the angelic intelligence.

The wide-ranging appeal of the enneagram is significant. Gurdjieff claimed that it could deal with anything that we might know. It is important that we remember this, because the purpose of the enneagram is connected with its universality.

Gurdjieff and His World

In his time, George Ivanovitch Gurdjieff (1866–1949) had an impact on a great number of intellectuals and artists in Europe and the United States. However, he was born and brought up in the city of Kars in what is now eastern Turkey, studied and traveled widely, and made his public debut as a "teacher" in Russia, in the period just before and during the Bolshevik revolution. He offered a summation or quintessence of certain "ancient knowledge" concerning human existence on this planet, carefully tailored to the rapidly changing conditions of contemporary life. He was not alone in doing this. However, he stood out as a man who appealed to understanding and practicality rather than to belief and romantic speculation.

One of his main contributions to contemporary culture was the establishment of himself as a "paradigm" of what a guru or teacher should be. He imported many practices from the East, where the teacher can exercise overwhelming control over the pupil, in the cultural tradition of "despotism" against which the Greeks fought more than two thousand years ago. A man of powerful and creative contradictions, he set the tone for much that came after him.

Since his death, he has been variously evaluated. Such evaluations tell us more about the people making the evaluations than about Gurdjieff himself. What matters to us is that he put forward a number of very striking ideas and approached the problem of understanding human life within the context of the universe in quite unusual ways. Part of this teaching contained a schematic outline of the structure and working of this universe. Use of this teaching does not require occult leanings, religious feeling, or mystical insight. At the time he was in Russia, the intelligentsia had a fad for Theosophy.[2] Gurdjieff made use of it because it was current in the culture, to attract and communicate with his intended audience.

Many years later, Idries Shah—in order to propagate his version of Naqshbandi Sufism—first approached leaders of the various Gurdjieff groups to recruit support. It is a standard technique in the field. Among his claims, Shah included the enneagram as a Naqshbandi derivative!

Now, decades after Shah's original incursion into England, we find Gurdjieff's symbol of the enneagram replicated in many documents, papers, and books of diverse qualities. It appears not only in the context of various residual followers of his ideas but also in business training, artistic enterprise, religious studies, and other fields. It has been adopted by Oscar Ichazo for his interesting typology, which has proved widely popular. Yet all the explicit teaching about the enneagram occupies only a few pages in Ouspensky's book, *In Search of the Miraculous,* and has a brief mention in the compilation of Gurdjieff's talks, *Views from the Real World.* It is not mentioned by name in any of Gurdjieff's own writings, though it appears in various guises in *All and Everything* and is represented in a number of his dances or movements.

The way in which Gurdjieff presented his ideas was unusual. He introduced them a bit at a time, left many aspects imperfectly defined, and gave out different versions at different times. Gurdjieff's ideas were always "work in progress" rather than the dissemination of some previously established system. Ouspensky, one of his earliest and most gifted pupils, resolutely refused to accept this and believed—until nearly the end of his life—that Gurdjieff had been hiding some complete teaching. Many others were persuaded to this view and spoke among themselves of there being a complete "system."

Ouspensky was pursuing a chimera. One of the tragedies of Western civilization has been the mutual disregard of the esoteric and the scientific. Even in mathematics, there can never be a complete and self-sufficient system. One of Gurdjieff's pupils, John Bennett, was almost alone in accepting the incompleteness of all our schemes of knowledge, of whatever kind. Following this through, he saw that uncertainty was irreducible and that this and only this made intelligence real and significant. His leading idea became that of *hazard,* which is when worlds clash and being can be gained or lost.

Although the distinction is somewhat blurred, we believe that Gurdjieff was essentially concerned not with propagating a system of doctrine but with a method of *active mentation,* a way of utilizing our own intelligence to a certain effect. Gurdjieff could not stand still. He openly declared that he had much to learn and far to go, as Edwin Wolfe reports in his *Episodes with Gurdjieff.* His "confessions" in *Life Is Real, Only Then, When "I Am"* reveal him going through many crises in which his whole understanding of the Work underwent dramatic transformations. This was something even more radical than the changes he made in the way he presented his teachings to others. Also, as Bennett has pointed out, he did experiment and learn from the experience. Many of the techniques he used at the Prieuré (his institute in Fontainbleau where he taught in the 1920s) were later abandoned as he came to understand the Western psyche in more depth.[3] The idea of Gurdjieff as a man with complete certainly is a myth. Gurdjieff's claim was that if he made mistakes in dealing with people, he was able to put them right.[4] At the end of his life, little remained of any systematic set of ideas, and all appeared as an action within the present moment responding to individual circumstance. Whatever edifice he constructed did not contain him. He remained intelligent to the end.

Gurdjieff himself absorbed a certain amount of Western science in his early studies but showed no sign of ever keeping up with the remarkable advances of the first half of the twentieth century. He did not consider this to be his province. Nevertheless, his ideas are broadly speaking in accord with modern views of relativity and uncertainty. In his own way, he was a revolutionary and, in the general historical perspective, a part of that great movement of thought which went through the nihilistic trauma of the breakdown of all classical and inherited systems at the turn of the century.

Nietzsche declared the death of God. Wagner smeared diatonic harmony into disarray. Freud rode the wave of realization that the human psyche was largely an unknown. Oswald Spengler came to regard human history as out of human control. Max Planck reluctantly abandoned firmly held tenets of classical physics and gave birth to quantum theory. Out of all these and similar undoings came the struggle to form a new vision. But the vision was multiple and complex. In philosophy, thought bifurcated into a polarity of absolute freedom in existentialism and absolute mechanism in logical positivism. In music, Arnold Schönberg developed a structural approach to master the chaos he had helped to release.

Meanwhile, Europe plunged itself into a mad war and Russia into violent revolution. It was a time that Gurdjieff would call *soolionensius,* a period of "planetary tension," arousing in people a thirst for freedom and direct experience that they could never satisfy through their idealistic fixations and tendency to violent revolution. Gurdjieff centered himself on the burning question: What is the purpose and significance of life on earth and human life in particular?

A battle was in progress behind the outward and meaningless struggles. This was a battle to establish some kind of new order in the emerging chaos of human life. The totalitarian states that emerged were evidence of a profound failure of understanding. Fascism was an attempt to enforce a rigid view of order, vying with communism for the destruction of meaning and the curtailment of transformation. Under all totalitarian regimes, freedom in art and science and religion was suppressed. Gurdjieff saw this as merely an expression of something that had always been in force in every epoch. Like many men of wisdom and compassion, he keenly felt the horror of truth giving way to force, and in his vision of history, the essential insights into the human condition were always in process of being lost and then only partially regained, over and over again, making any notion of overall progress suspect, even absurd.

In a time of soolionensius, of general planetary tension, while the greater majority would succumb to a kind of collective psychosis, there were opportunities for the relatively few to wake up to the human situation and gain something objectively good for themselves. This is an example of *hazard* on a planetary scale.

Just when we entered the era of uncertainty, the world split into retrogressive forces seeking to impose an imaginary certainty on reality on the one hand, and adventurous spirits on the other, seeking a totally new kind of mind capable of being in tune with changing reality. The former tend to impose their view on other people and as many as possible, while the latter tend to work on themselves. The battle continues, as we face the ever more reactive forces of fundamentalism and tribalism.

Just as Freud began to peer into the dark corners of the human psyche and Schönberg to foster the "liberation of dissonance" in music, Gurdjieff undertook an exposé of the then-current suppositions about the collective accumulation of knowledge of the human condition.

Thus, when he entered the public arena in the wake of Theosophy,

Gurdjieff presented himself as a new harbinger of ancient teachings. The-osophy can be considered unfounded and rampant speculation, but it was also a valiant attempt, over a very wide spectrum of approaches, to draw within one coherent compass an explanation of the human condi-tion and the range of human possibilities. It was also, we might say, an attempt to replace the terror of the "empty infinite spaces" felt by Pascal with something more encouraging. Theosophy, like many other occult movements, preserved a sense of meaning on a cosmic scale that was being lost in the general culture. Many artists such as Kandinsky and Mondrian found their inspiration in its teachings and held visionary no-tions of educating society to see and feel in a more integrated and mean-ingful way. It is usually the case that occult movements become strong in times of general distress and decay simply because they are needed as carriers of basic and important values that are in danger of being lost.

Theosophy was becoming absurd with its myriad schemes and doc-trines, hierarchies of masters, cycles of human evolution, "rays" of differ-ent natures, and so on. Its accommodation to physical science was becoming outmoded. However, many intellectuals, particularly in Russia as well as in England, were still greatly attracted to it while, it must be remembered, others of their contemporaries were becoming addicted to Marxism. It was into this milieu that Gurdjieff made his "descent." The culture of the time was already impregnated with ideas of "superhuman-ity" and the possibility of someone of a "higher order" descending into the marketplace to teach the people.[5] This Nietzschean idea has now de-volved into hunting mysterious shamans in third world countries, after passing through Himalayan masters (post-Theosophical) and Middle Eastern "powerhouses." The whole question of higher beings, guidance of humanity, secret influences, centers of spiritual power, gurus, and so on, was being experimented with and yet hardly debated throughout the century. Each culture, perhaps each generation, projects its own myths of the "wise ones," the "seers."

However, in some major respects, Gurdjieff's mission appeared to have been to bring people down to the nitty-gritty of human life and the inti-mate details of the functioning of their mechanisms, and to eradicate the spurious associations which had accrued from Theosophical excess. He advocated an experimental, reasoned approach to inner phenomena and the questions of personal development. Setting the scene for a kind of underground tradition, he turned the tables on expectations and often seemed, to ordinary eyes, to be radically *un*-spiritual.

In the story entitled "Glimpses of Truth," Gurdjieff claims that the Great Knowledge he is representing is "more materialistic than materialism."[6] In *In Search of the Miraculous* we see him (through the eyes of Ouspensky) building up a new vision of the universe and humanity's place in it in which everything is material. Thoughts are material. The emanations of God are material. A human being is a device playing a role in the functioning of the solar system. Angels are a cluster of what he calls "hydrogens." Using elements of nineteenth-century science, and the German tradition of *Kraft und Stuff* (force and matter), he puts forward a cosmology that is austere and gives the appearance of rigor. He insists that everything he teaches about the human psyche has to be verified by each person in his or her own experience and that every idea he puts forward has to be thought through.

People want to know: Where did he get his material? He himself spoke of sojourns in special monasteries, of the researches of a group he called Seekers of the Truth, and of becoming able to "read" certain relics or "messages" (legominisms) from wise people of the past. There have been many who have attempted to trace his sources, who have traveled and studied widely. Antecedents for particular ideas and formulations can be found—in Sufism, Christianity, Zoroastrianism, Buddhism, and so forth—but the central unity and coherence of them remains elusive. The critical sources have not been found. We ourselves do not know how he derived his ideas. In a sense, they are more than ideas, because they claim a connection with an "intelligent energy" (similar to the *baraka*, or "grace," of the Sufis) to which we need to find an access.

In putting forward his ideas, Gurdjieff could always claim that they had been preserved from ancient times. This has a strong appeal because few of us can fail to feel that important insights came to people in the past which have now been lost or covered over by more recent ones. Perhaps we are in awe of those first people who spoke, who thought, who painted, who observed the stars, who made irrigation canals, who built the pyramids, who first connected cause and effect. Our present-day technological wonders are built on fundamental breakthroughs that were made tens of thousands of years ago; but we can recognize that as we take in new information we lose contact with what came before. A truly historical sense is lacking in most people. Both in space and time, human culture is fragmented and dislocated. Because of this, Gurdjieff claimed that "there is no progress whatsoever." Every advance is canceled out by an equivalent loss.

Living in our present time, we are encapsulated in it. All the same, we now have access to material of the past which vastly exceeds in quantity and range any that was available in any preceding era. Yet it is one thing to have the data and quite another to understand what they mean. We still argue about the state of mind in which early people erected the great megalithic structures such as Stonehenge, or created the wonderful works of art discovered in ancient caves. We are like characters wandering at night from lamppost to lamppost. As we enter the circle of light from one lamp, we become blind to what is under the other lamps. The immediate light enhances the greater darkness.

Gurdjieff was inspired by the possibility that real insights that had arisen in the past could have been transmitted unscathed into modern times. There are hints of this in the sacred books of the world, in which we can glimpse the operation of technique of information transmission which have many parallels with those of modern information technology. Such techniques extend into sacred rituals, which Gurdjieff understood as "recapitulations," designed to reenergize precisely designed memories of real and important events, or discoveries of the "laws of world creation and world maintenance." He grasped that these techniques would have to involve "self-corrections" which could take account of the inevitable distortions made in the communication over time. We may think of the way that compact discs contain features that correct for errors in the reading of what is recorded on them. One of the most important techniques used in the sacred books of the Bible, such as Genesis or the Gospels, is the repetition of the same story in more than one version. This technique was used by Gurdjieff himself in his own teaching and writings. The very differences and apparent contradictions we find are in fact the key to understanding what he wanted to communicate.[7]

The material for understanding is available, if only we can read it. What does it take to be able to read? It is no easy thing. Even the ordinary reading which we presume to have acquired—that is, the capacity to register both what is said and the structure within which it is expressed—is, in fact, quite rare. Gurdjieff himself told Ouspensky: "A great deal can be found by reading. For instance, take yourself: you might already know a great deal if you knew how to read" (ISM, p. 20).

At a later date, he explained: "I will prove to you afterwards that *knowledge*" (he emphasized the word) "is far more accessible to those capable of assimilating it than is usually supposed; and that the whole trouble is that people either do not want it or cannot receive it" (ISM, p. 37).

We can see that the assimilation of insights that have arisen in the past requires a great compression of data, something similar to the modern concept of a compression algorithm. This is an action which is at the very heart of history. It cannot be achieved in a linear fashion. It belongs to a somewhat different mode of intelligence than the one we are used to. This means that the prevalent attitude of "The latest is best" has to be superseded. Gurdjieff expresses his scorn through the words of Beelzebub: ". . . is it not the same to the contemporary beings of planet earth what ancient savages did?" (BT, p. 389).

Besides the importance of diverse cultures in time, there is the equal importance of cultures in space. Gurdjieff lived in a part of the world which was a melting pot. He was poised between East and West, Europe and Asia. Nomadic people still wandered over frontiers. His formal education came from Russian culture, which he was able to contrast with what he learned from his father and the variety of people around him. Russia itself has always been poised between Europe and Asia, but bending more toward Europe—a tendency which contributed to preserving turbulence in the character of that region, an area sometimes still called the "shatter plane" of Eastern Europe.

Russian culture is of great significance in understanding Gurdjieff. There was in Russia, for example, a particular scientific school, the "cosmocists," whose members made several major contributions to twentieth-century thought. Up until recent times, however, its contributions have been largely unknown, neglected, or not properly appreciated by the West. In this school we can place three individuals who, while we cannot claim they directly influenced Gurdjieff, undoubtedly paralleled him. Gurdjieff himself was able to "use the energy of the time" and cannot be considered to be an isolated and completely idiosyncratic thinker. This does not mean that there was any meeting together to consciously develop a new program of thought. Something was spontaneously *emerging*.

Speaking chronologically, the first in our group of three cosmocists is

Dimitry Ivanovich Mendeleyev (1834–1907), who was mainly responsible for creating the periodic table of elements, which appears in today's chemistry textbooks much as it did when it was first published in 1869. Mendeleyev's discovery of the periodic law of elements was an astonishing achievement and formed the bridge between chemistry as it had developed in the nineteenth century and the discoveries of atomic structure in the twentieth century. There is little doubt that Gurdjieff aligned his early language of hydrogens, atoms, and octaves with Mendeleyev's work. It is, indeed, extraordinary that we find the term *octaves* used in describing the progression of the elements from the lightest to the heaviest.[8]

The second in the group of three is Konstantin Tsiolkovsky (1857–1935), known as the father of space travel. At the turn of the century, he wrote: "Earth is the cradle of mankind, but one cannot live in the cradle forever." He was already visualizing what would be needed to take humankind off the planet and settle on other worlds. These were realistic appraisals beyond the scope of a fantasist such as Jules Verne. In this light, it is not so surprising that Gurdjieff set his magnum opus, *Beelzebub's Tales,* on a spaceship.

The third character is an almost exact contemporary of Gurdjieff's. He is the biogeochemist Vladimir Vernadsky (1863–1945), father of biospherics. He was one of the first to grasp that life on earth had utterly transformed the state and distribution of matter on the surface of the earth. He recognized that life was an active force on the surface of the planet, and arose and developed as a cosmic entity. His vision encompassed life as a transmitter of the energy of the sun to work upon the earth. His main work on the biosphere, published in both Moscow and Paris, was written about 1926, much the same time as Gurdjieff was working on his own book. It is possible that Vernadsky met with Pierre Teilhard de Chardin in Paris and that both acquired the notion of the noosphere (the sphere of mind) from the philosopher Édouard Le Roy, who was a student of Henri Bergson. The idea is that the noosphere will develop out of the biosphere through the evolution of mankind.

The ideas of Vernadsky may not have been studied by Gurdjieff himself, but they were certainly studied by his followers, including Maurice Nicoll and John Bennett. Indeed, the currently available, though abridged, English translation of his book, *The Biosphere,* derives from a translation made by the cybernetician David Foster (who studied with

Gurdjieff, Ouspensky, and Bennett). This translation passed from hand to hand until it was published, as a key text, by the pioneers who built Biosphere 2 in Arizona in 1991, who were themselves deeply influenced by the ideas of Gurdjieff and Bennett.[9]

There are other scientists who could be mentioned—such as Famastin, Mereschkovskii, and Kozo-Polianski—who, a century before Western scientists woke up to it, recognized the importance of symbioses for evolution. In brief, the Russian cultural milieu was full of ideas of an ecology on a grand scale in both space and time. Gurdjieff's idea of "the reciprocal maintenance of everything existing" emerges naturally from this background.

Gurdjieff was Russian in his feel for the land. It is not surprising that, when he talks about what he calls "mentation by form," he says that this kind of mentation derives from our contact with the landscape around us and is organic to our being. This kind of mentation is contrasted with "mentation by word," which Gurdjieff regarded as superficial and relative, being an entirely cultural artifact divorced from the structure of the world. In mentation by form, we have a contact with ourselves and with the physical world in which we actually exist. It is this which enables us to have access to what we might call cosmic information, and Gurdjieff's "First Series" of writings, called *Beelzebub's Tales,* concerns this access.

Beelzebub's Story

The main character of Gurdjieff's *Beelzebub's Tales* is Beelzebub himself, the "false god" of the Babylonians, reviled by the Jews in the period of their captivity. In this way, Gurdjieff made it plain that he would not be conforming to established modes of thought or entrenched beliefs. He was also alerting us to the fact that a great deal of his inspiration was drawn from Mesopotamian civilization. In conversation, so Bennett tells us, Gurdjieff often referred to the Tikliamishian, or Sumerian, culture as the highest ever reached by humanity.[10]

The book's main title was originally the more extravagant *All of Everything.* Because Beelzebub is also Lucifer, the fallen angel, we might well surmise that this was Gurdjieff's answer to Goethe's Faust, who seeks his All in the Nothing of Mephistopheles. The regard which Gurdjieff affords this devil may surprise the average Christian, Jew, or Muslim, but there is a tradition for such reverence. It can be found in the writings of the Sufi Hallaj. Beelzebub was at one point an attendant on His Endlessness Himself, but then Beelzebub "interfered in what was none of his business" (BT, p. 52). Expelled for being a misguided revolutionary, he is exiled to our solar system. It is here that he finds the answers to the burning questions which obsess him.

Beelzebub feels passionately that the design of the universe, even though it stems from God Himself, is illogical. In the course of his exile, he does not simply become a reformed character, ultimately receiving a pardon from on high for the sins of his youth. Over centuries, he studies the "strange three-brained beings of the planet earth" and comes to understand that the universe is subject to uncertainty and hazard. He sees that it is for this reason that freedom and compassion are possible. What he comes to understand proves to have such significance that it is transmitted right up to the sacred individuals residing on the planet Purgatory, the place of residence of the most advanced souls in the cosmos, saints of old who still need to evolve, eagerly awaiting his latest discoveries. It is tempting to see Gurdjieff portraying himself as Beelzebub—exiled as he was in Europe, away from Asia, and, as he often hinted, sending messages (and even people) back to his "elders" in the Middle East.

In the course of the book every kind of idealism and liberal concept is attacked. Idealism is treated as the refuge of the arrogant and ignorant and not as a virtue at all. Every single dominant world-idea, such as "good and evil," is turned upside down and shaken violently. What builds up through the book is an extraordinary vision of God as Source of Reality: our Endlessness, our Common Father—even, at times, a *suffering god.* No précis can even begin to do justice to what Gurdjieff achieved, and I shall not even try.

But one important component of Gurdjieff's mythology must be mentioned. He says that after "men," or beings capable of awareness of self, first arose, there was a cosmic accident due to a mistake on a higher level. Higher intelligences then concluded that to correct for their mistake they should use men simply as devices for producing a certain energy. However, they realized, if men became aware of this ignominious servitude, their sense of significance of self would have been so outraged that they would have killed themselves. To prevent this, an organ called *kundabuffer* was installed, specifically designed to distort their perception: *men were no longer capable of seeing reality.* When the need for this arrangement had passed and the organ had been removed, the artificial environment which men had created for themselves (or "culture") had become so imprinted with this distorted perception that its defects were perpetuated from generation to generation.

Beelzebub's researches on earth convince him that people continue to suffer from this now self-inflicted malady. The "consequences of the organ kundabuffer" that continue to plague humanity result from a disconnection between will and perception. In order to begin to break free from its sway, people have to be totally disillusioned. Flying through the universe toward his destiny, Beelzebub regales his grandson, Hussein, with stories of his various descents onto our planet. In doing so, he explains the origin of the universe and its further development through later ensuing crises. This in turn is shown in the light of basic laws.

Gurdjieff's laws all concern the mutual relevance of part and whole. In a particular sense, they describe the relation between God and man, or the *perfecting of the part within the whole.* However, this is dramatic and uncertain: even the dwelling place of God was once vulnerable to time! In some ways, the greatest power represented in Gurdjieff's mythology is the *Merciless Heropass,* probably derived from the Zoroastrian *Zurvan,* or "infinite time."[11] Later, Bennett was to take up the theme of dramatic history as "the war with time." In many ways, as we shall see, the enneagram is a cipher for the "secret of immortality," or the overcoming of time, that same secret which eluded Gilgamesh, the Sumerian hero, because he fell asleep.

Intelligence

If, as Alexander Pope says, "the proper study of mankind is man," then equally the proper study of intelligence is intelligence. If we use the singular term *intelligence,* this is not to assert that it *is* singular. It appears in all domains of human life and experience and cannot be reduced to a single definition, such as the power of solving problems. We find intelligence in ecstasy as well as in decision-making, in play as well as in calculation. When we deal with the world, or when we *work* in the world, the various modes and organs of intelligence engage in different ways. The *operations* that we do change according to the nature of the task. In the workings of intelligence there is very much to understand. We can sense and feel intelligence in what we do, but for most of the time, we do not grasp how it works, nor do we know how or why it changes in its operations.

When we come to discuss the structures and operations depicted through the enneagram, it will be useful to remember that we are looking at our own intelligence in operation, which is *how we engage with the world intentionally*. It was somewhat disastrous for Western thought that the idea of intentionality became attached to mental consciousness and lost the connotation of *physical work*.[12]

Intelligence seems diverse. But this is not a simple multiplicity of parts—essentially for the reason that every facet of our intelligence can communicate, to some degree, with every other, which has led many to picture our intelligence as a *community* of partial intelligences. The whole of humanity can also be seen as a community of loosely coupled intelligences. As with our own personal intelligence, there is only a partial communication among its members.

The historical development of human intelligence—in language, society, invention, and discovery—has led to a kind of loneliness for the human being amid all the other manifestations in existence. The twin symptoms of this are that the human being has become divorced from the rest of organic life and also feels alienated within a cold and indifferent and vastly meaningless universe on the larger scale. We may credit other life forms with some kind of intelligence, but those who believe in the continuity of intelligence throughout evolution tend to take the position that human intelligence is no more significant than that of a microorganism. Equally, the planets, stars, and galaxies of our universe are regarded as the dying embers of the primal creation, totally removed from any possibility of intelligence.

From the perspective of human intelligence in isolation, all our purposes and values must appear as fictions, created to make life interesting or tolerable. We witness this in full force today as humankind acts as if in the grip of some global cult of humanity, with all of the worst excesses to which cults are prone. If there is no equivalent intelligence in the rest of life on earth, nor in the heavens above, then there is nothing that can serve either as guide or companion besides the things of our own invention.

We have been divorced from a sense of connection with life and the cosmos *because of* our own intelligence. For more than a thousand years we have been brought ever more sharply into *the world of fact*. Because of this new experience of fact, we humans were subject to two profound shocks. First there was that "terror of the vast, infinite, empty spaces," as Pascal described when, for the first time, it became evident that the structure of the real universe was not at all a divine invention embodying the same values that we hold dear. Second was the discovery of vast aeons of change—in geology and in organic evolution—during which we and our world developed from distant and alien beginnings. It then seemed that our connection with the rest of things might only be through the smallest details and an accumulation of accidents.

The mechanisms and the contingencies which are now evident in the physical world stand in contrast with the sense of freedom and purpose that our own intelligence conveys to us. It seems impossible to comprehend these two perspectives within a single view, even though it was due to our own intelligence that we came to discover the scope of mechanical and contingent forces.

One of the properties of intelligence is its capacity to discover what we call *mechanisms*. It finds them everywhere it looks—including in itself! It may even invent or produce mechanisms for its own functioning. This is very apparent in mathematics, where the creative steps result in precise formulations and rules which can, in principle, be operated mechanically. It appears that intelligence is capable of producing mechanisms which, to some degree or in a certain fashion, imitate or duplicate its own functioning. Artificial intelligence has been foreseeable since the very beginnings of engineering.

However, this does not mean that intelligence *is* mechanical. The general argument against mechanical intelligence has been made by many, including the English mathematical physicist Roger Penrose.[13] It proposes that no mechanism such as a Turing machine (or computer) can, even in principle, resolve certain questions which are perfectly transparent to us. Perhaps a more telling point is the one made by the Polish science fiction writer Stanislaw Lem, who wrote that if we managed to create a truly self-conscious machine, we would find that it had no more idea about the nature of consciousness than we have![14] Whatever the scope of the mechanisms that we produce, there is always something left out, or we are already seeking beyond its range *in response to another purpose.* If this were not so, we would cease to be intelligent.

In 1931, the great Czech mathematician Kurt Gödel showed that no mechanism (or formal system) can be complete and self-consistent in itself.[15] Put very simply, behind every explicit mechanistic scheme there is always something implicit which does not obey the same rules. This is why the idea of playing a game has such universal application. The rules are fixed, but the game only works if there are players with characters and motivations: the rules of the game are obeyed, but there are always at work more subtle, psychological, and implicit "rules" of another order. David Bohm expresses it in this way: ". . . the possibility of going beyond any specific level of subtlety is the essential feature on which the possibility of intelligence is based."[16]

This gives us the glimmerings of an idea that intelligence involves the co-working of different orders of reality. To say this is to say a great deal. It already anticipates the logic of the enneagram. It implies that there is a structure to the world in which intelligence itself is integral.

Intelligence, in its broadest sense, is as general a feature of the world as matter or energy. It is the function that connects two aspects of *information.* The first aspect is information as data, the "given," where it appears as something passive. The second aspect is information as instructions, or "commands," where it appears as something active. The two connect in intelligence as *meaning.* This does not ensure that the universe is divinely ordained or masterminded. Intelligence comes into operation subject to conditions: it cannot override the fixed relations of matter and energy, which relations are part of the informational universe and so cannot be asserted and denied simultaneously. As we have seen, intelligence is inoperable without mechanism, even though it transcends all mechanisms. How can a game be played if there are no constraints?

Intelligence involves both ends and means. The question "What *ought* to be done?" is a real one and wreathed in uncertainty. Intelligence is a combination not only of awareness and function, but of a *will* or *wills* also. In this respect, the question of higher intelligence—meaning an intelligence stronger or more coherent than that in a human mind—is relevant. We can picture to ourselves a chain of intelligence in which the *ends* of one link become the *means* of another, interleaved as it were.

A lower intelligence cannot understand a higher intelligence—that is, comprehend its vision and purpose—but this does not mean that the two intelligences cannot communicate. The higher intelligence can provide artificial means to bridge the gap. Artificial means appear in human life in the form of symbols and myths, sacred images, and so on, but they may also be inherent in some of the sciences that have developed. Both the enneagram and information theory fall into this category. The word *angel,* which means "messenger," depicts the higher intelligence in its mode of communicating with the lower realms. In cold-blooded terms, this means a device which translates from a higher-dimensional world into a lower-dimensional one. Put in this way, we can begin to appreciate that the phenomena of both science and religion have much in common.

Relative to the higher level, the lower level would appear to be "unconscious." This is at first difficult to grasp, since we consider our kind or degree of consciousness to be ultimate. The ordinary distinctions we make between ourselves and others cannot strictly apply in our relations with a higher intelligence. That is why we find tradition depicting higher intelligence sometimes as the higher powers of the mind and sometimes as consisting of another order of beings.

The possibility of communication between levels is also the possibility for intelligence to *evolve*. In the context of human existence: intelligence breaks free of biology in the form of mind; and it is in process of breaking free of mind in the form of something else again. This, I believe, is the implicit message of the enneagram.

Notes

1. There is an old saying: "He who teaches, learns." Gurdjieff insisted that initiation into the "esoteric circle" was only possible if we had brought at least seven people up to our own level. This is not so easy as it sounds. We are fortunate to find one person who is able to learn.
2. Theosophy was initially associated with the work of A. P. Sinnett and Helena Blavatsky (the latter an outrageous and intriguing figure in her own right).
3. See the chapter "Djartklom" in J. G. Bennett, *Talks on Beelzebub's Tales.*
4. Bennett reports in his autobiography, *Witness,* an incident in which Gurdjieff was psychologically tearing a young man apart. In the middle of his outburst of concentrated fury, Gurdjieff turned to Bennett and calmly pointed out that, if he was making a mistake and the young man was damaged, he would be able to make repairs.

5. Cf. Nietzsche's *Thus Spake Zarathustra*.
6. Published in the collection *Views from the Real World*, p. 21.
7. See the section "Legominism" in chapter 11.
8. This concept was first introduced by the English scientist J. Newlands. See John Knedler (ed.), *Masterworks of Science*, vol. 2, pp. 203–4n.
9. See J. Allen *Biosphere 2: The Human Experiment*, ed. A. G. E. Blake. Unfortunately, a true account of this experiment has yet to be written.
10. J. G. Bennett, *Talks on Beelzebub's Tales*, p. 25.
11. See Robert C. Zaehner, *Zurvan*.
12. Simone Weil escaped this trap, as is shown in her study of Descartes. See her *Formative Writings 1929–1941*.
13. In Roger Penrose, *The Emperor's New Mind*.
14. In Stanislaw Lem, *Microworlds*.
15. Kurt Gödel, "On Formally Undecidable Propositions of Principia Mathematica and Related Systems."
16. David Bohm and B. J. Hiley, *The Undivided Universe*, p. 385.

PART ONE

THE FRAME OF TRANSFORMATION

· 1 ·

The Symbol

The idea of laws of the universe is very grand, and initially it is difficult to see how a few lines scratched in the sand, or on a sheet of paper, can have much to do with cosmic realities. Actually, in some ways, the grander the vista, the simpler the depiction. At the heart of every attempt to make sense of things is a form, abstract or concrete, which is the glyph, the key, which lets you into the whole system. In Sufism, it is sometimes called the naqsh, *or design. Physics has something similar in, for example, the Feynman diagrams. In the same way, the enneagram is a key, a form of insight—but, into what?*

The Diagram

JUST BEFORE the outbreak of the Bolshevik revolution, Gurdjieff introduced his Russian pupils to the symbol of the enneagram (fig. 1.1). It has not been found in any document from before that time. The symbol is

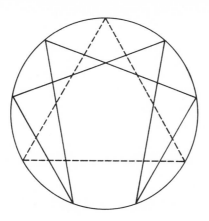

1.1. The enneagram symbol.

23

elegant, even beautiful. It is little wonder that it remains the main icon of the Gurdjieffian schools. Ouspensky reports Gurdjieff as saying: "All knowledge can be included in the enneagram and with the help of the enneagram it can be interpreted. And in this connection only what a man is able to put into the enneagram does he actually *know,* that is understand. . . . *Everything* can be included and read in the enneagram." At the same time, he claimed that the symbol as he gave it "is only in an incomplete and theoretical form of which nobody could make any practical use without instruction from a man who knows" (ISM, p. 294).

With that rather severe warning in mind, we can take it that any combination of ideas, any kind of insight, can be represented in terms of the enneagram. It has universal relevance. It can even be said that the symbol itself will compare, evaluate, and refine what is brought into it. It acts as both an organizer and a filter. However, it can be understood at many levels because it is made up from a fusion of several interlocking parts. In its most superficial form, it is a pattern made of nine points. Actually, the name *enneagram* strictly means "drawing of nine." Six of the lines derive from the number seven and three from the number three. These two numbers, as we shall see, are crucial for understanding what the enneagram is about and how it works.

There are three distinct forms combined in the enneagram (fig. 1.2), and it is useful to keep this in mind. As we shall see, these three probably have their origins in the mythic past.[1] "The circle is divided into nine equal parts. Six points are connected by a figure which is symmetrical in relation to a diameter passing through the uppermost point of the divisions of the circumference. Further, the uppermost point of the divisions is the apex of an equilateral triangle linking together the points of the divisions which do not enter into the construction of the original complicated figure" (ISM, p. 286).

1.2. Forms in the symbol.

The circle represents a unity, a whole. It is a definite region in space, time, and form. That is to say, it occupies a certain space and contains various activities. Hence, the circle is like an enclosure. The circle also represents a *present moment,* proper to the given whole: around the circle there is a successive movement, a "flow of time," while the circle as a whole is always "now." Finally, as an autonomous whole, it has its own pattern, or "signature."

Gurdjieff said: "The isolated existence of a thing or phenomenon under examination is the closed circle of an eternally returning and uninterruptedly flowing process. The circle symbolizes this process. The separate points in the division of the circumference symbolize the steps of the process" (ISM, p. 288). (See fig. 1.3.) The enclosure of the circle derives from the structure of its process. The circle represents the continuity of substance in circulation, so that *matter is conserved.* He also said: "The apex of the triangle closes the duality of its base, making possible the manifold forms of its manifestation in the most diverse triangles, in the same way as the point of the apex of the triangle multiplies itself infinitely in the line of its base" (ISM, p. 288). In other words, it is a *unity in multiplicity* (fig. 1.4).

When the two figures combine into one system, we have the main process, represented by the circle, punctuated by the points of the triangular figure (fig. 1.5). The triangle is not a process but a structure of intention or will. It is what is *informing* the process and giving it meaning.[2]

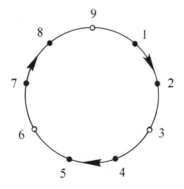

1.3. Process sequence.

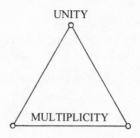

1.4. Unity in multiplicity.

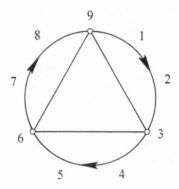

1.5. Triad in circle.

The points of punctuation—3, 6, and 9—are also where the main process is open to the influences of other processes. Just as point 9 can enter
into the workings of another process, so, too, the points which are at 9 in
other cycles can enter into the given process at either 3 or 6. This gives
us a picture of the interconnectedness of processes and cycles. Speaking
properly, only the point 9 *is* something in the given process: the other
two—that is, 3 and 6—with certain important exceptions, are simply
openings. The latter two are said to be "filled" from other processes.
Usually, we will show these points as open circles to remind us of this.
Having "holes" in a process is extremely important, because this allows
the nature of the process to change.

In general, the three punctuations are points of exchange (fig. 1.6).
However, Gurdjieff said on another occasion: "Each completed whole,
each cosmos, each organism, *each plant* is an enneagram. But not each of
these enneagrams has an inner triangle. The inner triangle stands for the

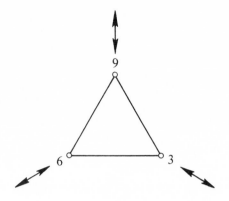

1.6. Openings in the process.

presence of higher elements . . ." (ISM, p. 293). There are certain wholes which carry in themselves the capacity to fill the openings at 3 and 6. Such wholes are "self-making."[3] The apex point 9 is unique. It represents the beginning and the end of the cycle. It is also the apex of the triangle, that which gives the form of the whole. It is the source of the purpose that has to be realized.

The periodic figure, usually given by the sequence 1-4-2-8-5-7, shows how the various steps are interconnected (fig. 1.7). The derivation of the sequence is given by dividing 1 by 7 (which gives the recurring decimal 0.142857 . . .). The idea is to represent unity as divided into seven steps. The seven steps include the apex point (as both beginning and end) as a special case, since 7/7 is calculated as 0.999 . . . recurring, and exclude the "openings" at points 3 and 6. The fact that the division of 1 by 7 gives

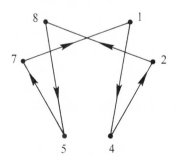

1.7. The periodic figure.

such a remarkable cyclic number is at first surprising and has been seized upon as a powerful way of conveying the sense of the working of an inner logic. Of course, the properties of numbers are nearly always interesting and often surprising. What the use of this division tells us, factually speaking, is only that the symbol cannot date further back than the adoption of the decimal system by the Arabs, particularly through the work of al-Khwarizmi, who lived in the ninth century.[4]

The substantial importance of the periodic figure is that it represents the cyclic integration of the process. We can think of the fundamental process, represented in the sequence of steps around the circle, as undergoing a *progressive harmonization*. The process can be corrected because it is repeated over and over again. Such improvement depends on making adjustments between the contents of the various parts of the process.

Here we come to a very important aspect of the structure of the enneagram. It is not obvious simply by looking at the symbol. *The completion of the main process depicted in the circle involves two extra processes combining with it.*

At point 3, we have what we called a punctuation, and something can enter from outside the main process. This is a second process. In its turn, at point 6, the second punctuation, a third process can enter. These two extra processes not only can but *must* enter if the main process is to be completed. The punctuations at 3 and 6 are *necessary*. This is just one example of what Gurdjieff meant by saying that the symbol as it is given is incomplete. It is an abstraction requiring an understanding of *evolutionary transformation* to make it meaningful. Otherwise, it is almost impossible to see why the inner lines are necessary.

Each of the three processes concerns a different working material or kind of substance. In the case of man, the three processes concern the three kinds of "food" that are necessary for survival: ordinary food, air, and impressions. ". . . It must be understood that, just as in many chemical processes, only definite quantities of substances, exactly determined by nature, give compounds of the required quality, so in the human organism the 'three foods' must be mixed in definite proportions. . . . Only by a strengthening or weakening of the different parts of the process, is the required result obtained" (ISM, p. 292).

In speaking of the periodic figure, we have made reference to the seven steps of the fundamental process. The idea of seven steps was a cornerstone of Gurdjieff's system of ideas. He referred to it as the law of seven and, sometimes, as the law of octaves. The triangle in the figure, in its turn, represented the other fundamental law of Gurdjieff's system, the law of three. *In the enneagram, the two laws are combined in their operation.*

The term *octave* is an obvious reference to the musical scale; however, it is also a reference to the arrangement of elements in the periodic table as it was developed by Mendeleyev, Newlands, and others. An octave is defined as a doubling of atomic weight such as the interval between fluorine (atomic weight 19) and chlorine (atomic weight 35.45).[5] The inexactitude relates to the inner structure of the atomic nucleus, which was not understood until the development of particle physics in the twentieth century. Gurdjieff utilized the idea of chemical octaves, even though he made disparaging and ill-deserved remarks about Mendeleyev himself and scientists in general.

In Gurdjieff's treatment of materiality, the heavier the atom, the lower it is in level. The highest level, then, is represented by an atom of hydrogen, or H1. All other elements could be regarded as denser versions of the prime element (that there are two kinds of nuclear particles, neutron and proton, was not known at the time, nor even the basic structure of atoms with a positive nucleus and orbiting electrons). Thus, Gurdjieff referred to various degrees of materiality in terms of *hydrogens.* H24, for example, would be twice as dense as H12.

A complete process of transformation proceeds from a lower matter to a higher one. Each step in this process consists of going from a given hydrogen to one of half the density. For convenience, each of the various hydrogens is given an integral number. We can picture the enneagram as a progression of hydrogens, marking stages in a process of transformation.

Calculations

A sense for the inner dynamism of the enneagram can be gleaned by going through various calculations with numbers. Doing these calculations is important for our understanding only if they can convey to us an experience of the power of *generation* contained within the symbol. Though the enneagram appears abstract, it is intended to represent substantial, self-organizing totalities. We have to bring to bear some physical sense or feeling for the *substances* represented by the numbers. A similar feeling is needed if we study the Kabbalistic Tree of Life and its ten *sefirot*. One of the meanings of *sefirot* is "numbers" or numerical potencies.

Gurdjieff introduces the enneagram after a discourse on the nature of symbolism, which we take as our guide: ". . . in symbology . . . *numbers* are connected with definite *geometrical figures,* and are mutually complementary to each other" (ISM, p. 283).

The three points of the triangle derive from the ratios 1/3, 2/3, and 3/3, giving the numbers 0.333 . . . , 0.666 . . . , and 0.999 . . . in the decimal system on which the figure is based. The six points of the periodic figure 142857 all appear in the same sequence in the ratios 1/7, 2/7, 3/7, 4/7, 5/7, and 6/7 as 0.142857 . . . , 0.285714 . . . , 0.428571 . . . , etc. Adding 0.142857, or 1/7, to 0.857142, or 6/7, gives 7/7 as equal to 0.999 . . . , showing that the 3 and the 7 unite at the apex point. The sequence of six digits repeats itself endlessly, which suggests a repetition of the cycle at further and further depths or finer and finer detail. All these numbers depend on the arithmetical base we are using and work out quite differently in other bases.[6]

There is another set of calculations we can do, once we have given the various points around the circle definite *values.* We picture the various points, proceeding clockwise, as a series of finer and finer "matters"— called hydrogens by Gurdjieff—so that, as we go round the circle (by our convention in the clockwise direction), we are moving upward in level. This is the picture of the enneagram as a *transformation device.* We can give definite numbers to each of the points, representing their level or quality of energy, and then work out what these must be relative to each other.

First we have to define one unit of change, such as going from point 0 to point 1. If we represent this as "doubling the rate of vibration" or "halving the density," then we can represent it terms of hydrogens. If point 0 has the value H384, point 1 will—by this convention—have the value of H192. The periodic figure has six points, and these correspond to the six whole tones of an octave in music. If we now have point 1 as H192, this leads to point 2 as H96, point 4 as H48, and so on, leading to point 8 as H6. The triangular figure has only three points, so we divide the interval between H384 and H6 into three ratios. Point 3 will then have the value H96, point 6 the value H24, and point 9 the value H6. (See fig. 1.8.) H192 (point 1) is midway between H384 (point 0) and H48 (point 3). Points 1, 4, and 7 can be seen to arise as the midpoints between 0, 3, 6, and 9. The value of point 2 (H96) is then halfway between H192 (point 1) and H48 (point 4). Point 2 arises according to the pattern 1-4-2. Mirroring this relation, point 8 appears as the source of the pattern 8-5-7 and has the value H6.

The triangular points represent openings where something of a new character can enter and further the transformation. But, as point 2 and point 3 have the same value, what extra thing can enter at 3? The answer, as we shall gradually see, is *information*. Point 2 has to be at the same vibrational level as point 3—that is, *energetically* similar—or it cannot be reached by the information transmitted through the opening at 3 (represented by the arrow).

The information flow of points 3, 6, and 9 means that each of these points gives a certain perspective or view of the whole enneagram. Strictly speaking, there are at least three versions of every enneagram, owing to this feature. Gradually, we may understand that point 3 gives a *spatial* perception, point 6 a *temporal* perception, and point 9 a perception of *direct cognition*.

The threefold division of the circle represents an "imprinting" of the law of three onto a process, and it is through this threefold "eye" that we

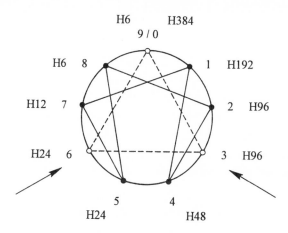

1.8. Progression of hydrogens.

can understand how the process of transformation works. The simplest expression of this in classical times was in Aristotle's *Poetics* where he describes the unity of a dramatic work in terms of having a beginning, a middle, and an end.[7] However, this implies purpose and intent of some kind, or some form of *will*. The threefold division means that the process is not just happening but is coming about purposefully. To take account of this, we need to have an intimate connection between past and future, a two-way traffic, as it were. Will is only effective in regions that are neither predetermined from the past nor preformed from the future. At points 3 and 6 we have such regions. Gurdjieff, in his book *All and Everything*, calls them "ways-in" or *mdnel-ins* (using Armenian).

They are openings in the *information field*.

To Feel and Sense

What is being measured in terms of level is sometimes called "intensity of inner-togetherness," or *being*. However, this is an abstraction from our concrete experience, where we have the relative scales related to something specific in our experience, such as a task. It is one thing to speak of relative degrees or levels of achievement and quite another to speak of relative grades in general. For example, how many times "higher" is a human being than a dog? Or how many times "higher" a star than a planet? Gurdjieff liked to pose such questions and said that there was a science which could compute the answers.[8] One day, we too might be able to answer such questions, once we have assimilated the implications of modern discoveries concerning complexity and organization.

What is represented just as a number of a hydrogen can also be felt or *sensed* through our own bodies. The link between concepts of number and sensation is provided by *music*. The musical canon of Gurdjieff's teaching was made possible by the remarkable talents of the Russian composer Thomas de Hartmann. Gurdjieff was, technically speaking, no composer himself and needed de Hartmann to realize his intentions.[9] De Hartmann was at one time closely connected with Wassily Kandinsky and Alexandr Scriabin, both of whom were concerned with the transmission of a philosophical system through the senses. Kandinsky was a student of Theosophy, while Scriabin researched the implications of synesthesia, the combining of the senses. We see the relevance of the prevailing Russian culture to the formation of Gurdjieff's transmission.

Included in the repertoire of pieces composed with de Hartmann was a corpus of music for movements or sacred dances. It was through such movements that Gurdjieff believed it would be possible for people to experience the cosmological ideas within the realm of sensation and feeling (see photograph). He told Ouspensky and others that this was the only way they could be understood—that is, experienced in all the three centers of thought, feeling, and sensation. It is not clear whether he thought he had succeeded; but, for the greater part of his active teaching life, he continued to work on his dances, and many of them were based explicitly upon the enneagram.[10]

G. said at that time that exercises of moving according to the enneagram would occupy an important place in his ballet, *The Struggle of the Magi-*

A movements class at Sherborne House, Gloucestershire, in 1972, working on the movement called The Enneagram. *Sherborne House was where Bennett ran intensive ten-month courses in the period before his death in 1974.*

cians. And he said also that, without taking part in these exercises, without occupying some kind of place in them, it was almost impossible to understand the enneagram.

"It is possible to experience the enneagram by movement," he said. "The rhythm itself of these movements would suggest the necessary ideas and maintain the necessary tension; without them it is not possible to feel what is most important." (ISM, p. 295)

The idea that dance can accurately convey the substance of a set of ideas is strange to contemporary Europeans, even though recognized in antiquity. Athenaeus speaks of Memphis, a famous mime, who could dance faultlessly the whole of Pythagorean doctrine. This was not to say that either he or his audience *understood* what the dance contained. It is pertinent to remember in this context that, according to Aristotle, what is esoteric is something that is learned long before it is understood.[11]

Gurdjieff spoke, however, of feelings and sensations and not simply of the pattern of movement. He brought to the character of dance an inward content, such that certain of his movements have to be executed with specific combinations of sensations, feelings, and thoughts. It is this inward content that makes a connection with the understanding.

However, the inner movement of the enneagram can be understood with the aid of *any experience of intelligent action.* All intelligent actions transform the situation in which they arise. A transformation—even of materials—is a "movement," a movement obeying impartial laws, organized according to a meaningful structure, and involving a *physical body.* To approach the enneagram without a physical base is to miss the point of it entirely.

"What [a person] cannot put into the enneagram he does not understand" (ISM, p. 294). For Gurdjieff, understanding was a question of what one can *do.* Understanding involves action. Gurdjieff also put it: "If a man knows how to make things well, then it is possible to talk to him." We should not forget the importance that Gurdjieff gave to practical abilities. He was deeply interested in how things were made and done. This is of great importance for any appreciation of the enneagram. The cover of the brochure for the *Institute for the Harmonious Development of Man* (which Gurdjieff founded as a vehicle for his work) shows the enneagram symbol, angel and devil (see illustration), and, besides, a large collection

A representation of a design for the program of Gurdjieff's Institute (1923).

*The nine-sided building based on the enneagram designed and built
near London by Bennett and his students.*

of instruments such as microscopes, sewing machines, and garden tools. Even a section of the movements themselves was devoted to representations of skills such as sewing shoes and weaving carpets.

Bennett and his students designed and executed a nine-sided building based entirely on the structure of the enneagram (see photograph). It was called the Djameechoonatra, a word taken from *Beelzebub's Tales* meaning "place where one receives second-being food" (air). The main function of the building was to house the performance of Gurdjieff's sacred dances. Frank Lloyd Wright visited the site (at Coombe Springs, near London) while it was being built. It had three levels, signifying the three worlds of action, built of concrete, wood, and copper; and all the internal angles derived from the inner lines of the diagram. The structure was destroyed after the property was given to Idries Shah.

The particular relevance of all this to the enneagram is to point out that it cannot be taken merely as a conceptual tool. Unless there is a feel for the substances involved, as living physical realities which we can encounter through our own bodies, we will *misunderstand*. The direct experience of struggle with recalcitrant material, the feeling of progressive coordination, the shock of discontinuous transitions—all of this and more which comes from work in the real world—is essential. Real work is hazardous, and this is what the enneagram describes.

Notes

1. In chapter 7 I speak of this triunity again. An interesting source of reference for the history of triadic symbolism is Jean Gebser's *The Ever-Present Origin*.
2. See Paul Klee, *The Thinking Eye*: "The triangle came into being when a point entered into a relation of tension with a line and, following the command of its Eros, discharged this tension" (p. 113).
3. In modern biological theory, the idea of *autopoiesis,* or self-making, has become important. First introduced by Francisco Varela, primarily in *Principles of Biological Autonomy*, it played a significant role in the generation of the Gaia hypothesis of James Lovelock and Lynn Margulis.
4. The decimal system based on the digits 0, 1, 2, 3, 4, 5, 6, 7, 8, 9, and place values did not get established in Europe until as late as the twelfth century.
5. Between these two elements, which have similar chemical properties, we can find seven other elements of intermediate atomic weights. Between chlorine and bromine, in the next octave, there are seventeen.
6. It is useful to keep in mind that the numerical patterns of the enneagram are based on calculations in the decimal system, that is, on the number ten. It is also significant that $3 + 7 = 10$. In the decimal system, there is no separate symbol for the number ten, which is written, instead, as 10 (a one and a zero). We count from zero upwards: 0, 1, 2, 3, 4, 5, 6, 7, 8, 9, 10, etc. If we use a different number system and divide one by seven, or by three, the results are different. In fact, there are a whole series of figures similar to the enneagram that can be derived using different number bases. For example, in the duodecimal system based on the number twelve: if we use 5 and 7 $(5 + 7 = 12)$ instead of 3 and 7 to make the inner figures, we produce a sixfold periodic figure similar to what we had before (deriving from the seven), but also a fourfold periodic figure (deriving from the five), in place of the triangle. In the number base of seventeen, we can use $13 + 4 = 17$ to derive two sets of figures. The 4 gives the triangle, while the 13 gives two sets of hexadic figures. This has very similar properties to those of 3 and 7 in the decimal system, since 13 and 4 are related as 7 and 3 are in terms of structure of subsets.

7. I take this up later in more depth, in chapter 11.

8. Perhaps the most famous example of this was when he calculated how many times more intelligent Jesus Christ was than a table! "If we are able to calculate how many times hydrogen 6 is more intelligent than hydrogen 1536 we shall know how many times man number eight [Jesus Christ] is more intelligent than a table. But, in this connection, it must be remembered that 'intelligence' is determined not by the density of matter but by the density of vibrations. The density of vibrations, however, increases not by doubling as in the octaves of 'hydrogens' but in an entirely different progression which many times outnumbers the first. If you know the exact coefficient of this increase you will be in a position to solve this problem" (ism, pp. 319–20).

9. Cecil Lytle, one of the newer interpreters of Gurdjieff and de Hartmann's music, writes: "Coming from Alexandropol . . . , Armenia, Gurdjieff's attitudes were textured by the fact that since the 3rd century bc, this area had become the literal cross-roads for the diverse cultures that ringed the Black, Caspian and Mediterranean Seas. The horizon of his musical art never widened. Instead, it grew gradually and inexorably, his gaze focused more and more on using music to gain mastery over the ethological resources of the human spirit and moral behavior. It is ironic, indeed, that someone with such an unambiguous and immediate use for music in furthering a prodigious philosophical narrative, was so ill-equipped with the general skills of the art." From his introduction to the CD of Gurdjieff–de Hartmann's music, *Seekers of the Truth.*

10. Such as "number 17" in the series of 39. Music for some of Gurdjieff's movements is now freely available on compact disc and in other formats. See note 8 above.

11. See Giorgio de Santillana and Hertha von Dechend, *Hamlet's Mill,* pp. 118–19.

· 2 ·

Overview

The enneagram is a subtle and interwoven teaching. It is a challenge to keep in mind its multidimensional perspectives. Here is an overview, before we embark on our further explorations.

Form and Content

THE ENNEAGRAM describes a pattern and a process, something invariant and something that changes in steps. Think of the pattern as the basic plot of a drama and the process as the action that unfolds it. Or, as the "idea" of a piece of art, which has to be realized through a line of work. In the enneagram, the plot or the idea is not a thing but a *relationship*, and it appears in the form of the triangular figure. The process, the action, or the work appears in the sequence of steps around the circle.

The primary relationship expresses Gurdjieff's idea of the *law of three:* nothing can happen without three forces (active, passive, and neutralizing). So threeness is the underlying *form* of everything that happens or can happen. The three of the triangular figure represents the specific "trinity" of the whole. There are scores of interpretations or images of the trinity—such as the "what?," "how?," and "why?" or the Father, Son, and Holy Ghost—or three aspects of Gurdjieff's "third force." All we need right now is the idea of the three as a primary *logos,* the core meaning that informs everything contained in the given whole.

The sequence of steps expresses his idea of the *law of seven,* which encapsulates common traditional ideas that can be found in the days of the week, the visual spectrum, and the musical octave. It is the idea that seven quite different qualities or states have to be gone through to complete an action. This encompasses both steps in succession, in time and space, and steps in level of being or quality, either up or down a scale.

In the enneagram, the threefold form is given by the triangle 3-6-9, and the sevenfold sequence by the points 1, 2, 4, 5, 7, and 8 together with the point that appears as both beginning and end, the point 0/9. At first glance, these two structures are just laid one on top of the other, tied together at the top point. But they are closer to each other than it first appears. One of the ideas we need to borrow from contemporary thought is that of *fractals*. In a fractal, we have a shape such that any part of it is similar to the shape of the whole. So we have the idea of a form that is echoed on finer and finer scales, reaching into the smallest region. It gives us a picture of something pervading throughout a complexity. The form, the primary relationship depicted in the enneagram, must be like this if it is to *in-form* the whole. Similarly, the enneagram is like a hologram, in that every point is itself an enneagram.

There is even more. The three elements of the triangle each carry their own version of the triangle. So we have *three versions of the three.* Point 3 carries 1-4-7, point 6 carries 2-5-8, while point 9 carries the primary triad, 3-6-9. In this picture, the primary triad is projected into the field of action where it is to be worked out. Each of the three main sectors or phases of the enneagram contains all three ingredients, just as in a fractal, though not in pictorial form, but in the shape of action. Each is a partial resolution of the working together of the three. They have to be brought together into a total fulfillment *progressively.*

Asymmetry and Buildup: Transformation

The three ingredients of the primary triad are different from one another. We are free to choose static or progressive models of this differentiation. The static view derives from Gurdjieff's own remarks about the line 3-6 expressing in duality what 9 has in unity. Looked at in that way, we are bound to see the whole cycle in terms of balance between left and right. The progressive model also stems from Gurdjieff, in the guise of the three foods needed for transformation. The transformation model suggests that the three ingredients build up successively, so that point 9 is the unique fulfillment of the work. We then picture three phases of the action, from 0 to 3, from 3 to 6, and from 6 to 9. The buildup is accumulative and discontinuous.

The main discontinuities come in with the points of the triangle. In the sequence of buildup around the circle (clockwise) these points represent the "shock of the new." The temporal nature of the sequence is such that the previous "new" then turns into the "old," which needs a further shock of the new in order to advance. In this way, the process is kicked into higher levels. This is similar to an old shamanistic image in which the sorcerer fires an arrow, stands on this arrow, fires another arrow, stands on it, and so on. This image of transformation is necessarily that of *accelerating* transformation.

The total process is also revealed as having three layers to it. The first layer starts at point 0 and goes right round the circle to 9. The second only begins at point 3, while the third only begins at point 6. These layers of the action have to be significantly different from one another and related to their points of origin. So we discover the primary triad again in the threefold sequencing.

The idea of transformation may be rather abstract until we have tied it down to something concrete, such as the transformation of materials. The first layer of process would be the mechanical actions of crushing, screening, washing, heating, and so on. The next layer would concern chemical actions of solution, precipitation, combination, and equilibrium. The third layer would reach the atomic and structural level, as in nanotechnology. It is fairly easy to see, in this example, that material has to reach a certain fineness or purity in a previous layer to be ready for entry into another layer of the transformation.

The sequencing in three sectors can be appreciated in the light of innumerable metaphors. A powerful one, also reflective of transformation but in a different way, is that of the quest. Here we only look at the straight lines between the three main points. The line 0–3 is leaving home and "looking for trouble." The line 3–6 is the journey in the new land, of discovery and experience. The line 6–9 is the coming home, the return and transforming experience into wisdom. We might well think of the voyages and life work of Charles Darwin in these simple terms. It is an *archetypal* quest.

The hazardous nature of the sequence as an *ascent* is reminiscent of John Climacus's depiction of souls tempted and attacked by devils as they ascended.[1] These devils may turn out to be no more or less than the inevitable result of a transformative process which must engender its own resistance, or dampening forces. The higher you go, the more severe the temptation.

Seeing in threeness is a powerful tool of the understanding. Putting the general form of the three into specific circumstances, where action has to be taken, challenges the general understanding to become more concrete, more related to what we can *do*. It is in this way that the enneagram can be said to be a *generator of intelligence*.

Intelligence

If we imagined each arm of the primary triangle as disconnected with the others, then the sequence of the action would simply go all over the place, like the "drunkard's walk" of a randomly moving particle. The first and second sectors and the second and third sectors have to be tied together. This is the task of *intelligence*. Intelligence lies primarily in the *will* that connects knowledge and action. In the enneagram, such acts of intelligence as correction, guidance, tuning, verification, and simulation are depicted as the inner periodic figure of six lines. The cyclic sequence 1-4-2-8-5-7-1 (etc.) contains in it the triads 7-1-4 and 2-8-5, which are the two other versions of the primary triad. At the same time, the linkage 1-4-2 ties the first and second sectors, in the sequence, while the linkage 8-5-7 ties the second and third. Both form and sequence are involved in the inner lines.

The inner lines are the intentional aspect, independent of environmental pressures and influences. If we adopt the metaphor of the triangle as representing the *will* of the whole, then the inner lines are its *inner life*. The range around the circle is its *outer life*. The three points of the triangle are like "openings" between inner and outer, like "mouths" that take in food and give out speech.

Triunity

The enneagram shows all similar occasions repeated in time or paralleled in space. It is rather like an action pattern. Imagine the action pattern of the flight of birds. Somehow, this is stored in brains and unfolds in complex behavior in space and time, according to the circumstances. In that sense, the enneagram is a multidimensional image. Unity or wholeness is not so easy to understand. In the enneagram, wholeness is

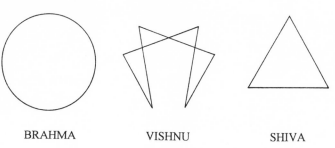

BRAHMA　　　　VISHNU　　　　SHIVA

2.1. The trimurti of the enneagram.

there at the beginning to begin with, *and* it is only realized at the end. This means that there are *three* dimensions of wholeness, or a *triunity*.

The cyclic character of the whole process, depicted around the circle in its return on itself, applies to the first layer of the action. If we remember, in the quest the hero returns home again, even though a changed man.

The inner lines weave their cohesion of memories and anticipations, eternally present, expanding the range and depth of the "here and now." This relates to the second layer. There is also a total dynamic in the way the three ingredients of the primary triad diverge from each other and converge into each other, like a cosmic pulse between life and death, day and night: this is in the third layer.

There are innumerable examples of threefold gods in ancient mythologies. One widely known is the *trimurti* of the Hindus, consisting of Brahma the Creator, Vishnu the Preserver, and Shiva the Destroyer. These three elements do not represent the forces of the triad, which we will be discussing later; they represent the meaning of the three main components in the enneagram. Brahma the Creator (or maker) is the circle. Vishnu the Preserver (and dreamer) is the periodic figure. Shiva the Destroyer (who makes the new possible) is the triangle. Such mythical understandings are an important part of the total view.[2] Remembering the image of the *trimurti* (fig. 2.1) can help us remember what is essential.

Notes

1. Climacus (c. 525–600) was an ascetic and mystic famous for his treatise *Klimax tou paradeisou* (Ladder to Paradise).
2. See the version Jung has in *Psychology and Alchemy* (p. 154), where Vishnu appears as a tortoise and Shiva as a lotus.

· 3 ·

Form of Sequence

It is a truism that nature does not proceed in straight lines. But though the processes of nature may be complex and unpredictable, we are finding out that there are nearly always patterns in the chaos. Whatever we try to achieve must take these patterns into account, and our success may depend upon the degree to which we can see them at work. Gurdjieff's idea of the octave is a metaphor for achievement. This metaphor is built into the enneagram.

In Music and Painting

INTELLIGENCE MAKES a difference. One of the important differences that it makes is in probabilities. What is unlikely to happen when things are left to themselves can be made to happen with almost certainty by intelligence. We have become used to this in the practical arts, or *technics*, where we are dealing with mechanical, or at least material, systems. When we, as intelligences, try to deal with each other or with ourselves, the results are not so predictable.

Broadly speaking, then, an intelligence can deal with a certain degree of uncertainty and complexity coming from the environment of its operations; but dealing with itself is another matter. This is important because intelligence begins and ends its path with an aim or purpose. Dealing with the world "outside," to keep to our aim, is one critical factor on the path. Dealing with the world "within," to *improve on the aim*, is quite another. This is now of urgent concern in the running of business organizations, which are mostly unable to catch up with the effects they themselves create.

A complete intelligent action has various stages or levels in it. It is constructed in steps. In Gurdjieff's system, the line between start and

44

finish has seven steps in it. These appear around the circle of the ennea-gram. The idea of a sevenfold division of scale or level is a very old one. Gurdjieff himself referred to its primitive expression in *Genesis*, where the "day of rest" refers to the last, completing transition. Of course, we come across the idea of sevenfoldness in such things as the spectrum of colors, where there are no actual transitions of state, leading from one condition to another, but the splitting of a whole (white light) into various comple-mentarities and degrees. According to Gurdjieff, this kind of structure is ubiquitous, but when it comes to bringing about change in some mate-rial, more is involved. There is no straightforward pathway between the start and the finish of a process. The initial impetus would fail part way through if there was only its own momentum. Without adjustments, the process would deflect and never reach its intended end point.

To convey this idea, Gurdjieff made use of the analogy of the musical scale. Numerous scales have developed over the centuries. All involve some compromise. The most natural interval to the ear is that of the octave itself, where the rate of vibration is doubled. The next harmonious interval is based on the ratio 3/2 (the dominant or fifth); the next on 4/3 (the fourth); and the next on 5/4 (major third). This means that we want to use these intervals to determine *notes* within the octave. The next simi-lar ratio, 6/5, is that of the *minor* third. The ratios 7/6 and 8/7 do not give results in harmony with the other ratios, but the next again, 9/8, gives the interval we accept as a *tone* or approximately one-sixth of an octave. If we keep the notes called the fifth, fourth, and major third, and also the tone as determined by 9/8, we find that the interval between the fifth and the fourth turns out conveniently to be 9/8. But the interval between the fourth and the third turns out to be 16/15 (or 1.066), which is close to, but not exactly, the square root of 9/8—that is, a *half-tone*. Similarly, the interval between the major third and the tone becomes 10/9, which is close enough to 9/8 to be accepted as a tone, but it is also not exact.

Dividing the remaining interval between sol and do (using the measure of a tone in its two approximations 10/9 and 9/8), we get la, which is 10/9 more than sol, and si, which is 9/8 more again. However, between si and do there is only room for a half-tone (16/15). It is fairly easy to understand, then, that this particular scale, which is called the major dia-tonic scale, is a compromise and that there can be many other alternative solutions; including the "even-tempered" scale, actually used in most

Western music. This also does not give *exact* intervals, though it allows for identical octaves starting on any note. (See fig. 3.1.)

We are free to divide the octave in other ways. One of the most simple and interesting of these is the whole-tone scale of six notes, which was used a great deal by Debussy. The six points of the enneagram excluding the triangular figure—1, 2, 4, 5, 7, and 8—represent this simple scale.

In all variants of the *diatonic* scales, there are five "whole-tone" and two "semitone" intervals. In subjective terms, we could call the diatonic scales "dramatic" in contrast with the whole-tone scale of Debussy, which is called "impressionistic." The dramatic scale has tensions and uncertainties in it that the impressionistic scale lacks. The two semitones can be seen as necessary adjustments which have to be made to preserve the steady sequence of tones in the rest of the octave. Many people hear the two semitone intervals (mi-fa and si-do) as *tense*. There is the sense of a "retardation" in going from mi to fa and a sense of "being urged on" from si to do. These subjective evaluations are, of course, no evidence for a physical theory. But they convey an *experiential* sense of what the two critical intervals mean. Gurdjieff's use of the musical octave combines art with science.

While science concerns what actually is, art concerns what we intend. Science uncovers laws, while art proceeds by arranging things "not according to law" or "otherwise." They go hand in hand, because it is only on the basis of knowledge of laws that we can construct the deviations

Note	Ratio
do	2/1
. . .	
si	15/8
la	5/3
sol	3/2
fa	4/3
. . .	
mi	5/4
re	9/8
do	1

3.1. The musical scale.

which impart a message. Hence, the significance of the musical analogy is to represent the fact that study of phenomena can uncover the traces of an adjustment in the laws which signify the work of intelligence. In this sense, the universe cannot be understood entirely as an object of scientific study. *It is also a work of art.*

The two semitone intervals represent something that deviates from the other sequences of notes. The symbology is fairly obvious: here are changes in functioning which are needed for the harmony of the whole. Through them, phenomena can communicate with and influence each other. In Gurdjieff's model, the half-tone intervals represent the hazards to be found on the way where something new or an act of adjustment has to be made. When the octave is put into the enneagram symbol, we see that the second hazard or interval does not appear where it should (fig. 3.2). This "error" is important because it enables a very important type of information to be conveyed.

Gurdjieff was not alone in his symbolic use of the musical scale. In medieval times, a mnemonic for the musical scale had a celestial symbology which prefigures a Gurdjieffian cosmology (fig. 3.3).[1] As this is not the place to make a historical survey of the subject of ancient and classical symbologies based on the octave, I shall only mention, by way of illustration, one example from Renaissance times. In 1499 Botticelli painted his masterpiece, the *Primavera* (Spring). In this painting, there are eight figures (or nine, counting the cherub). We can correlate them with a musical octave (fig. 3.4).

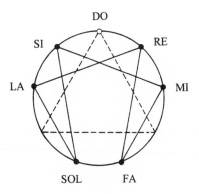

3.2. The octave in the enneagram.

DO	DOminus	The Lord, God
SI	SIdera	[All] Stars
LA	via LActea	Milky Way
SOL	SOL	The Sun
FA	FAta	Planets
MI	MIcrocosmos	Microcosm [Earth]
RE	REgina Caelum	Queen of Heaven [Moon]
DO	DOminus	The Lord, God

3.3 A celestial octave.

Mercury	Voluptuous	Contemplative	Active	Venus	Floris	Chloris	Zephyr
do	si	la	sol	fa	mi	re	do
	opposite					opposite	

3.4 Botticelli's octave.

Drawing based on Botticelli's painting Primavera.

Looking from right to left there is: Zephyr, who impregnates the next figure Chloris with his breath; Chloris, who turns toward him while flowers come out of her mouth; these flowers are those which adorn the next figure, Floris (one of the most beautiful female figures of Renaissance art); next, standing slightly back from the rest, with the cherub above her, is Venus, whose depiction intentionally evokes that of the Madonna; next are the three Graces, to be understood in this case as first active, then contemplative, and finally voluptuous love; voluptuous love turns and is gazing at the contemplative love; finally, there is Mercury, who raises his staff to pierce the very heavens beyond the trees. The sequence of figures follows the notes of one of the musical scales. In this case, the unusual or "discordant" intervals appear between re and mi and between si and do. They are clearly shown, because Chloris (*re*) and the voluptuous Grace (*si*) are turned the other way.[2]

As is now widely appreciated, the paintings of this period were intended to convey ideas and could be read as books. In *Primavera* even the particular flowers shown at the feet of the figures have significance. Nothing is put in for effect alone. Painting served as an mnemonic of ideas, compressing classical learning (and, sometimes, contemporary history) into its most attractive and elegant form, in which it could be appreciated by the feelings as well as by the mind. We mention this, because time and again Gurdjieff insisted that truly "objective" art should be read like a book, and he obviously wanted his own sacred dances to be taken in this vein. It was also his serious wish that "artists and poets in the future" would make use of his own writings in *Beelzebub's Tales*. If we look at *Primavera*, we can perhaps feel something of what this might have meant.

Another thing to realize is that painting such as that of Botticelli flourished in connection with a certain school. Under the patronage of Cosimo dé Medici, and the guidance of Marsilio Ficino, one of the rare Greek scholars of his time, a Neoplatonic school was established which sought to emulate Plato's own Academy. Many followers of Gurdjieff's ideas have delved into Ficino and the Neoplatonic school of Florence. Certainly, it was a remarkable flowering and of great importance for making a bridge between the classical heritage of the Hellenic world and Christianity. To this day, we still have little knowledge of what went into the making of the modern world and the role that might have been played by such small creative groups.[3] An important role must have been played by the Arabs—particularly by the Sufi orders—and Gurdjieff's connection with such groups in more recent times is undoubtedly important.

However, our concern is with the way in which Gurdjieff presented his ideas. We have seen that the use of the musical octave (in one or another of its possible diatonic versions) was an established tradition. But Gurdjieff was at pains to point out that his understanding of it went far beyond that of "the Greeks," whose ideas he often contrasted with those of "the Chinese." In this way, incidentally, he also reinforced his underlying message of retrieving real understanding from cultures on a global scale.

According to Gurdjieff's model of the octave, any given process needs assistance in two particular places in order to complete itself. Here Gurdjieff ranges far beyond the scope of musical analogy, which can only show us the adjustments needed to establish a harmony. When it comes to making an actual transition of state from a beginning to an end, we have to take account of a buildup *in substance.* The two critical steps then signify important transitions: in the first, the substance comes "alive," while in the second, it acquires a "will" of its own. These ontological steps (having to do with being) cannot be described within the framework of the musical octave. All we can know is that there need to be at least two critical adjustments; we can have no preconception of their content.

Change and Order

To approach Gurdjieff's understanding of the octave, it might be useful to consider a few basic principles. We start right away with the distinction between *causal* and *intentional* change. Causal change depends on what has already happened. Intentional change depends on what *will* happen. Causal change is inevitable while intentional change is conditional. Causal change goes on by itself, but intentional change has to be sustained.

Following Gurdjieff's indications, there is this distinction only in the relative world, the world commensurate with human experience. In the Absolute this distinction does not hold, a notion that comes up in theology. Hence, the "law of change" differs in the relative world from how it is in the Absolute. In the causal or mechanical sequence, to speak more scientifically, the entropy of the system increases; whereas in the purposeful or intentional sequence, the entropy of the system decreases (because it is expelled elsewhere). We all have the sense that when we want to achieve something deliberately, we have to go uphill against the stream of events. The causal sequences militate against the intentional ones. Going "against the stream" is intentional, while going "with the stream" is mechanical (and the notions of intentionally going downstream or unintentionally going upstream are both sheer delusion!). Gurdjieff made a strong distinction between these two sequences, "upstream" and "downstream," calling the first *evolution* and the second *involution*. On the personal level, he focused on the way in which our intentions fail to be realized and turn into their very opposites.[4] While involution goes "like a Pianola," evolution is hazardous.

On the cosmic level, the creation of the universe is involutionary, a successive series of steps which takes "what is" from some primal and pure condition toward a state of cold and meaningless inertia. Because of the mechanical associations of the term *creation*, we tend to feel that it marks an addition to reality whereas, more logically, it is a privation. In involution *possibilities decrease.* In this sense, a gallon of gasoline has more possibilities than its combustion products: it can be used to clean stains, produce a weapon, or fuel a car. In evolution *possibilities increase.* Evolution is only feasible for relatively individualized states of existence, which are localized and of specific form. The state with more possibilities is said to be on a higher level than the one with less. The critical question for any process is whether it increases or decreases possibilities, whether it is going up or going down in level. The "going down" and the "going up" are measured in terms of possibilities, not in terms of space and time.

Entropy is a measure of the disorder of a system. All causal (downward) sequences result in an increase of disorder. It is, therefore, possible to take entropy as a negative indicator of level. This was not possible for Gurdjieff, since the correlation of entropy with loss of information is a concept that first emerged in the 1940s. He was constrained to present these ideas through traditional and semireligious forms and used a concept akin to that of "relative conditioning" to represent what we now call entropy.

He considered that all states of existence are under a certain number of laws. The greater the number of laws, the greater the conditioning and the lower the level. If we picture a given state of existence as partitioned or divided up according to the various laws, then we can see that the lower levels are more divided. They are not divided in space but according to their possible states. The more laws, the more states. This makes the character of the lower levels more muddled than that of the higher levels. Muddledness is similar to entropy.

Gurdjieff considered that the muddle produced by relatively large numbers of laws diminished consciousness and will. This is the equivalent of saying that the lower levels are less intelligent. Conversely, the higher the level, the greater the degree of intelligence. An evolutionary (up) sequence results in a gain of intelligence. Involutionary (down) sequences result in a loss of intelligence. In Gurdjieff's cosmic scheme galaxies, stars, and planets are on various levels of intelligence. There are relatively few people who think of the galaxy as having a higher intelligence than the sun, or of the sun as having a higher intelligence than the planets. It will seem strange to most—and something of a relic from earlier periods of divine cosmic geography—to equate intelligence with scale in the universe. But this point of view has always been there, in different guises, throughout the modern era and has counted some of the major scientists among its adherents.[5] It is simply that, with our contemporary conditioning, it is very difficult for us to think in such terms. It requires something coming from the hidden side, the inner side, to help our minds.

Furthermore, if we think of change we might remember that it is multifaceted. There is change within a given world, and there is change as between different worlds, higher and lower. The two comingle. Intelligence is mixed with mechanicality.

If there are different worlds or levels, then there are intervals or gaps between them. Otherwise, they would collapse into each other. In his teaching on the cosmos, Gurdjieff first spoke about what he called the *ray of creation,* in which the different levels are established as distinct and quasi-autonomous worlds.

The organization according to scale is also an outer symbol for inner levels of operation. We need to pass from an outer and spatial representation to an inner and temporal experience. We then need to reconcile these two representations in our understanding. Gurdjieff's primary cosmic octave, stretching from the *Absolute* to *Nothing* is only an initial sketch of a dynamic and dramatic universe. Each of its levels is like a world in which everything it contains conforms to a certain logic or set of laws. If we are in one world, our consciousness cannot reach a higher world. The question is: How can these different levels or worlds be connected? and: What kind of connection is possible?

One of Gurdjieff's crucial questions was how *higher influences could reach into lower worlds*. The worlds are separated in a *hierarchical* order. What other kind of order is there that brings them into mutual communication?

Notes

1. I am indebted to William Sullivan for pointing this out to me. The topic is taken up again in chapter 14, where I discuss Gurdjieff's ray of creation.
2. My description is adapted from that of David Foster and Pamela Tudor-Craig in *The Secret Life of Paintings*.
3. John Bennett died while working on a book in which he intended to include this history.
4. This should be an obvious fact to any student of political history, indeed to any serious student of any kind of history. We might even call it a law.
5. See, for example, David Foster, *The Philosophical Scientists*. For a modern approach based on information technology, see Fred Hoyle, *The Intelligent Universe*.

· 4 ·

The Symbolism
of Making and Becoming

*When we propose to create something, there is the feeling that we are
only a subcreator, since everything we use has already been brought
into being by God or nature. This has uncomfortable ramifications.
Can we, then, aspire to make ourselves? We try to find out about this
by looking at the work we do with our hands and eyes. Do we bring
something into being? Unlike Allah, who simply commands* Kun! *(Be)
and it is, we have to go through a process if we are to make something.
In this process, can we go beyond the assembly of bits and pieces into
the realm of being?*

Octaves of Achievement

AN AIM HAS the promise of its fulfillment; an idea has the potential to
be realized; and a seed contains the fully developed plant. There is an
analogy here with properties of the musical octave: when any note is
sounded on an instrument, the equivalent note of the octave above also
sounds (though less strongly). We know, however, that the actual realization of an aim, or the growth of a plant from a seed, is not something
guaranteed. We have to water the seed, keep the weeds away, guard
against bugs and slugs, and have it in the right soil and light. Gurdjieff's
account of the octave puts these facts of life into their most general form,
and this form is built, with some modifications, into the enneagram.

Let us think, for example, of an artist starting with a blank canvas, an
idea in mind, and a set of paints. These components have to be brought
into a coalescence in which a value is realized. The finished work of art

54

has, to use a phrase of Bennett's, a greater "inner togetherness" than the state of affairs with which the artist began.

The transition from the starting point to the end point has many stages and does not happen all at once. If we have in mind that the completion of the process is not guaranteed, then we may think of there being certain critical stages at which, if the right thing is not done, the enterprise fails. Gurdjieff said that there were two such critical stages. In these, there is a change in the relation between inner and outer rather than anything happening in time.

The octave description is set against a backdrop in which there is a series of distinct levels, or degrees, of inner togetherness. In making the transition from beginning to end, there is an overall change in level. This change of level does not arise all at once, nor does it arise continuously; it occurs in definite increments. For example, in making a painting, it is possible to see at one point the general form of the picture emerging or, at another point, the colors coming into a definitive harmony. Of course, the changes in level may not occur in the same sequences as the changes taking place in time. The process takes place within a matrix composed of levels of inner togetherness and of sequences in time. This nonlinearity explains why Gurdjieff had to introduce discontinuities as focal crossover points. (See fig. 4.1.)

The matrix is rather akin to the game of snakes and ladders, in which there is a movement along the sequence of squares but also discontinuous jumps from one level to another.[1] In general, what we call "doing things" is like moving from one square to the next. The transition from one level to another appears more to happen by itself, or to emerge. It is like a change in perception, in what we see. Functionally, all the things that we

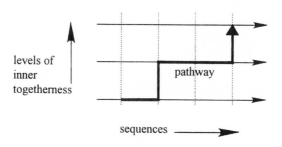

4.1. Changes in level and time.

do are much of a kind. The painter paints—though he may also prepare his canvas, mix his colors, use a palette knife, and do all manner of other things, as part of painting. He has to do things in a definite sequence, because of the nature of his materials and the conditions in which they exist. This sequential order does not appear in the final result. The final result is a realization of value which has another kind of order in it. The result is a *whole,* whereas all that is done is concerned with *parts.* At every stage of the process there is a certain state of combination of perception with actuality, of the whole with the parts, that we call the degree of inner togetherness.

Gurdjieff supposed that there were measurable gradations of inner togetherness. His steps involve both visible and invisible change, outer and inner alterations. The measure of the gradation of inner togetherness relies on something like the property of consciousness. In Gurdjieff's scheme, consciousness has a set of values in an objective framework. There is something beyond our subjective evaluations. The perception involved in the making of something meaningful has an objective role in enabling the thing to be made. If there is only a perception based on like and dislike, for example, nothing of value can be made.

As we have seen, Gurdjieff described the different levels in terms of various "matters" called hydrogens. These can transform into coarser or finer materials. The different levels of hydrogen correspond not simply to different gradations of materiality but also to their converse: to different gradations of awareness. This terminology emphasizes Gurdjieff's claim of objectivity and flies in the face of current attitudes toward art.

To take a familiar example: it is like saying that the very material of which a pot is made changes in "vibrational level" as the potter works it toward its completion and that this material acquires more of *the substance of perception.* We can say that the potter and the clay become mixed together, or that what happens is a blending of the causal and the intentional. In the causal domain we "push," while in the intentional domain we are "pulled." Gurdjieff referred to this frequently. In *Beelzebub's Tales* it is given the name *harnelmiatznel,* which is explained as the blending of the "higher with the lower in order to actualize the middle" (BT, p. 751). The definition goes on to point out that the result of this can serve as active or passive with respect to other forces. The relation of active and passive, or higher and lower, is the same as the relation of intentional and causal. The concept can even be extended into the relation of value and fact, or the spiritual and the material. The fundamental action is always the actualization of the middle. What is made by the potter out of clay is both a material object with definite properties and also an artifact which has a meaning in the human world.

The basic *action of making,* in which the human and the material world blend together, is actualized in a series of steps. These steps serve to link together what first appears as quite disparate. At each of these steps, the density of the higher and the lower, or the intentional and the causal, must be close enough together to blend. However, there have to be two critical transitions. In the one, the action of making is set free from the laws of the mechanical world from which it starts. In the other, it is made an integral part of the purposeful world in which it ends.

As the potter works on the clay spinning on the wheel, he gives it shape. The work proceeds from the simplest forms to the more subtle ones. However, a point is inevitably reached where no more can be done in this way. The clay must be removed from the wheel in order for the work of adorning the surface to be done. Fingers are now replaced by tools. The object is being turned into *something to be looked at.* It has moved from the world of things into the world of perception. This marks the *first kind of transition.* It is striking that, in this example, the transition is marked so clearly: at the point when the potter uses his wire to separate the pot from the wheel. The pot has changed from an amorphous state as a lump of clay indistinguishable from any other lump of clay, to a definite shape, capable of further transformation. There are intriguing parallels with our own prospects of transformation![2] It is sometimes said that at this point something of the soul of the potter can enter into the pot he is making.

After decorating and glazing the pot, giving it over to the furnace might first appear as the end of the potter's active involvement. But there is more to it than that. The pot is often left to dry out before subjecting it to the extreme heat of the kiln. We also need to keep in mind the peculiar role that fire plays. It alters the molecular structure of the surface, producing the final colors and quality of glaze. It is part of the decorating process, though on a deeper level. Just when the potter has no apparent physical contact with the pot, he or she—that is, as an *intention*—is having the most profound effect.

After being fired, the most sensitive pots require a careful cooling before the work is complete. At the end the pot has to be brushed and cleaned, checked for faults, and put on the shelf. It is this final set of operations which bring it into the human world as a meaningful object that can be sold or displayed. In relative terms, this brings the pot into "eternity"[3] and marks the *second kind of transition*.

My outline of the process of making a pot (see fig. 4.2) is the barest sketch of one of the most ancient and interesting of all crafts. Through the entire process, a lump of clay has acquired a beauty and a permanence that it did not have before. We say that it has evolved. We note that, if the first critical step is not made correctly, the whole inadequate pot will have to be squashed and returned to the clay store. If there is failure at the second critical step, then the pot will not be saleable.

Here is a way of thinking that takes a given whole—as symbolized by the octave—and produces fractions of the whole where each fraction plays a unique role in the whole. However, each of the *fractions of the whole* is still a whole, a fractal, because all of them are concerned with the overall action of blending the human and material worlds.[4] The shape or character of each stage reflects, in its own unique way, the shape or character of the total transition. It follows that when it comes to relating this symbolism of the octave to any actual situation, we have to identify the different parts *in relation to the whole*—and this is not something cut and dried.

In respect to Gurdjieff's treatment of form within sequence in particular, or the octave, Bennett came to the view that the universe was not only structured, but through and through *dramatic*.[5] This is because the more significant the process of change, the more hazardous become the critical points. Change—in our sense of a change in level—is not mechanically guaranteed.[6]

saleable pot
· · · · · · · · · *2nd transition*
decorating, glazing, firing, cooling, and finishing
· · · · · · · · · *1st transition*
throwing, shaping, and surfacing

4.2. Patterns of transformation in pot-making.

Shocks or Enablement

At the critical points something else must enter, or the process deviates or falters. This something else must be provided for, intentionally or mechanically, from outside the process itself. Gurdjieff's idea was that such things had been provided for in the creation and evolution of the universe, but that they were only partially developed. Humanity is a part of the incomplete interventions. These interventions at the critical points can also be taken to be points of maximum significance for intelligence. They create conditions in which evolution is possible.

In the first critical transition, there is a change in the relation of the potter to his pot. In the previous stages, his connection was through his hands. Now it comes more through his eyes. His powers of perception and his powers of manipulation are able to meet in a new way. He begins to see the pot as it will be seen by a customer. Thereafter, the pot begins to have a being of its own. In Judeo-Christian mythology, as a parallel, we have the notion that God "breathed spirit" into the clay from which the human being was fashioned to make it into His own image.

Gurdjieff referred to what enters at this critical point as a *shock*. What is a shock? First of all, it is a discontinuity. It is as if the process starts again, but from another point. Secondly, it is characterized by the meeting between two independent forces. At the beginning of the making of the pot, the potter with his hands on the clay is almost part of the clay: he is his hands, and what is operating is simply the intelligence of his hands. He could form the pot with his eyes closed. At the critical point, when the pot is taken from the wheel, he is separated from the pot. He can look at it instead of feel it. Because of this separation, something new is possible: another kind of intelligence.

Gurdjieff says that this first shock comes from outside the process. This simply means that it does not follow on what was begun but constitutes a new beginning. It appears that there is nothing "from outside" coming in at all when the potter removes the pot from the wheel; however, a new factor belonging to the potter "kicks in," and the process can take a new direction, because the potter has to look at the outside of the pot instead of working inside it.

Gurdjieff distinguishes two types of shock: the "higher" and the "lower." Through the use of the symbolism of the diatonic scale (see fig. 4.3),

DO

——— *higher shock*

SI

LA

SOL

FA

——— *lower shock*

MI

RE

DO

4.3. Diagram of shocks.

both of the critical points are placed where there is shortened interval, a semitone, between the notes; however, Gurdjieff said that they appear differently according to whether there is an ascending or a descending octave:

> In an ascending octave the first "interval" comes between mi and fa. If corresponding additional energy enters at this point the octave will develop without hindrance to si, but between si and do it needs a *much stronger "additional shock"* for its right development than between mi and fa, because the vibrations of the octave at this point are of a considerably higher pitch and to overcome a check in the development of the octave a greater intensity is needed.
>
> In a descending octave, on the other hand, the greatest "interval" occurs at the very beginning of the octave, immediately after the first do, and the material for filling it is very often found either in the do itself or in the lateral vibrations evoked by do. For this reason, a descending octave develops much more easily than an ascending octave and in passing beyond si reaches fa without hindrance; here an "additional shock" is necessary, though *considerably less strong* than the first "shock" between do and si. (ism, pp. 131–2).

Both of the two kinds of shock mark a discontinuity in the way of working. They are called shocks from the idea that such discontinuities must have some kind of cause. More generally, however, they are brought about by a change in the functioning of the system—that is, an alteration in the way in which its various components are linked together and how it is coupled to its environment. The crucial factor, therefore, is a change in the relation between the inside and the outside of the system. Like many of Gurdjieff's terms, the word *shock* draws on strong psychological experiences. In particular, this term draws on the fairly common and striking experience of "waking up" when subject to a strong emotional disturbance or sudden change in the sphere of perception.

Gurdjieff was to elaborate and modify his description of the two kinds of shock during the course of his teaching. For example, he later spoke of the first shock (between mi and fa) as coming "from outside" the main process, and of the second (between si and do) as coming from "inside" the do. The latter idea comes from the concept that the second do, which represents the completed state, has an extended realm of influence that encompasses the si-do interval. In this sense, there is the suggestion that the ascending process has to come within the sphere of influence of the final state itself in order to be made complete. In theological terms, this would mean that man cannot complete his self-realization "from below" (this would require energy of cosmic intensity) but requires the assistance of the Divine itself. For all that can be attained through works only grace can finally "save us."

The final stage, then, cannot be any kind of "making"; it is a pure act of will in which nothing is done but everything is accomplished. In the biblical story of Moses, after all his dramatic endeavors, God still decides that he will not enter the promised land. In the case of the potter, the final step concerns whether or not the pot is acceptable to a given market or customer.

I have introduced the idea of ascending and descending octaves without explanation. In the example of the potter, we were dealing with an ascending octave, which begins from an intention or aim. It is a response to value. The reverse kind of octave is sometimes referred to by Gurdjieff as "creation." This can lead to confusion, since we also tend to identify what the potter is doing as creation. The descending octave of pottery starts with the market. It is the market that makes it possible for the potter to pursue his craft. It is the market that says: "Let there be potters, and let them make these sort of things." Naturally enough, the market is not a person and has no single voice. What the market does have, however, is *authority*, though we must understand that such authority acts only within the domain of *fact*.[7] The market creates the possibilities for craftspeople by determining the availability of resources. This can be seen, from one vantage point, as exerting a pressure; but from another, it is exerting a pull. In this latter sense the market is dynamic and changing. The potter who fails to keep up with the market goes out of business.

It is from this special standpoint that we can say that it is the market (or customer) who "creates." But the market does not create any *thing*, any pot, as such. What it does is to activate the *possibility* of pots being made. Looking at the situation in this way, we can even picture to ourselves that the potter making the pot is performing the *structural* equivalent of an act of worship with regard to a creator figure. This would apply whether we regard the market as satanic or as divine!

We only see the descending octave if we have gone through an ascending one. The experience of going through an ascent provides us with data on the series of levels which have been generated "from above." Gurdjieff's descending octaves "go by themselves" without any particular aim. They automatically produce stages of lesser and lesser degrees of freedom. The various stages thus produced constitute "stages" in another sense: the theatrical meaning of *stage*, or sets of conditions in which different kinds of action are possible. This is why Gurdjieff quoted with approval the hermetic phrase "The way up is at the same time the way down" (ISM, p. 207). Gurdjieff's view of creation is incomprehensible without the experience of the structure of realization. We come to know the higher levels by realizing them through our own achievements. It is this, and only this, which can enable us to read the signs of a higher intelligence working within the sphere of human life. Once we do this, this same higher intelligence can begin to play an active part in what we do.

In practical affairs, such as making pots, we know that some of us can tune in to the dynamics of the market and become more successful. This is much the same as coming to "know the will of God." Gurdjieff's depiction of the octave was not restricted to mystical or religious beliefs but extended to the totality accessible through human intention.

The Evolutionary Sequence and Physical Science

As noted in chapter 2, Gurdjieff called himself an out and out materialist. In his view, everything existing in the universe is composed of matter and energy alone. His concept of energy is much simpler than that of a modern physicist. Besides differences in quantity of energy, he also distinguishes different rates of vibration in matter. This use of the idea of vibrations may strike us as rather quaint in these times, but we can accept it as a way of describing different *levels* of energy. Its nearest analogue in twentieth-century physics is the idea of discrete energy levels within an atom, due to quantum effects. In Gurdjieff's explanations, the idea of different rates of vibration, or levels of energy, is extended by implication to include hierarchies of different *qualities* of energy.[8]

In physics a distinction is made between thermal energy and energy available for mechanical work. The two energies are said to be of different quality. Only a fraction of thermal energy can be converted into work. This is the main distinction which allows us to consider a differential of quality. We can extend the idea of qualities of energy by saying that there are different kinds of work, cr organized energy. This extension is applied in ecology when different qualities of energy are distinguished as we go up a food chain. They can be given a relative measure by calculating the ratio of the amount of energy fed into a given system to the amount concentrated from that energy for the system's own functioning, or level of work. In this view, work such as reading and thinking is at a very high level indeed, since its cost in energy is extremely great.[9]

It is therefore possible to consider a Gurdjieffian evolutionary sequence as one in which energy is taken to higher levels. At each step, a certain fraction of the energy available is concentrated for a higher step. In the case of the food chain, energy is transferred upward from organism to organism. Needless to say, with every step made upward, there is an inevitable waste product which goes in the downward direction and is involutionary. Thus, the whole process has two results. One is the maintenance and evolution of the biosphere, and the other is the production of heat (which radiates into space).

In this view, what goes up an octave is related to the energy of the systems involved. Now, these various qualities of energy are concentrated in different organizations of matter (molecules, cells, tissues, organs, systems, and so on). These store, transfer, process, and transform energies. So we can also talk about the evolutionary sequence in terms of a transfer between different levels of material organization, each associated with its own kind of energy.

This leads us to introduce something which can help us understand—in a different way from before—what is meant by a "critical
point" in the development of an octave. If we picture to ourselves a chemical process whereby some more complex and highly organized molecules
are produced out of simpler and less organized ones, then we have to see
what makes it possible for these higher forms to endure when the overall
tendency is toward a degradation of energy. If we reduce our account of
this kind of process to changes in the chemical or potential energy of the
molecules—a relatively simple quantitative measure—then we come up
with graphs which look like the diagram in figure 4.4.

Along the horizontal axis we have the various molecules, from the most
simple to the most complex. Along the vertical axis, we have chemical
potential energy. If the graph were just an ascending curve, then we can
see intuitively that there would always be a tendency for the system to
slide back down again. However, what we find in chemical syntheses are
dips in the curves forming small valleys of stability. As the more energized
molecules fluctuate in state, they keep falling back to the minimal energy
condition (in the valley). Only some relatively high input of energy will
enable a molecule to go over the crest of a hill and get onto the degradation slope, down to the next valley of relative stability. At the same time,
this means that in order to reach this particular valley from below, we
have to put into the system more energy than this state requires, to get
over the hill in the first place. In either direction—up or down—more
energy is required to pass through a hilly region. This extra energy corre-

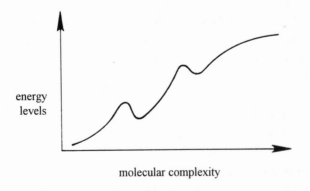

energy
levels

molecular complexity

4.4. Energy levels.

sponds to the shock of Gurdjieff's system. Interestingly enough, this also serves to show that crossing the critical point results in a new condition of stability. It is rather like reaching a ledge in a difficult ascent of a mountain. We do not have to keep going to prevent ourselves from sliding back. The extra energy is due to something like overcoming the action of repulsive forces, which come into play as simpler molecules aggregate, before they can lock into new positions.

We encounter similar phenomena in nuclear synthesis. We also find critical points associated with any phase transition, such as that between ice and water, where the temperature has to rise above the equilibrium value to set the change off. A simple and useful illustration of an ascending octave would start with ice and end with steam: in the first phase, the ice heats up and then goes through a phase change and becomes water; then the water heats up and reaches the next critical transition at the boiling point and turns into steam. In both critical transitions, the relevant two phases coexist. This already anticipates Gurdjieff's notion that two distinct substances are involved at these points.

The question of the second type of critical point is not so obvious in physical phenomena as the first. The notion is that of something "coming from the state of completion," enveloping and holding the final transitional state. A good way of talking about this is to see the evolved product merging into a greater whole. In our simple example of heating water, the greater whole is the atmosphere: when the water is turned into vapor, it diffuses into the atmosphere and becomes part of it. This is where Gurdjieff's teaching about *atoms* is significant. For him, atoms were not the units known in physics but the least particle of a given whole. For instance, one could talk of an atom of water as the least drop which could exhibit all the properties of water, such as wetness, surface tension, and so on: "An atom of water will in this case be one-tenth of one-tenth of a cubic millimeter of water taken at a certain temperature . . ." (ISM, p. 176).

Every member of a given organic species, such as a dog, is just such an atom of that species. In this perspective, an octave spanned between two atoms, and an evolutionary sequence took an atom of lower matter and transformed it into an atom of higher matter. Or it took the energy of a lower matter and transformed it into the energy of a higher matter.

The second critical transition can be understood on the lines of assimilation, rather as this takes place in the process of feeding in biological systems. Food taken in is processed until it becomes part of the organism. In this sense, when it crosses the si-do interval, the matter which is evolved enters another world. It becomes part of a greater whole. An atom of potassium present in the sea salt with which we flavor our food is one thing, but as an atom in a synaptic link in our brains, it is quite another.

In general, then, we can easily find physical phenomena which illustrate some of the characteristics of Gurdjieff's first kind of critical interval, for which a shock is required. The second kind of critical interval is best illustrated from the realm of biology, where the distinction between part and whole is significant. What we have at the beginning of a process of transformation is just like a piece of construction, of fitting bits together: it is relatively mechanical. In passing through the first critical interval, or in acquiring the energy of the first shock, the action moves into a chemical phase. The very material undergoing the process changes—just as in cooking! The transition of the second shock is rather curious. The process of transformation comes to stop, as it were, and its results "go elsewhere." In other words, it is no longer connected with the way it got to be what it is. It is like the case of a man who becomes free of his personal history, including his efforts and experiences in transforming himself. The higher do is *already there in the world of being,* and the results of transformation simply become identical with it. The efforts which belong to the first phase, and the experiences which belong to the process after the first shock, remain in their own worlds.

Notes

1. In general, games are useful analogues because they combine intention with hazard. Behind this lies the fundamental triad: intention-hazard-mechanicality, hazard providing the link between the other two. I discuss the logic of the triad in chapter 6.
2. Gurdjieff refers to crossing between two streams, the stream of mechanical life and the stream of conscious life. Crossing over is equivalent to making the mi-fa transition. See the chapter "The Octave of Salvation" in J. G. Bennett, *The Way to Be Free.*
3. In archaeology, pottery is often one of the major indicators of a civilization, and pots have been found which are thousands of years old and hence relatively "eternal."

4. A fractal is a shape in which every small part has a shape similar or identical to the shape of the whole.

5. Bennett said that it was only after he had come to understand the universal significance of *hazard* that he was able to understand Gurdjieff's description of the octave in these terms; cf. *Talks on Beelzebub's Tales.* The precise form of Gurdjieff's octave is not essential to this principle.

6. In *Beelzebub's Tales* Gurdjieff's portrayal of the law of seven goes further than his earlier description of the octave by extending the degrees and types of uncertainty inherent in evolution. Beyond the first critical transition, things get trickier and trickier as we go deeper and deeper into the intentional regions. However, the general interpretation I had given here of the critical transitions or "shocks" can easily be extended to enable us to understand these later refinements.

7. Hence, former prime minister Margaret Thatcher's terse comment: "You can't buck the market."

8. Gurdjieff's implicit scheme was made explicit by Bennett in his book *Energies,* in which Bennett carefully distinguishes between quantity, intensity, and quality.

9. See E. P. Odum, *Ecology and Our Endangered Life-Support Systems,* p. 78.

· 5 ·

Sevenfold Architecture

*Numbers are always connected with our ideas of wholeness. And whole-
ness is always connected with our visions of structure. There are several
basic ways in which mankind has looked at these things. Gurdjieff's use
of the idea of laws is a very structural approach, since we have a whole
that is divided into three or seven parts, each essential to the whole.
The tricky thing is to grasp what the whole is. We can call it the universe
or something like that, but that tells us very little. When we get hold of
what Gurdjieff is talking about, we see that his trick was to let us think
that the whole related to the law of three and the whole related to the
law of seven are exactly the same. This is actually built into the enneagram and is a challenging assumption. It may well be that it is true
only when it is made to be true.*

The Law of Seven

The idea of the octave as a universal analogical model is based on a
very general understanding of levels of organization, corresponding to
different scales. If we have an organized whole, then it will exhibit typical
properties and typical entities on a series of levels; it will have an organizational hierarchy. Typically, we describe such hierarchies in terms rang-
ing from the smallest recognizable constituent unit to the organization as
a whole, thus establishing a scale from least to greatest. Some examples
are shown in figure 5.1.[1]

Each of these widely known and used hierarchies happens to have a
similar number of levels. They are, of course, merely human labels, and
there are some widely different versions of the ones I have shown (especially of the military example). They correspond to structures in our perception and thinking that, if we accept the principle of universal

Taxonomic	*Physiological*	*Military*
kingdom	individual	general
phylum	organ system	colonel
class	organ	major
order	tissue	captain
family	cell	lieutenant
genus	organelle	sergeant
species	molecule	private

5.1. Sevenfold hierarchies.

intelligence, are there for a reason. Such structures are not unambiguous nor are they fixed: they encourage perception rather than condition it. The top level in each case appears at the threshold of something radically new, belonging to a new level of wholeness:[2] in the case of taxonomy, that of all life-forms on earth; in the case of physiology, the life of the organism in an ecology; and in the case of the military, the political leadership (such as that embodied in the president in the United States). In more detail, we can point out that, in the case of physiology, we can move on upwards as in figure 5.2.[3]

We should also note that there is a shift of emphasis as we ascend any of these scales. In the military example we move from the execution of commands up into the formulation and creation of commands, or from doing to commanding. It is interesting that in real life there are strong barriers separating the realm of the soldier in the trench from the realm of the generals at headquarters!

biosphere
biogeographical region
biome
landscape
ecosystem
biotic community
population (of a species)
organism

5.2. Ecological hierarchy.

The rudiments of Gurdjieff's two kinds of shock are implicit in such organizational hierarchies. Of course, it is not possible to derive the particular format that Gurdjieff used, but the correlation is striking enough: one kind of transition serves to bind octaves together into a higher-order scale, such as that encompassing the physiological and the ecological octaves; another kind marks the changeover region between the tendencies of one kind of operation to tendencies of another kind (officers are trained separately and tend not to be promoted from the ranks).

Gurdjieff's masterly step was in linking organizational hierarchies—such as those he first expounded in terms of the "cosmic octave"—in their various forms with a *progression of action,* so that we can see octaves developing "in time." In one stroke, Gurdjieff could then relate his description of the organization of the universe to humanity's attempts to produce change and improve its lot.

We can picture it in terms of the military example by considering ourselves as a private wanting to become a general. The steps we must take in ascending any octave are fraught with difficulty. As Gurdjieff put it, we have to "go against the stream." For example, it becomes imperative that if we are to leave the realm of the "poor bloody infantry," then we need to relinquish our old sense of camaraderie and consider many things, such as casualties and duty, in a different light. Taking over command requires a tremendous shift of attitude. Seeing what is needed at the critical point of transition means all the difference between advancement and failure, life and death.

The general idea we find in Gurdjieff's scheme is that some primordial will sets up a hierarchy, so that a movement from below is made possible which can progress back up the various organizational levels, *though in unpredictable ways.* The movement from below is temporal and successive: in relation to this, the structure of the various levels from above to below is "eternal." The octave is therefore a peculiar marriage of the *temporal* and the *eternal,* which two sides must always be kept in mind.

There is the question: Why should we have seven levels and not four or ten, for example? A perfectly valid reply is: Yes, why indeed not? Another, quite different response is that we find in practice that what we take to be organized wholes always have "about" seven levels; it may be a fact of life. For example, after years of intensive deliberation involving the work of hundreds of people, the OSI (Open Systems Interconnect) model for computer communications has finally settled on a scheme of seven functional levels. This is an entirely pragmatic scheme with no theoretical bias.[4] In the seminal work of Eliot Jacques, a theoretician of management and organization, there are seven levels of "time-span capacity," corresponding to seven levels of abstraction in logic and human action. Contrary to contemporary fashions in downsizing business to just four or three levels of responsibility, Jacques's scheme suggests that seven levels are necessary to cover the full range of possibilities a business might encounter. His seven levels are divided into three that are relatively concrete and four that are relatively abstract. (See fig. 5.3.)[5]

False egalitarian ideals have tended to obscure and even deny such hierarchies. In present conditions of turbulence and change, they are re-emerging as a necessary feature of effective organization. The sevenfold scheme is not arbitrary but, at the moment, we have no theory to explain why.[6] Gurdjieff portrays the discovery of sevenfoldness as a matter of observation of the similarity of diverse natural processes, much as present-day scientists have come to discover the "patterns in chaos."

It is possible that we have wired into us some capacity for perception in octaves, just as the linguist Noam Chomsky says that we are born with a capacity for generating language structures in ourselves. But we must remember that what is now wired into us arose by an evolutionary process and must in some way reflect the world in which we exist and how we operate in it. It is very likely that we see "in several," and that there is no mechanically precise number involved beyond the requirement that it be more than three, say, and less than ten. The musical analogy of the

Level	Time-span	Realm of Work	Level of Abstraction
7	20 years	global	highest
6	10 years	multinational	creation of institutions
5	5 years	national	intuitive theory
4	2 years	regional	conceptual modeling
3	1 year	50,000 sq. ft.	imaginal scanning
2	3 months	5,000 sq. ft.	imaginal concrete
1	1 week	500 sq. ft.	perceptual-motor

5.3. Levels of abstraction and time-span capacity.

octave helps us to see that there can be many different interpretations but that Gurdjieff's version represents an optimum. It is halfway between an oversimplification and being caught up in the myriad of details.

As yet we do not have any precise kind of science able to measure the properties associated with the different numbers in our perception. It is interesting, however, to note the experiment which René Daumal puts into his fantastic novel *Mount Analogue:* he challenges us to follow any sequence of actions we might do in our minds and see how many steps we can hold together at once. The general finding is that we fail beyond four steps.[7] It is possible to regard this result as supporting Gurdjieff's placing of the first shock after the first three steps. It is easy to keep three steps in mind but harder to keep four. That is why we switch from concrete to abstract after three.

It seems to be the case that we can perceive and understand things somewhere in this range of "the several"—just as we do in the range associated with connections and relationships, with regard to which Gurdjieff formulated the law of three. If this notion is correct, then Gurdjieff's concentration on just two fundamental laws of three and seven corresponds with the two main modes of understanding that every human being is born with. It is then possible to connect these two modes together—as surely they are connected anyway in ourselves—and use our powers of analysis to see how they are involved in the making of each other.

Seeing in Depth

It is because the two laws appear as intertwined with each other that we may suppose that there is an intermediary mode of understanding between the three and the seven which represents their difference: $7 - 3 = 4$. Thus would be a secondary fourfold law. We also have the possibility of the addition of the two laws: $7 + 3 = 10$. There may well be a law of ten. Indeed, this is what we find in the enneagram, which is based on the decimal system. To relate these abstract possibilities to the figure of the enneagram, we might suppose that they would appear as shown in figure 5.4. The law of ten appears above the circle because it is beyond the nine. The law of four appears opposite it, embedded in the bottom part of the figure. The law of four concerns the mixing and blend-

LAW OF TEN

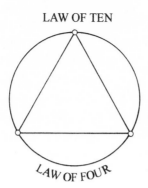

5.4. Implicit laws of the enneagram.

ing which was the province of alchemy. Our playing with numbers and symbols here is more than arbitrary, since we have to take account of the *progressiveness* which is a feature of the movement in the enneagram, signified in the sequence from 0 to 9.[8] I interpret this to mean that the degree of order at each stage is an advance over the preceding, and that there is a progression of laws of greater and greater intelligence. This will form the background to all our explorations in the following chapters.

What we have to fix in our minds at this point is the general idea of combining two distinct forms of understanding. This is an important key to Gurdjieff's intellectual method. What we have essentially is one mode of understanding connected with a small number, and another mode connected with a significantly larger number. It is only the two working in combination with each other that can provide us with an understanding in depth—just as we have a perception in depth through the conjunction of two eyes and a perception of color through the conjunction of short- and long-wave sensitivity. What we call color, depth, and understanding exemplify the structures of meaning that combinations of forms produce in a dynamic continuum formed in the process of their dialogue. The law of three concerns our grasp of immediate connectivity or relations,[9] while the law of seven emerges for us in such things as our fascination with narrative and with any time-factored structuring of our experience.[10]

One important thing we must keep in mind is that Gurdjieff, by his placement of the two shocks, clearly distinguished the form and sequence of descending and ascending octaves. In the octave as such, of course, we have eight notes, the last being a reiteration (though on another level) of the first. The final note, the higher do, always represents the unity of the whole. In Gurdjieff's treatment, the do's are always creators, though of different orders. Therefore, when the seventh note, si, is reached, we are at the threshold of the "god," or creator, of the octave. In the god of the octave, the threefoldness of the triad reverts back to unity again. But this reversion is only under the power of the do itself. That is why Gurdjieff says that a very great deal of energy is needed in the ascending octave to pass from si to do. In contrast, this interval is filled by the higher do in the descending octave and constitutes no barrier at all. This provides a technical distinction between creator and creature.

If we picture the lower do as an atom (such as an organic molecule) and the higher do as an atom on a totally different scale (such as the whole organism), then the idea is that the organism as a whole has an integrative power that cannot be provided by any ascent from the cell. If we reflect on this, we can begin to see that this is a necessary condition for there being organisms at all; otherwise, they would be dissolved in the general processes of evolution and involution. A do is a pause, a special nodal point, in the whole dynamic flux.

The lower interval represents a meeting of dynamics and substance: in any real octave the two sides of movement and becoming, dynamic and substance, are intertwined. But it is also the case that their distinction is echoed in the way that real things are accomplished. If we remember examples such as the potter making something meaningful from clay, these abstract ideas become clearer. The first stages have no permanence, no substance. In all human endeavors, these stages are just the thoughts and efforts working from the outside. A threshold has to be passed before this striving becomes substantial. It has to penetrate within.

A real process can be felt. It can be weighed. Among the Gurdjieff movements there are dances which contain an inner work—invisible to any audience—which makes them initially much more difficult to perform. The introduction of this inner work to the students has to come at the critical moment, when the striving has reached a certain level. It is so designed that this additional effort, of a different kind than which went before, enables the performance to be lifted into another region of development. The performance then no longer comes from effort directed from the outside but from an inner feeling. This corresponds to the first critical transition. Without the inner work, learning the movements would continue in a mechanical circle, and we would have trained dancers and not a living presence. As for the second critical transition, this—as Bennett has pointed out—is when the spirit of the movement is realized.[11] It is then that the "movement performs itself." It is in regard to these possibilities that Gurdjieff insisted that his sacred dances afforded the key to a real understanding of his ideas. The will-pattern of the dances, their *logos,* has to be realized within the functional process of the dancers, and the two can only be united in *being.* One of the best definitions of being was given by Madame Ouspensky when she said: "Being is what you can *bear.*"[12]

Seven into Three

In the enneagram, the law of seven is intertwined with the law of three. This means that the two laws can map into each other or reflect each other. It should be possible to see how the sevenfold architecture we have been looking at—the structure of significant change—is reflected in three distinct parts. There are curious mathematical relationships between three and seven, but we will confine ourselves to qualitative imagery.[13]

Reverting to the structure of the octave we have: three notes, then a shock, and then four notes before the final or second shock and the reaching of the next do. We assume that the octave is made up of three triads, or three groups of relations. We already have the first triplet in the first three ascending notes. Next comes a shock. Let us consider the next three notes as another triplet: what does that leave us with? We have another note, then a shock, and then the do of the next octave. If we consider si–shock–do as a triplet, we now have three triplets as desired (fig. 5.5).

In fact, Gurdjieff always links si–shock–do together, by saying that—in a descending octave—the "will of the higher do fills the interval and produces si." Further, his first three notes (do-re-mi) are always described as having a certain kind of momentum in common, a kind of movement that cannot of itself reach any higher. Thus, the first three notes are also bound together in their own way. This leaves the middle three notes, which signify a triplet equivalent to the first on the other side of the mi-fa barrier. The first transition brings together the first three notes into a whole. This is a step of progressive integration: without this transition,

```
do   |
 —   |  three
si   |
la   |
sol  |  two
fa   |
 —
mi   |
re   |  one
do   |
```

5.5 The octave in triplets.

these three would continue to repeat in succession, a condition that Gurdjieff called a deviation of the octave which results in going around in circles. (See fig. 5.6).

The three triplets make up a higher order triplet, each of them carrying a specific quality of the triad, such as passive, active, or reconciling. We are anticipating ourselves, because we have yet to go into the nature of the law of three, which we will do in the next part of the book.[14] I have added the terms *mechanical, intentional,* and *spiritual* also in anticipation of our later explorations.

```
do
 —      RECONCILING   spiritual
si

la
sol     ACTIVE        intentional
fa

 —
mi
re      PASSIVE       mechanical
do
```

5.6. The octave as a form of the triad.

Notes

1. See Odum, *Ecology and Our Endangered Life-Support Systems,* p. 27. The examples are just as they are given by Odum, who has no particular vested interest in looking for sevens! Gurdjieff, in his *Meetings with Remarkable Men,* describes a visit to a Sarmoun monastery where he sees a striking artifact made of seven branching limbs that indicate postures to be taken in sacred dances. As he points out in his introduction to the book, his intention throughout was to create strong emotional images related to the Work. It is not confined to rare and exotic people. Once you have the idea of events on different scales, you can analyze your day and see it as an intricate branching structure of behaviors that define your life. But first you have to be convinced that there is an underlying structure.

2. See chapter 4. I am treating the relation between higher and lower do's as that between different degrees or kinds of wholeness. The simplest picture of this I can make treats the lower do as an atom and the higher do as an organism. Every level has its characteristic elements, which may be taken as atoms relative to some higher level of organization.

3. See Odum, *Ecology and Our Endangered Life-Support Systems,* for explanations of the terms in the figure.

4. Private communication from Chris Thompson. There is no existing theory which accounts for this kind of structuring. Very likely, however, we will come across such structures when there is a strictly linear-hierarchical arrangement. But contemporary business organizations, which actually concentrate on tasks and make rapid adjustments to changing economic forces, tend to flatten to three or four levels.

5. This table is adapted from the table "Summary of Strata and Levels of Abstraction," which appears in Elliot Jacques, R. O. Gibson, and D. J. Isaac, *Levels of Abstraction in Logic and Human Action,* p. 294. Jacques and J. G. Bennett exchanged ideas at one time, and Bennett is referred to in Jacques's book, a unique and extraordinary collection of studies that should be more widely known. What is not touched upon is how organizations only work well if they include nonhierarchical relationships as well as hierarchical ones.

6. Whereas in science we have laws largely expressed in mathematical equations, in the realms of will and consciousness there are patterns largely expressed in symbols and numbers.

7. Others have pointed out that the maximum number of distinct elements we can keep in mind, without reference to sequence, is seven. Putting these two pragmatic findings together gives an astonishingly close approximation to the basic ideas of the octave.

8. The sequence of integers is obviously one of the easiest ways of indicating a stepwise progression. Structure arises when we take only a limited set of numbers. Again, in the simplest representations, the starting point must be zero or

one, with corresponding consequences. The numbers, then, are in no way funda-mental but simply part of the symbolization.

9. The work of the American philosopher Charles Sanders Peirce is particularly important for the study of relations, work which was taken up later by Bertrand Russell; see *The Principles of Mathematics*.

10. See Alexander Marshack, *The Roots of Civilization*. This was a very original book in drawing attention to the amount of detailed, shared, and structured knowl-edge required for any advance. It is far removed from mystical cant about ancient wisdom, insisting that the real ancients found things out through hard work just as we do today.

11. Described in the chapter "Doing Movements" in J. G. Bennett, *The Way to be Free*.

12. Reported in J. G. Bennett's autobiography *Witness*.

13. The most intriguing is that seven is the largest number of objects that can be formed into subsets of three, each having one and only one member in common with every other subset of three (pointed out by Oswald Veblen to Arthur Young; see Young, *The Reflexive Universe*). If we have seen objects labeled *a, b, c, d, e, f, g*—then the subsets are *abc, ade, afg, bdf, beg, cdg, cef*. There can be no more than seven such subsets. This property vividly suggests the fundamental interconnec-tivity of the law of three and the law of seven. However, it is important not to lose sight of the fact that these are just properties of numbers like countless others. For example, three is the largest number of objects from which we can take subsets of two, such that only one member is common to each pair, and there are three such subsets. Thirteen is the largest number of objects within which we can form subsets of four with a similar property, and there are then thirteen such subsets. Quite possibly, then, there is a law of four that combines meaningfully with a law of thirteen.

Indeed, if we treat four and thirteen similarly to the way three and seven are treated in the construction of the enneagram, then we use as our number base (see note 5, chap. 1) $13 + 4 = 17$ and calculate the ratios of 1:4 and 1:13 in this base. The result is the same kind of recurrent figure of six points as in the ennea-gram (though there are two of them!) and a square connecting the force points 4, 8, 12, and 16 in place of the triangle at points 3, 6, and 9. It is almost as symmetrical as the enneagram and, perhaps, quite as intriguing. It is simply that four and thirteen are harder to handle than three and seven!

The central point to realize is that the numerical aspect of the system is not its foundation but used by way of illustration. Gurdjieff's incessant reference to various scales points the way. If there are such fundamental laws as three and seven then there must be other corresponding laws. The enneagram is a kind of paradigm and not a formula. Bennett was one of the few followers of Gurdjieff who realized this and began to explore in an open manner the various possible laws and their combinations (such as in the enneagram).

14. Reading the sequence of the three elements from the bottom upward, we have

the sequence passive-active-neutralizing, which Ouspensky, and later Bennett, saw as signifying the basic pattern of evolution. Conversely, from the top downward, we have the sequence neutralizing-active-passive, which Bennett understood as order or the generation of order and considered to be the basic pattern whereby conditions are set up within which a type of action is made possible (much as the determining conditions of space and time make motion possible). As we saw in the pottery example, the market forms a nesting set of conditions for the production of pottery.

In the Samkhya system of India, attributed to the sage Kapila in about 200 BC, nature is described in terms of the workings of three *gunas* (literally "strands," or qualities). These are *tamas* (dark, inertia), *rajas* (red, energy), and *sattva* (light, consciousness). In the orthodox interpretation of Samkhya, liberation or transformation amounts to a lessening of *tamas* and an increase in *sattva*. We could construct a scale starting with pure *tamas* and ending in pure *sattva*, with six stages of various mixtures of the three *gunas* in between: t-r-s, t-s-r, r-t-s, r-s-t, s-t-r, s-r-t. These would correspond to re, mi, fa, sol, la, si. In this way, we could use the triad to construct the octave. Bennett and others, under Ouspensky's direction, undertook a study of the Samkhya system in the 1930s and were probably influenced to think of combinations of the three forces of the triad according to Gurdjieff. In the Samkhya system, the three *gunas* mix according to various proportions or dominance, and the order in which they are shown in the combinations reflects this. Bennett took *dominance* in the sense of "taking the initiative." A full circle was made when the sage Sri Anirvan, an outstanding Vedic scholar and associate of Sri Aurobindo, connected Samkhya back to Gurdjieff (see Lizelle Reymond, *To Live Within*). A more important point is that there are other interpretations of Samkhya which are not so materialistic in their thinking. See A. G. E. Blake, *The Triad*.

· 6 ·

I Put Three Together

Threeness is one of the master ideas of human culture. It is integrally linked with a vision of creativity, of making the new from the old. It draws upon our intuitions of a spiritual order intervening in the workings of the world—without violating any of the restrictions under which we exist, such as cause and effect. When we speak of it as a law, we can become too fixed. It is an open-ended principle, capable of endless interpretations. Gurdjieff's formulations of the law of three are masterly works of art in their own right. We should remember his injunction that to understand is to think, feel, and sense together: to have the law of three working in us. We understand the law by making it happen in ourselves. It is this that enables us to link with the phenomena of the physical world and begin to see how real change is possible.

The Law of Three

THE IDEA of a law of three must at first seem pretty strange to most people. How can the number three have a law? If we now seem headed for some abstruse region of number theory, appearances are deceptive: threeness is implicit in nearly all our human relationships. Our linkages with other people in relation to our various purposes show what is at stake.

The old adage "Two's company but three's a crowd" points out that threeness is not automatic. Whenever there are three people in a situation, the tendency is for two of them to gang up on the third, or exclude him or her. Gurdjieff expressed the same thing, though in a more profound and technical way, when he said: "Man is third-force blind." We cannot, on the whole, accommodate a third person in our relationships, because we do not see what other role there is to play. It is only when

80

something needs to change that we entertain the idea of third force. Couples whose marriage is breaking down turn to a marriage counselor, parties in a dispute turn to arbitration, and so on. Perhaps more important, nearly all couples accept that their relationship has to change when they have children; otherwise the marriage fractures.

To associate three with change is the first part of the law of three. Gurdjieff asserts that change can happen only when three independent forces come together. If there are only two forces, they either affirm or deny each other, and the situation is static. If there is to be a real change, there needs to be something independent of yes and no, plus and minus. When a third force enters, the other two forces are no longer locked into each other in the same way as before. There is an extra degree of freedom and a higher level of awareness. This idea was known in ancient times, and we can find it particularly in the Indian system called Samkhya, one of the earliest systems, which taught that the workings of nature (*prakriti*) arose by the combination of three qualities, or *gunas*.[1]

Our terminology moves around between *people* and *forces* and *roles,* but these amount to the same thing in the law of three. The three components are all active, otherwise one of them would be swamped by the others and would then not be independent. To be independent, they need to be both equally strong and also of distinctive character: this is the second part of the law of three. It was this part that strongly came into Western civilization through the Christian doctrine of the Trinity. In this doctrine, God is three persons of coequal status (see fig. 6.1).[2]

The psychological importance of the law of three can hardly be exaggerated. It can be made into a truism: that if we merely react to what happens, we can never learn and will remain slaves. When there is only reaction, the situation is polarized and static. (If there is no reaction, of course, then we are brain-dead and nothing counts anyway!) Someone insults us or attacks us, and our reaction is to fight back or defend ourselves. In classical physics we have the clear idea that action and reaction are equal and opposite. It is a null situation. The reaction is a mechanical response to the action and adds nothing new. If something is to come out of this painful event, something besides reaction must play a role.

Typically, this involves a kind of honesty that brings out more information, that reveals or shows more. For example, we might express the pain we feel at being attacked and the effect it is having on us. In order to do

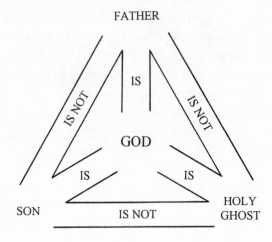

6.1. Holy Trinity.

this, we cannot be completely identified with the reaction. Or we may go even further and appear to side with the attacker, deepening that person's criticism of us! In the extreme, we follow the various injunctions of Jesus such as "Love thine enemies" and "Agree with thine adversary quickly while thou art in the way with him." Such injunctions depend on the reality of the law of three to be true. There has to be a third independent force that gives the freedom to make a change. This does not take away our reaction. It can still hurt, but we need not be slaves.

The pain we feel on being attacked can very easily bring us down into a mechanical world. The mechanical world was brilliantly analyzed by Newton centuries ago. In his three laws of motion (note the three again) we can read exact intimations of mechanicality in human life. To crudely paraphrase:

1. Things keep going the way they are until something else disturbs them.
2. The amount of disturbance is dependent on the energy brought in from outside.
3. Action and reaction are equal and opposite, and the whole situation remains the same as before.[3]

In the world of mechanics, there are only plus and minus forces, only pushing and resisting. Whatever disturbances result are just that—

results—and do not play a role in the initiating action. Imagine the pushing and resisting forces coming together and then the effect this has escaping away into the surroundings. When the law of three is in operation, what was just the disturbance appears as an independent force of its own, taking part in the formation of the action. There are various ways of picturing this, and no single way covers all the angles; but figure 6.2 is useful. Whereas before we had *A* acting on *B* (and the resulting disturbance passing away), now we have another operation: *A* acts on *B through C*.[4] The total action is twofold: the result at *B* is now uncertain and, in place of the mechanical disturbance, remains within the field of the three factors. A simple and useful way of thinking about this is to imagine *C* as a mirror in which *A* and *B* can see themselves *and the action between them*. We have to add here that the arrows can point either way, giving us the sense of a resonance within the three.

The nature of this nonmechanical resonance is such that the three forces mutually define one another. They may even refine one another. What they do not do is reduce one another to their common denominator. We have to acquire a feel for this, since it is not possible to give a completely logical definition of the forces. In Gurdjieff's system, he often speaks of an active, passive, and neutralizing force, which conjures up images of an electrical battery with a conductor between the poles. Bennett tended to use the terms *affirmative, receptive,* and *reconciling.* There is a whole corpus of alternative terms, which suggests that the three forces are not something cut and dried: "the first, the 'Affirming-force' or the

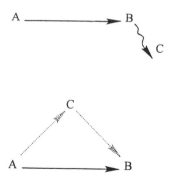

6.2. Uncertainty and the third force.

'Pushing-force' or simply the 'Force-plus'; the second, the 'Denying-force' or the 'Resisting-force' or simply the 'Force-minus'; and the third, the 'Reconciling-force' or the 'Equilibrating-force' or the 'Neutralizing-force'" (BT, p. 751).

If we start with the idea of active and passive (in spite of the second part of the law, which says that all three terms are equally active), then the idea of neutralizing is so close to that of the result or effect of the other two coming together that it loses much of its sense of being independent. It is much the same with the idea of reconciling, because we expect the reconciliation to come after what it is reconciling! This is why it is often useful simply to refer to *third force*.

What any of the terms "really" is depends on the specific situation we are looking at and what we are looking for. For example, if we are looking at physical bodies from the standpoint of motion, we are going to look for forces. If we are looking at people from the standpoint of values, we might look for ideas. There is always an aspect which stems from the concrete and specific character of the situation and the kind of entities contained in it. In addition, there is an aspect which stems from the kind of purpose or meaning we are looking for in that situation. This issue illustrates the ubiquity of the triad. Again we have three factors: the entities in the situation, its purpose, and the nature of the forces.

When we speak in general terms about the triad, this is only an abstraction, and we might as well speak of force 1, force 2, and force 3. We need to be able to view the third force as equally capable of initiating the action as either of the other two. It is not just the result of the two coming together. It is helpful to keep in mind the resonance model and picture to ourselves that each of the three forces is mutually adjusting to each of the others. However they happen to come together, once they are linked they tend toward a triadic equilibrium. The linkage serves to keep the results feeding back into the initiatives, making for the various adjustments that are possible. These adjustments Bennett called the laws of the triad, and they constitute a whole other study.[5]

What we see in the enneagram is both the law of three and the laws of the triad: the coming together of the three and their mutual impact on and adjustment to each other. In the enneagram, there are three octaves. The three come under a triadic attractor, which is represented in the triangle of the figure. The three octaves in the enneagram are of different natures, and their integration into a whole is called a *synergy:* an action in which elements of different kinds and on different levels cooperate and work together (*syn* = together; *energeia* = working).

It is when all three have come into balance with each other that synergy is possible. As in traditional theology, Gurdjieff often associates this condition with the Holy Ghost. A similar way of looking at it is that the three attain the condition of the Holy Trinity, or that the whole is *perfected.*

The Three

Although, as I have said, there are inherent limitations on any generalized version of the three forces, we can form some conception of what the three elements represent in terms of physical reality. Gurdjieff himself says that nothing exists but matter and energy, which leaves us devoid of the third category. In general, we can ascribe the active role to energy and the passive role to matter: energy provides motive force, while matter is characterized by inertia. What can be the nature of the third force?

Here is introduced what is, for us, a fundamental and necessary addition to the Gurdjieffian scheme: the category of *information*.

The proteins working in our bodies are extraordinarily specific. Specificity means information. A more extreme example is DNA, which carries the information from which the enzymes are synthesized. In every organized system we know of, it is essential to take into account the role of information. This is not to say that what information is is at all understood or conceived of in a generally agreed way. However, for some scientists, information also exists, and it is no longer correct to assume that nothing exists but matter and energy.[6]

We say that information means *in-forming,* or putting the form in. In recent times, this more active and organizing view of information is gaining ground; it is central, for example, to Bohm's interpretation of quantum mechanics. Parallels with the action of language may help us understand the nature of information. The whole universe can be seen as one great sentence or statement—such as *fiat lux*—a vast articulation of matter and energy. Information informs the world of matter and energy, and in a sense, matter and energy are unified in information. A contemporary physicist such as Wheeler offers the slogan "it from bit," meaning that objects, forces, and so on, arise out of quantum information.[7]

The articulation of the universe is usually understood in terms of laws—whether those of physics or the more metaphysical laws of Gurdjieff. *Laws* is just another name for primary types of information. Primary information brings into effect and then permeates a series of levels. On each level, there is a trinity of information, energy, and matter that establishes what exists (fig. 6.3).

Matter and energy can interchange, and my scheme suggests that information and energy can also interchange, though this has yet to be demonstrated in the realm of physics. More accessibly, every energy transformer, whether natural or manmade, involves information processing. An energy source, such as the sun, can also be regarded as an information source. This is because the radiation from the sun is of a higher order than the radiation the earth sends into space. The difference of order between input and output amounts to an input of information. The biosphere has arisen by capturing some of it, and it has evolved devices such as plants, which can transform solar energy. Information comes from information and energy processing comes from information. Information with a small amount of energy can control energy transformations involving vast amounts of energy. This is what happens when we drive a car.

The very arrangement of material things in space is information. We know from experience that the very shape of buildings can produce a definite state in people. One of the most important pieces of information in the universe concerns the arrangements of matter that we call galaxies. Our own solar system, with its sun and planets, is also a repository of information. And every biome (such as a rain forest, desert, or savannah) on earth, with its historical soils and dynamic ecologies of populations, is

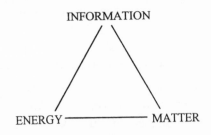

6.3. Three categories of existence.

like a library for our biosphere. Gurdjieff himself said that the same matters mean something different according to *where* they are.[8]

Information is present both in process and in structure. In a process, where energy is transformed, it can appear as a control or program. Natural and artificial processes can be looked at as computations. It is even said that the whole universe is one vast computer. Information as structure appears as *form*. This was understood in an abstract manner by the scholastics, building on Aristotle's conception of matter and form. In modern times, it is taken in a more tangible way, as in D'Arcy Wentworth Thompson's *On Growth and Form*.

I am advocating, then, a tripartite scheme of *matter, energy,* and *information:* matter being equated with the passive force, energy with the active force, and information with the third force. But we must also remember that these three factors are so intertwined that what is information in one context or set of conditions may become energy in another. This metaphysical idea becomes obvious if we consider a practical example such as insider trading. Insider information converts into vast monetary gains (money is a form of energy). These gains can be converted into acquisitions (matter). Not only can the three appearances of existence change into each other, they do so according to the context or world in which their combinations are experienced.

Creation

In Gurdjieff's scheme of Creation, there is an initial triad or combination of three forces out of which develops succeeding triads. These succeeding triads correspond to lower and lower levels of "vivifyingness" or intelligence. The first triad entails all the others that follow. It is rather as if the secondary, tertiary, and succeeding triads are echoes of the original one. We might think of them as fractals.

In the initial triad, the highest active force combines with the highest passive force to produce the primary third force.[9]

The first third force is of particular importance. The task of this first third force is to permit the arising of evolving intelligence while preserving the overall mechanism of the universe. It is, to personify it somewhat, a designer or primordial mind. In the further stages of the creative descent into lower levels, it appears with less and less vivifyingness until it becomes simply a mechanical principle of conservation.

When the primary third force arises, or is actualized, it is, in religious terms, the Word of God. It is pure information. It is the "I am the I Am." However, at the next step, in the succeeding triad, it appears not as information but as energy. This is similar to a transition from witnessing to acting and is an ancient Samkhyan idea. *The first third force becomes the active force of the next triad.* The Word becomes the command such as is expressed in Genesis: "Let there be light." It is only then that it acts as a creative power, but it can only do this if there is a new degree of matter, or a new passive force, to combine with it. The only possible source of this new matter is the previous or primary triad. There is nothing else. Gurdjieff says that the whole of the primary triad now appears as matter, or as passive.

The picture that Gurdjieff gives evokes an image of the primary third force turning into an active mode and finding an echo of itself within the primary triad. Such metaphysical talk is not entirely addressed to cosmic issues. What is focused on here is how *any whole whatsoever creates forms of itself within itself.* As with much of Gurdjieff's cosmology, what he speaks about is the logic of wholeness, which enters into all of our experience. The various representations and images are for the sake of visualizing the action of the creative power within ourselves and within every whole in nature. They are of urgent meaning.

We can complement Gurdjieff's picture by considering what happens inside the nucleus of an atom. The basic particles are *quarks.* Three of them bind together to form a proton, or nuclear particle. A proton cannot be broken up into its three constituent particles. The binding force of the proton, called the color force, also acts outside of the proton to form *mesons,* which serve to bind the particles of the nucleus—the protons and neutrons—together. So we see the primary relation of quarks giving rise to a secondary relation of nuclear particles.[10]

Gurdjieff described the three forces as "striving to reblend." In the physical world, this appears as forces of attraction. The color force holds the quarks together; the strong nuclear force holds the nucleus together; the electromagnetic force holds the atom together; and the gravitational force holds the universe together! However, there is also a factor of repulsion, otherwise all matter would collapse into itself. At the atomic level, this is due to quantum effects such as the Pauli Exclusion Principle. We can visualize the succession of triads in terms of an interplay of repulsive and attractive forces, operating at different strengths and on different scales.

In consequential triads, the third force becomes progressively weaker, signifying a decline in intelligence. So, also, in succession the other two forces diminish. Each triad generates its own message, its own informing for the next lower triad.[11] Just as in a human organization, the succession of levels means that the lower levels are cut off from the higher levels by a shielding effect.

It may help to remember occasions when we had a creative insight and it ran away with us. The initial idea is simple and clear, but its implications become so attractive and interesting that, before we realize it, we are involved in connecting everything we know with the idea. Interest is at a lower level of understanding than insight. The initial clarity becomes lost in a welter of activity. Sooner or later, our steam runs out.

We may also take an illustration from religious history in which there is an initial phase concerning a revelation or manifestation of God, followed by an initiatory action involving a very small number of people. This, in turn, is followed by various cultural manifestations such as writings, art, and even wars—manifestations which are all too often taken as the very apogee of the revelation but which are, in fact, only weak echoes of it. An example is Islam.

We cannot see the "tristinctions," or logic of a higher world, from the standpoint of a lower world. A lower intelligence cannot understand a higher intelligence. This accords with the realization that what is highest and most powerful *must* be invisible to us, because otherwise we could not exist.[12] In his first expositions of the Creation in triads, Gurdjieff says only the first triad has free intelligence. But he labored for many years in the writing of *Beelzebub's Tales* to convey a more subtle picture in which free intelligence is present, though only weakly or in an uncertain way, throughout the whole of the universe on all its levels. Maybe then, it is its probability that rapidly decreases with decrease in level.

Evolution

What does creation mean? It represents a movement from the highest informational level to the lowest informational level, from the most active to the least active. This movement is given the name *involution*. We tend to picture this in terms of above and below, but it might just as well be depicted as within and without, or deeper and more superficial.

There is a contrary movement from the least active toward the most active, which is then called *evolution*. This other kind of movement is not just involution backward.[13] We can think of evolution along the lines of eating and digestion. The matter of a triad progressively decomposes, liberating its energy. It acquires a higher degree of organization, or information, as it is assimilated. If we imagine each step in the creative involutionary process as a degree of coagulation, then each step in the evolutionary process is a degree of dissolution—and begins from the passive aspect of the triad. This enables some of the weight of the triad to be eliminated as a waste product, which is equivalent to an awakening, or release, of intelligence from conditioning.[14] An alternative description is that of "separating the fine from the coarse," which presupposes a mechanical model in which particles of varying fineness are mixed together and have to be selectively sorted. Materialistic atomism is an ancient concept and hard to shake off.

Gurdjieff says that we have to struggle with our denying parts to liberate consciousness. We return to our basic example of a human interaction. A clarifying light can break through, changing the whole tenor of the conversation. Or a moment of insight can come that surpasses the ineffective attempts to solve a problem. This might be simply the realization that we can try a different approach! The struggle alone does not produce this result. The evolutionary process, then, is an awakening which arises from below and is supported from above. We can see the subtle and close connection between the idea of shocks and the awakening which liberates the next higher third force beyond the confines of the given triad. This is what happens at the critical points in the enneagram.[15]

The Logos

What operates in the triad works rather like a combination of rules. Saying this is to look at the triad from the perspective of information, and I can illustrate what I mean by work being done on what is called artificial life. In this work, the key is to set up a combination of rules which can generate lifelike behavior rather than to specify what happens.

Imagine the flight pattern of a flock of birds, which often amazes us by its coherence. A computer program can now be written that produces this beauty and order.[16] It is composed of three rules: (1) the birds should continue to fly in the same direction, (2) they should not get too close together and (3) they should maintain the same speed as each other. That is all that is needed. Everything else can vary except for these three rules. In our interpretation, rule 1 represents the active force; rule 2, the passive or denying; and rule 3, the reconciling. It is rule 3 which brings rules 1 and 2 together.

Rules provide a model for what is meant by will. The forces that Gurdjieff speaks of are not things at all. The field of information technology, especially as it has developed in computer science, makes great use of information in the form of instructions (or rules which can be programmed). On the surface, an instruction is just a string of data; however, in its operation, it commands other data. Where there is a triad, three commands come into combination. They have to interlock. As is partially shown in the above example, the third command serves to bring the other two into connection, yet it is something in its own right. It is the combination of three commands that we want to consider as the *logos* of a situation. In Newton's physics, for example, there are three fundamental laws. From these three laws comes all the logic of motion which applies throughout the whole of classical physics. Refining the complexity of the world down to the working of just these three laws was an incredible feat. The logos of motion is given by Newton's three laws. In this light, the law of three is a *metarule*, a rule that deals with combinations of rules.

It is when we think of the combination of rules that the idea that there are just three basic factors begins to make sense. Nothing happens unless there are three forces. If we have any two rules, then *they cannot operate on each other without a third.* In the case of the flight of birds, the first two rules without the third would eventually result in the birds becoming ever more distant from each other, in which case the second rule would have no meaning. The basic fitting together of rules is triadic. Could there be more than three rules? Yes, there could, but these would consist of overlapping units of three.

In an enneagram, the three commands, the *logos*, define a space of permitted or relevant creative action (fig. 6.4). The triad governs itself. There is no need for any external guidance or control. In this sense, it is

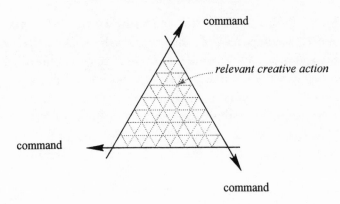

6.4. Action space defined by the logos.

at least self-steering, or cybernetic. Cybernetics is the relatively mechanical view of self-organization. The idea that relative wholes can evolve their own structure and govern themselves is now almost commonplace. It was not so commonplace when Gurdjieff taught in Russia and in France.[17]

Triamazikamno

One of the words that Gurdjieff uses in *Beelzebub's Tales* for the law of three is *triamazikamno*. Roughly, it means "three together I do" (from *tria* = three; *mazi* = together; *kamno* = I put/make/do). This has enormous bearing on the relation between the laws and our own will.[18] What can we do about the workings of a triad in which we are involved? Are we just hapless observers? If we are drawn in to either the passive or the active role, we are governed by the prevailing third force coming from the context or environment. If, on the other hand, we are able to participate in the third force itself, we can influence the form of the triad as a whole.

Participation in the third force is understanding. Through this, we can become a source of order. This is what happens in all our constructive work, as in design. It is from this that technology is possible, representing a creative descent into the material world, or a transition from information to matter.[19] There is also a participation in the third force in which something is set free. This happens in what we call art. In his *Sonnets,*

Michelangelo says that he releases the form from the marble which held it obscured. This is a transition from matter to information. The making which we find in both technology and art (though in complementary ways) is essential for our understanding.[20]

There is a further mode of participation which obtains in history or, more strictly, the history of conscious acts. Here, we have literally "I put three together." This mode of participation in the third force draws the other two forces together. In saying this, I am asserting a great deal and can offer little in the way of evidence. It is, after all, the very essence of there being any *conscious direction in history*. The important point is that such a direction cannot work by either affirmation or denial.[21] That is why it is sometimes associated with the power of ideas. Such ideas are neither true nor false, new nor old, good nor bad.[22] The synergy I briefly mentioned in relation to the enneagram is concerned with bringing the reconciling power of ideas into manifestation.

Notes

1. The ideas of Samkhya can be found in the Vedas and the Upanishads as well as in the *Mahabharata*. The central idea is dualistic, that there is both spirit, or *purusha,* and matter, or *prakriti. Purusha* does nothing. All doing is in *prakriti* and results from an imbalance between the three *gunas* of which it is composed.

2. The term *person* was taken from Roman law and does not mean the same as it does today. It meant playing a role in a transaction.

3. The three laws are, in Newton's own words: (1) Every body continues in its state of rest, or uniform motion in a right line, unless it is compelled to change that state by forces impressed upon it. (2) The change of motion is proportional to the motive power impressed and is made in the direction of the right line in which that force is impressed. (3) To every action there is always opposed an equal reaction, or the mutual actions of two bodies upon each other are always equal and directed to contrary parts.

4. This is discussed in cosmological terms in Bennett, *Talks on Beelzebub's Tales*, p. 52. In quantum mechanics, Bohm suggests a similar scheme, whereby a wave path combines with a particle path, affecting the final state; see: David Albert, "Bohm's Alternative to Quantum Mechanics," *Scientific American* (May 1994).

5. See the chapter "The Triad" in Bennett, *The Dramatic Universe*, vol. 2, part 11. Allowing initiative to pass equally among the three terms gives rise to six combinations. Each of these represents a form of action that adjusts the balance of forces in a specific way.

6. Bohm uses a similar scheme of matter, energy, and meaning; see Bohm, *Unfolding Meaning.*

7. In W. H. Zureck, ed., *Complexity, Entropy, and the Physics of Information.*

8. Gurdjieff, *Views from the Real World.*

9. The two forces are much the same as those envisaged thousands of years ago by the Sumerians, when they were called *apsu*, the "sweet waters of the abyss," and *tiamat*, the "bitter waters of the ocean." In Gurdjieff's cosmology, *apsu* would be the Holy Sun Absolute and *tiamat* the substance *etherokrilno*, or empty space. We should, of course, also connect Gurdjieff's etherokrilno with the modern conception of the vacuum state, which, though no-thing, is far from empty! In Samkhya (see note 1) the two forces are *purusha* and *prakriti*. In the abstract system of surreal numbers invented by John Horton Conway (see Knuth, *Surreal Numbers*), they are "nothingness" and the "empty set." He has a previous stage of "nothingness and nothingness," to create the empty set!

10. The formation of nuclei may be then superseded by "strange quark matter," relatively vast clumps of matter, which may constitute the as yet unidentified "dark matter" of the universe—and so on, up to the neutron star of incredible mass and beyond into quasars which lie at the heart of galaxies.

11. This amounts to the establishment of a set of possibilities. A good example is that of the market, which makes possible an interplay of consumers and producers. The successive triads are like coarser and coarser media. We might imagine a descent from communion to communication, to exchange, to interaction, etc.

12. The notion that higher worlds are more substantial than lower ones is vividly portrayed in C. S. Lewis, *The Great Divorce*. Another approach is to realize that binding structures which exist in lower worlds cannot hold together in higher-dimensional worlds. As Bennett put it: "You cannot tie a knot in four dimensions."

13. Gurdjieff himself does not give an account of it in *In Search of the Miraculous*, and his description in *Beelzebub's Tales* is not explicit. Bennett and others seized on the point that involution begins with the affirming force, while evolution begins with the receptive force. But they very early on realized that the two were not the inverse of each other. Evolution proceeds from sacrifice, even if just the sacrifice of quantity for quality, while involution proceeds from acquisition. The active contemplation of the distinction between evolution and involution was a primary discipline in the Gurdjieff tradition.

14. Gurdjieff called the act of dissolution or "waking up" *djartklom* (*djart* corresponds to the Armenian for "break" or "kill"!). This generally means, of course, the breaking of conditioning, but it has also all the connotations of the Ch'an (Zen) injunction: "If you meet the Buddha on the way, kill him!"

15. See my comments on this question under "Shocks and Enablement" in chap. 4.

16. As described in Steven Levy, *Artificial Life.*

17. In the concept of *autopoeisis* or self-creation, which plays an important role in the modern biological theory of autonomous systems, we have something much

more powerful. Gurdjieff had much the same concept in his *autoegocrat* (I make myself). However, he says that this principle was replaced in the creation of the world by the *trogoautoegocrat* (I make myself by eating and being eaten). In other words, a being or cosmos sustains itself only by participation in the welfare of the whole (a concept much closer to the realities of living beings than autopoeisis). This is the synergy we spoke of earlier. Bennett says that Gurdjieff "sometimes personifies the trogoautoegocrat as the Holy Spirit," and we should remember that the Holy Spirit is the essential source of communion. Gurdjieff's writings suggest that, although we cannot say that God speaks to everything that exists, His Word echoes throughout the cosmos. The Word is both personal and impersonal. Nothing can really happen without the Word, as is asserted in the Gospel According to John. Gurdjieff addresses the issue of how the Word is transmitted through his idea of the trogoautoegocrat. However, as we shall see, the process of "eating and being eaten" that he speaks of is not only a question of nutrition but also of the "daily bread" spoken of in the Gospels. When, in the sacraments, we partake of the body of Christ, this is to eat the Word of God. In more prosaic terms, it is symbolic of Gurdjieff's assimilation of finer impressions, which is crucial for understanding his system.

18. See J. G. Bennett, *The Dramatic Universe*, vol. 2, p. 77.

19. See "Backward and Forward" in chapter 11.

20. Without experience of these two modes, much of what Gurdjieff has to say about the law of three is incomprehensible. William Blake expressed the same thing when he said: "If a man or woman not an artist or poet be, they cannot be a Christian."

21. "I must not be a slave of either affirming or denying force. But this is difficult." J. B. Bennett, unpublished diaries, 1953.

22. Gurdjieff's ideas transcend even moral imperatives and cannot be understood without the act of freedom.

PART TWO

THE HAZARD OF
TRANSFORMATION

· 7 ·

Four Paradigms
of the Enneagram

The enneagram as a cosmic structure must be embedded in everything. We usually come to recognize the structure only if we attempt something new and significant, when we come up against the laws which maintain the integrity of existence. Through doing, we learn how to cooperate with these laws instead of trying to fight against them. The making of reality is contrary to our expectations, and we tend to encounter reality only through hazard, *which puts us on the spot. This unexpectedness tells us that there must be something radically against common sense in the enneagram, something that appears to us as impossible.*

The four paradigms are four ways of visualizing the workings of the enneagram, each emphasizing some particular aspect. They embody some of the main ideas used in this book. They are not explanations, but aides memoires. *To "have them in mind" means to change the way you think.*

The Simple Action

THE STRUCTURE and meaning of the enneagram is rooted in our experience and is not simply a matter of cosmic speculation; but the way of talking about our experience that is represented by the enneagram can at first appear rather mysterious and seems to go against common sense. This is only because we have habits in talking about our experience which are so ingrained that we fail to notice the obvious about even the simple things we do.

To illustrate the point, let us consider the action of filling a glass with water.[1] Nothing could be simpler:

99

Turn on the tap.
Water comes out.
It goes into the glass.
The glass gets filled.
Turn the tap off.

Yet something important is left out of this description, something that is
hidden in the innocuous phrase "The glass gets filled." We turn off the
tap *because we see* the glass is full (in fact we *anticipate* the water reaching
full). We are able to do this because we can *see* the water reaching the
right level. Our perception of the amount of water in the glass is an
important part of the action. A more complete description of filling a
glass with water would be:

Turn on the tap.
Water flows into the glass.
Monitor the level of the water until you judge there is enough . . .
and then turn off the tap.

The more complete description incorporates our perception. The enneagram teaches us that there is a mechanical side and an intentional side
to *every complete action:* a side to do with the movement of things in
space and time and a side to do with purpose and perception. On page
91 I talked about a triad of commands, or *logos,* governing a complete
action. The *logos* arises out of the top point of the enneagram where we
have the desire for a glass of water. We happen to be thirsty. Along the
line 0-3, we have the command to switch on the water and, along the line
6-9, we have the command to switch off the water. Between 3 and 6 the
glass is filled.

The part of the octave between 0 and 3 has to do with the actual flow
of water from the tap. Between 3 and 6 the water level rises in the glass,
and between 6 and 9 the flow of water is made to stop. Nothing complex
about that, surely? Why should there be anything between 0 and 3, for
example, other than just tap on / water flow? Just think about the practi-
calities. We don't want the water to flow too quickly or too slowly. We
want to optimize the flow so that it doesn't splash or take forever to fill
the glass. There has to be a mechanical adjustment of the rate of flow.

This corresponds to the line 1-4-2 in the inner periodic figure. By means of this linkage, the rate of flow of water is adjusted to the capacity of the glass. Point 0 is switching on the tap; point 1 is having the water flow out; and point 2, the adjusted flow.

What of the rest of the octave on the other side of the enneagram between 6 and 9? Here we *anticipating* the water reaching the desired level. The image of the desired level is at point 8. This enters into our perception of the actual level of the water at point 5 and emerges at point 7 when we begin to close the tap. This is an example of the inner line sequence 8-7-5. At point 8, the glass is full. At point 9, the tap is completely closed—with a final touch of pressure to make sure—and the glass of water can be drunk. (See fig. 7.1.)

It is not surprising that the fine structure of the enneagram only comes into view when we are precise. Ordinarily we do not notice the structure of an action because our desire *is locked into the apex point.* Thus, the whole action is reduced to an atom, and the filling of the glass happens automatically. We do not notice what we really do or how it works. Common sense is a matter of taking things for granted and it obscures *consciousness of structure.* If we take the trouble to notice what is actually involved in even our simplest actions, we immediately become aware of the world of structure.

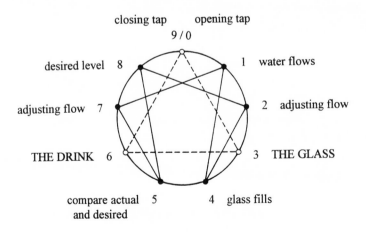

7.1. Filling a glass with water.

Let's look at the three octaves that interact in the enneagram of filling a glass of water. The first octave concerns the water flowing from the tap. We can see that the flow of water increases, stabilizes, and then decreases. The second octave concerns the glass, which is brought in at point 3. The glass does not change per se, but the amount of water in it gradually increases, until point 6. In common parlance, we speak of the glass as "becoming full." The third octave takes us entirely into the realm of perception and intention. Here we reach a correspondence between the desired and the actual, a matching of information.

The simple task of filling a glass with water has all the ingredients of the enneagram. This should not be surprising, because the enneagram is simply a combination of intention (*logos*) and process in time. Out of intention, an actual course of events is set in motion (0-3) and a frame of perception is activated (9-6). Actualization and perception comingle in the middle ground between 3 and 6. Point 5 is more closely allied with perception than point 4. This corresponds to the fact that in filling a glass with water we only need to pay close attention at point 5, when the glass is nearing full.

Our simple example tells us a lot about intention. We see that it gives rise to both action and perception. And when the intention is clear, we go in a circle. We can even say that intention is quantized. Because this is so, there is closure, and because there is closure, we have a structure. The intention penetrates into the action at every point, and in different ways from point to point.

With the complete story of what we do, we see that the description goes in a circle. It parallels what Mircea Eliade has called the myth of eternal return.[2] Because this is ubiquitous it is not noticed, just as we imagine a fish does not notice the water in which it swims. When we begin to notice what is actually going on and tell our story accordingly, it appears as if we are saying something strange full of hidden cosmic secrets. This is only so because the secrets are in fact blindingly obvious!

Everything in the enneagram can be grasped by paying close attention to any action we choose. But this requires that one see *oneself* inside the action and be part of it. The action cannot be viewed as being entirely "out there." We are involved in an action when we *work*, which means a combination of doing and seeing. This is true even for simple actions in the physical world, such as filing a glass with water.

Looked at from outside, such simple actions as filing a glass with water are merely mechanical and repetitive. It is bringing ourselves consciously into our actions—or *understanding*—that renders these actions transformational.

The Impossible Object

Some people are puzzled by the circular form of the enneagram because it seems that the progression around the circle from point 0 to point 9 is like an ascent, rising further and further away from the starting point. How, then, can the sequence of steps enter into itself such that point 0 and point 9 appear to be the same? To grasp the paradox better, we can look at a drawing made by Oscar Reutersvärd (see fig. 7.2), which focuses on the essentials. Here we have three interlocking cubes. Any pair of these cubes appears to make sense in terms of three-dimensional space. However, all three cubes taken together do not make sense at all. In a more elaborate work, *Homage to Bruno Ernst,* there are nine cubes, perfectly duplicating the structure of the enneagram. This is echoed in a 1994 work by Leander called *Statue of an Impossible Tri-bar* (which, unfortunately, we cannot reproduce here).[3] The three cubes represent the three

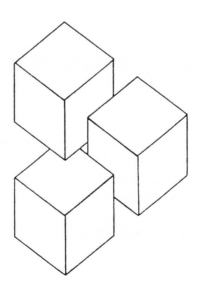

7.2. An impossible object, after Opus 2B *by Oscar Reutersvärd.*

phases of the enneagram. Our eye-brain sees any two of them arranged in space in a plausible way. However, it is impossible for all three to actually exist. Reutersvärd, like M. C. Escher, Bruno Ernst, and Roger Penrose, made a study of such impossible objects, and they have opened up a new chapter of man's investigation into the nature of his seeing. Better known is the image of the endlessly ascending staircase, first invented by Roger Penrose and exploited by M. C. Escher in his famous work *Ascending and Descending*. Although this image is usually presented in a form which has four sides, its relevance to the enneagram representation is fairly clear. Such images are more to the point than the attempts which have been made to render the enneagram in three dimensions as a spiral, with point 9 above point 0. Viewed "from above," then, points 0 and 9 appear to be the same. Such attempts reduce the significance of the symbol because they destroy the wholeness—the closure and cyclicity—which is an essential property of its structure.

Viewing the enneagram as existing in an impossible space is very suggestive. Impossible space is not a higher space of four dimensions, nor is it a non-Euclidean space. It is created by the translation process the eye-brain performs between two and three dimensions. It may well be that this corresponds with a similar translation process the thought-brain performs between twofold and threefold logic. In this book, I will often make use of the concept of a threefold order that is somehow superimposed on a twofold order.

The triadic impossible object belongs to a family of structures of similar character. Another member of this family is known as the Borromean Rings (fig. 7.3), where three rings appear to be linked together in spite of the fact that no two of them interlock. Such a linkage is perfectly possible in ordinary Euclidean space, yet it is counterintuitive. It may help us grasp that there is a connectivity of a higher order than the linear ones we are used to. Geometrical experiments of this kind, which challenge our habits of perception, can also indicate the need for a deeper *conception*.

Throughout this book, we will find ourselves dealing with a combination of sequence and cyclicity. Sequence is linear while cyclicity is circular. The sequential mode of understanding time is dominant in our era and has superseded the earlier dominance of cyclicity as the master idea for our understanding. Combining the two modes requires just the "impossibility" or the counterintuitive linkage we have seen in a spatial sense. This

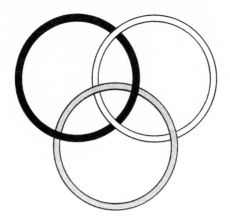

7.3. Borromean rings.

must be kept in mind during all that follows. The enneagram describes not a mechanism but a process of transformation and realization. Always, something new and significant is made out of the existing materials and circumstances. What draws these elements into a new meaning is a call or invitation from the realm of values, from that which does not yet exist.

The Problem Solution

In a famous parable of the work of transformation, a man has a wolf, a sheep, and a cabbage to transport across a river. These three represent parts of his nature. According to the story, he can travel across the river with only one of them at a time. The problem is that, if left alone, the sheep will eat the cabbage and the wolf will eat the sheep. How does he manage to transport them all across without losing any of them?

In all, he needs to make seven journeys. These can be plotted around the enneagram as the steps between the numbered points. The points themselves represent the different combinations of the three creatures appearing on the far bank of the river:

1. —
2. S
3. S
4. SW

5. W
6. WC
7. WC
8. WSC

Between points 4 and 5, the man has to bring the sheep back or the wolf will eat it. When we come to study the structure of stories in chapter 11, we will meet this retrograde motion again.

The triangular figure represents the man. If the cabbage, sheep, and wolf represent his physical, emotional, and intellectual nature, then the "man" himself is the "I," or will. Point 9 is the unity of the three and the "I" and is reflected in point 8, where all the characters are together again.

The condition of this story, that no *two* creatures can be left together, parallels what we have found in impossible objects. The feature that only *one* of the three can be moved at a time imposes the logic of linear sequence. It is all the more striking, then, that such constraints automatically produce a structure of seven steps. In the pseudo-enneagram in figure 7.4, the seven steps of the process are capped by the three terms made by points 1, 8, and 9. These three terms represent the abstract possibility of shipping the creatures across the river without any constraints.

Thinking analogically, the realm above the line 8-1 is that of the empy-

7.4. *Problem-solving sequence.*

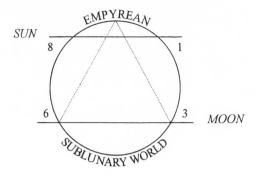

7.5. Celestial analogue.

rean, the angelic order beyond the sun. the realm below the line 6-3 is the sublunar world of corruption. (See fig. 7.5.) In our puzzle, this is where the sheep travels in the reverse direction, for example.

The Three Versions

In the process of any event, the same event is happening in three different ways. This has been wonderfully portrayed in Carlos Castaneda's books where he introduces gradually, step by step, the idea of a second and then a third *attention.* The very way in which we construe our world depends on the attention we are in.

The first octave is the way in which we ordinarily see our world and the sequence of events in it. This is the octave which is built into the way we are constructed and goes by itself. If we call to mind the structure laid out around the circle of the enneagram, then we might remember that the first shock at point 3 is considered to be mechanical. This means that it happens automatically.

The first octave is something that we all have, no matter who we are and what we do. It is the basic form of being human in this time.

When it comes to the second octave, we are in a predicament. We have to construct this octave for ourselves. The passions and energies of life take us only so far (to point 5). In order to live in this octave, we have to make it happen *artificially,* that is, with artifice or design. In terms of the Gurdjieff Work, we have to separate ourselves from ourselves. We are concerned with going through experience "otherwise" than that to which we have become accustomed. This is essential if we are going to be able to liberate our intelligence from mental conditioning.

There is a Zen saying: "First I thought that mountains were mountains, rivers were rivers, and trees were trees. Then I saw that mountains were not mountains, rivers were not rivers, and trees were not trees." Finally, after enlightenment, the narrator adds, "Now I see that mountains are mountains, rivers are rivers, and trees are trees." The strangeness of the second octave has to be superseded by the reconciliation of the third.

It seems that we have to go through the second octave in order to be in a place where the third can begin. I remember the inspiring mathematician Spencer Brown once telling me: "When I do mathematics, I never think." Thinking is the very emblem of artifice—but unless one learns how to think, one is dumb and blind in the higher worlds. Or, in Gurdjieff's language, one turns into a "stupid saint."

The struggles with oneself, the turning upside down of one's conceptions—these artificial labors and exercises serve only to bring us to the point where they are not needed.

In the "third attention" all that we need is at hand, and there is no longer any need to be divided. This exacts a severe price: we must be able to get out of the way. Such an outcome may seem to us impossible or an expression of some absurd self-denial. On the contrary, it is the root of understanding.

I take understanding to mean "standing under." I stand under what I understand so that *it informs me.* Gurdjieff called this "reason of understanding," and it is in utter contrast with "reason of knowing," which obtains in the first octave. Between the first and the third octaves we have to go through a revolution in ourselves. This is the task of the second octave. What is conscious has to be seen as unconscious, and vice versa. It is hardly surprising that we can lose ourselves in the process.

Without the grace of God we would be lost forever. As we struggle to transform, to understand, to come to be, there is constantly flowing through us the Word of God. The Word moves in counterclockwise direction around the enneagram. It is the stream in which we can be transformed. But first we have to go against the stream.

Outer work and inner work are never enough. The outside and the inside are incomplete. As we enter into the third octave, all that we have been and done becomes God's work.

To avoid spurious associations with such grandiose terms as "God," we can speak in terms of any situation of transformation. In fact, we must do this. What is at stake is the discovery of a language, a mode of expression, which is universally true and contains no bias.

Notes

1. This example is taken from Peter Senges, *The Fifth Discipline.*
2. See Mircea Eliade, *The Myth of Eternal Return.*
3. For a fuller account of this fascinating area of study, see Bruno Ernst, *The Eye Beguiled.*

· 8 ·

The Metabolism of Perception

*The theme of eating and being eaten reverberates throughout Gurd-
jieff's cosmology. It can be taken in an ecological way, reminding us
that we, too, must be part of a food chain and that there is something
beyond us in the scale of being. Such idealized cosmic speculations may
mean nothing if we do not bring such possibilities into the sphere of
actual experience. For this reason, the restaurant provides an appro-
priate challenge. Most of us have battled with waiters, and many have
sat through meals where the only objective was to get laid or drunk.
Cuisine is a part of culture, but we may want to remember the agape
or love feast of earlier religious people, when the meal was an occasion
of worship.*

*Eating together can be a sacrament and a sacrilege. Without any
moralizing, we need to look at the structure of this recurrent event of
human experience objectively. What are these waiters and cooks and
customers? Cooking is a transformation of raw food into meaning. Can
this teach us anything about the transformation that may take place
within us?*

The Secular Ritual of the Kitchen

IT IS TIME to discuss the workings of the enneagram in situations with
which everyone is familiar (yet which are more complex than pouring a
glass of water). In doing so, we can come to understand that the enneagram is exemplified at every level and on every scale. The sole condition
is that we must have a *cosmic formation:* any whole that renews itself and
is capable of evolving. Let us use the shorter term *cosmos* for the sake of
brevity, though it will not be used in the precise sense that Gurdjieff used
it, but in the more colloquial sense of a "world of its own."

A cosmos does not exist in isolation but is coupled to other cosmoses, greater and smaller than itself. It *transforms* what passes through it. Let us also emphasize that a cosmos in this sense is *physical* and not merely a set of operations or qualities. It is not abstract. This is often missed by those people attempting to study the enneagram who use it as system of concepts rather than as a means of assessing the structure of a concrete, physical, living whole. A cosmos might be a whole class of situations, represented by innumerable examples; but it is nevertheless physical. This also means that the cosmos is limited in time and space. It will occupy a certain scale of existence and also exemplify a certain quality of being. We suppose that all human inventions and productions approximate to cosmic formations.

Where the cosmos is more than physical is in its *realization of a value*. This comes from its coupling with a greater or higher cosmos. In our simple example of filling a glass with water, we had to take into account that it is for the satisfying of thirst that the whole enterprise exists. Nevertheless, there is also a value that the cosmos has in its own right—when it may be regarded as a work of art. As William Blake says, "Everything that lives has meaning, needs neither suckling nor weaning." Every true cosmos is both machine and art. Its function then becomes ritualized so that we see only the pattern of styles or forms and not the underlying transformational action, or why it exists at all.

Cooking is perhaps the most common experience of transformation, akin to alchemy and reminding us that we ourselves have to be "cooked" in order to develop a soul. With its interesting actions of mixing and blending ingredients and bringing these into the making of a new whole on a higher level, cooking exerts a fascination in its own right. When we realize that cooking is the transformation produced in a certain kind of apparatus working within a certain kind of environment, we can use it as an example of cosmic laws and processes. It was a favorite theme of Bennett, who often used it to illustrate the enneagram.[1]

People require food that is brought into a certain state before they will ingest it. The raw ingredients have to be processed or cooked, and the food must be presented in a convenient and attractive way. The transformative purpose of cooking is to provide edible food. There are three basic commands:

1. Get (raw) food.
2. Cook food.
3. Serve meal.

The primary command is to "feed me" (or "us"), where there is reference to the concrete individual desire. Each of the three commands has a distinctive role in the totality. The first command—to get food—is crucial when we think of the importance of the categories, quality, and origin of the raw ingredients. The second command—to cook food—is crucial because it involves the skill and tradition of the cooks. The third—to serve the meal—is crucial in that it implies the whole ambiance of the restaurant: its setting, decor, and manner of service.

The total process is authorized by the three commands, and the action-space is defined by their triangulation. If we place the three commands into the circle of the process, it is possible to see three different phases of operation (fig. 8.1):

preparation: all that has to be done to be able to process the foodstuff
execution: all that has to be done in cooking
realization: all that has to be done to bring the food into the realm of
    consumption

The cooking apparatus is the kitchen, while the environment in which this apparatus operates includes sources of food (which reach back into

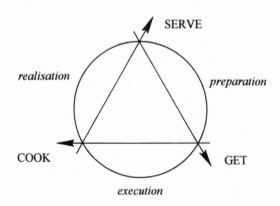

8.1. Commands in the circle of the process.

the workings of the biosphere) as well as customers (and all the complexity of their cultural and economic life). The relevant cosmos is the restaurant which we can visualize as existing within other, larger cosmoses. There is a similar setup in any business, not only in a restaurant. In the general case of a business, the point of the organization of activity is to bring something into a market. A concept is "made flesh" and brought into the world of the consumer.[2] The same pattern is to be found under the most primitive of conditions as well as in sophisticated settings.

It might at first seem strange to limit the actual cooking of the food to the middle phase. This was done because of the scale of operations established by the command structure. If the primary command had been "Cook food," then we would be constrained into the world of cooking alone, a world smaller than the world of providing meals to people. In this smaller world, we would find analogies with the process of making a pot as discussed in chapter 4.

In the world of the restaurant, there are three octaves. The first concerns the functioning of the kitchen; the second, the transformation of the food; the third, the fulfillment of the customers' needs. In Bennett's terms, these had the character of function, being, and will. Function is what we can know; being is what we can experience; while will is what "in-forms" us. My description of the three octaves in terms of *matter, energy,* and *information* can be explained as follows.

In the *first octave* there is nothing but the movement, selection, and combination of materials. In the *second,* there is a transformation which produces finer energies. Just as a heat engine (such as we might find in a car) produces work out of heat, so cooking produces meals out of raw food. In the *third octave,* the process concerns impressions. A restaurant that pays no attention to food as impressions never makes the grade. Customers do not only eat food; they also "eat" the way it is presented and the setting in which they eat it.

The given whole is the functioning restaurant. At the apex point of the enneagram, the customers and the kitchen staff correspond to the value and the fact of the situation and face in opposite directions (fig. 8.2). From the standpoint of the customers—who give the waiters their orders, which are then passed on into the kitchen—the kitchen is there to fulfill their wishes. The nature of this relationship is involutionary. The custom-

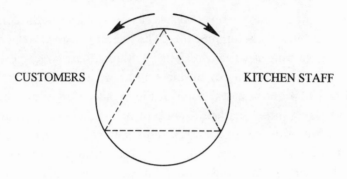

CUSTOMERS KITCHEN STAFF

8.2. Face-off at the apex.

ers have the active role and the kitchen staff the passive role. It is the customers' demand on the kitchen staff that determines the meal.

From the standpoint of the kitchen staff, they are there to anticipate and influence the wishes of the customers. The nature of this relationship is evolutionary. Again, the kitchen staff is passive in relation to the customers, but now the initiative is with them. This *also* determines the meal.

The two relationships or tendencies meet in the middle region, in the realm of cooking. I suggested in chapter 5 that there might be a law of four, and it is here that we would see the operation of such a law. Bennett describes this law in terms of the combination of ends and means. This is precisely what we have. Ends and means are not fixed but blend together, rather like the two just "rubbing together" as if two "sticks"; and this is signified as fire. We can see how the periodic figure divides about this region. The part 1-4-2-8 corresponds to evolution, while the part 8-5-7-1 corresponds to involution. The region between points 4 and 5 is the turning point between the play of external and internal forces. It is, therefore, sometimes associated with *chaos*. The law of four is *antichaos*, in which self-organization begins.[3]

The next transition in the evolutionary sequence is the most tense. It is poised between the two different worlds of the kitchen and the dining room. Gurdjieff, speaking about transformation in *Beelzebub's Tales*, introduced the idea of a disharmonization which is produced by the two kinds of critical interval. According to the principle of the octave, the first kind of interval is at point 3 and the second kind is hidden between points 8 and 9, so that this disharmonization is associated with points 5 and 6.

However, the workings of the enneagram are usually only considered from the point of view of evolution, in the clockwise direction. This means that it is point 5 that is *felt* as the point of maximum disharmony.[4] From an "objective" point of view, however, the critical step is at point 6. This will become clearer as we go on.

Involution and evolution go together. The setting up of the kitchen and the cooking of the food would not take place unless there were customers (it is generally agreed that it is very difficult to cook for oneself). More than this, the stream of information coming into the kitchen from the customers—the orders for food—is actually blending in various ways with the operations at different stages. If, in this process, the information is not transmitted, the restaurant ends up being at variance with its customers, and it will go out of business. This blending of information with operations—or of ends with means—we put under the heading of "intelligence."

Of course, the stream of information is also altered on its way down, in particular at the critical points 6 and 3. In fact, at these two points there are important "step-down" functions (akin to the stepping down of voltage from the power company to the domestic appliance). Thus, each of the three phases is characterized by a distinctive information stream. For example, the information stream from points 6 to 3 is less specific than it is from 9 to 6. It concerns an assessment of trends on that particular evening. From 3 to 0, however, it concerns even more statistical trends, which affect the tuning of the kitchen to a certain line of cuisine and service.

A restaurant is an interesting example to take because it has scope for undergoing major adjustments in its construction, cuisine, and staffing. Here, we need to take account of the manager. It is he who unifies the command structure. He is responsible for the getting of the food, its cooking, and its serving to the satisfaction of the customers. As the one person able to go freely anywhere in the whole restaurant, he is ubiquitous. He may even sit with the customers. He overshadows the waiters, advises the cooks, checks on the state of the kitchen, and sees to the condition of the dining room. He needs to establish the right relations between customers, waiters, and cooks. His shape is that of the triangle.

However, there may well be someone who stands behind him, the "big name" who actually owns the restaurant but only appears at its launch. This person—a film star, say—then represents the cultural and economic dimension.

The chief cook, on the other hand, lives in the periodic figure (1-4-2-8-5-7). A chief cook is more than an expert chef. He should be able to manage the state of the kitchen, oversee the assistant cooks, design the menu, and influence the waiters in their presentation of the dishes to the customers. The assistant cooks enter the action at point 3 of the ennea-gram and the waiters at point 6. These two points are the gateways. Corre-spondingly, food enters the action at point 3, and passes from the kitchen to the dining room at point 6.

We said that the restaurant exists and operates within other, larger cosmoses. One of these is the socioeconomic cosmos, which can be thought of as a point 10. It is in this medium of finance, glamour, and reputation that the restaurant has to find its place. (If we were thinking not of a commercial restaurant, but of something like the refectory in a monastery, then this medium would include the rules of the order.) Points 0 and 9—the kitchen as a material object and the kitchen as mean-ing—are embedded in this greater cosmos. The owner of the restaurant is also a part of it.

The principle can be extended to the two openings represented by points 3 and 6. The working of the biosphere, the world of life, is an equivalent point 10 with respect to point 3. What is implicit at point 6 is particularly interesting, because it is here that humans engage in role-playing. The people involved in the process are aware of themselves as part of the process and, as a consequence, are projecting themselves as specific characters. The equivalent point 10 here is that of psychology.[5] (The idea of a point 10, which is only sketchily introduced at this point, will become important in later chapters.)

Centers of Gravity

I have already said enough to show that restaurants are complex wholes. When it comes to representing all this complexity by means of labeling an enneagram, the terms we use must be summary ones; but one of the most important and useful methods is to look for the centers of gravity of the whole action. Every such center of gravity can be represented as a point on the enneagram yet is itself a whole, or monad. Each has in it the potential to be a smaller, more limited enneagram. There can be simple and fixed meanings of the points only when we are dealing with an artifact, such as an automobile. It is for this reason that we speak of centers of gravity rather than of things or particular operations. These monads with their centers of gravity correspond to Gurdjieff's hydrogens. We can begin make sense of this in terms of the different states of material, which we can relate to the first octave.

The process begins with the first person entering the kitchen and, maybe, switching on the lights. Point 1 is making sure that the kitchen as a whole is together: that it is clean, the tools and utensils are in the right places, and the working surfaces are made ready. Point 1 also represents the assembly of the staff. This meaning is reinforced by the line 7-1 which signifies the restoration of everything that has gone out into service back to its rightful place. It is also at point 1 that the ovens are switched on to bring them to the right temperature in time for the cooking.

Point 2 is the region of selection. There is a selection of utensils—pots and pans—which will serve to cook the anticipated foodstuff in the anticipated way. This is reinforced by the line 4-2, which signifies that knowing what one is to cook influences the way that things are laid out. Thus, point 2 is "more intelligent" than point 1. It is here, corresponding to the line 2-8, that the menu is decided. At point 2, the material of the kitchen is more highly organized than at point 1. What has been assembled at point 1 is now divided in intent. Different people have different tasks.

Point 3 is where the new octave of the food itself begins. At this point, the food is in the same state of organization as the utensils. The food is simply a kind of material. The all-important distinction between organic matter and inorganic matter only arises later on. Therefore, the "hydrogen" of the food is at the same level as the "hydrogen" of the kitchen. It gives the kitchen something to work with; otherwise the process stops here.

What comes to pass in the transition through point 3 is the creation of a connection between the kitchen and the food. The first transition from opening the kitchen to assembling the instruments and people is echoed in opening the supply of food and assembling the ingredients. The second transition in which the assembly was divided into different tasks is also reflected in the discarding of inedible or inferior ingredients (fig. 8.3).

At point 4, where we have all the mechanical processes involved in cooking—such as cleaning, cutting, and mixing—there is an added intelligence. The center of gravity here is technique. The food is brought into a condition which fits the type of meal, and the second octave is underway. This is an important transition for the kitchen, too. The work being done by it is finer than before. The people involved are specialists.

Between points 4 and 5, the material of the food enters into irreversible transformations, which we can summarize as blending. It is somewhere in this region that the restaurant can be opened to the public, because the food is approaching the state in which it can be served. The customers will, of course, sit at the bar while they look at the menu and wait to be called to a table. Before this can happen, the dining room must be opened to the staff so that it can be made ready. We associate this opening to the staff with point 3, because of symmetries which will emerge. In the region between points 4 and 5, the kitchen is at maximum activity while the dining room is at minimum activity.

At point 5, the ingredients blend together as they undergo their irreversible transitions (we can no longer separate the seasonings from the meat) and the action penetrates into the cellular level. It is the blending process that makes the food into a meal, a meaningful whole. (In the

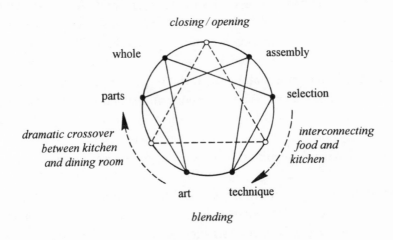

8.3. Centers of gravity.

further stages from point 6 onwards there is a blending according to impressions, rather than a blending according to composition). Here, at point 5, the food becomes increasingly separated from the cooking vessels: it changes, and they do not. Here we have the art, which often expresses itself in the final touches of the sauces and garnishes and the way in which the dishes are to be presented. The sauce cook is often the highest in the hierarchy of cooks. But what of the kitchen itself? It has become more and more alive. It has become something like an organism in its own right. It has moved from the realm of things to the realm of life. In this sense, a kitchen is only fully alive when it at the peak of activity. At that stage, the kitchen can become a world of its own and turn in on itself.

The transition associated with point 6 brings about a dramatic changeover as between the kitchen and the dining room. Between points 5 and 6, the garnishes and sauces are finished. Between points 6 and 7, the dishes are presented to the customer, and often the waiter plays an active role in their presentation. Even when he plays no part in their arrangement and appearance, he is responsible for conveying to the customer what they are by description.

The third octave, which brings in the *wishes of the customers*, begins at point 6. What is taken out of the kitchen is what is carried to the tables. It is obvious that at the start of the new octave at point 6, serving the food is at the same level as preparing the food was at point 5. However, it is *in a different world*.

It is at point 6 that the equivalent of an act of reproduction by the kitchen occurs. However, this "seed," if we can call it such, will reproduce not the kitchen per se but the life of the kitchen. This is because it will enter into the experience of the customers. As the food moves from the biochemical to the experiential world, the kitchen propagates itself. The life of the kitchen dies to become experience and memory. This idea is important in Gurdjieff's teaching. He spoke of the sacred *rascooarno*, or death, by which organisms release an energy that is needed for the functioning of the whole biosphere and the local part of the solar system.

In more prosaic terms: if there are a few sittings, then the cycle of cooking for one sitting can close at point 6, allowing the kitchen to be restored or renewed for the next. This restoration takes place up to and including point 9. The customers are given their food, eat, and depart, and the dining room is closed.

What develops through points 7 and 8 is the "soul" of the kitchen. The kitchen is becoming more than alive. What can this mystical-sounding idea possibly mean? We know part of the answer as the reputation of the restaurant, or the renown of the cook, or even that of its speciality.

At point 7, the customer sees the meal brought to his table as a series of dishes (a mirror image of point 2, incidentally), at which stage the meal is in *parts*. He checks that these parts are what he has ordered. The dishes are served onto his plate and combined into a meal, making the "form and sequence" of the meal.

At point 8, the meal as a *whole* is on the customer's plate, and he is ready to eat.[6] Perhaps he tastes to see if the meal is actually as he imagined it would be. In doing this, he echoes what the cooks may have done at point 5, as signified by the line 8-5. He may send something back if it is not satisfactory. Again, point 8 is a mirror of point 1: something is about to begin.

Though it is hardly common in a restaurant, point 8 is the moment of prayer and giving thanks (corresponding to the si-do interval). In an ideal setting, both points 1 and 8 are united through point 9 to the sources of the action. In an ordinary case, the sources are the booking of table and the settling of the bill—a commercial transaction.

Between points 8 and 9, the customer takes the meal in: he eats, assimilates, experiences. At point 9, the food enters into his organism. The owner of the restaurant, or a waiter, might inquire if everything is to his satisfaction. The kitchen fulfills its destiny as it becomes "visibly absent but invisibly present." In this last phase, the hunger of the customer is added to the material of the kitchen. (It is hunger that makes food delicious. The skillful restaurateur manages to enhance the hunger of his customers, without making them suffer through prolonged waiting.) It is just here, when the meal is passing into memory, that the kitchen acquires an atom of "satisfaction energy" that gives it being.

In the case of a dining room with a series of sittings, at point 9—when the sitting is over—the dining room has to be cleaned in the interval between points 0 and 3, while the kitchen springs into action once more for the next sitting. The great significance of the apex point 0/9 is that it represents opening and closing. The dining room and the kitchen open and close in a relation to each other that involves customers, kitchen staff, and waiters. If we picture the situation in terms of a series of sittings—which makes it easier to visualize—then the opening and closing go on around the circle of the enneagram, approximating to the diagram of perpetual motion that we will refer to again later, in chapter 13.

The descriptions in figure 8.3 are an amalgamation from all three octaves. They also include a sense of the nature of the transition from one point to the next. The first octave needs some further explanation: it is not merely the kitchen as a material construct but also the people involved. The principle lying behind this is a little difficult to grasp at first, because it entails seeing that the people are, as it were, just "thoughts" at the beginning and that they, too, come alive in the process. According to many spiritual traditions, thoughts are at the same level of being as material objects! This gives the clue: that the thoughts in the first part of the process are lacking in being, in substance; they are only possibilities. What happens as we go around the enneagram is that the thought of a meal becomes a real one.

There are two especially important transitions around points 3 and 6. In the first of these, the thought of the meal makes a step toward concreteness by coming into relation with the actual stuff of the food. Such a transition is found in all transforming processes. In the second of the transitions, there is something even more dramatic, because there is always "conflict" between the world of the kitchen and the world of the dining room: the meal prepared in the kitchen must be given up to be "destroyed" by the waiters and customers as it is served and eaten.

The other transitions indicate a step-by-step progression toward concreteness. In the last (from 8 to 9), which we can call remembering, the meal is able to enter the stream of history: we speak of a memorable meal. In its ideal form, the enneagram suggests that the activity of the workers, the transformation of the food, and the experience of the customers all blend together. This is what is meant by fulfillment. It is, of course, a relatively rare thing. The kitchen may be a hellhole and the customers indifferent or just there because it is the "in thing." In Gurdjieff's parody of American restaurants, all we have in the back is someone opening cans and heating up their contents.[7]

The Intervention of Point 6

Going beyond point 6 is like entering another world. There is the saying "It is not what you eat that matters but with whom." The gathering of people has a power of its own. There may be a couple in a relationship of seduction, or businesspeople trying to swing a deal, or people in a hurry, or others who just want to be seen. In a way, the motives of all these people may be totally foreign to the concerns of those working in the kitchen. The food, however, has a power too. And the interplay between the two worlds—that of the kitchen and that of the dining room—can become very dramatic.[8]

Gurdjieff says: "The apparent placing of the interval in *its wrong place* itself shows to those who are able to read the symbol what kind of 'shock' is required for the passage from si to do" (ISM, p. 291). The explanation which follows this statement shows how the three "foods" of a completing process must enter at the points they do because this is their position according to three octaves. In other words, each of them enters into a corresponding mi-fa interval.

However, there is something else to be seen, which can be illustrated by the workings of the restaurant. Every enneagram process produces a result which is completed in being applied. Looked at in this way, the point of application is where we have the si-do interval of the main octave. However, in order for any "machine" to function in a harmonious way, it requires the workings of the engine in the machine to be adjusted according to the load by feed back from the point of application: the point of feedback as the load engages with the engine is represented by point 6 on the enneagram. In the case of a motorcar, it is here that we have the clutch that serves to connect the revolutions of the engine with the transmission and, thence, with the wheels and the road (gear selection is at point 5).

In the case of the restaurant, the equivalent feedback comes from the taste of the customer. This, like a car's traction between its wheels and the road, serves as the point of application. The customer needs to inform the kitchen what he likes to eat. This has to be brought in at point 6.

All of this, and much more besides, comes from the fact that we have a completing cycle of processes—which maintains itself in operation, can prosper or deteriorate, and does not simply serve as a transition from one state to another.

Going Beyond

An interesting possibility foreshadowed in our example of the restaurant is that the transformation process can go further and develop in a still higher world. It is sometimes said that every realized enneagram feeds forward into another one. As Gurdjieff said: ". . . do can emerge from its circle and enter into orderly correlation with another circle, that is, play that role in another cycle which, in the cycle under consideration, is played by the 'shocks' filling the 'intervals' in the octave . . . the octave can be penetrated to make connection with what exists outside it" (ISM, p. 290).

What issues from point 9 of one enneagram can act as a shock or enablement in another. Gathering together and eating can enter at point 3 of an enneagram of a community undergoing transformation. This is at the basis of many religious rituals, such as the ancient agape or love feast. It was used in this way by Gurdjieff himself. He, like many other teachers, used the occasion of eating together to impart insight. In Gurdjieff's case, this utilized alcohol (similar, perhaps, to Bektashi practices), table talk, and his famous "toast of the idiots."[9]

Eating together energizes a kind of information-engine. In communities there are nearly always rituals, and in transformational communities these rituals are put to intentional use. They become a means of remembrance and perception.

In speaking about the enneagram of the restaurant, I said that prayers could properly be offered in the interval between points 8 and 9. This was to hint at the further development in the higher enneagram of community. We give thanks for our food while *remembering ourselves:* we come into contact with ourselves as a community through eating together. It is the thankfulness for the food that energizes the further transformation. This is the enablement that penetrates at point 3 of the higher enneagram. What, then, could the next point 6 of this enneagram mean? In the strong sense, it means that there the community itself—as food—is given over to be eaten! To most people, this notion may appear absurd or incomprehensible. It supposes that the community is assimilated into a higher realm of intelligence. In Christian terms, it is being infused by the Holy Ghost—by which act the community becomes the true Church.

There was a widespread belief that this could only be accomplished through the blood of martyrs. Gurdjieff himself often spoke of the significance of death for the release of higher energies but was always at pains to point out that there was an *intentional* way of releasing or tapping into these energies that was far superior to bloody sacrifice. Bennett savagely criticizes the early church for its advocacy of martyrdom. He argues that it was this, above all, that closed the doors to the church's access to *gnosis*.[10] The issue at point 6 is whether the community will accept to enter into the domain of higher intelligence, when such an entry is offered.

A community that accepts the Holy Ghost becomes "overshadowed" and a vehicle of a higher intelligence or wisdom. Great historical communities, such as the Jews, have felt this—and suffered the hatred of people who feel themselves excluded (fig. 8.4).

There is an intrinsic connection between the prosaic task of cooking food and the conduct of religious ceremonies, between the most basic nourishment and the most mind-blowing substances, and between eating and communing. The world of "eating and being eaten" merges into the world of communication. Although eating and being eaten concerns the exchange of energies and not of information, there is a sense in which

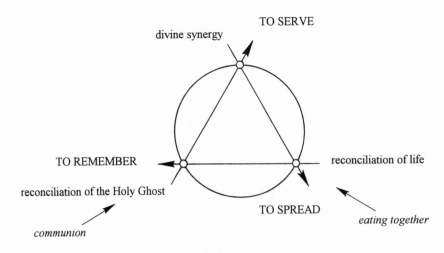

8.4. *Transformational community.*

these two aspects meet: if we can make contact with the *essences* of the life-forms that have provided our food.

Gurdjieff himself appears to have had a vivid sense of the interiority of other kinds of organisms. In particular, he made reference to the particular powers inherent in certain plants which yield psychotropic substances. This is to associate a kind of perception with these type of plants. That is the clue: the enneagram represents the way in which things come alive and then *rise in perception* through a kind of death.

Eating or consumption of any kind need not be a passive thing. There can be a certain consciousness in eating. Without this, the whole cycle returns back to the mechanical process. It is similar with any kind of consumption, for example of manufactured goods. Where consciousness is lacking in our consumption, we are rather like headless chickens. The idea of eating as a sacrament is very ancient but now almost totally non-existent. We have very little sense of the value of what is provided for us by the world of life. Our role in eating is to become more aware of the process, in this way connecting life with what is beyond life.

All of this is implicit in the original idea of there being a scale of intelligence. The enneagram points out that the transformation of food can serve to provide a fuel for a higher kind of perception. In this, we do something that all our studies of the world of life and sympathy with other living things cannot—that is, make something which touches on our thought and feeling an integral part of our *physical existence*. This is what Gurdjieff meant by transubstantiation, when ideas are made flesh in a totally literal sense.

The Restaurant (at the End of the Universe?)

One important aspect of the reality of cooking I have not brought out is also connected with time. When food is brought into the kitchen, the action becomes irreversible. Time takes over. The quality of freshness begins to deteriorate. The food has to be used or it is wasted. So we might regard the actual bringing of the food into the working spaces as point 3. As soon as this is done, something is set in motion that must be taken account of.

This deterioration accelerates when the food is prepared. For example, the potatoes are peeled and have to be put into water or they will go brown. Even the simple act of cutting produces an effect. Of course, the critical act is the application of fire or heat. This is something that affects the cellular and even molecular structure of the materials. It is the application of fire that marks the transition from point 4 to point 5. Then, what happens at point 5 is determined by an overall consideration of synchronicity. All the various ingredients must be made ready at the same time. Point 5 is a point of coming together of different actions involving different substances. Thus, what we can witness along the line from 3 to 6 can be well described as an acceleration. Actions become increasingly committal. The culmination is in a convergence of various actions. (Of course, it is possible to "cheat" and create dishes from ingredients held in a kind of quasi-stasis, like those taken from the freezer or tins.)

What happens across point 6 is also interesting. This transition is straddled by the waiter. We have to speak of something entering at that point, and this is represented by the wine or the aperitif. Sometimes, the customer sits at the bar before being called to the table, or the waiter says: "Would you like a drink while you are waiting?" As Karl Popper points out: "The materialists, down to and beyond Democritus, regarded the soul or spirit of man as analogous to the spirit of wine."[11]

In a restaurant where there is at least the semblance of a choice, the role of the waiter is crucial. He has to know how to interpret the menu, to know what dishes are available, what they are like, how long they will take to be prepared, and so on. He has to be able to communicate this to the customers. At the same time, he has to be able to communicate with the people in the kitchen. We have all had experiences of a waiter failing in his role and having to send back dishes which we did not order.

There can be various kinds of waiters. Besides specialists such as the wine waiter, there can be those who lead customers to their seats, those who remove the finished dishes, and so on. However, the important function is the interpretation of the menu. Here, the waiter echoes the chief cook, who also undertakes the practical interpretation of the menu, but for the purpose of organizing the cooking. The points 2 and 7 in the enneagram echo each other, but whereas the cook has to translate the menu into action, the waiter has to translate it into something meaningful for the customer.

Besides wine, there are various features which contribute to the ambiance. Some restaurants include music (even Muzak), or a floor show.

Some restaurants strive to make every evening an occasion and are eager to promote the birthdays of their customers. All of this has to do with the inherent need of making something out of the eating of the meal which is more than energy maintenance. We can see why it was that Gurdjieff made so much out of the possibility that humans could transform energies beyond the level of survival needs and that this is not always cultural imagination but another kind of physical reality.

Returning to the topic of religious communities, we should also note the widespread use of readings during the meal. This is a direct application of an insight into the third "food" of man as consisting of impressions. In part, the practice is to occupy the mind so as to prevent spurious associations and daydreams. In its higher meaning it is to make use of the energy released in the act of eating and transform this energy into understanding.

Point 9 has yet another interest. It is here that the customer pays up! That is part of the reason why the ownership of the restaurant is positioned particularly at this point, because it is here that the owner gets the cash. But what of the cases in which we do not have a restaurant as such, but just the kitchen in the home with, for example, the mother providing fare for her husband and children (only in a chauvinistic household, of course)? What kind of payment does she get? There is the old saying that "the way to a man's heart is through his stomach." Providing edible and attractive food is a function that has its rewards in affection and bonding. We can instantly feel that it is here, at point 9, that the circle is completed. At point 9, *the energy is passed over which enables the process to be repeated.* (See chapter 19.)

In the first phase of the process, the food was an abstraction. In the second, it has a tangible chemical reality. In the third, it has value. Each of the three phases requires a different approach. The maintenance and efficiency of the kitchen is one thing. The use of the kitchen for actually making food is another. In the third phase, the kitchen is out of sight and is only a supplier. Just as the cook need not be concerned with the source of the foodstuffs, so the customer need not be concerned with the source of the meals. It is only a conscious person who is concerned with the source of things he is consuming and how they have come to be what they are. This individual has a true historical sense. He is able to see the enneagram in reverse.

It was the unusual sage Pak Subuh who pointed out the significance of what happens in eating.[12] According to him, there is an encounter between the supposed human forces of the man or woman and the animal or vegetable forces of the food. For the food, it is like the attainment of heaven. For the human, it may well be an entrapment in a lower world. According to Pak Subuh, it is in sex that there can be an encounter of human forces with human forces.[13]

This is something that is almost completely foreign to a Western mind. But we have to make a place for some action which is taking the nature of the foodstuffs a further step. If we regard what happens to the food as something in its own right, as objectively happening (besides what we know of this in terms of calories, and so on, in terms of the subjective reactions of humans), we must subjectively enter into the experience of the food itself. Gurdjieff got away with a great deal by talking abstractly about further gradations of hydrogens; however, we must remember that the higher the hydrogens, the more we are involved in what we take as subjective experience—and even beyond experience as we know it. It is in this sense that we can look at the restaurant as a hell for humans and as bliss for the living essences which are transmitted along with the food.

The title of this section includes the name of one Douglas Adams's books (*The Restaurant at the End of the Universe*) partly because of a scene in it in which the raw food offers itself to be cooked and eaten. Jokes have a way of being true! The line from 6 to 9 is connected with a very deep possibility of realization. This concerns the fact that other living beings have died to give us our food. We may "know" this, but we do not realize what it means. To realize it would be to have compassion, to see the inherent mutual relationship of all beings.

The fact that Adams positions his restaurant at the end of the universe—in time—is no accident. The restaurant, as an exemplification of the enneagram, is at the ending of time. It represents the only kind of realistic immortality we can have, which is through "eating and being eaten."

Notes

1. See J. G. Bennett, *Enneagram Studies*.
2. See Clarence King, "The Manufacturing Process" in J. G. Bennett, *Enneagram Studies*.

3. A simple way of thinking about this law is as the cybernetic combination of four factors: the process under way, or the material; the operations on the material, in this case such things as cutting and mixing; the intention or teleology in the minds of the operators; and the goal, or standard, which is qualitative. Between points 4 and 5, these are mixed.

4. Called the *harnelaoot* ("mixed with eight" in Armenian) in *Beelzebub's Tales*.

5. This point would include the existential psychology of Sartre; cf. his portrayal of the bad faith of the waiter in *Being and Nothingness*.

6. The ideal meal contains the entire spectrum of qualities: it is at the right temperature; it has the right appearance; it has the right taste; it nourishes the body; it nourishes the feelings; it nourishes thought; it nourishes the community; it is a sacrament.

7. In the chapter "Beelzebub in America" in *Beelzebub's Tales*.

8. For example, Arnold Wesker's play *The Kitchen,* Peter Greenway's movie *The Wife, the Cook, and the Lover* and Gabriel Axel's *Babette's Feast.*

9. Some impression of the scene may be garnered from various books, such as Elisabeth Bennett, *Idiots in Paris*. See also James Moore's note on the "toast of the idiots" in his biography *Gurdjieff: Anatomy of a Myth*.

10. J. G. Bennett, *The Self and Its Brain.*

11. See the chapter "A Thousand Years of Love" in J. G. Bennett, *The Masters of Wisdom*.

12. Pak Subuh, *Susila Budhi Dharma.*

13. Ibid., p. 350.

· 9 ·

A Computer Running on Air

*The kitchen is a traditional representation of the transformative appa-
ratus by which we are "cooked" to produce being-substance or soul. We
are going to follow through the analogy and extend it in many directions, particularly in terms of the modern paradigm of the computer.
This will give us an opportunity to investigate what might be meant by
the transformation of man and the formation of the inner bodies that
Gurdjieff many times referred to in his teachings.*

The Analogue

THE TECHNICAL ARTIFICE of kitchens and dining rooms on the one
hand, and the natural ingestion and processing of food in our organisms
on the other, should be related. The kitchen has its counterpart inside us,
in our own organism. Although cooking includes the breaking down of
raw foodstuffs, making them more digestible, and the elimination of un-
wanted parts, it is not simply an extension of digestion. As an art, it is
also the construction of the food we eat in "impression-space," so that it
looks, smells, and tastes good. Cooking enhances the experience of food.
We can say that the equivalent to cooking in ourselves produces and
processes *experience*.

If, in this analogy, the organism is similar to the kitchen, and experience to the food being cooked, what is the dining room? It is the realm
of *assimilation*. Instead of the productions of the organism going out into
experience and being taken up by passing impressions, leaving our present moment, something can be formed out of them that remains. This is
similar to the Gurdjieffian idea of an inner or subtle body. Only, the
question rarely addressed is: *Whose* body is it? Gurdjieff might say that
the dining room, the realm of our experience, is occupied by a variety of

customers but rarely ourselves![1] If we manage to attain an inner body, this is rather like becoming our own permanent customer.

We come to the point of picturing the possibility of dining on experiences instead of letting them be swallowed up by the world at large. Nothing is wasted in the scheme of things. What we do not consume is consumed by something. This suggests that we have to learn the art of cooking, to make our experience more digestible for an inner metabolism. We have to be able to assimilate a food that comes as much from inside as from outside. The generation and assimilation of experiences could also be called the generation and assimilation of energies, once we understand the connection between experience and energy. This is important, because we need to understand that energies can be subjective aspects. They are not just thinglike. When we feel, this feeling carries us along in its wake, it has subjectivity in it. Equally, experiences have a quantitative aspect. Gurdjieff says that we should be "economical with our experiences."

In one of his talks, Bennett asked the question: What is experience for? A student answered that it was *to see.* Just as food in the kitchen is translated into experience in the dining room, so this experience in its turn can be made into seeing. Hence, the title of the previous chapter, "The Metabolism of Perception," leads us into this one.

Three Bodies

In the abstract, it is easy to see that Gurdjieff's idea of three foods implies the possibility of there being two other bodies besides the physical one. Just as we develop an embryo and attain the formation of a physical body, so we can, perhaps, "conceive" and develop two other, finer bodies. These will drive from the air and the impressions of the second and third octaves depicted in the enneagram. By analogy, the conception of the inner bodies must involve a seed and an egg coming together, the joining of the similar but different. Gurdjieff himself says nothing about this.

In general, the physical body is understood to derive from the earth, while the third or divine body is said to derive from above, to be God-given. If there is a second or in-between body, then this arises from between heaven and earth—that is, from the *air,* or the *spirits,* or from some other intermediary realm that mediates between above and below.

Besides questions of conception, there are questions of nourishment and development, protection and guidance. Biological parents are responsible for the physical well-being of their child. Perhaps there are equivalent roles in respect of the other bodies as well. Beyond their conception, bodies also require nourishment and guidance.

In his writings and talks, Gurdjieff speaks of these possibilities in a variety of ways, and no single one can do the theme justice. One example is his idea that the second finer or subtle body develops under the stimulus and guidance of a teacher. In the first series of writings, *Beelzebub's Tales*, he ascribes this role to the *oskianotsner,* a notion that is a compound of our ordinary ideas of tutor and guru. In his third series of writings, *Life Is Real Only Then, When "I Am,"* he quotes a Persian text: "The soul is the sediment of education." Here, education is to be understood as a bringing out of what is otherwise latent. If there is an inner or subtle life, then the life needs to become organized and conscious in its own way. It may even need its own language and modes of communication. In his second series of writings, *Meetings with Remarkable Men,* this idea is subtly explored through various characters.

At another point, he says that this body arises through the assimilation of finer substances. At yet another, he says that it arises from a struggle with the impulses of the physical body. The two perspectives are connected. Gurdjieff calls the energies or substances of the physical body negative and those of the inner body, positive. Hence, separation from the forces engendered in the physical body actualizes, or invokes, those of the finer body. This amounts to what Gurdjieff called the struggle between yes and no. The basis of renunciation and practice of austerities is not moral but realistic. Unless there is a suspension of the powers arising from the physical body, inner powers cannot develop.

The idea of something arising from such a friction is suggestive of the generation of an energy or heat. In Hindu schools, this is a strong motif associated with the spiritual exercises known as *tapas,* which means both asceticism and *fire.* This is the inner cooking I spoke of earlier, which nourishes the inner body before it is born. The birth of this body is associated with a death. This is usually the death of attachment, or belief. This may mean that we have to cut the umbilical cord which links us to the external world. It requires us to acquire our own mind and detach from the secondary construct which has been derived from the external culture into which we were physically born.

The sheer variety of perspectives available to us from the world's traditions is very important indeed. It is a sign that what is at stake is not any easily understood mechanism but something inherently uncertain. It is entirely misleading to aim at any simplistic formula. The reason for this is that, if there are higher levels of existence, then they are far more individualistic than our form in the physical world. The development—or realization—of the higher bodies is not possible without the participation of our own conscious intention, and is not guaranteed by life.

Spirit and Soul

Gurdjieff calls the second-being body the *body kesdjan,* which can be translated as "spirit body." Sometimes he calls it the astral body. It develops out of air. The word *spirit* derives from the same root as respiration. The other, the "third-being body," is called the soul. We can say that it develops out of impressions, but these are the finer impressions coming from higher worlds that we discussed before.

There is no established agreement in Western tradition of what the two terms *soul* and *spirit* mean in relation to human beings. Sometimes soul is the higher, and sometimes spirit. Sometimes both soul and spirit are associated with the air and breathing. Sometimes the soul is understood as the form of the body, while spirit is akin to its life or energy. Bennett himself reversed the meanings to be found in *Beelzebub's Tales* and called soul the "coalescence of mind-stuff" and spirit the "will-pattern of value."[2] However, Gurdjieff's usage agrees with the terminology of the worlds we met before, where the second world or domain is called the *alam-i-arvah,* or world of the spirits. Interestingly enough, Bennett translates this as the world of energies. In contrast, he associates spirit with will—or the world called in Sufism the *alam-i-imkan*—more usually translated as the "world of possibilities." We ourselves characterize the third world as "of the substance of information." The first world, the *alam-i-ajsam,* is of the substance of things.

It is well known that the second body of man has been associated with breath and the air in nearly all traditions. If we go back to the father of Western literature, Homer, we find that he portrayed the stuff of the inner bodies as both airlike and firelike. The latter idea was amplified by Heraclitus. Karl Popper comments: "That we are flames, that our selves are processes, was a marvelous and a revolutionary idea. It was part of Heraclitus's cosmology: all material things were in flux: they were all processes, including the whole universe. And they were ruled by law (logos):[6] The limits of the soul you will not discover, not even if you travel every road: so deep is its logos.' "[3]

In the Pythagorean doctrine, two kinds of soul are distinguished. The one associated with the second body as process—that is, with fire or energy—is related to the idea of tuning a musical instrument, and it is not, strictly speaking, immortal. It is an extraordinary representation that the tuning of an instrument can last beyond the existence of the instrument, as if we were a melody that can linger on after the instrument on which it has been played has perished. We may think of the not-so-uncommon feeling that the dead are in the air all around us. The other soul, associated with the third body, belongs to the pretemporal order of number and, contrary to Gurdjieff, has no beginning or ending. However, we should note in passing that the concept of number here is related to that of information.

The uncertainty of nomenclature can be seen in terms of the nonlinear type of hierarchy of the three realms. This was suggested earlier (in chapter two) by our picture of the enneagram as an impossible object. *The three bodies are intimately related.* It is this that makes them difficult to describe separately.

Matter, Energy, and Information

Energy and matter are interrelated. Energy can be seen as a state of matter. It is processed by means of material constructs. Nevertheless, the two are distinguishable, as they are in physics. What is called matter appears as a kind of coagulation of energy, and energy as a kind of release of matter. Hence the famous equivalence relation of mass and energy first expressed by Albert Einstein. In this respect, it is quite permissible to regard Gurdjieff's "fine matter" simply as energy. The processing of matter gives rise to energy, which includes experience. This energy or fine matter, in its turn, can be processed to give rise to information.

It is highly likely that there is some equivalence between information and energy. Only, we need to picture information not in its usual representation as mere strings of symbols but as the very substance of relationships. Thinking of energy as a coagulation of information corresponds to the picture of the triad derived in earlier chapters. We must understand that consciousness in its deeper sense is more than the organic awareness we share with the animals. Through consciousness, we see relationships. To make this point clearer, Bennett spoke of the organic awareness as *sensitivity.*

Consciousness and Sensitivity

What makes consciousness comes from the third octave of impressions. We only generate or release consciousness through influences from above, from the realm of finer impressions, such as those we associate with creativity. Gurdjieff also proposes that only "self-remembering" makes true consciousness *our own.* If we turn to the enneagram model (see fig. 9.1), we can associate pure consciousness with point 7, while sensitivity, properly speaking, is to be associated with point 4. The intermediary point 5 is where consciousness is collapsed into sensitivity. It is this which gives us our ego-sense even though we exist just in surface awareness. The mixup of consciousness and sensitivity is sorted out by the inner linkage 8-5-7. Point 8 is creative-conscious, in contrast with point 5, which is conscious-sensitive. Our own special role in the process is self-remembering, which means to bridge the critical interval of point

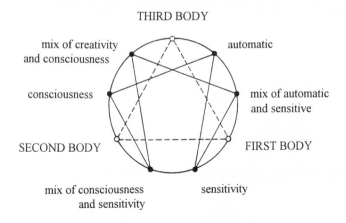

9.1. The dynamic of awareness.

6. While the creative incursion (from point 8 to point 5) is *spontaneous,* it has to be matched or complemented by an *intentional* practice. It is interesting that, in the structure of lines in the enneagram, it is only in the transition from point 5 to point 7 that the inner and outer lines proceed in the same direction.

Hence, this transition signifies the elementary act of synergy in the classical medieval sense of a cooperation between man and God. It casts a whole new light on the meaning of creativity, which is usually understood in only the outer sense of new productions in the external or cultural world. As noted in an earlier chapter, creativity needs to be understood as something capable of organization and not entirely gratuitous. What comes to us "out of the blue" needs to be made our own. Otherwise, we are not transformed by it. In tradition, creativity is usually somewhat oversimplified by treating it in terms of the transformation of sexual energy.

Our understanding of the realm of consciousness and creativity is obscured by our location in mere sensitivity. Sensitivity is rather like a surface phenomenon. Just as with the surface of the planet, it can form a mirror. In this mirror, objects are reflected back to us, while what is beyond us is reflected away from us. We do not really *see.* To see beyond the surface, consciousness is needed. This kind of seeing renders our experiences translucent and intelligible. It is a radical displacement of perspective.

We have talked about the possibility that humans can assimilate "higher hydrogens" of impressions. It is hard to grasp quite what this means. In ordinary language, we tend to say that we are aware or we are not aware of something. This concerns our sensitivity. In some way, the sensitivity is still quantitative. It also has an intensive measure—so that we can be more or less aware of something, while remaining only sensitive. The step that comes with consciousness is somewhat radical. In Bennett's language, this is a step into the *cosmic energies.* These cannot be measured by quantity or intensity. They are entirely qualitative in relation to the other energies. A useful analogy to make is one between the cosmic energies and the *transfinite numbers.* The step from sensitivity to consciousness is like going from the world of the finite to the world of the infinite. We can take consciousness to signify the first infinity, usually called omega.

This is not all that mysterious. The mathematician Rudy Rucker points out that this is very much like the step from the endless regress—which we would call sensitive—to direct connection. In meditation seeking self-knowledge, he says, there can be a jump from looking at oneself looking at oneself looking at oneself . . . to a direct sense of the whole, to "I."[4] This is true consciousness. The change of state is sometimes called *satori* in Buddhist literature. It may be the same as Gurdjieff's self-remembering. It changes our understanding of everything; but it is not the end. There can be a further, even more radical change, known in Sanskrit as *samadhi*. This is probably the same as Gurdjieff's *objective consciousness*. In Bennett's scheme of cosmic energies it is associated with the creative energy.

The idea that there is more than one definite distinct level or *kind* of consciousness is crucial. Equally important is the understanding that these are not to be confused with different intensities of sensitivity. This has been emphasized in certain traditions where the state of objective consciousness or creative energy is called the *black light*. Similarly, the Hindu tradition associates this level with dreamless sleep, which appears to our sensitive minds as an absence. It is not. It is simply that the finite is not able to see the infinite.[5]

Sensitivity gives us a great deal. It has the property of bringing us into contact with phenomenon. One of the most powerful contacts we have with our own organisms is through the breath. Ouspensky observed that breathing is closely connected with our sense of time. The process of breathing, the state of awareness, and the transformation of energies are intimately connected. As the kind of energy working in us changes, so does our sense of time, of the here and now. This has great significance. It is possible that the person who exists now can be intimately related to the person who was born and the person who will die, in a way quite different from that of memory or anticipation.[6]

It is important to note the twisted logic whereby the flow of breathing—the sense of ourselves as energy—becomes translated into something fixed. For some reason, the perspective of a flow in life becomes associated with impermanence, and we are led to search after some superior order of *things*. This is like valuing the musical instrument more than the music it plays. Incidentally, this comment suggests yet another analogy for our situation: We have to be able to *listen* to ourselves as *beings*.

This is reflected in cultures like that of the Lapps, before it was destroyed by Christian missionaries. In such cultures, everyone discovered and practiced his or her *own song*.

The experience of flow (or music) can go very deep. It is connected with the basis of true consciousness in what mystical traditions call the heart. The flow is less trapped in existence than the physical and conceptual objects which occupy the physical world. Yet we want to pin it down. Even in Gurdjieff's metaphors, we see attention being directed toward some kind of precipitation out of the flux of enduring atoms or particles, and not to the flux itself. The metaphor of finer particles is a holdover from Theosophy. It is far better to consider David Bohm's interpretation of the *subtle* as "finely woven." It is in this world that our treasures are to be laid up, beyond corruption. This is so even when we cease to be aware of them in our sensitivity.

Gurdjieff says that when a person expands his consciousness, he can assess a lower cosmos as well as a higher one. Bringing awareness into the body requires consciousness. True consciousness provides a link between the worlds. Most people have little awareness of what their bodies are doing or how they are breathing, just as they have little awareness of the food they are eating. However, such an awareness is possible. In *Beelzebub's Tales*, Gurdjieff makes much of what he calls *cognized intention*, which is his term for awareness with consciousness. It is not surprising that we find this kind of awareness featuring in what are called "spiritual" practices. Such practices entail a greater awareness of physical realities, not less. This is particularly significant when we become conscious of our own breathing, which usually goes on automatically, by instinct. If we bring only sensitivity, we are liable to produce a reaction that mechanically alters the breathing. Consciousness does not do that. Without altering the functioning of breathing in the least, it brings about a change in what it *is*.

State and Station

It is one thing to have experience of the various energies and another to be established in them. This is the Sufi distinction between *hal* (state) and *makam* (station). To be established means to be able to endure in higher worlds. The higher energies are available to everyone without exception, but almost as soon as we are in them, we are displaced out of them. This means that we lack the higher bodies. In his parable *The Great Divorce,* C. S. Lewis vividly describes people in the second or astral world walking in pain over grass which cuts their feet because their bodies have little substance. Similarly, the content of higher worlds is unbearable to us, and any access to it renders us "unconscious."

The higher bodies enable us to have a presence in higher worlds. If we recall our discussions of the different levels of existence in the universe, we can see that this means having a place in realms which are far more highly interconnected than the physical one. We need to organize for ourselves a different kind of state, one in which we are able to endure these extensive interconnections. This state is said to come about through *suffering,* but it must be emphasized that this suffering has more to do with bearing the impact of higher energies than with being miserable. In Gurdjieff's earlier teaching, much was made of the idea of the transformation of negative emotion. Quite rightly, this idea has always been treated with some respect and caution, for it has staggering implications. Some of these were publicly expressed by Bennett in his coupling of the advent of Love through Christ with a *necessary* "explosion of hate."[7] This kind of coupling of the negative and positive had its place in the Eastern traditions of tantra, and some have found many tantric traits in Gurdjieff's teachings and practices.[8] The lower self and the higher self have to fuse, even though they are of contrary natures. The more common idea that the lower self has to be removed or neutralized misconstrues transformation. Transformation does not cheat the economics of life. *Everything* has to be used. There is no escape clause.

Hardware and Software

If there are objects and processes in the inner world, then these will obey a logic different to those of the physical world. Such a logic is hinted at in dreams, though most people draw the false conclusion that the inner world is only subjective. However, we can extend our concept of information to suppose that the logic of the inner world can exert an influence upon lower levels. The strength of this depends on the degree of organization of the inner body.

We can represent the relation between worlds as similar to that between matter and information in our human experience of technology.

In this latter relationship, we regard the physical world as *matter* relative to the inner or subtle world of *information*. This highlights the distinction in a stronger way than the contrast of matter and energy. Now, the structure and processing of information has its own *physical* laws. Information has weight and is subject to thermodynamics. The physics of information has an enormous influence on the physical world; it is far from abstract. Of course, scientists who study the world of information almost entirely reject the perspectives of advocates of cyberspace, who believe that this world can be colonized by human *experience*.[9] In my view, cyberspace is the modern equivalent to the traditional notion of the astral world, the world of the second body, and arises because of the prevalence of information technology as a source of metaphor.

Traditionally, the astral world is associated with the stars. The reason for this is that, in the past, the celestial bodies played a role similar to that of information technology in our own time. They were the basis for the computation of patterns and cycles. But just as the cyberspacer seeks a personal experience of the abstract realm, so did the astral voyager of yesteryear.[10] Gurdjieff's materialism made him identify this participation with the assimilation of definite particles emanating from the sun and planets. Gurdjieff's pupil A. R. Orage speaks in this way:

> We fish in time's "ever-rolling" stream; what we can catch is ours, but what we don't is gone. Time does not wait for us to catch everything in the stream, but if we catch enough we shall have enough to form the higher bodies—and thereby become enduring. . . .
>
> Essence is a chemical deposit from the sun and planets of the solar system, which enters earth-beings at the moment of conception. In man this affects the region of the solar plexus. It is unlike any of the chemicals found on this planet, and links man to the cosmos. As the chemicals of the physical body return to this planet after death, so do the chemicals of essence return to their sources."[11]

The differences of language may be partially explained in terms of the enneagram itself. The combination of three processes is also the combination of three perspectives. It is possible to look at all the points of the enneagram from the standpoint of the first one. This, as we have seen, has the character of matter and things. It is, then, not surprising to find that the substance of the inner subtle body will be represented as another kind of matter. In Orage's poetic description, we have "atoms" coming from the sun and planets to fill this role. For the third higher-being body, the soul, the necessary atoms have to come from higher sources beyond the sun. If, however, we adopt the perspective of the second process, we find ourselves in a world of energies and experiences. We have to open the heart, burn with remorse, struggle against desires: fasting, breathing, dancing. The language is emotional. William Blake says: "He who kisses a joy as it flies, / Lives to see eternity's rise." We speak of an order of time other than the one we know physically.

In the light of the third process, emotion and experience do not count, only understanding. It is a difficult and profound point. In completing the cycle, we have to admit that real understanding has an effect on the nature of the world. The presence of "One who knows" alters the fabric of reality. But this, in its turn, may be experienced only by those who have developed something themselves.

It may appear that we have traveled very far from our starting point, the processing of food. Only, we have to keep in mind the radical departure from our ordinary ideas about food that Gurdjieff proposed. If the world of impressions is also to be considered as a food, this alters everything. We have to consider food not simply as material but also as energy and as information. We have to extend our physiological picture of digestion and metabolism into the realms of psychological and spiritual processing. As we pass from the physiology of digestion into the psychological realm, the step we make is rather similar to that between the hardware of the system and its software. The terms *software* and *hardware* are not fixed. What is software in one world is hardware in another.

Gurdjieff himself used this concept, though in other words. In his account of the creation, he distinguishes the material production of the different worlds from the action of what he calls influences from higher worlds upon lower ones. These influences have the nature of information. Modern physicists such as David Bohm speak in much the same way.[12] Gurdjieff's cosmological theories have their counterparts in his psychology. Thus, there is a problem connected with the coupling of higher and lower worlds both in the universe at large and in ourselves. If we revert to our language of software and hardware, we must remember that the usual picture of the computer, for example, is that the one is unrelated to the other. In other words, it makes no difference what the computer is made of, physically. It can consist of paper and pencil or of silicon chips; it can run on air or water, or whatever. One of the first computers ever built by the pioneer Alan Turing utilized columns of air with acoustical standing waves acting as memory stores![13] However, there is a minority school of thought which claims that this is merely a special case and that, in the natural world, software and hardware interpenetrate. This is just what appears in Gurdjieff's account of the processing of the three foods in man. To repeat, the relation between the substance of one food and the substance of the next finer food is similar to that between hardware and software, except that there is a region of identity between them, where they are highly coupled. This region is just the place of the critical interval, the interface. A third concept is needed, akin to that of energy, to provide this interface between software and hardware.

In our open-ended information processing, we human beings have almost unlimited possibilities. However, these remain only possibilities unless there is a way to connect them with our actual existence in space and time, at a particular point in our history. This is fairly obvious when we look at the way in which our ideas and insights float on the surface of our existence as beliefs and images. The penetration of these ideas into our living cells makes them real. They can only penetrate if they are enabled to do so.

Sometimes the link is said to be provided by something akin to a communication cable or thread. Gurdjieff provides some fascinating stories based on this idea, which supposes that the second body, the energy body, is not confined inside the organism. According to Gurdjieff, its natural place is in the atmosphere, which is where it goes after physical death. This body, then, is a necessity for us if we hope to attain some perception of the global situation in which we exist. It would enable us to see the "memories" of humankind in time, as well as the surface of the planet as a whole. People who enter into this sphere of perception often report a sense of looking down on the earth.

The third and highest body is supposed to have a similar function with regard to the whole solar system, and has its natural place in the sun. These cease to be simply metaphors once we realize that planets, suns, and so on also have their counterparts in the inner worlds. Looking at it in this way, we can begin to appreciate why Gurdjieff often spoke of higher development in terms of objective reason.

What Are the Bodies Made of, and Who Has Them?

The structure of the enneagram gives us three different bodies, or worlds, or spheres. These are not of the same nature, though they must be compatible in their transformations. That is why we must be careful how we take the idea of "body." What a body is depends on our perspective—that is, from which body we are looking. From the perspective of the physical body, the subtle body simply looks like our experience of time, or feeling, and the third body looks simply like a thought, such as the thought of God.

It is quite difficult to give neutral terms to the three bodies. If we persist in calling the first physical body, or our function in space, then the second can be called the present moment, our being in time. The third must be capable of encompassing these two. Further, if we remember the circle of the enneagram, we can ask: What is it that can *contain* or *own* all three bodies? This must be the *will,* and the will is identifiable with (but not the same as) the third body.

will in knowing	individuality	information
being in time	present moment	energy
function in space	physical body	matter

Bennett once said that the will is "infinite in its essence and finite in its operations." Remembering our earlier reference to the cosmic energies and the transfinite, we can think of the will not just as some spiritual atom but as an *infinite information.* Rudy Rucker helps us again by suggesting that we, and any feature of the universe, require an infinite string of information to specify ourselves. It is thus infinity that makes us individual.[14] The importance of this definition is that it brings the will into the realm of the concrete.

These various descriptions of inner transformation may leave us bewildered, but they help us appreciate the question asked at the beginning of this section. *Whose* is the higher body? The second, inner or subtle body *cannot* be the possession of something identified with the physical body.

By analogy, the third higher-being body *cannot* be the possession of that which is identified with the second body. Hence the traditional notion of having to "die" before being "born" into an new sense of life.

The triad of commands in the enneagram may be thought of, as in the language of the Yaqui sorcerer Don Juan, as kinds of *intent*. This is very much as Bennett construed the centers operating in man. He distinguished three forms of will acting in us: the will to *do*, the will to *be*, and the will to *see*.[15] (See fig. 9.2.) Without these forms of will, nothing can develop in us. We will not be able to assimilate the corresponding foods. However, in the case of the second and third forms of will, we need to learn how to connect with them. If we are identified with rushing about the world and doing things all the time, we cannot develop a being-body. We need "time to breathe," as people often say without realizing how accurate the expression is. If we are identified only with being, with unity of consciousness, we cannot develop a will-body. This takes us not only inward but also outward, though in a way markedly different from that of the physical body. The logics or laws pertaining to the three bodies are not the same.

In the Sufi tradition, the transition from a locus or center of one type to another is associated with the idea of *fana* and *baqa*, or annihilation and being. There is a peculiar kind of nothingness that enables the transition to be made. This nothingness appears in the guise of the critical interval in the enneagram model. The self-remembering we spoke of begins with nothingness. It is always unique and cannot be made the product of training. That is why it is almost impossible to describe.

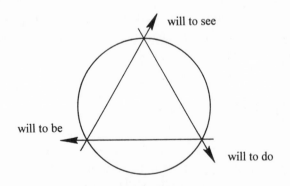

9.2. The will forms of the three bodies.

Active nothingness is a good way in which to think of will. It should be fairly obvious that, if will were "something," then it would be subject to the laws of things and therefore not will at all. At the same time, we cannot really speak of *our* will either, because it cannot be subsumed under some agent other than itself. The conclusion is that "we" belong to something which does not exist! *Will has us.* Will has the bodies. It is the everlasting consumer, enjoying the meal made of our reality. When we say "Thy Will be done," this is not slavish conformity to an external authority. The will is more truly who we are than "we" are!

Notes

1. In his favorite metaphor, we are likened to a carriage driven by a drunkard, available for use by any passerby: "The whole sum of the manifestations of human thought, with all the inherencies proper to its functioning and with all its specific characteristics, correspond in almost every respect to the essence and manifestations of the typical, hired coachman" ("From the Author" in BT).
2. See the glossary in J. G. Bennett, *The Dramatic Universe*, vol. 3.
3. See Popper and Eccles, *The Self and Its Brain*.
4. See Rudy Rucker, *Mind Tools*, pp. 255–56.
5. There is a very important and interesting analogue between the sensitive screen of our minds and the surface of the planet. Consciousness in mind is equivalent to the life which enables the earth to perceive. See chapter 8.
6. This theme is taken up in a historical context in chapter 15.
7. See J. G. Bennett, *The Masters of Wisdom*, p. 86. This astonishing assertion is connected with Bennett's understanding of the "path of humiliation." It is only this that can overcome the egoism which holds us personally, or the social fixation which holds us collectively. In the case of the birth of Christianity, the hate enabled this path to become a universal one—hurling it out, so to speak, into the world beyond the confines of Israel. See chapters 16 and 17.
8. This is referred to in passing by Bennett in his *Gurdjieff: Making a New World*, p. 254.
9. See, e.g., fantasies such as *Neuromancer* by William Gibson.
10. See, e.g., Bauval and Gilbert, *The Orion Mystery*, which details a ritual of stellar identification in the time of the Pharoahs.
11. A. R. Orage, *On Love, with Some Aphorisms and Other Essays*, pp. 55, 59.
12. See David Bohm and B. J. Hiley, *The Undivided Universe*, chapter 15.
13. See Andrew Hodges, *The Enigma of Intelligence*, p. 315.
14. In some remarkable passages, included in his book *Creation*, Bennett draws striking parallels between the different worlds and the transfinite numbers as discovered by Georg Cantor. Different aleph-numbers (zero, one, and two) correspond

very closely to the qualities we seek to define. Again, the concept of transfinite number might remind us of Rudolf Steiner's "plane of infinity"; only Bennett's use of Cantor's ideas lead us to begin to understand that there are important differences in the realm "beyond counting." All higher worlds are transfinite but some are more transfinite than others. This is not mystical but perfectly intelligible. Remember Bennett's early recognition of the importance of what he called in a general way "information theory," mentioned in the Preface.

15. See chapter 3 in J. G. Bennett, *Deeper Man.*

· 10 ·
Being in Life

Is it possible that there are patterns in the way that life works out? Can we see a necessary structure to what we go through, without cramping our authentic existence into some conceptual mold? The basics are that we are born as out of unconsciousness, fresh and new; then we grow up and form minds and purposes, which eventually deteriorate or etherealize, until death finally catches up with us. Our minds are full of dreams of other lives: life after death, or previous lives, or existence in other worlds, or worlds of perfect communion. After all the labor of growing up and learning how to do so many things—does it all come to nothing, or is it just something that has to be passed on to future generations, however best we can? Can we make the dream real? Can we have All as well as Nothing?

Sophocles warned: "Call no man happy until the time of his death." It is hard to see the whole while we are in the throes of life. We strive after meaning. We have to make sense of what is happening to us and what we are doing. And we have to find what it is that our division into two kinds of bodies—two sexes—means for us. The search for meaning can become urgent at any time of life. It may rise in a crescendo of burning concern until it becomes the core of life, instead of a momentary disturbance. A life is like a kitchen, but we do not know what it is that eats what life produces. And we do not know if we are able to digest this produce for ourselves.

The Human Life Cycle

IT IS TIME to look at the *shape of a human life* through the eyes of the enneagram. This shape is a *vision of itself.* We can quote the prayer of Saint Paul: "That I may see even as I am seen."[1]

Making "seeing" the fundamental attribute of the enneagram is extremely important here. It is all too easy to split the human condition into spiritual and material parts, leaving us arguing among ourselves as to whether one or the other is real or not. What is evidently and experientially true for human beings is that our lives are saturated with how we see ourselves. The seeing of our lives enters into our living. The form of the whole enters into the whole and has to make its entry into itself through our actions. The "form of the whole" is the *logos,* or threefoldness, while the "entering of the form of the whole into the whole" is the structuring of events, or sevenfoldness.

We perhaps remember a time when we did not know ourselves as we are now, when we were infants without speech. Perhaps, too, we anticipate or hope for a postadult phase of certitude, in which the external knowledge and words we have acquired blend perfectly with the original energies with which we feel we were born.

In the ordinary, residually religious frame of mind, this further state is placed after death; but in the heart of all religions has been an echo of the Islamic injunction "Die before you die"—a reference, obviously, to some further state within this life. Gurdjieff said: "When a man awakes he can die, when he dies he can be born" (ISM, p. 217).

There is no particular age at which this "should" come about.[2] It can come in early childhood or very late in life. In a sense, it is much easier later in life, when the breakdown of the preservative mechanisms that gave us strength, concentration, and vitality removes a barrier; but then we may no longer be able to make use of what we see. This is a frightening prospect.

In contrast, the ideal way would be to enter a third phase of life in the full vigor of existence by an intentional act of death, which is a setting oneself free of the law-bound materiality of an inferior world, held fast in mental structures, to enter another kind of world, a spiritual reality beyond the mind.

The second phase of life has all the attributes of artificiality that we have encountered before. It represents the image of a person. It is how he is in the context of the artificial environment which governs the social mind. In the third phase, this artificiality must die if there is to be an objective result of having lived. ("Artificiality" and "mind" are here synonymous.)

Because we are biological organisms, there must always be a limit to our productive activity; and so, ultimately, there has to be a kind of crisis point when the active life must give way. Different people take this in different ways: some people can persist in being active right up until the end; others deteriorate, because they are dependent upon external structures. Those people who live vitally right up to the end of their lives have managed to learn how to be self-organizing.

Continuing mental development is possible in old age: the brain by its nature as organ of information need not decline at all. But this is very far away from giving any substance to the idea of a breakthrough into a spiritual domain. And we have to admit that, as we look around, it is hard to find any living examples of the wisdom of old age. T. S. Eliot puts it clearly: "Do not let me hear / Of the wisdom of old men, but rather of their folly."[3]

It is interesting to consider that growing up is also a kind of death—the death of innocence, perhaps as inevitable as the final exhalation. When we grow up, we find childhood hidden from us by a veil. Interestingly, the old find themselves remembering their childhood more vividly than their adult life (which is a hint of the significance of the 7-1 line in the enneagram). So we have two partial deaths in life, the death of innocence and the death of powers, as well as the final biological death.

Leonardo da Vinci wrote in his notebooks: "While I thought that I was learning how to live, I have been learning how to die."[4] The biological drive to seize hold of life is overtaken by the imperative: "Awake, the day of judgment is at hand." In Gurdjieff's scheme of things, the active second phase of life is for waking up, so it then becomes possible to die consciously. This requires an initial acceleration of artificiality, which may include the taking up of special practices. There is a door to another kind of life, which Gurdjieff portrayed through the figure of Prince Lubovedsky in *Meetings with Remarkable Men,* to whom he bids farewell in the Sarmoun monastery.[5]

In contrast to the West, Asian societies have established a pattern which echoes the three stages. Thus, for example, the orthodox Hindu will enter adult life (at point 3), marry and have children, and acquire a profession; and then, when his children have entered their own adult lives and he has come to the end of his active career, he may abandon home and family to become a *sannyasin,* a wandering renunciate who devotes himself to religion (point 6). Point 2 represents the awakening of the sexual powers and is a cluster of potentials. Point 4 is the domain of personal relation-ships, centered on the family, while point 5 is the domain of achievement in the world, of professional success.

We must remember, however, that the idea of reincarnation is en-trenched in Hindu culture. Adult life can be left with such relative ease because there is the conviction that it will all be back again. Such a view was never encouraged by Gurdjieff. Either, he said, one develops a being strong enough to survive death, in which case one "goes elsewhere"—or one does not, in which case one "goes nowhere." Gurdjieff was well aware of the perniciousness of Asian fatalism and optimism.

So far, I have not defined what the three octaves of the enneagram of the life cycle are. It is important to feel them already from within our own experience before we resort to verbal formulations. As a first indica-tion, we can think of the general significance of marriage and procreation, which enters into view after point 3, and the passing beyond that sphere after point 6.

In general, the interval 3-6 is concerned with the productive years; and hence also includes professional accomplishment. However, it would be artificial to conclude that nothing is to be accomplished in the last phase of life in the world. What we tend to see is that a professional makes a shift into the world of values and is no longer so concerned with success in the existential sense. A scientist, for example, will become philosophi-cal and look for the meaning of the world rather than for its factual content—often to the disdain of younger colleagues who regard him as going soft. A businessperson will discover that ethics or ecology are im-portant to him and will wish to serve instead of exploit.

It is from this perspective that we can regard the first octave as primar-ily biological, the second as primarily cultural and social, and the third as spiritual. The third octave may have for a particular person no specifically religious content, but it will always embody some feeling for the uncondi-tioned world. In this guise, it can take two main forms: in the one, it is renunciation of the world and concern with inner reality; in the other, it concerns the transcendence of personal life in the sense of working for the welfare of the whole—but not in an ordinary social sense, because the whole is then something cosmic and not the perpetuation of the social-cultural fiction. That is why the third octave appears as something close in spirit to the first. It contains the mature innocence of being born again.

The two terms of the first phase of the enneagram center on growth and the awakening of powers (usually identified with puberty and adolescence). In the second octave, the first two terms concern human relations and external efforts. In all three octaves, the first term concerns stabilization. In the third, it is a matter of being at peace with oneself. The second term of each octave concerns emergent phenomena and marks a kind of instability that invokes the next stage. The penultimate point 8 is that of a greater vision, a transcendence of all that has gone before.[6]

In the first octave, we see a rise in powers followed by their decline, just as in an ecological system we see rising complexity having to be balanced by a reduction to enable material to circulate. The second octave feeds into the social pool from which it derives: the ethos of a population. The third octave feeds into the spiritual pool, the reservoir of spiritual energy from which the third octave derives: the "communion of saints."[7] We can speak of the second octave as arising from outer society, while the third arises from inner society. In the third octave we enter into a communion which is beyond the scope of external communication.

Meanwhile, serenely (or so we might imagine) at point 9 of the enneagram the hidden master of our lives sits and contemplates the whole—seer first and doer only by proxy. This master is our essential will, the unmanifest point 10 being the spiritual medium in which this will lives. Here we should emphasize that the "form of the whole" is not some abstract pattern but a dynamic generator of information. The essential will is not a blueprint for action but a gateway to seeing the greater whole in which we can participate.[8] We can think of this as a cosmic society, or the realm of higher intelligence. This top-down representation—in which the true self is supposed to be already there as some kind of absolute invariant almost totally detached from the troubles of life—is made sense of by the inner lines, the lines of learning. It is what is gathered along these lines that can remain.

Doris Lessing, in her book *The Making of the Representative for Planet 8*, portrays the essence of this in a most moving and convincing way. She does not subscribe in the novel to any theory of an immaterial individual soul, but envisions the making of a certain quality or essence, set free from time and space. This quality is able to enter into and guide living souls on other planets. It is similar to Gurdjieff's explanations of the sacred *rascooarno*. The core of this picture of things is that a life can make something which is not explicable in terms of succeeding memories among the living. This is the difference between the second and third octaves. It is true that we only live on in the memories of people, but this is strictly true only in the second octave. The real *soul* is born in the third octave, and that is another story altogether.

By distinguishing the three octaves we can separate out three different frameworks of explanation.

If it is true that, at point 6, we really have a death, then this means that what endures cannot, even in principle, be the property of the human remnant (alive or dead). To die to oneself means to relinquish all those claims of possession and identity which enable ambition and attachment to play their coercive roles. All such roles and attitudes stem from the second octave, the sociocultural one, which operates as I have said before in the medium of the artificial environment from which we derive our ordinary personalities and knowledge.

Put like this, it is a beautiful paradox: the essential immaterial soul belongs neither to the living nor to the dead, and as it is acquired, so we lose ourselves. Such a conception must lead us to suppose that soul is taken up by something, somewhere, that it does not just disperse into the meaningless void or return, as in Advaita Vedanta, to the Source "as if it never was." Gurdjieff spoke of all the living beings on earth providing an energy to the evolutionary and regulative matrix through their sacred *rascooarno*, or deaths. It is hard to imagine what this means when we consider intentional, inner death and the making of soul.

Coming back to the enneagram (see fig. 10.1), the region between 6 and 9 has to be filled intentionally, from within. The interval from 3 to 6—which Keats calls the vale of soul-making—is to arrive at a capacity of dying by an act of will, which means to suspend a lesser order and permit a higher order. The realm from 3 to 6 is also, on the other hand, the karmic arena (the middle phase of the enneagram being where two quite different modes of operations act side by side). It is the realm of compounding effect, which does much to explain both the fixity and turbulence of life.

The important thing is that the soul is not a matter of belief but of accomplishment. If we lose sight of the possibilities of a further realm, then we stagnate and poison ourselves. We may not see the nature of the fruit which can be set free by the arising of consciousness in life, but it is

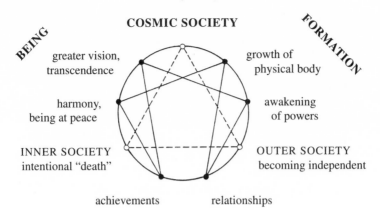

10.1. *The circle of a human life.*

a task of being human to investigate what this might be. What can come into play in the third phase of the enneagram is always individual and not general. In spite of appearances, children and adults are not usually individuals at all but biological and cultural exemplifications. It takes a very great deal to wrench oneself out of the role of "being played" by the environment. Here is Gurdjieff's response to the heedless nihilism that has led to the derangement of social man. This is our true ecological role in the functioning of the intelligence that spans the stars and worlds.

The World of Sex

One of the major powers that is awakened in the formative years is that of sex. In figure 10.1, sex belongs in the region indicated by points 4-2-8. It can be taken as a world in itself. As something pervading human life, it should afford an interesting illustration of my interpretation of the enneagram.[9]

First of all, we have to find some expression of the *logos* of sex. In D. H. Lawrence's novel *The Rainbow,* one of the characters gives a speech in which he says "the union of a man and a woman is an angel." In Chinese tradition there is the concept of *tsing,* a substance created whenever a man and a woman meet.[10] Religious people might say that a man and woman can become one soul in sexual contact. The *logos* of sex probably has to do with overcoming the polarity of the sexes. The biblical term "to know" suggests that sex enables the man or woman to know the other *from inside* in a stronger sense than physiological sensation. However, our picture of what it means for the two to come together, or be united, depends on our understanding of the nature of the human being. The enneagram perspective simply tells us to look for three different aspects.

My description of sex will be limited to heterosexuality and centered on penetration. I am working within this limitation because this form of sex is founded in the biological reproductive process. In contrast, from a cultural standpoint, all forms of sex are equally valid; and, from a personal standpoint, a kiss may be more significant than an act of intercourse. The wide-ranging possibilities are not excluded from my treatment; only, they have to be translated into its form.

The primary process we follow through around the enneagram is close to that of the process of reproduction. There is: meeting, consent, copulation, conception, and birth. The first two occupy the first phase; copulation, the middle phase; and conception and birth, the third phase. To make the picture more concrete, we can point out that, when contraception is used, this is tantamount to putting a barrier at point 6—that is, the reproductive process stops there. As far as the biological world is concerned, the process is terminated. The social and cultural world allows for enormous variations. For example, a childless couple can adopt or can engage a surrogate mother to have their child. A physiological blockage at point 6 can be circumvented by drawing on help from outside.

The primary process is *physical.* In our minds, in our feelings, in our imagination, we may follow a different path. In the form of the enneagram, this is signified by the inner lines, which show the sequence of events as "otherwise." This is where the passions can travel. In the middle phase of copulation, in the line of the circle, they tend to be attached to physical events. They only come into their own beyond orgasm. Bound neither by biology nor by psyche, there is the spirit or will. It is this that makes us "free," or "one," or "responsible." Independently of the first two processes, the spirit or will can intervene at points 3, 6, and 9. This is an infinitely subtle area, for the spirit works in a diversity of ways. For the moment, we can illustrate the idea of intervention by thinking of point 3 as where we are freed, or released; of point 6 as where we can commit to responsibility; and of point 9 as where we can become unified.

In what follows, we shall build up a complex picture of sex by repeated though changing descriptions. We will be following the inner lines as well as the outer circle.

In the general experience of the majority of humankind, sex has the structure of courtship, copulation, and the consequence of conception. In courtship, the man and woman come into closer and closer proximity. In copulation, their bodies are joined, giving rise to intense experiences. If conception results, then they enter the new relation of being parents. We see that the conception and nurturing of a child appears in the place of the realization of the unity of the man and the woman. But what I have described is merely the *functional* aspect of sex, which has a structure in time. It is, therefore, only the material of the *first octave* of the complete enneagram.

We look for a second octave, beginning further on or higher than the first. This connects with the onset of copulation. It is fairly clear that this must concern the *experience* of the sexual act. Therefore, in comparison with the first, the second octave concerns the psychological and, specifically, the erotic. The movement of this second octave is toward greater and greater intensity, just as the movement in the first was simply toward greater and greater proximity. We might question the positioning of this movement as starting after the first: sex in the imagination can be more powerful than actual sex. Most of the vast amount of sexual fantasy and associations which go on are largely outside the enclosure we have drawn. It is only when there is a precise connection with an actual relationship that we have the new independent *do*. The accumulated program of sexual imagination has to be downloaded into the actual occasion. A fit has to be arranged between actual and imagined. That is why the sexual act is full of artifice.

More important, the second octave is linked with the inner lines. Quite simply, the act of sex is linked with what comes before and after. The erotic passions weave into seduction and responsibility for its consequences. The experience of actual sex feeds into the inner movement, which is stimulated by the release or sense of freedom that comes in at point 3.

The third octave must, in its turn, begin further on than the second. It is neither physical nor psychological. Let us provisionally call this the *spiritual* octave. Just as the experience of the couple is within their bodies, so the spiritual element is within their experience. Giving this octave the name "spiritual" may be misleading, because most of us think of spirituality as associated with religious beliefs. It might be better to think of this third domain of sex as the relation between the man and the woman *at a creative level.* This means that we are looking at something that is more than a convenience of copulation, and suggesting that something is made or realized that marks a definite step beyond the range of subjective intensity of experience. Whether we regard this as the making of a common soul or in terms of the possibilities of conception and children, whenever the *question* of the relation between the man and woman arises, we then have a third octave. This is when we have *responsibility,* which starts "for real" at point 6.

As with the second octave, the material of the third largely resides elsewhere outside the enclosure of the first octave. Dante, catching sight of Beatrice, is enraptured for life, though he never even sees her again. Only when the recognition comes that "this is *she*" or "this is *he*" does the third octave activate in the other two. This recognition brings an added degree of *cognition,* of an order different from that expressed in the biblical "to know."

Sex has been taken, in a metaphysical sense, as representing the very principles by which the universe is created and balanced, as can be seen in Hindu depictions of the gods in copulation. At the same time, it is a mere mechanism which is a by-product of the reproductive needs of the species. Thus we have two different aspects or sides of the complete process, which have to come together in a creative realization. In terms of the enneagram, the metaphysical reality of sex is concentrated in point 9, while its purely biological and contingent reality is concentrated in point 0. Our experiential connection with the higher or metaphysical side has to be *intentional,* while our connection with the reproductive urges of the species is only *mechanical.* Out of these two kinds of connection comes the whole gamut of sexual experience—in common parlance the experience of making love—which can be visualized as occupying the middle part of the enneagram.

To have the completed action of sex, we need the actual combination of male and female bodies (the first octave), which is felt or experienced by them intensely (the second octave). This conjunction of the physical and mental (or emotional), or of the bodily and the experiential, then acts as a *field of realization.* It does not make the realization happen. It is only in the third octave of sex (starting at point 6) that a man or woman can overcome the separation between their natures, because men and women differ both physically and psychically. In this realization, the man and the woman find themselves "in each other." For a man and woman to realize their unity—that is, to both know it and make it happen—is a big thing. It means that they know each other not only as bodies and minds but as *will.* In this respect, the will of the man and the woman involved in sex is the same, and there is, and can be, no difference. They both gain contact with the triangle or logos of sex.

We can now suggest that the *logos* of the enneagram of sex can be expressed in terms of the threefold character of will. This means that it is constituted out of the interplay of the *affirmative, receptive,* and *reconciling* impulses which govern all relationships. These are related to release, responsibility, and unification, respectively. It is usual in most cultures to take the man to be the affirmative and the woman to be the receptive in the relationship. However, this convention misses the point: what is involved is a *transformation of a relationship* in which both partners participate. *Both* of them are affirmative; both of them are receptive; and it is through entering into the experience of each other that both of them can be reconciling. However, the word *both* changes according to which phase of the total action we are looking at.

The images of this changing relation, which we can find in literature, are nearly all biased toward regarding the man as affirmative. His task as a lover is to overcome the original denial of the woman—first through seduction and then through domination, until they reach the point at which she surrenders totally. In the extreme, the woman loses all separate individuality, while that of the man is enhanced. On the other hand, in erotic classics such as Pauline Reage's *Story of O*, the submission of the woman is so powerful that she attains the individuality that the man forfeits by his sadistic acts. The picture of woman as a being of receptivity obscures the drama of the will. In place of this caricature, it is better to picture both the woman and the man as first becoming aware of something missing or lacking in themselves. In the next stage, when they come into contact with each other, they feel powerless in front of each other. After that, when they come together as lovers, what concerns them is giving to each other and then surrendering to each other. Beyond their

making love—that is, in the realm of love itself—they first give up themselves and then give up each other. Step by step, they bring themselves—by means of each other—*under* an increasing affirmation (they
come to under-stand). They become able to bear a deepening transformative action that acts from within them.

In speaking about the *logos* I am speaking about the essential values
that inform the process. It is difficult to capture the right degree of real-
ism in my descriptions. An easy but facile formulation of the triangular
figure of commands would be: to fall in love (0-3); to make love (3-6);
and to be in love (6-9). But this cannot satisfy our experience of the
tensions and uncertainties that affect sexual relationships. It is fairly obvious that a harmonious integration of all three octaves is a rare and unusual event. This would be a perfect marriage. However, all of us who
have some kind of sexual life are willy-nilly part of its dramatic and uncertain logic. Part of the pain and suffering we go through stems from
the combination of the three quite different processes which sex involves
us in.

The enneagram directs our attention toward the need for *closure* and
recurrence, the essential conditions symbolized by the circle and the inner
lines. It is easiest to think of closure in terms of the generic concept of
marriage, but this should not be taken too narrowly. It is possible to
conceive of an entirely erotic path, unconnected with reproduction and
social life in general. Whatever the case, there must be some form of
enclosure of sex: some constraint such as monogamy, or some discipline
such as tantra.

Even the point 0 on the enneagram is significant. This represents, for
the individual, an acceptance of his or her sexual nature. It is to belong
to the "world of fuck," as Henry Miller succinctly puts it.[11] It is activated
by the sight, sound, touch, or even thought of the other sex. Biologically,
almost any man and woman can have sex together. Psychically, there are
cultural factors and subjective conditions to do with attractiveness and
access which vastly narrows the field. There is also the question of professionalism, in respect to which the role of the courtesan is significant.

At point 0, the common will of the man and woman is only a possibility, and the ensuing process may well lead toward conflict. We may well
cast the "war of the sexes" between points 4 and 5. But the fulfillment of
our sexual nature does not end with erotic experience; it lies in the real-

ization beyond it. We begin with a sense of what we lack and come to understand that what we need cannot be taken but is given freely.

The possibilities in sex are similar, but not identical, to those we discussed for eating food. It is usual to eat purely for the satisfaction of eating. It is rare to eat with an attitude of compassion toward all life. In sex, it is usual to aim for orgasm while ignoring the essence of what is involved in producing this experience.

Bennett argued that sex always involved the essence, the reality behind the social self or personality, and that it was irrevocable.[12] In a similar vein, the sage Pak Subuh said that sex involved the meeting of truly "human forces."[13] In such views, it is believed that something irrevocable happens, whether or not the participants themselves are aware of it. However, it is common for most people to practice serial or contemporary multiple relationships. This is a shadow of the higher level, where sex may be considered as a marriage of wills, and the union of one man and woman is not a closed system but one able to provide a home for other wills.

The marriage of will is only possible through mutual sacrifice and is not ended by death. It is a paradox that what comes into being through rigorous exclusion can become all-inclusive. The psychological realm cannot match this combination of uniqueness and universality. A man or woman may have many physical sexual partners, but only a few will be regarded as having a relevance to his or her inner life that, in ordinary Western parlance, is referred to as "being in love." It is rare for this love to spread out and be able to contain or cherish others.

In the ordinary view, too, the spiritual octave is disregarded or considered as something utterly different from the erotic. We may regard the relation of Saint Teresa and her confessor Saint John of the Cross as one of sublime spirituality, but there can be little doubt that the grille between them was scorched![14] When sex is taken in a symbolic or idealistic sense, it is easy to cast aside the gross mechanics of copulation; but if we are to assemble an enneagram, it has to include the mechanics. Every enneagram has a substantial physical base. The first process would begin from the meeting of the man and the woman (point 1) and what passes between them (point 2) before they engage in sexual congress. It is the act of penetration which typifies the shock in the first octave (point 3) which, at point 5, reaches the stage of orgasm. It is just there that the third octave becomes possible, at point 6. This possibility is usually spoken of in Eastern traditions as where orgasm is held back or ejaculation prevented (the sexual fluid actually then goes into the bladder). This holding back has many aspects; for example, it is a technique whereby one partner can take the energy of the other (that is why in the Chinese Taoist tradition, the men take younger partners who have not learned the deeper skills of sex). However, this only concerns the second, or energy, octave. It does not advance perception, as might be the case in tantra.

There is the possibility of a deviation at point 3. This may, perhaps, be represented by the practice of mutual masturbation, in which the sex organs are stimulated without penetration. One of the main drives behind this practice stems from the fact that many women experience orgasm primarily through the clitoris and only secondarily through the vagina. (This fact has led certain male-dominated cultures into the barbaric practice of female circumcision.) Similarly, many men prefer oral sex. I am not suggesting that there is anything inferior in clitoral orgasm or oral manipulation of the penis, only that they are restricted in terms of the sexual communication between the man and the woman. There can be a kind of dialogue between penis and vagina that some couples approximate when they are separated, by masturbating while they are connected by the telephone. As far as the *experience* of sex is concerned, the actual organs used are a secondary consideration.

The orgasm has to have something spontaneous in it, or it is not an orgasm. This means that there is always something paradoxical about the use of technique in attaining it. One of the delights of sex is in the interplay of control and letting go.

In Chinese eroticism the act of penetration (which we associate with point 3) is assisted by another woman, who of course represents the third force in the equation. This enables the couple to feel entirely free in the sexual act, the mechanical part taken by someone else. In Western eroticism, a recurrent idea is that deep sex is not possible between a couple and there needs to be a third person involved. This is an extraordinary manifestation of the truth of the triad. At the moment of orgasm, the third person takes the role of witness. Naturally enough, it is possible for the role of the third person to be taken up internally.

The point of maximum tension, point 5, is where both intensity of involvement and also detachment have to be at their peak. The orgasm, which is so often considered to be the culmination of the sexual act, appears like that only from the perspective of the movement from point 4 to point 5. Between these two points lies the fire of sex, which seeks a fulfillment. But point 5 is also connected with the dramatic crux of the action, which is focused on point 6 and poised between two differently natured relationships. Point 5 is the beginning of the structure of the intentional component, which can enable the crossover between the second and the third octaves. The important issue is whether point 5 is governed more by the beginning or by the ending.[15] It is the most difficult thing, because the further action has to take us through the peak of intensity into something of another order. Erotic intensity can be seen as the culmination of the whole process. It is only from another, completely different perspective that it can be seen as a kind of death, a perspective in which both the physical and the psychological are seen as limited forms of existence.

In figure 10.2, I have labeled the various points in summary ways and suggested the character of the inner lines. Since there are three octaves which intertwine together, of three different natures, the nature of the points—particularly on the left-hand side of the enneagram—is far from simple. For example, when we call point 7 "rest," this can be taken as (a) the transcendence of the physical organism, (b) the passing from consciousness into creativity, and (c) the stillness in which the will unifies. The shift in experience I shall speak of later, when it will appear that I

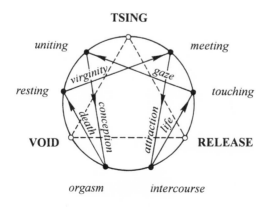

10.2. Enneagram of sex.

contradict myself by speaking then of a journey. However, as we shall see, this journey is when the outer action has ceased to be dominant.

In labeling the line 5-7 "death" we mean it both consciously and unconsciously. It is not for nothing that the event of orgasm has been called *le petit mort*, the "little death." In contrast, the line 4-2 is called "life." This is an allusion to the interplay between life and death that sex entails. The meaning of the other inner lines will emerge.

Gurdjieff mocked those who lose self-awareness at the peak of orgasm. The reason they do this is because, for them, *there is nothing more.* They can only go back into the ordinary states, as if they had hit a wall and rebounded. Hence Sartre's dismal "taste of ashes in the mouth" after coitus. In this respect, point 6 appears in its guise as a mirror instead of a lens. We need peak experiences because they challenge our perception, not because they are ends in themselves. Gurdjieff claimed that sex is a kind of "shit" that eliminates certain psychic poisons that accumulate in the brain. Certainly, many people find that they can think more deeply after orgasm. In general, the creative power in sex divides into creation, destruction, and wholeness and can become the gateway to different perceptions. A change in perception is radically different from having experiences. Using our own terminological categories, it is the difference between information and energy. Sex *can* enable one to see more, although it is usually a light that blinds. It is radically uncertain. Perhaps very few can go through sex into another kind of perception.

In the more profound erotic traditions, the line of attention follows the inner lines and is not fixated on the outer sequence. It is this which can take the process *into our being.* That is why, for example, we can find the exceptional use of the gaze in Indian eroticism, which is an expression of the 2-8 linkage. At point 2, the man and woman look *into* each other's eyes and not *at* each other.[16] In the deepest sense, it is an opening of the heart to each other and to the possibility of uniting together. At point 2, it is also significant to put the *kiss.* In ancient societies, the kiss was a mark of worship.

The line 1-4-2 encompasses just about everything to be found in sex manuals, such as "foreplay" and determining the position of congress. It is only on the right-hand side of the enneagram that we have the dominance of the ordinary human powers of thought and imagination. The line 1-4 is about the potential inherent in any encounter between a sexually active man and woman, when they meet alone. Always implicit is the possibility that they will sleep together. Hence the tendency in traditional Eastern cultures to have a third party present, capable of neutralizing the situation. In its simplest sense, the line 1-4 is mutual attraction. Whether the attraction is mutual or not is tested out at point 2. If the two willingly touch each other, this allows the process to go forward.

Point 1 is always a kind of virginity or innocence, meaning that it has to be fresh and not conditioned. A significant sexual event only arises from an innocent beginning. This is crudely emphasized in the taking of a virgin female. Point 7 symbolizes the *essential* virginity, while point 1 represents the *existential* kind of virginity. In a deep sexual relationship, the man and the woman become virgins again, no matter what their previous experience. This derives from the contact with creative energy. The line 4-2 comes into play when the merest touch is sexual. All the senses become conduits of sexual energy: seeing, hearing, touching, smelling, tasting.

On the left-hand side of the enneagram, we have the essential or more objective aspects. The line 5-7 requires an inward rather than an outward surrender—a relinquishment of the immediate satisfaction of orgasm for the sake of a deeper union. Point 6 then signifies the conception of the third force in a third octave (which, ordinarily, does not come into being at all). The conception, which is made possible according to the inner line 8-5, can be either that of a child or something of another nature altogether. Essentially, they are the same. This is only because the fulfillment comes from the same source of the unitive energy, the energy of objective love. When the man and woman "die" in the movement indicated by the line 5-7, they have surrendered their separateness. This is an action in the deep regions of the worlds beyond imagination. It means that the body is as ready and potent as it was in the initial stages: it is rendered virginal. Hence, in the perfecting of sex there is never any loss of innocence. *The conception by the virgin is a natural part of complete sexuality.*

Between points 7 and 8, the action enters into meaning. It is here that it becomes increasingly or decreasingly significant. It can wax or wane in being. The issue is whether this relationship grows stronger or weaker in the face of the prevalent environment of sexual multiplicity and also of social friction, or "noise."

As in the case of the restaurant, there is a flow of *information* coming from point 9 right around to point 0. In this regard, point 5 is the sexual image, from which the sexual fixation derives, such as a man being attractive to certain women because he has power, say in politics or finance. Point 2 is then to be associated with the paraphernalia of seduction: low lights, sweet music, or the more severe and exacting rituals of tantra. In traditional times, even astrology played a role, serving as a transmission from point 7 by providing information on compatibility of types (of which I shall say more later).

Besides the first world in which the bodies take positions and perform various acts, there is another. This is the world of images (which, in the ordinary case, is the world of fantasy and includes pornography) in which the man and woman perceive each other and, therefore, reflexively see themselves. This world is bound to come under the various archetypes of man and woman, whether these are unconscious or social. It is common for the second phase of the sexual process to be characterized by struggle and conflict, and there is an inherent uncertainty focused in the interval between point 4 and 5.

If we look at the enneagram as a whole, we can see the first octave as acting as a container for the second, and the second in its turn acting as a container for the third. We have to understand that the enneagram operates as between two extremes, but that both these extremes cohere in an implicate order or substance of a particular nature. As I have said, the apex point is something like *tsing,* or an angel, or the third force; but it has to be that which arises as a possibility between a man and a woman. In passing from the material condition of two bodies, with different sex organs, to the spiritual condition of a union of opposites, we do not proceed in a linear fashion. The Jungian notion of the anima and the animus are a reflection of this: the realm of the psyche is intermediate between the spiritual and the material and, in this part of the integrated action, the roles of the two agents can invert in relation to each other. This crossover between the sexes embodies an important principle and one which lies behind much of alchemy, which concerns how the created world can be creative.[17] We must remember that each of the octaves continues to develop. In terms of the first octave, it is unnecessary to go into the physical changes taking place up to the point of orgasm. It is then possible that conception takes place at point 6 and the ensuing stages concern the nurturing of the new being. As far as the participants are concerned, point 7 is, as I have said, the stage of rest. Point 8 then refers to something that probably does not exist for them at all. This would be the physical base of union, a substance that Gurdjieff called *resulzarion.* Whereas point 7 represents the stage of nonactivity, point 8 represents the stage of nonbeing or pure will. From here, all kinds of extensions of meaning can escalate. For the moment, it is enough to remind ourselves of the Sufi concept of *fana,* or annihilation. At point 7, the couple rest. At point 8, they *disappear.* This strange-sounding notion may simply mean that "they" are drawn back into the general genetic pool, concerned with the species.

As for the further stages of the second octave, the poet Rainer Maria Rilke tried to pierce the veil that life draws over the erotic transformation:

> . . . every one of our deepest raptures makes itself independent of dura-
> tion and passage; indeed, they stand vertically upon the courses of life,
> just as death, too, stands vertically upon them; they have more in com-
> mon with death than with all the aims and movements of our vitality.
> Only from the side of death (when death is not accepted as an extinc-
> tion, but imagined as an altogether surpassing intensity), only from the
> side of death, I believe, is it possible to do justice to love.[18]

The second octave of sex can develop beyond point 6 if something of a different order intervenes. The experience is then like taking a journey through different spaces and times, to become travelers in other worlds. The man and the woman "ride" each other's bodies as free spirits. They become "wild" not in the sense of thrashing about but inwardly. They have an access to the cosmos. In their journey, their freedom, they be-come companions on the path of the void. *Eros* becomes united with *agape.* It is not neutered but enhanced beyond recognition. In this experi-ence, it hardly matters if the two never meet again in worldly terms. They are always together. Any hope or expectation of repetition simply gets in the way, but it is for this that we long. We wonder if it will even happen to us once in a lifetime. Once is enough, because it can change everything. It is identical with the core of our transformation. Transformation is not some solitary and grim labor accomplished by denying life. By con-sciously accepting another—physically and concretely, totally and imme-diately—we have the taste of real freedom, beyond the subjective release that begins at point 3.

What is involved in the third octave is not personal. That is why it is generally disregarded, even though it is universal. The third octave brings in the purpose of sex. None of our descriptions can do it justice. However, Rilke's words are useful in suggesting to us that this comes from beyond life, or from death itself. Sex is then no longer a matter of personal experience at all. When Saint Paul says that "there is no marrying in heaven," besides its obvious connotation that physical sex is left behind is a more subtle one: that there are no longer any men or women. This is the realm of the reconciling force. Men and women differ not only physically but psychically: their animate souls are not of the same type; however, in the end, the distinction is no more—in the third octave.

What is at stake is a marriage of will, something that is inherent in the possibility of every individual. It is this which makes possible the seeing of the third force. Bennett, in his book on sex, draws attention to the realization through the union of a man and woman of communities or dwelling places in which other souls may find a home. However, these are all in a higher cosmos than sex itself. In the case of what Gurdjieff calls the conscious production of a result outside of oneself, realization is taken up by the will of the child. Carlos Castaneda asserts that having children produces a "hole" in the energy body. Hence we have the notion that a child represents a new source of perception in the world (and the hope of its renewal) and also the notion that the child robs the parents of the power of vision. Bennett says:

> The affirming and the denying force take place through the man and the woman, but the third force, the *helkdonis,* comes independently of them and this third force is what makes conception possible. . . .[19] The role of the helkdonis is that it brings in an individualised will-pattern. This is the very core of the being but, as it arises from a different dimension or a different world, it does not have a place in the material existence. We can say that it remains in the unconditioned world. A place has to be prepared for it. A great deal of our work consists in preparing a place for the entry of our true individuality that will remain in its own world until we have prepared a place of it here.[20]

The human has, as subordinate aspects of itself, both man and woman. It is through being a man or a woman that the human in us can see, but only partially. Sex exists so that we may experience the other side of human reality: the movement toward completion is that which enables us to be human rather than being one or the other sex.[21] In *Beelzebub's Tales,* Gurdjieff uses the metaphor of a special planet (Modiktheo) in which reproduction of the three-brained beings proceeds through *three sexes* and in which understanding of the laws of the universe is guaranteed.[22] However, on earth, humans are bisexed, and this necessarily means that what is harmoniously and almost automatically guaranteed on the special planet, on ours is subject to hazard and uncertainty.

The sexual logic of the special planet Modiktheo is represented in the triangle of the enneagram. On the outside of the circle, there is all the mess and confusion of our sexual lives. Within the compass of the enneagram, there is a *transformation.* What this transformation does is to provide a substantial link between different worlds. For example, if we speak of man as body, soul, and spirit, then these three will not be living separate lives, governed by separate laws, barely touching upon each other. There will be the know-how—the intelligence and understanding represented in the inner lines of the periodic figure—that weaves these three strands of our being together.

Uncertainty remains. This we feel most strongly at the moments of committal, which are indicated at points 3 and 6. The rest of it largely goes by itself. It is interesting that we have the "professionals" in sex, exemplified by the courtesan and her assistants, who take away the hazard of the sexual act. There is something similar in relation to the second point of hazard, the far stronger one, which is to do with marriage or union. This kind of professionalism was associated with astrologers, who were capable of determining the compatibility of the man and the woman and of giving some measure of the worth or significance of their sexual union. Thought of in such terms, incidentally, point 7 appears as the matching of their charts, while point 8 is finding an auspicious time for the marriage (consummation) to take place. In this context, the parents take on the role of the influence entering at point 6. Just as in the case of the kitchen in the restaurant, the lovers are to provide something which has a meaning maybe far removed from their own. The demands of families—their histories, their finances, their genetic and social tendencies—bring in quite other laws.[23] Traditionally, the couple require the consent of their parents in order to marry, and they have to conform to the religion of their community.

The transitions required at points 3 and 6 are powerful. We may not believe in souls or a spiritual reality, but we know, directly from experience, that in making these transitions we change the laws under which we live. The question of the relationship between the man and the woman is, as we have seen, not something confined to their isolated encounter. It is something embedded in a nexus of interrelations, and it is also open to a variety of realizations. *What is brought to our attention by the enneagram is not the mechanics of the world but the meaning of what we do in the world.* The various sets of laws I have spoken about are simply an expression of what is *possible;* but this, of course, verges on what is allowable or permitted in a cultural, ethical, and religious sense. Whether or not some kind of "tangible intangible" can be made through sex, we may never know. It is all, then, part of the quest for the imperishable through the perishable, the immortal through the transient. As Shakespeare, in one of his sonnets, writes of time and love:

> Or what strong hand can hold his swift foot back?
> Or who his spoil of beauty can forbid?
> O, None, unless this miracle have might
> That in black ink my love may still shine bright.[24]

The Physical Symbol

In addition to being a symbol of transformation, the enneagram serves as a symbol of wholeness. Looking at transformation, our attention is on the progression of the action: the build, the commitment, the climax, the resolution, and the fulfillment. Wholeness appears to us in a different mode. One of the most common symbols of wholeness is the completion of man and woman in each other. Imagine the enneagram as an embrace, the woman on the left and the man on the right. The line 3-6 is the dominant sexual link: point 3 the penis and point 6 the vagina. The cross-links of the inner lines that join right and left are through the eyes and lips. Their limbs entwined make up the circle that surrounds them both. The man's testicles are represented at point 4 and the clitoris of the woman at point 5. In relation to these, the two brains are at points 1 and

8, and they are linked into the cervix and the prostate respectively at points 7 and 2 in orgasmic behavior. If we picture the enneagram as a series of levels—4-5, 3-6, 2-7, 1-8 and 1-9—we go more and more inward. There are layers of wholeness. The core is at point 9, where essences meet. (I take this up again in the last chapter.)

Notes

1. In chapter 15 we will look at the important transition from "real" images to "virtual" images in the workings of a microscope. This transition is echoed in human life. The images we have of ourselves as we mature are "real" while those that come through further transformation are "virtual."
2. In China it is commonly thought that this happens at the age of sixty. The example of Christ puts it at thirty. Many Sufis do not even marry until they are fifty!
3. T. S. Eliot, *Four Quartets*, II.
4. *Notebooks of Leonardo da Vinci*, p. 63.
5. The whole of this book is concerned with the various attempts of Gurdjieff's friends to find a solution to the problem of human life, it should be read to illuminate this section.
6. This is symbolized in the confession of faith at the moment of death and the giving of the last rites.
7. I take up the theme of such "reservoirs" in chapter 13 (see pages 235–36). The phrase "communion of saints" is not intended to convey a simplistic idea of a paradise, but a state of existence in which individuality and the many are not disjoint. This has been excellently expressed by William Pensinger, in his novel *The Moon of Hoa Binh*, as "identity transparency," implying a condition of hyperorgasm or "supersex." It is a transfinite condition.
8. Bennett used the term *will-pattern* in this sense.
9. Stanislaw Lem estimates, in his satire *One Human Minute*, that 4.3 million liters of semen are discharged into vaginas worldwide every minute, which may or may not be accurate but makes the point.
10. Julius Evola, *The Metaphysics of Sex*, p. 23.
11. Henry Miller, *The Tropic of Capricorn*.
12. J. G. Bennett, *Sex*.
13. Pak Subuh, *Susila Budhi Dharma*.
14. As Elizabeth Bennett once remarked to me.
15. Gurdjieff calls this *harnelaoot* ("middle of the eight").
16. This also relates to the metaphysics of procreation. The highest form is through the gaze, the next through the breath—as in the case of the impregnation of Chloris mentioned in chapter 2—and only the lowest form is through physical

contact. Of course, these three forms in their turn relate to the three octaves of the enneagram.

17. In chapter 3, I postulated a law of four for the region between points 4 and 5; the tetrad is highly significant here.

18. Rainer Maria Rilke, *Briefe an eine junge Frau*, 21–22.

19. The word *helkdonis* roughly means "I give mind." Bennett connects it with the Semitic root HLK, signifying order or cosmos. He also says that it is food for the highest or third being-body and arises only when we have undertaken something of objective significance.

20. J. G. Bennett, *Talks on Beelzebub's Tales*, p. 116. The sexist view that man is active and woman passive, which Bennett, after Gurdjieff, constantly espoused, should not detract from his insight here.

21. An excellent evocation of this is in Virginia Wolf's *Orlando*, now to be enjoyed as a movie.

22. G. I. Gurdjieff, *All and Everything*, pp. 771–2.

23. Hence, the potential for tragedy.

24. Sonnet LXV.

· 11 ·

Drama

The theatrical act is sometimes discussed as a way of mirroring life. Just as we might look into our experience and begin to see some shape—even if not much rhyme or reason—we might imagine that the stage is like a consciousness reflecting the turmoil of life in a starker light than we can afford with our limited energies. So we pay someone to perform. In the Medea of Euripedes, we have a speech lasting ninety minutes, though it is spoken through different characters: a complete and seamless articulation of a human event. Intentions are announced, carried through, and then again stated as accomplishments. We know what will happen. What is happening is precisely said. What has happened is revealed. The conscious mirror does not judge, only sees.

Perhaps we go to the theater because we sense that we do not know what has happened to us or what our lives mean. We are unable to practice the austerities and disciplines which will give us enough consciousness. We hope that the experience of the drama will rub off on us enough so that we can have a semblance of understanding. Our judgments and the affectations of this or that playwright or genre are secondary. It is the phenomena of theater as a whole that makes its effect. The human story is being told.

Legominism

GURDJIEFF WAS deeply concerned with the issue of how real knowledge could be transmitted from the past to the future without being lost through distortion ("noise") or by material destruction. His explanation in terms of legominism has intrigued many since. He argues that intentional transmissions worked by altering the structures involved (in works of art, rituals, and so on) so that at certain places something "not according to law" is inserted. In ordinary terms, this must simply mean that the higher knowledge is inserted where something *unexpected* occurs. This makes theoretical sense in the context of traditionalist art, where there were exact canons of execution—but very little sense in the context of recent art.

Gurdjieff himself cites his father as an example of how accurate oral traditions could be: his father knew songs of the Gilgamesh epic even before they become known to the Western world from the decipherment of cuneiform texts—an epic of transmission over thousands of years![1] It seems that similar endurance is evidenced in the written word, which is first of all puzzling since transmissions through written texts are notorious for being miscopied as they are passed down through the ages.

Here is where the evidence of remarkably exacting numerical structures in biblical texts is relevant. For example, recent studies have shown that Genesis is a text intricately constructed upon the golden mean.[2] The point of this is not any supposed property or significance of the golden mean but that this can serve to ensure an accurate transmission of the text. Those in the know could develop checks on the veracity of any version of the text. They would expect to find a precise correlation between the content of the lines, their position in the text, the number of lines, the numerical analogues of key words, and so on. Any deviation would become apparent. "Did not Rabbah b. bar Hanah say, 'They did not stir from there until a scroll of the Torah was brought and they counted them?' They were thoroughly versed in the defective and full readings, but we are not."[3]

Gurdjieff himself was well aware of this. In his account of symbolism as reported by Ouspensky, he says ". . . in symbology . . . *numbers* are connected with definite *geometrical figures,* and are mutually complementary to each other. In the Cabbala a *symbology of letters* is also used and in combination with the symbology of letters a *symbology of words.* A combination of the four methods of symbolism by numbers, geometrical figures, letters and words, gives a complicated but more perfect method" (ism, p. 283).

It is more than astounding that similar procedures have grown up recently in the domain of information technology. For example, our compact discs contain functions which check that the disc is being read correctly. Errors in the disc itself can be compensated for. Now, of course, the information residing in these functions is not itself a part of the music we want to hear, but it enables the machine to reproduce the music accurately. Thus, we have two different but interconnected sets of information. Similarly, in the case of Genesis, information concerning the golden mean may be woven into the structure of the text. We read Genesis not to learn about the golden mean but to learn about the Creation. However, the scholars who transmit such a text over time could know how to correct for accumulated errors by using its structural information.[4]

The test of Gurdjieff's hypothesis would be to find texts in which we can discern not only the error-correcting program but also *deviations* from the program in relation to significant items of content. This is an intriguing prospect. In our present culture, even the search for structure is regarded by most Western scholars as disreputable. This is largely because most scholars have no contact with contemporary science and technology, as used to be the case for archaeologists; also, contemporary scholars are under the delusion that techniques of structure inhibit creativity. So the hope of finding deliberate errors in the error-correcting programs is very small.

There is a well-known Islamic custom of "intentional imperfections," whereby the pious craftsmen admit their imperfection in relation to the Creator. Gurdjieff in his usual inimitable style put this on its head and turned it into the idea of an intentional transmission of higher knowledge. One of the ways in which we can begin to approach what is truly esoteric is to think of the cases in which we have more than one version of the same story, or more than one explanation of the same issue. Putting the one over and against the other highlights their divergence. It is this that can open the doors of understanding.

One may be asking: What has this to do with the enneagram? The enneagram helps us here, because what we have discussed falls into the pattern of three octaves. First there is the octave of the content of the text. Second there is the octave of the regulating program. Third there is the octave of higher knowledge. In going around the circle, we first read the content; then we uncover the underlying program; and only then are we able to discern the hidden, in which the apparent story is made to reveal another kind of story. In electronics we have something similar when we have a carrier wave by which information is transmitted. As an additional illustration, we may think of autostereograms where we may have a picture ostensibly showing a landscape, but which can be looked at in such a way that it reveals a hidden three-dimensional message.

It is interesting to meditate on the nature of the higher knowledge, which is "esoteric" in Aristotle's sense, as that which is learned long before it is understood. That is to say, we can have the text *exactly* and still be none the wiser. First of all, we must be very clear that the hidden knowledge is *not* the error-correcting program itself. However, the vast majority of occultists spend their time looking into such things as if they were of cosmic significance! *No numerical scheme of whatever nature has any significance beyond the use to which it is put.* However, this use has two quite distinct sides, just as we have two sides of the enneagram, of different natures. On the right-hand side we have the program entering to perform its function in regulating error. On the left-hand side we have the same program enabling us to discern a hidden intention.

The recent investigations of Mary Douglas, Simon Weightman, and others are relevant here.[5] The twelve-term structures found in Genesis and *Numbers* highlight the technical usage of critical terms such as *Lord, God, unclean, Israel,* and so on. We can see that such terms are used intentionally and, presumably, to convey something important. The readers' attention is directed in a specific way without their being told anything by this. They have to *find the explanation themselves.* Idries Shah drew attention to this feature by means of his teaching stories, one of which, the story of Dhu'l-Nun the Egyptian, illuminates our theme: It was said that a certain statue indicated where a hidden "treasure" lay buried. Many had searched where the pointing figure of the statue pointed, but to no avail. Dhu'l-Nun observed the statue and then, on one particular day at one particular time, dug where the *shadow* of the finger fell, and discovered the treasure of ancient knowledge.[6]

The nature of the hidden, more intentional knowledge cannot be separated from our own involvement. It does not consist of abstract, general information, nor of mathematical patterns. It is always unique and concrete, and it addresses the reader who finds it directly and purposefully. It involves the will. This is all that can be said here, since the very basis of the idea of legominism is open to question. However, we might bring to mind certain parallels with genetics. The genes, carrying the information which will direct the growth and characteristics of the organism, have their own type of error regulation that guards against misreading by the RNA sequences. This regulative program obviously has limits and can misfunction; only, such a misfunction appears critical for the possibility of *evolution*. We can even picture a crossover between the two sets of information—genetic and regulative—so that the one interferes with the other. In the context of orthodox biological theory, such misfunctions can only mean randomness. For us, it means the *unexpected*, which is the gateway to higher information. Hence the continuing fascination of fairy tales.

Of course, no text exists in isolation; we read a text in the context of other texts. When we come across two differing texts with the same content, we should be alerted. Such is the case with the two versions of Genesis that begin the Bible. Having two versions means that we are led to look "between" them. This is, as we have seen in another context, the basic stereoscopic functioning of intelligence. We may just think, by way of another example, of how God appears both as plural (Elohim) and as singular (Lord).

The method of legominism that Gurdjieff discussed relies both on radical conservatism and radical innovation. There is no perfectly stable structural form. Modifications enable messages to be "sent to the future." This has been pointed out by William Sullivan as a result of his researches into the astronomical language of South America. People of wisdom have used this language to encode data on significant events.[7]

This century has seen a progressive appreciation of ancient intelligence, no matter its detractors. Some of this appreciation has been closely reasoned and investigated, such as that of Alexander Marshack on the written notations of Palaeolithic man, Giorgio de Santillana on the origins of science, Paul Feyerabend on early science and, most recently, Robert Bauval on the astronomical foundation of the pyramids. As we go back through the texts received from the past, we reach a horizon of extraordinary astronomical learning associated with the power of number. Feyerabend says that "there existed a highly developed and internationally known astronomy in the old Stone Age, this astronomy was factually adequate as well as emotionally satisfying, it solved both physical and social problems (one cannot say the same about modern astronomy)."[8]

The recurrent sense of an original and high understanding of the cosmos may prove a lesser realization than that of the enormity of the invention—or discovery—of language and number. Santillana suggests that just as we can go deeper than words and stories to number and the stars, we can go further still to where "there are only thought forms thinking themselves. With this progression, the ascensional power of the archaic mind, supported by numbers, has reestablished the link between two utterly separate worlds."[9]

My suggestion is that, with language and number, a new order was created on earth.[10] Reciprocally, when we pass through their domain into their source, we arrive at higher intelligence. Naturally enough, this intelligence is articulate and speaks to us, *informs* us. However, access to this domain is problematic on account of distortions we have inherited from our beginnings. The correction of these distortions is one of the functions of the Work.[11]

Weaving a Plot

The enneagram tells a dramatic story. In fact, it is archetypal of all stories that capture our interest. Just think of one of the most basic plots used by Hollywood: boy meets girl, boy loses girl, boy finds girl. Variations on this plot encompass some of the greatest love poetry of the world and some of the most important works of literature. The religious archetype is simple: from the One, or God, comes the lover (0-3) and the beloved (6-9); the lower suffers longing for the beloved (3-6) and is united with her only in the One (9). In psychological terms, the lover is the outer person and the beloved the inner soul, and their relation is the key to transformation.[12] The open-ended character of the third phase allows for all kinds of variation. A common one is that the lover finds the actual beloved inadequate for his love! Or, as in Dante's *Divine Comedy,* the beloved becomes the eternal feminine who draws him unto God. This is in Ibsen's *Peer Gynt,* too, when the blind Margaret saves Peer from dissolution at the hands of the Button-Molder through her prayers to the Virgin.

All these themes are found in most profound forms in Sufi love poetry, in which the lover is man and the Beloved is God. One of John Bennett's pupils, Simon Weightman, has discovered a poem of the Shattariyya order composed of 540 lines, in which two subsidiary stories come precisely at one third and at two-thirds of the way through.[13] Relating these to the scheme of the enneagram, we can regard them as the second and third octaves. The first octave concerns the love of Manohar and Madhumalati and runs right through the story. The second octave concerns

Manohar and another beautiful maiden, Pema (love), whom he saves from a demon and through whom he regains Madhumalati. The third octave concerns another prince, Tracaner, who restores Madhumalati from her state as a bird, into which she was turned by the spell of Pema's mother. In the culmination, Manohar is united with Madhumalati, and Pema is united with Tracaner. The two additional octaves are all completed within the story, a variation which shows that the poem is primarily based on a twelve-term system, that shows through with startling clarity.[14] This agrees with the corpus of analysis we will discuss later in this chapter, showing that many classical texts, such as the *Iliad,* and religious texts, such as Genesis, are deliberately constructed according to certain rules. Most have symmetrical forms, in which the first half of the text is reflected in inverse order in the second half. The most frequently used structure is twelvefold.

In its most primitive form, the enneagram is rather like an expression of Aristotle's view of drama as consisting of beginning, middle, and end.[15] If we imagine that these three are significantly demarcated, then we have the three phases. If, in addition, we suppose that the action of the drama builds, then we can see each of the three phases as marked by a new content and direction. In other words, we have octaves. These are acknowledged in the convention of three acts.

It is also easy to picture to ourselves that in drama we must have a character becoming increasingly involved in a problem or danger and then finding his or her way out. In a comedy everybody might live happily ever after. The laughter induced by comedy corresponds to the neutralization of yes and no. There is the tragic alternative in which the main character comes to doom and destruction. If we have a coherent story, then the seeds of destruction must be already sown in the beginning, made apparent in the middle and, possibly, neutralized in the end. Theater has been a long meditation on the structure of significant events.

In the zero point of the dramatic structure we have the setting, the relative normalcy against which the more interesting events will be portrayed. The first point of the dramatic action identifies the element which will be subject to transformation; and the second, an anticipation of its culmination. These appear in the enneagram as the points 0, 1, and 2, and their implications are given by the inner lines: point 1 is connected to point 4, where the transformation becomes actualized, and point 2 is connected to point 8, in which the ultimate meaning of the action will be found (fig. 11.1). An educated audience can read the implications, so that the whole drama is configured in the first phase.

This interpretation of the initial points of the enneagram shows itself clearly in the dramatic art, because we have an audience which must be made aware of the *whole*. But such an interpretation is not something confined to this art; it arises from the very structure of the enneagram, which is a reading of experience.

If we regard the first process as the relatively stable component, the second process concerns an *external* disturbance of the course of events. Suddenly, the hero or heroine is plunged into a different world. This lifts them out of the normal and subjects them to risk. They live more interesting or more dangerous lives. Something happens to them, or they lose something, and this opens up a "hole" in their world. The third process concerns an *internal* disturbance of the course of events, which makes possible a new realization (passing "through the hole into the whole"). Thus, there is a first mechanical disturbance and then an intentional disturbance, on a different level—just as in Gurdjieff's scheme.

We can see the form this can take even in a popular film such as *The Terminator* (although perhaps this is too easy an example, since it is based on a theme of time travel, and we are concerned with connections "out of time"!). (See fig. 11.2.) In the first phase of the film, the Terminator, a cybernetic killing machine, and its adversary Rees, a soldier from a future that is fighting against artificial intelligence for the very existence of the

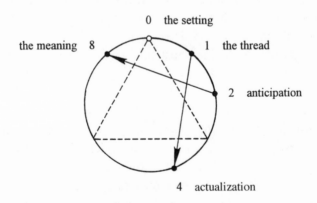

11.1. Implications of the initial points.

(10) The Future World

TIME TRAVEL

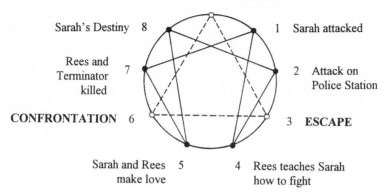

John Connor born   9 / 0   Rees sent

Sarah's Destiny   8 — 1   Sarah attacked

Rees and Terminator killed   7 — 2   Attack on Police Station

CONFRONTATION   6 — 3   **ESCAPE**

Sarah and Rees make love   5 — 4   Rees teaches Sarah how to fight

11.2. Plot of The Terminator.

human race, materialize in 1990 in Los Angeles. Both of them are searching for Sarah Connor, who is to be the mother of the savior of the human race, John Connor, who in the future sends the soldier back to protect her. Saving her from the Terminator, Rees is arrested by the police and imprisoned. Now, here comes point 3: the Terminator, in pursuit of the woman, who is also at the police station, unleashes a holocaust of violence and inadvertently allows them to escape together. This is the turning point of the change in Sarah's life. She will become pregnant by the soldier and come to assume responsibility for the future. The second octave consists of Sarah and Rees together. Then, at point 6 both Rees and the Terminator are destroyed in another orgy of violence. This marks the beginning of the third octave, because it creates the condition for fulfilling the whole cycle of events.

Two important events ensue. Although Rees and Sarah defeat the Terminator, at the cost of Rees's life (point 7), a piece of critical silicon circuitry from the future is preserved. This is essential for the story, for it is this piece of circuitry which is to be picked up by a technician and result in the cybernetic system that will bring about atomic conflagration. The other important event is when Sarah drives into Mexico, contemplating her future in a world of destruction and has her photograph taken (point 8). This is the same photograph that will, in the future, inspire her soldier lover to risk his life to save her.

The whole action represented by the enneagram may be seen as a bubble of space-time events embedded in the future world. This future world, with its capacity for time-travel, represents multiple possibilities, or alternative enneagrams. It is an example of point 10, which is implicit as the medium in which any given complete action takes place. The law of ten was briefly discussed in chapter 5 (see fig. 5.4) and in reference to the milieu of a restaurant (see page 116) in chapter 8.

Sarah Connor is first portrayed as a "loser," working as waitress in a cheap fast-food restaurant and failing to find a decent boyfriend. She is transformed into a smart, hard, and pregnant woman. For this she has to be shattered out of her wits and forced to believe in the terrible realities of the future. She has to wake up and die to her previous life (much as Hedda Gabbler in Ibsen's classic play). It is her choice—though she is guided by Rees, the soldier.

The role of the guide is itself a major archetypal theme. In the context of the enneagram, guidance belongs to the second octave. The guide in the second octave provides what we called the software in relation to the hardware of the first octave. In the second octave, Rees is there to provide information (including genetic information!).

The linkage 1-4-2 indicates how it works. This is part of the cyclic sequence corresponding to the character of Rees, the soldier. The soldier knows the future, while Sarah is the innocent. We see him "remembering" events in his past but in her *future*, being driven by both the terror of the situation and his love for her. Gradually, we realize that the future savior, John Connor, recognizing his father, has knowingly given the soldier the photograph of Sarah. All of the sequence 1-4-2-8-5-7 is endowed with knowledge of the future; but it is not the precise future of the main characters, who have to be left in the freedom of relative ignorance, in order for their actions to be meaningful.

The plot thickens! The unseen character of John Connor acts in the triangle. His place is at point 0 (9). From there, he sends the soldier to be with Sarah (0-3). Connor is born as result of his mother and the soldier spending one night together (6-9). The line 3-6 represents the intervening struggle which will make it all possible.

I have associated Rees with the hexadic inner lines. He is certainly intermediary between the world of command—the triangle of the master of the situation, John Connor—and the world of blind experience, the circle of Sarah Connor. Quite obviously, he anticipates fighting by her side (1-4), and he has to find a way of taking her with him (4-2). But what he sees in her (2-8) is the mother of the savior of the human race, a person whom he is both willing to love (8-5) and to die for (5-7). His death fulfills his basic commitment (7-1).

We see the terrible state of affairs in the future through his eyes, first of all in his reveries and secondly in what he tells Sarah. These two scenes of "memory" take place in the intervening phases between points 1 and 2 and between 4 and 5. In the corresponding phase between points 7 and 8, the original film left it nearly all unsaid. This, in fact, enabled a second film to be made (*Terminator 2—Judgment Day*), since this phase of "memory" concerned the linkage between the special circuitry left after the destruction of the Terminator and the whole future of the human race. It also included the fate of Sarah, isolated in a world of disbelief.

In both films, the same central technique is used: driving the main sequence of action through a literal machine, a terminator, with single-minded aim. This makes the flow of action very clear and well defined. In the first film, the machine drives Sarah into action, but it is only when she acts together with Rees that her transformation begins. This transformation goes right to the end of the film but, quite obviously, extends beyond. The third process, interestingly enough, is literally concerned with information. There is the genetic information produced by the conception, and there is the technical information accessible through the remnants of circuitry. This third process will go even further into the future than Sarah's transformation.

In the second film, point 9 of the previous one becomes point 0. The first process is driven, as before, by the ruthlessness of the new kind of Terminator and concerns Sarah's son, John. The second process begins with the freeing of Sarah from the lunatic asylum in which she has been incarcerated, so that she, her son, and the "reprogrammed" Terminator of the previous film (actually assuming the role that Rees had) are brought together. The third process concerns the new possibility that the future is not predetermined but can be changed. At the culmination, all the material and data which would have served to create the cybernetic monsters of the future are destroyed; the savior family is united in a kind of love just when the reprogrammed Terminator has to sacrifice itself. The two Terminators join in a common meltdown in a pool of liquid metal, leaving the way open for a sequel, making a classic trilogy. We could regard a trilogy as a triplicity of enneagrams, capable of providing a complete resolution to all the problems that have arisen.

At point 8, Sarah wonders whether in fact the future is an open question and not yet determined; whereas, in the first film, she looked into the future as the coming of a storm which would bring about an atomic conflagration in 1997.

The basic line of the first process leads to the expectation that John Connor, or Sarah Connor, will be terminated somewhere around point 3. This is the mechanical line. What happens, in fact, is an unexpected (from the mechanical point of view) synergy between the relevant disparate characters: John, Sarah, and the reprogrammed Terminator, who manifests as the perfect father for John! It is the new synergic entity that pursues the second process. We find, however, that this process cannot be taken beyond a certain point without the act of self-sacrifice mentioned before: the "good" Terminator carries in itself the very self-same circuitry which is the cause of all the trouble.

So we see that the second and third processes do bring in quite new elements, without which the action could not be fulfilled. The tying together of these three processes appears as something which is intentional—based on knowledge of the future—and not predetermined or mechanical. The emergence of what I have called synergic groups corresponds to what we will find in physical processes, that is: dynamic self-organizations only existing within conditions of a certain flow of energy!

The dynamic of the triangle in itself is of some interest. Here, John Connor reprograms the Terminator to save himself in the past (0-3). But there is a new ingredient in the attempt to change the future: the true welfare of John, the child, lies in there not being any future with Terminators in it at all (6-9).

In the intermediary connection (3-6), John the child finds himself loving the Terminator as a father. This is a most interesting version of the saying "The child is father to the man." Thus we see, though only in a qualitative way, how it is that the central core meaning (represented by the triangle) is brought into expression through the inner lines, which represent all that is purposeful—and hence hazardous—in the unfolding of the action.

Since we are dealing with a story and not a scientific experiment, we find that the functions of the various structures—outer circle, inner lines, and triangle—are portrayed by an invisible being. We find exactly the same thing in Greek drama, where the triangular role is taken by the gods!

We might briefly mention the special role played by Tireisias in *Oedipus Rex*. He is our "inner lines" character. Poor Oedipus is forced to go through the travail of the outer circle, bringing himself inexorably towards his doom. In other Greek dramas, such as the last of Aeschylus' Orestian Trilogy, the gods intervene to resolve the conflict that cannot be resolved on the human level. Euripedes went further in providing a *deus ex machina,* a "god out of the machine" for this purpose (quite literally, a "god" would be lowered onto the stage on a movable platform). This is the helping hand from heaven referred to in the last chapter. It is a device which recurs throughout Western literature and finds its more modern equivalents in the works of Dante, Goethe, and Ibsen. This device is a representation of assistance from a higher level, entering the action at point 6, just the point when it can make a difference to the outcome.

The Art of Interpretation

The foregoing interpretations of plays and movies can easily be criticized. It would be a mistake to assume that they are offered as final truths. Any enneagrammatic interpretation of a movie or play must itself be judged aesthetically. Practitioners in the field follow their own understanding of what makes for a good story. This understanding is both implicit and explicit. There are traditions, conventions, cultural values, unconscious patterns, and much else that implicitly inform every work. There are also explicit analyses and structural models.[16]

The aesthetic field is important for understanding the enneagram because it takes us away from mechanistic conceptions of law. In one of his letters, the serialist composer Anton Webern wrote of his discovery that the Greek word *nomos* can be translated as "melody" as well as "law." He, like his colleagues Schönberg and Berg, composed whole works on a single note row—a specific sequence of notes taken from the chromatic or twelve-tone scale—and thought of this sequence as the underlying *nomos* of the work; much as we have taken there to be an underlying *logos* in every coherent situation.

In our own lives, we experience series of events and strive to "hear the music" that underlies them. We look for repetitions, similarities, contrasts, and relationships. The more we find this music, the more meaning we feel in ourselves (fig. 11.3). The enneagram is a systematization of this inherent search for meaning. It draws on what we already feel and sense. Its main virtue is that it brings together in one whole *all* that we might feel and sense.

The sense and feeling of a moving pattern in life akin to music may well lead us to imagine a meaning only partially realized in the course of events. Similarly, in watching a movie, sometimes we become aware of the more meaningful movie "behind the screen." When we come to look into the structure of a movie, we can also become aware of multiple interpretations. We may have more than one event as candidate for a point on the enneagram. The octaves can be read in a variety of ways.

This does not mean that such interpretations are merely subjective or a matter of opinion. There are stringent aesthetic criteria, among which are a regard for symmetry, consistency, and elegance. These are also to be found in the construction of scientific theories. In order to show what this might mean, we have to make an excursion into ancient and classical times.

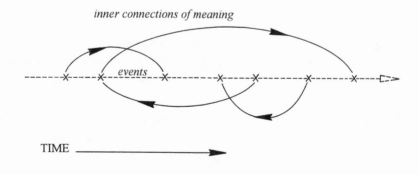

11.3. Sketch of the "music of life."

The Turn and the Latch

The importance of the affinity of points 0 and 9 cannot be overemphasized. As we shall see in the final chapter, this is the key mystery of the enneagram, and all others are subservient to it. This unity of beginning and end reflects into correspondences between the left- and right-hand sides of the enneagram. For example, the third phase of the enneagram parallels the first. It is a repetition of the first: on a higher level and in reverse. The second phase effects a transition between the first and third rather like a turning inside out. The traditionalist René Guénon always insisted that true analogy meant an *inversion* of the principles of the lower world to correspond to the higher, and vice versa. Each is the mirror of the other. Hence, in this case, while the first phase moves toward greater complexity, the third moves toward greater simplicity. The whole process demands a "decreation" of mechanical order and a "creation" of meaningful order. Similarly, in the reverse direction, there is an increasing privation of meaningful order and an increasing acquisition of mechanical order.

In most ancient literature, the structure of texts follows this pattern of inversion. The *Iliad*, for example, which takes place over six days and five nights, is divided around the third night into two parts. The first part is paralleled by the second but in reverse order. The anthropologist Mary Douglas calls the passage which makes the division the "turn." She also refers to the ending of the text in a special way, calling it the "latch," because this is where the two halves are joined together. Another commentator says that this kind of structuring produces "a circular effect, the acoustical analogue of the visual circle" and that it was a natural technique to repeat at the end of a story the formula which began it, to bind the whole together. If we place the various verses or sections around a circle, a pattern of correspondences emerges,[17] as shown in figure 11.4.

Also, we find a widespread use of a technique in which a series of phrases or verses are repeated in a very similar way but in the reverse order. This is called a chiasmus (from the Greek letter *chi*, which has the shape of a cross), the simplest form of which is ABB'A', as in: "If only we had died / in the land of Egypt / or in this wilderness / if only we had died" (Numbers 14:2). Where we find chiasmus with a central line, verse,

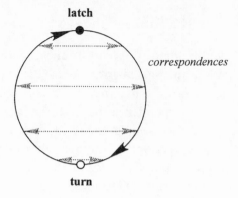

11.4. Turn and latch.

or passage (for example, ABCB′A′), then this central member will probably contain "the main point of the author, climaxing what precedes and
anticipating what follows."[18] It is then interesting to ask what the mid-
point, if any, of the enneagram "text" is. In one sense, it is the whole of
the middle phase. In another sense, we have to see that Gurdjieff introduces *two* central members, and that these are the critical points 3 and 6.
The "text" divides into two at point 3 and then divides into two again,
but otherwise, at point 6. What is divided at point 3 becomes reunited at
point 6. What is united at point 3 becomes divided at point 6.

This shows something important about the meaning of the enneagram.
While there is a temporal and sequential action, represented around the
circle, there is also a nontemporal and recurrent action, represented by
the inner lines. It is in the latter kind of "nontime" that what is represented by points 3 and 6 *harmonize,* such that the one corrects for the
incompleteness or even distortion of the other. The power of harmonization develops out of the primary contact with uncertainty that is given by
these critical points. It is intentional but it cannot be reduced to any
technique. If we associate this with "method," this does not mean that
there is any winning formula to be found. It is something that comes out
of and is transmitted through living experience.

The structure of ancient texts indicates only the way in which people
then agreed to represent meaning. The formation of a text into two
halves, "hinged on a turn," is evidently a simple device for restoring
wholeness. The technique leads naturally into further refinements. It is

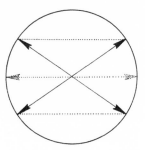

11.5. Diagram of text with crossover links.

not necessary that the two halves mirror each other linearly. Indeed, in the early books of the Old Testament, it is not hard to find examples of links which cross over from side to side and do not operate in parallel (fig. 11.5).[19] This appears in an elegant way in the enneagram. The inner lines 1-4-2 are reflected across into the lines 8-5-7. Through this reflection (as if in a mirror) the line of flow appears reversed—for instance: the line 1-4, which goes from lower to higher (or forward), is reflected in the line 8-5, which goes from higher to lower (or backward).

The most usual system of structuring texts has twelve sections and not nine. The zodiacal signs of astrology reflect a long tradition. Any tradition which has its roots in the classical or biblical world will carry these ways of organizing information. The structural devices of ancient times are, in fact, analogues of present-day computer programs. Such a program is a piece of information that organizes information. However, our culture has tended to lose sight of the significance of the *arrangement* of information. A computer program is a set of *linear* instructions. There are as yet no computer-based devices which can handle patterns. A computer program is a left-brained device, whereas the story devices of the ancients were right-brained.

The Measures of Interpretation

The ancient scheme gives us a way of making a start. A storytelling movie will contain scenes that repeat or echo each other so that the viewer can grasp the work as a whole. We will look at *Total Recall*. The story for this film was taken from a short story by the brilliant gnostic science fiction writer Philip K. Dick called "We Can Remember for You, Whole-sale" (and it is not accidental that I choose this example). In the movie, the main protagonist, Quaid, goes through a radical transformation. The events are broadly as follows:

Quaid is first seen dreaming of being on Mars. He walks with a lover over the Martian landscape, and falls and breaks open his helmet, suffering agonizing asphyxiation.

Following his attraction to Mars, he goes to Recall, a "travel" business that gives complete experiences by means of "mind implants."

Before the treatment is complete, he goes beserk, claiming that his "cover is blown." He is drugged and dumped near his home, only to be attacked by his workmates and then by his wife, who tells him that their whole marriage has been an artificial mental implant.

Fleeing for his life, he is given a suitcase that contains a message from "himself" telling him to go to Mars. He is told that he is really Hauser.

On Mars the dictator Cohagen is determined to annihilate the rebel forces seeking to break his control. Many of them are mutants, made such by bad air caused by him. Their leader is Quawato.

Quaid meets with the woman of his dreams, Melina, but without remembering her. She rejects him, disbelieving him, threatening him with a gun.

He learns of the existence of "alien artifacts," which had been mentioned in a TV broadcast from Mars at the beginning of the film.

In his room in the hotel on Mars, he is visited by someone who claims to be from Recall and who tells him that he is lost in an hallucination. His wife joins them to reinforce the message. Seeing through the deception, he is overcome and about to be delivered to his enemies, when Melina appears to rescue him.

He and Melina are chased into the mutant zone. There they enter the rebel headquarters, while the zone is cut off from the air supply.

He meets with Quawato, a being growing from a man's belly. Quawato opens Quaid's mind to reach the information that the rebels need. Just then, the rebels are invaded and Quawato is killed, but not before he tells Quaid to switch on the alien reactor.

Brought into the presence of Cohagen, Quaid learns that the whole series of events have been planned to gain access to Quawato and destroy him. He sees himself on video again. "Hauser" tells him that he is going to claim his body back.

Quaid is put into another mind implant machine. But he breaks free and, with Melina, flees to fulfill Quawato's instructions. In the vast alien reactor he kills his pursuers and, Cohagen also dies, gasping for air on the surface of Mars.

Quaid switches on the reactor before being blown with Melina onto the Martian surface. As he struggles for breath, the reactor releases air from an underground glacier, and he is saved, as are the mutants. He and Melina walk on the surface. They kiss.

The first thing that we can do is set up the parallels according to the "turn." (See fig. 11.6.) Then we look for (1) the primary octave, (2) the critical dramatic moment, (3) the *logos,* and (4) the other two octaves, commensurate with the first.

The primary octave concerns Quaid and what happens to him. It is a series of events, much as I have already outlined.

The critical dramatic moment is ambiguous. It is either the moment when Melina suddenly appears to rescue him or the moment when he is opened by the mysterious Quawato.

The *logos* concerns the archetypal question "Who am I?" First, the protagonist is Quaid. Then (after point 3) he believes he is Hauser. Finally, he realizes himself as Quaid (after point 6) when he becomes him-

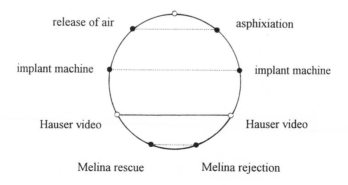

11.6. Design of Total Recall.

self. This is, of course, the equivalent of the primal structure of boy meets girl, boy loses girl, boy finds girl.

The other two octaves are represented by Melina and Quawato. Melina signifies the people of Mars, the suffering population which longs for liberation. Quawato is of the same unknown nature as the aliens who provide the way out of the predicament. Melina represents the second force, both as denial and receptivity. The alien or mutant contribution comes as a reconciliation. The whole theme of the alien reactor is precisely equivalent to the *deus ex machina* of the Greeks.

Any well-crafted story contains indications to the reader or audience about how to "read" or understand what is going on. After seeing the movie, the audience is able to go back over the sequence of events and find a coherent pattern, using these indications. They give us the aesthetic pleasure of knowing what we feel. However, the art of drama is rooted very much in a dislocation between thought and feeling. Out of this is born a yearning for reconciliation—or, at least, for *catharsis*.

Dramatic Progression

A drama can be viewed crudely as just a series of ups and downs. (See fig. 11.7.) But there can be more at stake than merely a succession of different intensities. A drama can take us deeper and demonstrate a certain progression in depth. At the outset of a play, we have the key charac-

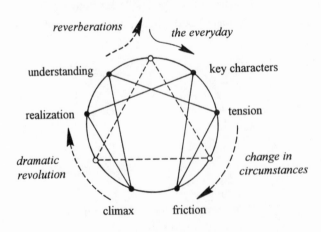

11.7. Basic structure of drama.

ter or characters living out their lives within an overall context, like motes in a sunbeam. We see them as they are in their typical setting. However, in the next stage we begin to see them differently. They do not quite fit in their circumstances. Something is not right, there is a tension.

The first critical transition is a precipitation from this state of inertia and unease into a new set of relationships. The way in which this usually comes about is through a change in circumstances, or in learning about something not known before. This change progresses, through increasing friction, until everything comes to a head, which introduces the dramatic crux of the play and another critical transition. If this transition is passed through, we enter a quite different realm. In place of the conflict comes insight and understanding. The key characters see a truth they have never seen before. The misunderstandings between characters give way. Even through the events portrayed are on a small scale, a reverberation of meaning is sent through the totality. The particular drama, restricted in space and time, can *signify* important changes in the social fabric. This can be dampened down, as in the classic comedy or, as in the case of such plays as *Hedda Gabbler,* can be left unresolved, an open question. In any event, something concerning the fabric of the whole has been brought into question.

There are obvious parallels with the structure of organic evolution. The point is to grasp the underlying progression of the evolutionary process and *feel* its nature. This has been, and always will be, dramatic and open-ended. It is a big mistake to consider evolution as a purely factual process. It cannot be understood outside of the context of values, because it is not indifferent to purpose. This we have to feel and not simply think. Going even further: history comes out of the dramatic; it is the *transformation of the whole from the interplay of its parts.* This is a reversal of what we might expect but is at work in evolution. We have to remember that it is quite possible for there to arise spontaneous mutations out of the genome which originate with localized transformations.[20]

Naturally enough, all this must make us consider the dramatic form of the story of Jesus. We can see the crucifixion as associated with point 5 of the enneagram; then, as always in the complete structure, it is the prelude to another kind of action, in this case the resurrection and ascent. With this comes the universalization of Christianity.

It is quite astonishing how close the form and sequence of the Terminator films are to the story of Jesus Christ. If we read the Bible as if it were made of the scripts of an interlocking series of films, certain things stand out. Just consider the apocalyptic books at the end of the New Testament: these are precisely the equivalent of the storm that is coming in *Terminator*. The human race has yet to find the script for its *Terminator 2*. Behind all these stories lies the same question: what does it mean that "time shall be no more?"

There is always, at all times, in human life the quest for redemption. This is the question of the third octave and what it entails. The third octave is how the third force comes from above into the action of human life. It is characterized by the peacemakers of the Beatitudes. We are in a situation where we feel and begin to acknowledge that we do not know how this can happen: we do not see how we can make peace on earth. It was a staggering claim by Gurdjieff that wars are no longer necessary, and his references to war are among some of the most important things he has said.

The telling of stories has a great power in human life. From time to time, the structures built into storytelling have been adjusted just so that it can become possible for us to think straight about what is happening to us, and what we can do about it. We ourselves are driven by a Terminator. In some guises, it is the "Merciless Heropass" (the name that Gurdjieff gives to the flow of time in *Beelzebub's Tales*). At present it is the megamachine of technology.[21] In front of this, the whole human race is just like Sarah. There are things that we can do; we can struggle to overcome our fate. But in the end, even this will not be enough. We need information from the future, the third force coming from above, salvation, or the like. Like the Greeks, we may resort to the concept of a god out of the machine, such as some help from artificial intelligence, but this is not very realistic. It is more realistic to begin from the standpoint that we are loved, that God seeks after us. This was Simone Weil's submission, that nowhere in the Gospels do we find any reference to man seeking God, only to God seeking man![22] There is a greater present moment in which our own smaller present moment subsists. All the teaching of the octaves and the enneagram concur in saying that only through a voluntary connection with this larger present moment can we hope to resolve the impasse in which we find ourselves.

Form of Recurrence

There is something irreducible and basic in the sense of a core meaning. It is precisely this that Heraclitus called the *logos*. In science, it is some basic law of the universe. In drama, it is the will or obsession of some central character, portrayed according to the culture of the times. We might conclude, at this point, that what I have been representing as the inner lines of the enneagram has a universal significance. These characterize all our intentional actions and disciplines, by which we hope to relate ourselves to the core meaning through what we do and suffer as participants in the world process.

Taken as something in itself, the inner line sequence becomes what we know as ritual. Gurdjieff said that certain rituals that still exist—such as those of the Christian church (particularly in the Easter forms)—contain in them a deep knowledge of what we may call the intentional way. It is, he said, by such means that important knowledge has been conveyed from generation to generation concerning the way in which real events come to be created.

This is important in respect of the prophetic reading of history. History is the outer sequence of events, while prophecy is their inner connection. When we describe events in terms of a series of contingencies or proximate causes, we cannot have any sense of connection with a purpose that extends beyond the time frame of their human protagonists. Prophecy, of course, concerns knowing the will of God in respect to particular events. It is not only an anticipation of the future but also a way of seeing the past.

In the Judeo-Christian tradition, the prophets spoke of the judgment of the Lord. This judgment concerns the relation between the different levels of events, or the events as they operate in different worlds. It speaks of what is allowed into a higher world, the world of harmonious reconciliation where God and man "agree." The triangle 3-6-9 in the enneagram figure represents the thresholds for passing from one world into another. The periodic figure represents the cyclicity in which the promise of human life on earth is renewed. Where we find people like Newton or Bennett investigating the prophetic cycles, we should not imagine that the aim is to find some underlying spiritual mechanism: the important principle is the renewal of evolutionary possibility.

A brief survey of some of the connections in the periodic figure may illuminate this idea (fig. 11.8). The connection 2-8, for example, is that of eschatology, or the study of "last things," while the connection 7-1 is that of prophecy in the sense of the study of "first things": the first looks to the future, while the second interprets the past. In the Bible, the Epistles (concerning the early church) are at point 7 and Revelations at point 8. The Gospels occupy points 4 and 5. Point 0 is Genesis and the genealogies. The key stories of Abraham and Moses and the formulation of the laws of the faith occupy point 1 (the arising of the chosen people), while prophetic books of the Old Testament such as Isaiah appear at point 2. Point 2 is informed by point 4, and hence, we find in the Prophets an intimation of the coming of the Messiah. The connection 8-5 indicates the coming of the new order, the kingdom of heaven.

The contrast between the left- and the right-hand side of the enneagram is between the relatively unrestricted or global savior and the relatively restricted messiah of the Jewish people. Hence, we associate point 3 with the line of David, while point 6 is associated with the injunction to "go unto the Gentiles." This leaves us with point 9 as "time shall be no more," which can only mean a transition into connection with a history that is not governed by any human culture.

Prophecy reinterprets history in the light of a vision of the relation between the human being and higher levels. Similarly, we also reinterpret

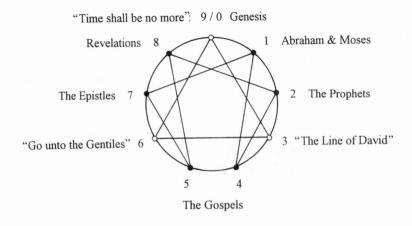

11.8. Enneagram of the Scriptures.

our own life histories in relation to a core meaning. In doing this, we have to bring about a marriage between fact and value, between what actually is and what should be. For this, we have recourse to some archetypal image of the meaning of human life, secular or spiritual. Part of the appeal of astrology arises from such a need. Equally, life can be seen through novels, or through sociobiology for that matter.[23] Some, such as the psychotherapist Victor Frankl and the advocate of intentional genius, Ted Matchett, have made *meaning* the fundamental criterion.[24] To say that all we are doing is a question of mere "invention"—subjectively interpreting the past and future—is to miss the point, because it is not arbitrary. We have built into us, by the very form of our perception and understanding, an access to the nature of higher worlds. This is usually regarded in terms of values, to the neglect of recognizing that it is a type of real information.

The approach of rational science and the approach of religious prophecy are diametrically opposed, but only in the abstract.[25] Though the majority of scientists simply soldier on in their narrow specialities, following the disciplines of their field, advancing increment by increment, there remains an element of the prophetic, because scientists are bound to reflect on where science is going and the question of whether or not it has an ending. Just as Francis Fukuyama has developed the myth of the "end of history," so many scientists are convinced that they are in the last days of science and that soon the ultimate equation will be written. In contrast, there remains the enigma of why science (in the effective form that we know it now) arose in Europe in the first place. This is something that continues to puzzle scholars such as Joseph Needham, the world's expert on Chinese science, who was forced to conclude that Western religion may be a critical factor.[26]

It is of practical and urgent importance that something more than the play of external causes and human motivations be allowed as real in history. The will of God in relation to our history is the promise that there is a purpose for human life on earth that is compatible with both external reality and the human spirit within, but goes beyond both. We need to tell stories which remind us of this.

When a story is repeated over and over again, something is built up along the inner lines. The outer sequence carries the inner one within it. However much the details of the story might change in its telling, if the structure of the inner lines is maintained, then the power of the story grows. But there is more here than a question of preservation. At the heart of every real story is its *logos*, a creative source of meaning. Just as, according to Gurdjieff, certain plants have their own *logos*, so do certain stories. These cease to be the product of any man and they become self-generating, replicating the structure of the worlds.

In a study of the great Finnish epic *Kalevela*, an old storyteller, after reciting the origin of the world, says to the scholar: "You and I know that this is the real Truth about how the world began."[27] He has no doubt that this is so, by the very power of the recitation itself. *This* is esoteric. The storyteller, the *laulaja*, is in contact with the inner *logos* of the story, which has ineluctable power. It takes generation after generation of story-telling to arrive at such an invariant conviction. And we must remember that all these great epics and mythologies derive from echoes of the past, always from recitations based upon recitations. In contrast with modern concerns over originality, the tradition always began from *the origin*.

In this context, Gurdjieff spoke in general of "objective art" a concept that has irritated most Western artists. However, this degree of art, "requires at least flashes of objective consciousness; in order to understand these flashes properly and to make proper use of them a great inner unity is necessary and great control of oneself" (ism, p. 298). This leads us to explore the nature of objective consciousness, which means to investigate the structure of perception. The key is in realizing that there are higher substances of perception and that what is at issue is the capacity to assimilate them. If we focus on the idea of consciousness we are simply liable to be confused by the emotional impact of more intense states. Gurdjieff's insistence on objectivity is no mere rhetoric.

Notes

1. G. I. Gurdjieff, "My Father," in *Meetings with Remarkable Men*.
2. David Howlett, quoted in Mary Douglas, *In the Wilderness*.
3. It is significant that this passage from the Talmud shows a concern with accuracy and not esoteric meaning.
4. Many years ago Bennett explored similar ideas in his research into structural communication. He realized that any effective message must not only transmit pieces of information but also the way in which they had to be put together. Hence, the *structural* idea. Bennett was obviously inspired by Gurdjieff, particu-

larly by *Beelzebub's Tales,* which is written according to the form and sequence required for *reason of understanding.* This is something I discuss in the last chapter. It is the key to all effective communication.

5. Mary Douglas, *In the Wilderness: the Doctrine of Defilement in the Book of Numbers.*

6. Ahmed Abdulla, "The Pointing Finger Teaching System," in *The World of the Sufi,* introduced by Idries Shah (London: Octagon Press, 1979), pp. 255–56.

7. William Sullivan, *Secrets of the Incas: Myth, Astronomy, and the War against Time.*

8. Paul Feyerabend, *Against Method,* p. 306.

9. Giorgio de Santillana and Hertha von Dechend, *Hamlet's Mill,* p. 346.

10. A colleague, Richard Heath, has proposed that the Greeks marked a transition from a previous epoch into the modern age of information. The original understanding of structure was "downloaded" from the skies. "We propose that the Pythagorean corpus was a coherent remnant of techniques that allowed the megalithic age to conduct an efficient mathematical and astronomical quest." "Some Possible Achievements for Megalithic Astronomy, from Harmonies of the Sky," unpublished paper.

11. In *Meetings with Remarkable Men,* Gurdjieff has Father Giovanni define understanding as the product of "real knowledge of past events and experiences personally experienced." Real knowledge of past events is not so easy and rests very much on the *reading* of ancient texts. In *In Search of the Miraculous,* Gurdjieff says: "You must understand . . . that every real religion, that is, one that has been created by learned people for a definite aim, consists of two parts. One part teaches *what* is to be done. This part becomes common knowledge and in the course of time is distorted and departs from the original. The other part teaches *how* to do what the first part teaches. This part is preserved in secret in special schools and with its help it is always possible to rectify what has been distorted in the first part or to restore what has been forgotten" (p. 304).

12. In *In the East My Pleasure Lies, and Other Esoteric Interpretations of Plays by William Shakespeare,* Beryl Pogson also makes this point that spiritual influences are represented externally as woman.

13. "Symmetry and Symbolism in Shaikh Manjhan's *Madhummalti,*" in C. Shackle and R. Snell, ed., *The Indian Narrative: Perspectives and Patterns.*

14. It is as if the enneagram acquires a *fourth* phase, turning it from a nine- to a twelve-term system. This amounts to a resolution of the incomplete octaves.

15. See Aristotle, *Poetics.*

16. For example, the screenwriter Robert McKee offers an extraordinary seminar in the structure of story. I have found that his understanding accords very closely to that of the enneagram.

17. I use this pattern in chapter 16 when discussing the centers. In the diagram, the number of points or lines is not significant. The usual structure in ancient tests is twelvefold, six to each half of the cycle.

18. Douglas, *In the Wilderness.*

19. Private communication from Simon Weightman, concerning the story of Noah in Genesis.
20. See Stuart Kaufman, "Antichaos and Adaptation," in *Scientific American,* August 1991.
21. See chapter 9.
22. See the chapter "God's Quest for Man" in Simone Weil, *Intimations of Christianity.*
23. John Berger's marvelous study of a doctor, *A Fortunate Man,* shows how the doctor fashions the meaning of his life on the basis of Conrad's novels and is an illuminating document in this respect. For the use of sociobiology, see E. O. Wilson, *On Human Nature.*
24. See Victor Frankel, *Man's Search for Meaning,* and Ted Matchett, *Journeys of Nothing in the Land of Everything.*
25. See the quotation from Leonardo da Vinci in chapter 10, page 149.
26. As attested by Needham's monumental work *Science and Civilisation in China,* still in progress after his death.
27. Quoted by Giorgio de Santillana and Hertha von Dechend in *Hamlet's Mill,* p. 111.

· 12 ·

An Enneagram of Crisis

"Where have we come from and where are we going?" is the question of every intelligence becoming aware of itself. Like every living being, we feel the force of history, the inexorable march of events, which drives us along, willy-nilly. Events on a vastly greater scale than that of our own lives shape our ends. Our own actions are encompassed by a design that emerges in the world process. Yet, on the scale of the biosphere within which we exist, collective human power has become a major factor. An individual, awakening to the situation, can find his greatest danger in the collective mass of humanity. This chaotic totality of more than five billion entities intervenes between ourselves and the greater cosmos.

When the pioneers of the Biosphere 2 project in Arizona—an attempt to mirror the complexity of the biosphere on a relatively minute scale within a few enclosed acres—asked one of their Russian precursors, Professor Joseph Gitelson, for some guiding thoughts, he replied: "Have courage—and remember that man is the most unstable part of the biosphere." We can also quote the anonymous humorist who said: "Humans are just God's attempt to pass the Turing test." (The Turing test is the test that can determine whether a machine is intelligent.)

Rise of the Technosphere

LET US TURN to the larger scale of things and focus on the biosphere and the *arising of humanity* within it. With the enneagram as our lens we bring focus what is significant. What we see depends on the settings we choose, and in particular the choice of the three octaves. Different choices will bring into focus different aspects of the whole. This capacity to be adjusted is inherent in the enneagram and is similar to what we find in a telescope, microscope, or camera. We can make adjustments according to what we want to focus on. We can do little more here than sketch out the situation, but we will still arrive at a *vision* of the *whole*. Work with the enneagram proceeds by *progressive approximation*. The symbol enables us to bring together all of the important elements. No matter how crude our first atempt is, it will contain most of what is significant and will point us forward to better approximations. With the biosphere, my first approach will be to consider which three octaves sum up the present situation and our place in it.

There is no guarantee whatsoever that human life on earth will progress. Human destiny and, hence, the destiny of the biosphere, in other worlds beyond the earth is not assured. The impact we are having on the biosphere has engendered a sense of crisis. I will center our perspective on this. There is an early history of the biosphere, before man, and a possible future of the biosphere, which may lead beyond man. We thus place the role of mankind in the *second octave*.

The working of the biosphere, which has gone on for at least 3.8 billion years before humans appeared, constitutes the *first octave*. Nearly all the material and energy available to us now derives from this working. Going back to our most simple example of pouring a glass of water, we can picture the biosphere as a flow which is being gathered and concentrated in a glass. The glass is humankind. The material and energy generated by the biosphere is increasingly being diverted into the human realm, by-passing the recycling loops that keep complex ecosystems alive. As a consequence, many species are being eliminated. Humans did have considerable impact on their environment thousands of years ago, but only in the present era has our impact attained global significance.[1] This is because technology has magnified and multiplied our effect on the environment. We need to take account of the rise of technology within the biosphere as part of the second octave.

Point 3 of the enneagram will mark the beginning of this human disturbance of the global ecosystem. Point 6 will then signify the beginning of a *resolution* of this problem. The region beyond point 6 is that of harmonious reconciliation. This may be occupied by a new type of "knowledgeable mind," which some have called the *noosphere*.

As we might expect, the bare idea of a sphere of mind has given rise to as many interpretations as there are of man's origins and purpose. All of these interpretations are part of the noosphere: the noosphere has to interpret itself in diverse ways. It is not at all like a thing, but is, so to say, on the other side to all our concepts, beyond the empirical world. If the noosphere has a substance to it, then it is the substance of *intelligence,* which is not to be identified with mind. Most interpretations agree that a certain threshold of global significance must be passed if there is to be a noosphere. In this sense, almost all that is encapsulated in our various cultures and traditions hardly foots the bill.[2]

It is an old idea that intelligence touched the earth and gave rise to life and the mind that seeks to communicate with intelligence. In this perspective, the arising of a noosphere is completing the circle. We might expect the transition to mind, or humankind, to mark a dramatic moment in the history of the earth.

Alfred North Wallace, who arrived at the principles of organic evolution at about the same time as Darwin, persistently argued that human evolution should be treated differently from that of other species. This stems from the basic insight that, with humans, evolution took another turn, acquired another method. This new dimension is *culture.* In the language of the materialistic biologist Richard Dawkins, culture consists of "memes," which correspond to the genes that are the crucial ingredients of organic evolution. Memes are the particles of culture which combine, mutate, and propagate themselves through institutions and communities.[3]

The crucial step in human evolution is often taken to be the emergence of language (that is, language as we know it today). It enabled people to share information in an abstract, symbolic way. One person could find something out and pass that on to others. This made it possible to accumulate and transmit information over generations. According to prehistorians such as Marshack, this then made it possible for social structures and innovations like agriculture to arise.[4] It was the accelerating trigger of all technology and discovery.

Naturally enough, the vast majority of scientists want to regard language as arising gradually, imperceptibly, and haphazardously over countless generations. Those with a religious or spiritual orientation want to regard it as a gift of the gods, or, even, a satanic intervention that ruined the human soul![5] Finding the connection between culture and genetics is the central problem. It develops through different, though related, modes of evolution. Once mind, culture, and language exist, they become self-referential. We can only explore them using our own mind, culture, and language. We cannot step outside ourselves to look in and see the border between the organic and the mental.

We have no clear and agreed-upon evidence of the sequence of species participating in human evolution. What makes us human is something we know from the inside, not the outside. Evidence of works of art and early notations have led many people to regard a period about forty thousand years ago as the most important evolutionary transition toward modern man. But focusing on such a period shouldn't distract us from seeing how it was made possible by previous steps. The principles of self-organization show that there can be quite abrupt transitions between one level of organization and another. It doesn't happen bit by bit. In fact, it cannot happen like that. This is important for looking at the emergence of language. We need not go to the interesting extremes that Bennett did when he argued that language was inculcated into the human race by superhuman magicians.[6]

Bennett argued that language in its main groups recognized today goes back to circa 10,000 before the present. Recent studies have suggested that there were earlier language groups, such as Nostratic, dating back more than fifteen thousand years, and protolanguages reaching back at least one hundred thousand years to the original sapiens coming out of Africa. The crucial step we look for is more radical than that proposed by Julian Jaynes in his theory of the arising of the modern type of self-consciousness three thousand years ago.[7]

Wallace was right in arguing that something radically new and different entered with human evolution. This was no more and no less than the creation of a new world on the earth. It is what the philosopher Karl Popper calls World 3.[8] World 3 is the world of *intentional objects* such as pieces of music, buildings, theories, and so on. World 2 is the world of subjective experience, and World 1 is the world of things. Sometimes World 3 can also be called the world of *meanings*. Do not make the mistake of thinking that this world is composed of people's states or emotions, even though emotion may be necessary to make contact with it. It is not just subjective and is governed by its own kind of laws. The emergence of World 3 brought different rules of process into action. Gurdjieff was aware of the implications of this world and considered it to be a subset of the universal world of impressions. He says: "Neither food nor air can be changed. But impressions, that is, the quality of impressions available to man, are not subject to any cosmic law" (ISM, p. 321).

The emergence of World 3 enabled life on earth to tap into open-ended information processing. This means that human beings became creative in a way that is independent from life as it had been operating up until then. It led to the formation of technics. Technics are the systems of information processing, which exert control over transformations of matter and energy. Gradually a whole new environment became established on the earth, interpenetrating and coexisting with the organic-material one.

Technics have emerged naturally in the course of evolution. Wasps build nests, ants organize raiding parties and cultivate fungi, and so on. Technology—the aggregation and organization of technics—is not artificial but is an inevitable outcome of the evolution of life. During the course of natural evolution technics arise as by-products of the interplay between matter and energy. It is when they acquire consciousness, or a degree of freedom peculiar to themselves, that acceleration begins. When technics can be manipulated in their own right, when people *become aware* of World 3, the rules of the game of evolution change. This is the probable evolutionary significance of consciousness.[9]

Semidetached from the already existing processes of organic life, technics are autocatalytic: that is, they induce their own production. Technics use information to gain control over the natural flux of matter and energy. Any gain of control releases further information, which increases the capacity to control. There is a positive feedback loop. With such geometric growth comes increasing instability and the emergence of new forms of self-organization. The American historian Lewis Mumford argues that technology has become a megamachine proceeding under its own steam, almost independent of human initiative. This is the picture of technology as out of control. In *Man and Technics,* Spengler describes the inevitable drive toward increasing complexity in human life. Every creative step aimed at solving problems simply exacerbates the crisis. When language developed to the point where plans could be formulated, a radical division emerged between those who make plans and those who carry them out. Social classes, based on information hierarchies, were born. This made society more complex but enabled specialization to advance. Specialization led to the emergence of cities and accelerating human control over the environment, which, in its turn, led to the inevitable expansion and intensification of warfare, when it became possible for wealth to be accumulated.

We have now reached the point where an autonomous technosphere exists which interpenetrates the biosphere. Spengler points out that there is no culture on earth capable of encompassing the forces embodied in the technosphere. Today this technosphere is fueled by the West (including those "Western" nations which are in the Far East). It creates stress between the so-called developed and undeveloped nations. Even within developed nations there is a rift between those who remain at the level of superstition and magic and those who have an understanding of science and technology.

Our present-day cultures are like dream worlds, and it is a very big thing to awaken from these dreams to find the objective world. Cultures—and, indeed, the whole second octave of our biospheric enneagram—are fueled by *imagination*. Imagination is both a way of accessing higher worlds and a source of self-imposed bondage in delusion. It is a power that enables us to do remarkable things in the material world, but there is a cost and a risk.

Technology is now studied as if it were made of species emerging and struggling for survival within the ecology of human economics. This was first explored by Samuel Butler in the late nineteenth century. Anything complex enough begins to act organically, having no rhyme or reason other than its own perpetuation; that is, it becomes autonomic. You can look at so-called human artifacts as parasites on the human population equivalent to domesticated animals. It now appears that domestication was at least as much a strategic survival move on the part of those species as it was an innovative step on the part of humankind.

The technosphere is reaching an intensity which is severely disturbing the balance of energies on the earth. We speak in terms of pollution, extinction of species, population explosion, and so on. We contrast the workings of technology with those of the natural ecologies, but we must remember that both are expressions of the same forces acting on the earth's surface.[10] It is only that, with the advent of our contact with open-ended information processing, the rules have been changed. This is the arising of *mind*. The consequence seems to be a situation out of control, whether or not this is manifested in technology.

There is an accelerating rate of innovation which has thrown every-thing into chaotic change. If we chart this, we see that we are more and more rapidly approaching the point where innovation will become virtu-ally instantaneous. This hair-raising possibility has been given the name of "technological singularity." The two sides of this singularity, past and future, are divorced from each other. The future beyond this singularity is outside any sphere of expectation that we can generate from this side, in the past. Already, general world culture is saturated with a sense of time in which progress in every sphere—from art to economics—is felt to be an illusion. The assurance of comprehensible step-by-step progress has almost vanished. Instead, people live in expectation of radical discon-tinuities.[11]

In order to complete our first approximation of the enneagram of the crisis of humanity and the biosphere, we introduce the *noosphere* as the third octave. I referred to this before as "knowledgeable mind" to suggest that it is seen as something capable of dealing with the situation. At this point, we are indifferent to whether it is something spiritual or something material. The great Russian scientist Vladimir Vernadsky saw it in entirely materialistic terms, while Teilhard de Chardin made it into a mystical concept. The biosphere suffers under the impact of the technosphere, but this phase may only be the prelude to the noosphere's emergence.

Let us now look at the enneagram with its three octaves: biosphere, technosphere, and noosphere (fig. 12.1). Each of the three is related to evolution, but *the meaning of evolution is different in each of them.* Each octave builds on the octave already established. The technosphere exploits the biosphere, and the noosphere can be expected to rely on the tech-nosphere (for example, for accessing needed information). Our perspec-tive in the enneagram of crisis is centered on the critical impact of technology on the biosphere. The technosphere offers a challenge to the biosphere which causes the opportunity of the noosphere to emerge. But the realization of the noosphere through this opportunity is not automat-ically assured.

The technological singularity represents one way in which we can see the transition of point 6 on this enneagram. If things continue as they have been doing, we are headed toward a point of maximum uncertainty and hazard which might even destroy most complex life forms on the planet! Many people think that a reduction of momentum will prevent

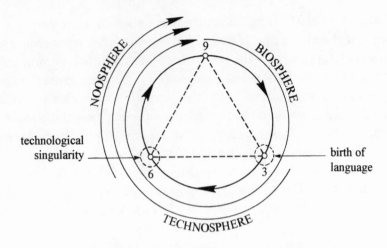

12.1. Biosphere, technosphere, and noosphere.

us from reaching this crisis. An ultimate limit to the amount of energy that can be made available might curtail the rate of growth of technological innovation. There is an uncertain relationship between energy expenditure and innovation. Three billion bollars is about to be invested in nuclear fusion research to produce a prototype that might actually work by 2020. This comes after almost thirty years of research.

There is a feature of technology which has gone unnoticed until recently: it has a tendency to decay. In place of the chromium-bright and tunic-clad images of the future that dominated popular culture a short time ago, we now picture dark futures full of hi-tech decay and tyranny.[12] In the movie *Bladerunner* the cutting edge of technology had been transferred to other planets, leaving a remnant population living in technological degeneracy. This is not just science fiction. The majority of people in the world today are living "downstream" from technology. Technology as we know it today requires a shock to enable it to develop further along its own octave. If we picture ourselves standing at point 5 in the enneagram, then our technology is faced with a critical interval. It has increased in intensity and tempo, but now it needs to change in quality.

Information technology and artificial intelligence are key factors in this drama. There are important trends toward organic, evolutionary methods in design. These promise to greatly shorten the time required for effective improvement, but this is only the faintest help compared to what is needed. The potential of artificial intelligence is broader and more powerful than anything we have seen to date. What is needed is nothing less than an integration of human, technological, and organic intelligence in a noospheric totality. In this respect Lewis Mumford expressed something very well: "Our capacity to go beyond the machine rests on our power to assimilate the machine. Until we have absorbed the lessons of objectivity, impersonality, neutrality, the lessons of the mechanical realm, we cannot go further in our development toward the more richly organic, the more profoundly human."[13]

The Three Octaves

First Octave

On the scale we have chosen, the articulation of the six points—1, 2, 4, 5, 7, 8—is broad in scope. In dealing with the biosphere, the first octave which continues right around the circle, we have to take the global character of the terms into account. We cannot simply speak of the various species, or even of the kingdoms. The biosphere is not the aggregate of living species but an intricate and dynamic coupling of living and non-living matter. We have to speak of *biomes,* which are its natural units.

After the rise of organic life in the first place (point 0), came the emergence of the "wilderness biomes" (point 1). These are those broad ecological systems like deserts, rain forests, savannas, and tundras, where species, geography, and climate intertwine. These did not exist in the early stages of the biosphere.

The biomes give rise to "successions." In this phase climatic and terrestrial changes spur the succession of differing ecologies as they respond to and exploit the varying environmental conditions. These successions take place within wilderness biomes, but they are capable of initiating major evolutionary changes on the scale of the biomes themselves (such as those which established the biomes in the first place). It is in these successions that we find the major spurts of evolution and the rise of the new evolving stem (point 2) of the biosphere. When dinosaurs disappeared through drastic climatic change or the impact of a large meteor, there was an

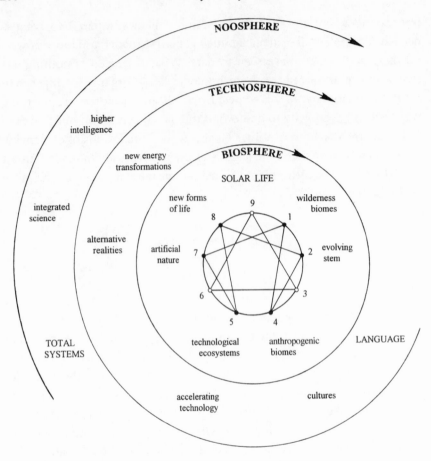

12.2. Nine points of evolution.

opening for mammals to evolve into the dominant species. In our present era the evolving stem is humankind.

In general, we find that the first point in a phase of the enneagram has a spatial character and the second, a temporal one.

At point 4 we see the emergence of the *anthropogenic biomes,* classes of artificial, man-made ecology such as we find in farms and cities. At point 5 we see included the emergence of new kinds of ecosystems, which are created with the aid of technology and are as far removed from the anthropogenic biomes as these were from the wilderness. They are artificial, engineered, closed ecological systems such as those constructed in Russia and the United States—approximations to total, global systems. Also, we see the beginnings of a synergic management of ecosystems—in which economics, ecology, culture, climate, transport, production, and so forth are considered together. This is an anticipation of the third octave, the noosphere.

The prospects for the biosphere beyond point 6 are largely unknown. There has been speculation that we may well have to undertake a *terraforming of the earth*. This seems to be a contradiction, since the earth is already earthlike! However, the impact of technology is becoming so great that even the wilderness may need to become a man-managed artifact. This corresponds to point 7, which I call artificial nature to highlight the apparent contradiction. The prospects associated with point 8 are even more extraordinary, involving production of biospheres in the depths of the ocean, in the Arctic, or in space. They would employ aspects of life's potential that have not yet been seen on earth.[14]

At the end of this process, at point 9, we must have a solar life, a kind of life capacity capable of spreading throughout the solar system. Although this kind of life must evolve through the intervention of human-technological forces, wherever it enters a new world, the nature of that world will take over the shaping of the new wilderness.[15]

Second Octave

The second octave begins with language (point 3). Point 4, we associate with *cultures* or civilizations, and point 5 with accelerating technology.[16] The cultures of point 4 echo or parallel the biomes of point 1, just as the accelerating technology of point 5 echoes the successions (and evolutionary spurts) of point 2.

The meaning of technology and culture change when we reach point 7. We have only hints of this from the potential of global digitalization: instant global communication is already changing the nature of cultures and political systems, as well as developing new alternative realities, sometimes called cyberspace. Point 8 may involve intuitive powers which have hardly been tapped until now, manifesting in the exercise of new energies. At this point technology and biology may well be reconciled again.

Third Octave

In the third octave, at point 6, a new age is initiated through the influence of total systems. What follows is the start of a global or total system, of integrated sciences and technologies (point 7). We can look at the macrosphere of astronomy, the biosphere, and the microsphere of nanosystems to see the emergence of total systems science.[17] At present we have no methodology capable of managing such enterprises. What can emerge out of these at point 8 are nodes of *higher intelligence*. That is why, in the more traditional language of Gurdjieff and Bennett, this point is associated with "conscious men and women." Such men and women are tapped into what Gurdjieff called objective consciousness, the impersonal wisdom that informs the universe.

We have moved into the realm of speculation, and it takes further speculation to consider that this whole process has a destiny on other worlds. The biosphere has a role to play in the larger solar system and even beyond that. But this is beyond the threshold of point 9. The traditionalist Réne Guénon would call point 9 the Lord of the World.[18] It is most interesting that we seem unable to decide whether or not this lord has any *power* over events or even if he (she, it) should be considered personal or impersonal.

We are forced to speak of all this as if it was separated from us in the future. This can be misleading. What lies beyond point 6 is already an influence on the present. Remember that both points 7 and 8 are connected to point 5 by inner lines. When we enter into the domain of the third octave, we are entering a kind of present moment which is not strictly parallel to our own ordinary experience. Something may already be going on that *we do not see*. If we do not see it then, not only is it not real for us, *we are not real for it.* That is truly terrifying.

The Inner Lines of Regulation

We move from the octaves and their stages to the inner lines that regulate the enneagram's function. These inner lines suggest that intelligence can regulate the mutual impact of the octaves. The octaves do not interact simply in a mechanical way. The linkages are *forms of control,* which means that they are related to intelligence. The inner lines of the enneagram actually do represent something inner.

The inner lines connect in the sequence 1-4-2-8-5-7, and the pattern is cyclic: 7 connects to 1. In pouring a glass of water, point 8 appeared as an image of the completed action. It is the *guiding vision* of the whole process. It is one of the three innovative or dynamic points along with points 2 and 5. The stable or conservative points are 1, 4, and 7.[19]

When we think about the inner lines, it is advantageous to take them in threes, because this best corresponds to a control linkage. The linkage 1-4-2 refers to one of the basic biospheric laws postulated by Vernadsky: "The evolution of species, in tending towards the creation of new forms of life, must always move in the direction of increasing biogenic migration of the atoms in the biosphere."[20] This rule governs the whole of the right-hand side of the enneagram. We have also noted that an increasing amount of matter and energy made available by the biosphere is being short-circuited through humankind. The anthropogenic (manmade) biomes are coming to dominate the biosphere.

The 1-4-2 linkage shows an anticipation of the future: the development of point 2 is linked with the outcome at point 4. The idea that something in the future has an effect on the present is not at all accepted by most biologists, who prefer to regard evolution as resulting from a succession of contingencies. Vernadsky's concept of the biosphere presupposes a definite direction to evolution. This suggests that we can speak of an *attractor* working on the biosphere which pulls it toward more complex dynamical states. The term *attractor,* as we saw in considering the nature of the triad, is used in chaos theory to describe patterns of equilibrium. A *strange attractor* is understood as a very complex kind of pattern, not at all like a blueprint or a single-valued design. What actually comes about is not predetermined. It can oscillate between various configurations, or suddenly jump into a completely new configuration.[21] Periods of near-turbulence alternate with periods of relative order.

As the biosphere changes, so does its possibilities. In some respects, we can think of the inner linkages portrayed in the enneagram as kinds of information processing or computation, since Gurdjieff spoke of them as concerned with balancing the contributions of the three octaves. Here I want to emphasize the temporal aspect of this balancing: that the inner lines link what has happened with what might happen, to affect what is happening. The idea of computation as an integral part of the natural order is fairly recent, and it is not an anthropomorphic projection. Once we accept that information is as much a part of existence as matter and energy, every entity can be seen as a computational device, including the whole universe. Computation has an effect on the succession of events and is not a mere reflection of what actually happens. It is a necessary function in self-organization. Gurdjieff speaks of Great Nature being compelled to do certain things or as adapting certain things—for example: "Great Nature most wisely adapted the inner organization of beings" (BT p. 788). Such adaptations arise out of computation which, obviously, must allow for innovation and foresight of some kind. Gurdjieff's description of the dramas surrounding early human history suggests that nature's ingenuity was stretched by the interference in human development from higher intelligences. Put in our terms: certain computations coming from a higher sphere overrode those taking place through the biosphere (Great Nature), forcing it to adjust.

In this enneagram point 6 is the point of entry of the noosphere. According to the principles of the enneagram, this presupposes a harmony with the processes of the first phase, the biosphere, and a resolution of the dilemmas created by the second phase, the technosphere, in which we are now living. This is represented by the linkage 2-8-5. These three points usually concern the emergence of the new. There is a science and technology of the biosphere which is now emerging. It is a departure from the mechanistic approach which is part and parcel of the megamachine. It is to be expected that the majority of scientists view this latest development with suspicion. The apparatuses in this field (for example, artificial biospheres and cyberspace) cannot be controlled according to the entrenched methods of machine design. They require use of complex and, to some degree, unpredictable systems. In other words, they need to take account of the computational power of nature itself and work in harmony with it.

In terms of the existing, dominant megamachine, the arising of biospherics (a new science concerning the properties of this newly discovered class of entities called biospheres) is both unexpected and inevitable. It is unexpected in the contemporary milieu, since it concerns the harmony of the whole. It is inevitable, because we are beginning to suffer and understand the effects of the technosphere on the biosphere. It is also important to recognize the great significance of intelligence creating intelligence. This goes far beyond the present crude attempts at computer-based intelligence to include artificial life.

Each of the three points 2, 5, and 8 indicate something with radical significance for the future. At point 2, we have the evolving stem. This represents the best bet the biosphere can make at the time. The material and energy resources of the biosphere are focused disproportionately. At point 5, where we engage in the human story, we have the radical impact of technology. The cultures of point 4 are, in a sense, left behind. Their atavistic trends act to put a brake on the acceleration of technology as a conscious control of the environment and its matter and energy. There is a kind of tenuous global culture of science and technology, but it is looking to the future for its development. The power of point 8 is in its capacity to operate with everything all at once. It supersedes the technological power of point 5, ultimately based on consciousness, with a transformative power ultimately based on creativity.

The 7-1-4 points concern *stability,* and their inner linkage represents the concerns of conservation. There is a need to reexperience the nature of ecosystems in order to learn what works. This is to take nature as our teacher. There are already signs of this in the application of ecological principles to industry, where the waste products of one industry become a resource for another. Coupling industries together in this way greatly reduces pollution, is energy-efficient, and supports communities. In the larger picture, the linkage 7-1-4 indicates our role as *steward of the biosphere.* Our responsibility is to foster the welfare of all life on earth.

We have associated the stable points with the biomes. There is a structural parallel between the wilderness biomes of point 1 and the cultural biomes of point 4. Each represents an optimum under its given constraints. At point 7 we would have intelligence biomes that cannot be subsumed under the cultures. A feature of these biomes would be fast, global information processing, unhampered by local barriers due to mindsets.

An injection of intelligence is needed to resolve the underlying crisis which we and the biosphere face. We look for more information and build faster computers of ever-increasing capacity, but what is required is *intelligence of another order.* This is indicated in the linkage 8-5-7. To get us through to the next phase, nothing less than a hookup with higher intelligence is needed. This means that the mind which appeared in the second octave has to be transformed into something new. A new form of mind implies a new form of information and communication.

The Structure of Sustainable Development

As I have intimated throughout this book, the enneagram is thoroughly compatible with twentieth-century systems theory. This is true of the structure of development, particularly economic development. The dominant attitude of politicians and media imagemakers is that development should just go on and on, but those who understand systems see this as theoretically and practically untenable. Actual events are constantly showing the lie of unbridled development. Unfortunately such occurrences, like the recession of the 1980s, are interpreted as merely aberrations which can be put right by fiddling with the monetary systems. Such aberrations have, in fact, been a feature of economies for as long as we have records.

The technological singularity that I spoke of can be seen as a point of catastrophe. This is not necessarily a destructive or bad thing. A *catastrophe* has the technical meaning of a sudden shift from one state into another—a break in continuity, like a wave curling over to break into turbulence. Our present-day economic systems tend to crash, in smaller or greater degree, because of their very nature. The dynamism between capital, resources, and markets must contain a certain degree of self-destruction. The more we manipulate money and resources to control the economy, the more it is likely to crash. The reason for this is that these manipulations are not based on the holistic principles that actually govern self-organizing systems like the biosphere.

Without an *inhibitory*, regulative element, stemming from a corresponding perception, we end up with a system out of control. The action of opening up the tap to fill a glass with water needs to be balanced by a perception and a means to close the tap. Without these there is no system, only a movement toward chaos. Our present economies work like taps turned on. When water begins to flow, it provides positive feedback which then makes the flow even greater. Such a one-way feedback system can only break down. If we do not learn how to reduce the flow from the tap *intentionally*, we can rest assured that it will be reduced *mechanically*.

This is particularly important now because we face breakdowns which can affect the infrastructure of the biosphere and cause irreversible damage. In human society these manifest as wars, poverty, and disease. These are not causally linked to what is happening in the biosphere, as we understood causes in the past. They are systems-linked.[22] Consequently, some people see the connection directly, while others have to be persuaded by circuitous arguments.

In place of the technological singularity, where the rate of development approaches instant change, we can strive for a sigmoid pattern of development. In the S-shaped sigmoid pattern, when development speeds up toward insupportable proportions, it then levels off, reaching a stable plateau. (see fig. 12.3).

In the enneagram model, the turning point in the middle of the S-curve lies between points 4 and 5. If the turning is not achieved, the system heads toward insupportable behavior and ends in chaos. Point 6 in the enneagram represents an input of superior information. This makes point 5 a point of critical significance. It represents the point at which the rate of development can no longer be increased without heading into catastrophe. It is the crunch point. If we are only aware of what proceeds along the outside circle, this won't be apparent. Without communication from point 8 (in the inner line connection 8-5-7) we have no vision, no pattern which enables us to assess our situation.

The critical role of point 6 is to blend an extra dimension of perception

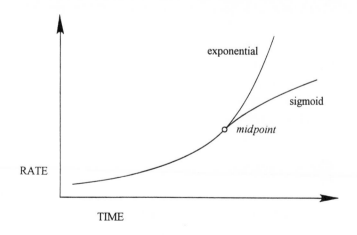

12.3. Developmental curves.

into the system. Such a perception "sees the forest for the trees," is aware of the total system properties, and is capable of giving rise to intelligent regulation. This intervention can only work when point 5 and point 6 can come to an agreement. This did not happen with the first Club of Rome report (a potential carrier for point 6), which was derided by critics centerd on point 5.[23] The abstract information of the report did not match with the concrete complexity of the situation.

Interestingly enough, the critics made a fundamental error in confusing creativity with chaos. They argued that the increasing complexity would always generate its own solutions, indefinitely. It is still a popular fallacy that creativity takes place unintentionally and with no relation to ethical or spiritual factors. This is only true for a low level of ongoing, random, piecemeal, and often violent innovation. The Club of Rome, on the other hand, failed to relate the gross simplifications of their model to the real situation and fell into the trap of making explicit prophecies of a collapse which failed to materialize.

The intervention of point 6 has to be engineered with precision. It is probably insufficient to advocate a slowdown, without offering some other, new form of development. We see a hint of this in the growth of information technology as the more gross manufacturing arena slows down. Now we have the prospect of linking technologies in an *ecological* manner with synergetic payoff. Of course, every new line of development, *after* it has been set in motion, becomes the playground of the corrupt and narrow-minded (the inner line 7-1 shows that the new idea stimulates a new line of exploitation). The intervention at point 6 has to be continually renewed. A point to be made here is that humankind tends to take itself too seriously. We are obsessed with the tragic option of destroying everything that is of value. A cosmic sense of humor would give not only relief but also much-needed insight. God's greatest gift to humanity may have been a sense of humor. It is, at least, an antidote to self-importance and even has the potential to detach us from the realm of mind.

Much of the first part of Gurdjieff's *Beelzebub's Tales* deals with intervention at point 6. Beelzebub's task of stopping the escalating trend of animal sacrifice is an exact parallel to the requirement to tone down rampant development before it reaches overwhelming catastrophe. He is successful—through the implantation of certain *new ideas*—but problems such as war continue. Beelzebub represents a higher intelligence. This intelligence, though constrained by particular circumstances, draws on an inexhaustible creativity and sense of the absurd.

The realm of the third octave of the enneagram represents something that is beyond space and time. In his writings Bennett called this the *hyparchic future*, a creative kind of future that is not the resultant of the past.[24] It might well be described as the *creativity of the whole* in contrast with the creativity of the parts, which is what we see in the random innovations taking place around us. What has so far been missed in the advocacy of the sigmoid pattern of development is that this is only possible with a *creative* input. The bare notion of regulation will never be enough.[25] There needs to be a creativity which addresses the concrete situation in all its complexity by being in the future, ahead of the game.

What we see in the existential problems of economic development is only a shadow of the dramatic issue of the human soul. By our very nature, we must become ever more involved in the workings of the material world, but we do this at a cost. There is a wonderful gnostic tale of a young prince from a divine kingdom being sent by his father down into the lower world to recover a precious pearl. The prince has to disguise himself to pass as one of the lower beings. But then he forgets who he is. The vestments take him over, like a mask. Only when his father sends him a message, a bird that whispers to him who he is, does the prince remember what he has to do. He recovers the pearl and returns to the rejoicing of his parents in the heavenly kingdom.[26]

The father in the tale needs to redeem his son. We too need to be redeemed. Our involvement in the material world puts us at great risk. Redemption is nothing less than a necessity given the human situation. No piecemeal efforts of whatever nature or extent will ever be able to assure man of his link with the divine, or his own higher nature, or with *who he really is*.

Of course, the majority view in present culture is that we have no need of redemption at all. We simply are what we are, autonomous beings, with no need for justification from a higher realm. This, in fact, emphasizes the crisis we are in, corresponding to point 5 of the enneagram. Here we see ourselves locked into the consequences of our own inventions. As such, we *cannot* evolve any further: whatever our intentions, whatever the degree of progress in invention, we remain the same. Constantly, we are pulled back into limited cultures and belief systems. In base terms, no one can pull themselves up by their shoe laces.

The kind of impasse we are in illustrates the nature of point 5 in general. It always can be taken as an *end point* instead of a transitional hiatus. In the individual human, this is sometimes associated with egoism. It is powerful stagnation.

The Logos of the Biosphere

I am not presupposing any higher-order pattern which contains all the answers. What could such a thing mean? The difficult point to grasp is that the higher intelligence concerned in the fate and destiny of the earth requires the cooperation of human life. This is not attained by either coercion from above or by rampant heedlessness acting from below. It is the crucial historical factor. All that has been so far produced, both in religion and in science, serve, at best, only as preliminary exercises or provisional explorations.

The law which is in operation is the *logos* of the enneagram, represented in the triangle. It can be viewed as a triad of commands and equally of values. The three commands *inform* the three octaves. In terms of the nomenclature of the enneagram, these are represented as the lines 9-3, 3-6, and 6-9. The point 0, which is in the same place as 9, does not appear, because we are not concerned with the *facts* of the situation as much as with the *values*. The *logos* concerns values, while the octaves concern facts.

To give some form to our discussion, I propose that the three commands are:

9-3   Survival (shared with all life)
3-6   Emergence (the historical force "seeking the new")
6-9   Unification (synergy of values)

The crisis we are in is described by the opposites to these imperatives: extinction, stagnation, and disintegration. It has been suggested that technology could make it possible to colonize the solar system, possibly through controlled use of fusion reactions, a source of energy independent of the organic biosphere (which can only process solar energy). This would divide humanity into populations with different environments *and values*. The possibilities for radical divergence between subpopulations, based on changes in both biology and technology, have been explored in literature.

The significance of the third process of the enneagram is that it introduces a totally new player into the drama. This is something in its own right. Gurdjieff said that we humans have to serve something, be food for something.[27] This means that we cannot, even in principle, be self-sufficient. Not only do we rely on the rest of organic life for our food; we rely on what is beyond life for our evolution. This might be literally true in a very stark and frightening manner. In an empirical sense, what is beyond life is simply *death*. The evolution of complex life such as ours depends almost exclusively upon death. It is important to acknowledge this in relation to our conceptions of higher powers. In a very real sense, these powers are dead, but they are *consciously dead*.[28] An animal, in contrast, is unconsciously alive. Life is only an intermediary condition, if we imagine life to be like that of an animal or plant. There is something beyond life, of another order. Maybe it is like a planet or a star. And, in some sense, this other order *eats us*. It must be fed!

From such primitive intuitions, the ancient ideas of sacrifice must have arisen: by giving captives or animals unto death, the rest, the people, could be spared. Exploration of this idea is one of the first and greatest themes of Gurdjieff's *Beelzebub's Tales*. There he argues that the idea of sacrifice is misconstrued—that what is required as food for the higher is not the aroma from the sacrificial fire, nor the energy of palpitating hearts torn from their owners, but a certain energy or substance that can be generated by conscious work and intentional suffering. It is because so little of this energy is produced intentionally that the whole earth suffers and that people come up with monstrous ideas such as that of ritual sacrifice.

In this respect, the arising of *conscious individuals* on the earth can make all the difference between success and failure in the evolutionary stakes—and, maybe, even in survival. A conscious individual is one who is able to produce subtle energies intentionally and, *through this work of transformation*, communicate with what is beyond life and be given the *sight* of higher worlds. The future of life on earth depends on the attainment of higher perceptions, the ability to assimilate the higher hydrogens of impressions. Only if we have men and women who are of the nature of point 8 do we have a chance of making the next step. The traditional role models—variously called avatars, saviors, buddhas, and the like—are probably totally misleading, since they now belong to the world of expectations and are embedded in existing human cultures. The real action from point 8 may have little to do with enhancing our life-based dreams.

Notes

1. It is estimated that 40 percent of biospheric production is now involved in human systems.
2. Vaclav Havel, the Czech president, said in 1994 that a "single interconnected civilization" is emerging, but that this is only on the surface of human lives. Below that surface, he sees a countervailing reassertion of local cultures and a clinging to the "ancient certainties of their tribe." Havel appeals to the sense of being a cosmic citizen: "We are not here alone nor for ourselves alone, but. . . . we are an integral part of higher mysterious entities against whom it is not advisable to blaspheme." As one might expect, he has been criticized for lack of specific proposals. This only goes to show that people are still stuck in wanting answers before they have acknowledged the significance of the questions.
3. See Richard Dawkins, *The Blind Watchmaker.* This idea was intimated earlier by C. H. Waddington in his book *Man: The Ethical Animal.*
4. Alexander Marshak, *The Roots of Civilisation,* pp. 12–3. Much the same picture was given by Oswald Spengler in *Man and Technics.*
5. We can find this reflected in the teachings of Krishnamurti under the theme of: How did man make a wrong turning? See J. Krishnamurti and David Bohm, *The Ending of Time.*
6. J. G. Bennett, *The Dramatic Universe,* vol. 4, pp. 259–63.
7. Julian Jaynes, *The Origin of Consciousness and the Bicameral Mind.*
8. See Karl Popper and John Eccles, *The Self and its Brain.*
9. See my comments on participation in the third force in chapter 4.
10. This point is well made in Dorian Sagan, *Biospheres.*
11. See, for example, the Korda movie *Things to Come,* based on H. G. Wells's novel *The Shape of Things to Come.*
12. In a similar vein, Gurdjieff speaks of various "transapalnian perturbations," or "cataclysms not according to law," taking place through human history and radically altering it.
13. Lewis Mumford, *Technics and Civilisation,* p. 363.
14. See my discussion of artificial biospheres in "Artificial Worlds: The Enneagram of Closed Engineered Ecological Systems," in *Impressions* (Journal of the Claymont Society) 8, no. 1.

15. Organizations like the Nature Conservancy are already acquiring land and managing is as wilderness havens for endangered species.

16. In Arnold Toynbee's scheme, as set out in his monumental *Study of History*, civilizations are considered in terms of religious vision and stretch of empire. It would be more relevant to consider them in terms of scientific and technological innovation and implementation.

17. *Nano* means nine and refers to the scale of one centimeter divided by ten—nine times. Nanotechnology is the technology of using machines on this minute scale. At this scale, technology and life would become indistinguishable.

18. See Réne Guénon, *Lord of the World*.

19. These distinctions were introduced in chapter 1.

20. See Vladimir Vernadsky, *The Biosphere*, Appendix one. The term *biogenic* means "produced by life."

21. Our own global weather has two main attractors, one of which corresponds to an ice age. Relatively small perturbations may flip the planet into this configuration.

22. For example, both Gurdjieff and Bennett believed that the development of electrical energy has had a deleterious effect on the human psyche.

23. See Club of Rome, *Limits to Growth*.

24. The hyparchic future was one of Bennett's most original ideas. In this realm, nonthermodynamic operations could change patterns. This means that there is always far more that can be done than we expect! If we look at the enneagram in terms of time, taken in a broad sense, then the first phase deals in ordinary linear time, the second in eternity, or nontime, and the third in hyparxis, or antitime. Each phase has its active and passive modes. The total of *six* factors which conjoin through the inner periodic figure constitute what Bennett calls the *present moment*.

25. In the last chapter, in discussing the points as they appear in the inner lines, I associate regulation with point 7 and creation with point 8.

26. Jonas, *The Gnostic Religion*. Perhaps the classic work in this genre is David Lindsay's *Voyage to Arcturus,* in which different moral philosophies and religions are shown to arise from different sets of sense organs. A more recent expression is Bruce Sterling's *Schismatrix.* Kim Stanley Robinson's trilogy on the colonization of Mars, beginning with *Red Mars,* is a masterpiece of imagining the complexities of the future once humans move into space. Of course, different races and cultures arose in the first place out of differences in geography as well as of language and belief. Hence, we have the intriguing prospect of passing through a relatively homogenous global phase to a reversion into quite separate and mutually incompatible groupings. In this perspective from the future, the present century might begin to look like the Golden Age!

27. A highly sensational form of this idea was produced by Charles Fort in his famous statement, "I think we're property" in *The Book of the Damned.* This was used as a theme in the science fiction novels *The Puppet Masters* by Robert Heinlein and *Mind Parasites* by Colin Wilson. It is not all that far from Orage's answer to the question "What is the purpose of man?"—which was: "Mutton and wool!"

28. See Bennett's description of planetary existence in *The Dramatic Universe, vol. 1,* where he takes the phrase "consciously dead" from Douglas Harding and quotes him as saying: "Many-sided death is the condition of her [the earth's] vitality" (Harding, *The Hierarchy of Heaven and Earth,* p. 89).

PART THREE

THE PURPOSE OF TRANSFORMATION

· 13 ·

Wheels within Wheels

Every whole we can discover or create is a reflection of a cosmic reality. Cosmic means more than "applying everywhere." It is the informing principle that is ahead of existence at every point in the universe. Bennett divided reality into the subjective, the objective, and the cosmic. The subjective is what we find in our own experience. The objective is in what we discover outside of ourselves. The cosmic is what informs them both. David Bohm also insisted that both mind and matter come out of a common and deeper source. All schemes of thought postulate an ultimate cosmos from which we come to understand particular cosmoses as reflections of the whole. In ancient times, people used the template of the heavens to read events in their local history.

Cosmos is structured in depth. As the archetype of the whole, it contains the many. In the realms of evolution, it is threefold.

Into Eternity

AN ASCENDING OCTAVE requires a boost at a certain point. *This is provided by the influx or start of another process of a different kind.* The critical transition in an octave (mi-fa) is assisted by the addition of a note of another octave, acting as do. The newly originated octave develops side by side with the first one. In its turn, the second octave requires a boost at its critical point, for which a note of a third octave, again acting as do, is needed. In the enneagram, we have three octaves, linked in this way. Each one represents the structure of a distinct process. They build up on each other in the way shown in figure 13.1, where the numbers are those of the points of the enneagram. The completion of the second and third octaves, shown in parentheses, is outside of the frame of reference of the given action.

0	1	2	3	4	5	6	7	8	9
						Do	Re	Mi – Fa	(Sol La Si–Do)
.	.	.	**Do**	Re	Mi	–	Fa	Sol La	(Si–Do) . .
Do	Re	Mi	–	Fa	Sol		La	Si – Do	. . . .

13.1. Three octaves.

In an ideal, abstract world we could picture the enneagram as completely self-contained. Each of the three octaves or processes would proceed around the circle, the one reinforcing the other. The shock of the first octave would be given by the do of the second, and the shock of the second octave by the do of the third. And the shock for the third octave would be given by the do of the first octave. This would enable the cycle to go on forever, and we would have perpetual motion (fig. 13.2).

Real beings in our universe are not isolated but depend on their environment. The material for the assisting octaves is introduced from outside. An organism takes in food, air, and impressions from the world in which it exists. It also gives something out. For every breath we take in, we give out matter and energy. Thus, the enneagram represents a transforming device in which each of the dos is a *point of exchange* (see fig. 13.3, depicting a real entity in a concrete situation).

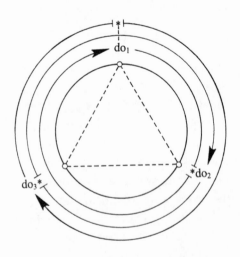

13.2. Enneagram of perpetual motion.

13.3. Enneagram of concrete situations.

In chapter 9, we introduced the best-known example of the three-process enneagram: the transformation of food. Gurdjieff distinguishes three kinds of food: ordinary food, air, and impressions. Without the participation of the process of air, the process of ordinary food does not develop beyond a certain point (point 3); similarly, without the participation of the process of impressions, the process of air does not develop beyond a certain point (point 6). Gurdjieff says that the first change of process at point 3 is arranged mechanically for us. The change at point 6 is not. It has to be brought about intentionally. The fruit of transformation appears in the third phase of the enneagram, and it is here that the *making of the soul* begins.

The points of the enneagram can be associated with parts of our physiology. These associations have always been controversial because they give us something tangible to visualize, and the processes evolving in the left hand of the enneagram must be increasingly psychological, or even nonmaterial. Figure 13.4 is a typical representation of the transformation of food enneagram from the 1930s.[1] Air enters into contact with the processing of food at point 3, and impressions into contact with the processing of air at point 6. The terminology of *conscious shocks* emphasizes the intentional character of the transition at point 6 and that there is a possible realm of further transformation beyond the range of this enneagram. This enneagram represents the start-up motor of our self-realization.

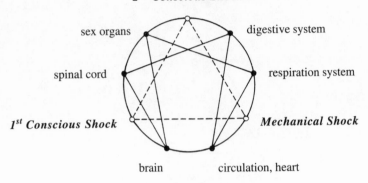

13.4. *Enneagram of food transformation.*

The physiological sequence in the left-hand side of figure 13.4 is interesting. Historically, it derives from the classical physiology of the second-century Roman doctor Galen, whose ideas dominated the field for more than a thousand years and would have been still prevalent in Gurdjieff's environment. In Galen's scheme, food is transformed until it goes into the brain and from there enters into all the nerves concerned with voluntary motion (the nerves were pictured like hollow tubes). Thus, there was a sort of "voluntary motion stuff." In moving (point 7), we are going outside the confines of the body into the world. This is the physiological underpinning of sense perception or "impressions," which belongs to the third octave. Sex (point 8) is a further kind of step, and Gurdjieff and his pupils emphasize the significance of the gametes as sources of new beings. Placing the brain at point 5 makes it the ground of action. In the line 5-7 there is a hint of the brain reaching out into the world just as in modern theories based on the concept of "quantum touching." Point 6 becomes immensely significant as the interface between organism and environment.

Acceleration

We can picture how the three processes link up with each other by imagining ourselves passing from one to the other. Picture a set of moving trackways—flat, parallel escalators such as the ones found in airports, but moving at various speeds. To get onto a faster track from a slower one, people have to walk fast enough to be able to transfer without falling. It is useful to associate the different octaves in the enneagram with different speeds or rates of change. There is a gradual acceleration along a given trackway or octave—and a sudden jump in speed when passing to the next.

In the passage from 0 to 9 in the enneagram we go from one domain (or world) into another. These are of different natures; it is not as simple as stepping from one room into another. We have to step onto a *moving* trackway. In the first domain we are walking on still ground. When we step onto the moving trackway, we still continue to walk, but our overall speed is increased. By walking fast enough on this moving trackway, we come up to the speed of the next trackway. We can then enter the third domain. If we say that the first domain is at rest, the final domain is moving at great speed. But if we reach the final domain, we ourselves can remain at rest *in a new way*. This new kind of being at rest is sometimes associated with *being in eternity*.

Associating domains with different speeds is a metaphor for different kinds of experience. Rodney Collin, a follower of Ouspensky, spoke of there being molecular, atomic, and electronic worlds.[2] His description of the human life cycle and the action of death is vivid and telling. He says that if people are not established in the electronic domain, then at the moment of death (point 9), they will be thrown off the circuit and forced into repeating their lives all over again (thrown off the fast trackway back onto the stationary ground).

The three octaves have a cumulative effect. The second octave comes in on top of the first, and the third on top of the second, culminating in a shift in level (fig. 13.5). If we remove the lines of the octaves, what we have is a set of *steps*. The step symbol (fig. 13.6)[3] is found all over the world but is particularly important in the Andes. The idea of stepping up

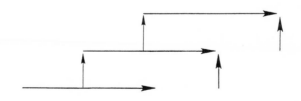

13.5. Cumulative effect of octaves.

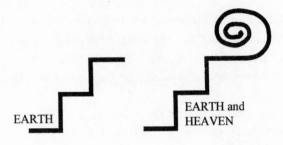

13.6. Step symbol.

into higher levels is intuitively obvious, but in Gurdjieff's enneagram we can see something of *how* this is to be done through the idea of octaves. Our tendency is to read symbols in a spatial way. It is a critical moment when we convert space into time and see the symbol of the enneagram as a pattern of movement. When we see it as movement, we become aware of the second octave in particular as an *acceleration.* The second octave is intermediary between the first and the third. If we regard the first as arising in a domain which is essential static, an unmoving trackway, then we can regard the third as arising in a domain which is essentially time-less. It is because the third is moving so fast in relation to the second, and the second to the first, that events in the third appear, from ground level, as if they were happening *all at once.*

The three lines of the triangular figure indicate the intention or direc-tion associated with the three octaves. They form into a cycle of outgoing and return. Between the outgoing (0-3) and the return (6-9) is the path of maximum acceleration (3-6). If we get caught up in this middle track-way, we are liable to fall off the edge, as it were. We *have* to come back to our starting point. The art is to step from the second track to the third *intentionally.* If we do not do this, the third phase of the enneagram is more or less empty for us, and we reach point 9 in a state of turbulence, to be thrown back into the first domain. In psychological terms, this means that something has to develop in the second octave which enables us to remain conscious in the third phase of the enneagram.[4]

From the perspective of what Gurdjieff called the chemical factory, a human's middle octave comes from the world of air and begins with breathing. We can alter our breathing mechanically by exertion, but it can also be altered from within as a natural result of changes in our attention.

Speaking about the octaves in terms of speed is, of course, a gross simplification. There are very important qualitative differences. As mentioned in chapter 1, Gurdjieff uses the metaphor of hydrogens of different densities. As we proceed clockwise, the hydrogens decrease in density and *increase in rate of vibration.* Rate of vibration corresponds to our more elementary idea of speed.

The Design of the Enneagram

The enneagram is not flat. Though it appears to be just on a surface, it is actually in a complex space of representation. The first thing to realize is that there are several elements which are superimposed on one another. We have to picture the diagram as a set of overlays, each dealing with a different facet. The most important aspect of this concerns the three octaves, which we have just been discussing.

The first octave, which goes right around the circle, can be represented in simple form like the one in figure 13.7. We have marked the first (mi-fa) shock and the second (si-do) shock.[5] The octave touches the inner triangle at points 3 and 9 (0), and not at point 6. At point 0, it *begins;* at point 3 it *changes* (shock); and at point 9 it *ends.* Point 6 is significant only for the other two octaves. We can represent the second octave in a similar way to the first, as in figure 13.8. We see that it touches the inner triangle at points 3 and 6. At point 6, it has its first shock. At point 3, it

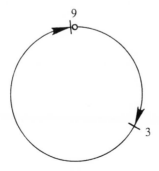

13.7. The first octave.

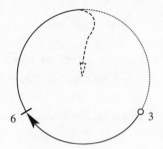

13.8. The second octave.

begins, and at point 6 it *changes* (shock). It does not touch at point 9. This is very strange. Perhaps it ends "inside" the enneagram, at some other level (as we have suggested by the dotted line)?[6] We can represent the third octave as in figure 13.9. It touches the inner triangle at points 6 and 9. At point 6 it *begins* and at point 9 it *changes* (shock). There is no suggestion of what can happen after that.

This representation of the design of the enneagram shows the three octaves as very different from each other. The first touches the triangle at points 3 and 9; the second, at points 3 and 6; and the third, at points 6 and 9. They are, therefore, associated with distinct lines of command

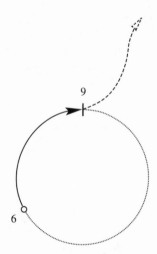

13.9. The third octave.

coming from the *logos*. In terms of what is encompassed by the ennea-gram figure, only the first is a complete octave. The other two are quasi-octaves. The second, for example, is really a *five*-term system (points 3, 4, 5, 7, 8); and the third a *three*-term system (points 6, 7, 8). If we consider point 9 to be a part of these, then they have one more term. It is am-biguous.

Point 9 turns out to be very complex. We are not sure how the second and third octaves participate in it. At the same time, it is the *transitional* point through which the cycle of the first octave is renewed. We imagine that the operation of the enneagram is recurrent: it repeats itself. What-ever is brought about in the first octave has to be brought about again. This means that the conditions for the starting point at 0 have to be reestablished. If we are thinking of eating and digesting food—we have to become *hungry* again.

In terms of the third octave, we do not know whether or not point 9 serves as shock (mi-fa) for it. If it does, then the *final product* of the first octave and the *first shock* of the third octave coincide. Point 9 has all the characteristics corresponding to the Sufi injunction to be in the world but not of it. The triangular figure represents a possible synergy between the three octaves. This corresponds to Gurdjieff's statement: "And thus, every man, if he is not just an ordinary man, that is, one who has never consciously 'worked on himself,' has two worlds; and if he has worked on himself, and has become a so to say 'candidate for another life,' he has even three worlds."[7]

It is important to realize that this also means that such a person *unifies the three worlds in himself.* How one does this is a matter of one's true intelligence, which is represented in the inner periodic figure. The multi-ple ambiguity of point 9 becomes more and more significant.[8] It says to us that the unity at stake can *either* be thought of as a product, somehow extracted out of life, *or* as something coming from Above, God-given. In the first, we think in terms of the first octave, while, in the second, we think in terms of the third octave. The relevance of the second octave is that *we ourselves have to bear the contradiction in our own work so that it can then be resolved by the third force.*

The design of the enneagram, therefore, contains an important mes-sage.

They Leave Our Story Here

There are often characters in stories who do not remain as part of the action to the end. They may play an important part in the action which revolves around the main characters, but they have their own destinies which take them somewhere else. A relevant example is that of Prince Yuri Lubovedsky, Gurdjieff's aristocratic friend, to whom he bids farewell in the Sarmoun monastery.[9] In a structured process that comes to completion, the work that is done involves processes which are left incomplete. We solve a problem by initiating processes which have ramifications beyond the scope of our concern. This often happens unknowingly, sometimes with unexpected results.

In both literature and mathematics, the process of reaching a result or conclusion generates other lines of development which cannot be completed within the intial framework. Any narrative is set within a greater narrative, on a larger scale or of more mythic depth. Any piece of mathematics is set within the evolution of its mathematical methods or even its philosophy.

The completion of a given task is a kind of closure that enables it to be something in its own right. It does not exclude the greater whole but lives within it, just as a type of organism lives within an ecology. The enneagram shows how *events* are produced within a given *history*.

Similar principles apply in the case of our own totality. We are living beings of the type Gurdjieff calls three-brained, referring to the three main functions of thought, feeling, and sensory-motion. Yet we are more than this and extend into realms beyond these functions. If we picture ourselves as an enneagram, then the processes associated with feeling and thought can be seen as having implications in another sphere beyond that of our ordinary perception. This is represented in the step symbol by the spiral glyph for heaven (see fig. 13.6).

Point 9 is a crucial *point of organization*. It is the "I" of which the content of the enneagram is the "am." Looked at in this way, there are things beyond "I," and the "I" is a point of meeting between greater and lesser worlds. The greater worlds are those in which the second and third octaves of the enneagram come to completion. On a few occasions I have referred to a point 10. This transcendental point refers to the greater world in which the transformation of the enneagram reaches full completion.[10]

In strictly individual human terms we should consider Gurdjieff's teaching on the higher centers of man. Besides the basic functions of moving, feeling, and thinking, he spoke of two higher ones: the "higher emotional center," or the "heart" spoken of in mystical tradition, and the "higher intellectual center," the "intellect." According to Gurdjieff, these are already at work in us, but our lower centers are disconnected from them, so they never enter our awareness. Making this connection depends on completing the higher octaves in us.

Ouspensky offers a striking image of this possibility: "There was yet another drawing of the enneagram which was made under his direction in Constantinople in the year 1920. In this drawing inside the enneagram were shown the four beasts of the Apocalypse—the bull, the lion, the man and the eagle—and with them a dove. These additional symbols were connected with 'centres' " (ISM, p. 295).

The fulfillment of the unfinished octaves may also be in some sense *outside* of us and on a *bigger scale.*

We have three inputs and three octaves in the enneagram. One of these is geared to a recurrent cycling that keeps the system going, while the other two go outside the system into a relatively unbounded domain. We can have a feeling for this domain by contemplating the biosphere. In considering the cycles of the biosphere, we have to take into account the existence of *reservoirs* of matter (and, to a lesser degree, of energy) residing outside the sphere of life—including the necrosphere, or sphere of death. By analogy, this can be extended into the idea that there are *reservoirs of experience and meaning.* In general, we have to assume some kind of "buffer store," which is not explicitly shown in the enneagram symbol.[11] This store contains the circulations of the enneagram—of matter, energy, and information—and their products of nutrition, experience, and meaning so that the sum of all the inputs and outputs is conserved in the total system.

In his own working of the cosmology of Gurdjieff, Bennett proposes a "soul-stuff pool," a reservoir of experience, which was drawn upon in the formation of every sentient being on earth and to which the "stuff of experience" was returned.[12] This is outside the temporal and spatial framework contained in the enneagram. Implicit, therefore, is a gateway to the *total* world of terrestrial experience (a store of memories, perhaps). At point 3, something is drawn in from this reservoir. Along the second octave, some work is done on the stuff of experience before returning it to the soul-stuff pool. We have no picture of how this is done because it takes place beyond point 9. Further, it is only through the third octave that something can catalyze this *stuff* of soul to coalesce into an *individual* capable of communion—which belongs to yet another domain, another kind of reservoir.[13]

We can connect with the formless reservoirs, or pools, by an enneagram. Here, we can think of sacred sites, sacred images, and sacred rituals which harbor or connect with higher energies. These energies may be more deeply structured than those of our usual world of experience. *They are more intelligent.* We cannot approach what is more intelligent than ourselves as if it were either an object or a person. Bennett, in his discussions of sacred influences, says that it is by the participation of people—in prayer or ritual—that the necessary energies accumulate in a sacred image or sacred site.[14] It is ecological. Here, he expresses his belief that it is the role of the higher intelligences to utilize the free energies of the mind to build enabling and helping energies. These energies are freed not only by death or external shocks (or crises) but can also be liberated in acts of worship. In a similar way, they can be accessed to enable the individual to be what "he" or "she" is. This is not a matter of one's separate self, but of one's essential individuality. It is only through help that we can bear to lose ourselves and enter into freedom.

Worlds and Cosmoses

We return to the picture of the three different trackways consisting of the stationary ground and the two moving belts. They can be seen as representing three different worlds. *World* can mean many things, but here it is simply a set of possibilities. What is possible in one world may not be possible in another.

What distinguishes the different worlds is not that they are in different places or at different times but that their basic structure is different. Gurdjieff describes this by saying that they are subject to different laws (or different numbers of laws). Computer games offer a simplistic analogue: as the game advances, the player enters different domains where the rules change, allowing for greater difficulties and greater possibilities; they are sometimes even called different worlds. To get into a higher world, the player has to reach a certain level in the world he is currently playing in.

We are picturing the complex play depicted in the enneagram as a movement through different levels of different worlds. If a certain level is not reached within a given world, then the transition cannot be made into the next. If, however, the transition is made, then the "player" acquires added powers.

The different worlds also contain different kinds of entities. For example, we can speak of going from the world of things to the world of life, and of going from the world of life to the world of mind. In the world of things, there is nothing living. Similarly, in the world of life there is no mind. However, just at the points of transition, there is some kind of overlap or meeting between the two types of entity. In the course of evolution, a class of chemicals arose similar to an organic totality and, later, an organic being arose similar to a conscious spirit. These are transitional forms.

My use of the terms *things, life,* and *mind* is simply by way of illustration, and I have made no attempt to define them in a strict way. Many other triplicities can be found such as that in Sufism, where we encounter the *alam-i-ajsam,* or world of bodies; the *alam-i-arvah,* or world of spirits; and the *alam-i-imkan,* or world of possibilities. Bennett has interpreted these as the worlds of matter, energy, and will.[15] In the enneagram, the different worlds are associated with the three octaves.

How can we picture the accumulative overlap of the octaves which takes place as we go around the circle? One way is as the successive addition of greater degrees of freedom. This is what it means to reach higher levels of *organization:* organization is the integration of different degrees of freedom within a whole. Thus, we can think and create while we remain subject to physicochemical laws. What thinks and creates we call mind, while what is subject to physicochemical laws we call body. To think of mind and body as two separate things is a mistake; nor are they the same. As an organization, we are both mind and body. Thus, in the enneagram, we see a successive organization of first one, then two, and finally three worlds.

Gurdjieff made much of the notion of man as a chemical factory in which three *foods*—food, air, and impressions—are utilized for the functioning of the whole. Here we must think of these three foods as being associated with different worlds. The first food that we take in gives us the material for our existence; the second, the energy we need to process this material and open the way toward perception, while the third food gives us the information for fulfilling our destiny. The processing of the three takes place at different degrees of awareness.

When the three worlds of an enneagram are integrated together, we have what Gurdjieff calls a *cosmos*. Hence, a cosmos is not monolithic, all of a piece, but involves the coworking of different worlds, each of which has different levels. A cosmos is like a living being. When Gurdjieff first presented the idea of cosmoses, he said that this was the beginning of knowledge (ism, p. 205). In his general presentation he speaks of seven cosmoses, each in the likeness of the greatest or *protocosmos*. The cosmoses are included one within the other. I am taking the idea of a cosmos in a more general way, as any class of autonomous wholes, or self-organizing totalities; so my description of cosmoses is not precisely the same as Gurdjieff's.

Gurdjieff says that when a man extends his consciousness into a higher cosmos he must at the same time extend it into a lower cosmos. And he adds:

> In looking for parallels and analogies between the cosmoses we may take each cosmos in three relations:
> 1. in its relation to itself,
> 2. in its relation to a higher or a larger cosmos, and
> 3. in relation to a lower, or a smaller cosmos. (ism, p. 207)

These three suggest that each cosmos has a lower, middle, and higher aspect. I have ascribed these three aspects to three different worlds, meaning three different sets of possibilities. Man is a cosmos, and we speak of him as *body, soul, and spirit.*

A cosmos partakes of different worlds, so it can interact with other cosmoses, including the cosmos above and the cosmos below. This interaction takes place within a world that is common to the two cosmoses concerned, so that we can look at the worlds as various mediums of exchange. If a cosmos does not have the given world within it, then it cannot connect with anything that world contains.

In the most general sense, what Gurdjieff calls air is not oxygen but something corresponding to the middle world of the cosmos, which is what it "breathes." Cosmoses can be on different levels. The first food (food) of one cosmos comes from the same world as the third food (impressions) of another cosmos.

In general, *food* signifies an exchange between cosmoses. There can be exchanges with a cosmos on a lower level, with a cosmos on the same level, and with a cosmos on a higher level. Without exchange with a lower cosmos, a body cannot be sustained. Without exchange with a higher cosmos, a mind cannot be sustained. Without other cosmoses, an individual cosmos cannot live or breathe.

It is wrong to look at this model in terms of the subservience of a lower cosmos to a higher, as the Sumerians did, seeing humankind as an instrument made by the gods to do their work for them. However, this idea is very reminiscent of Gurdjieff's own conception of the higher powers treating humankind as an energy producer that has to be kept in the dark by the organ *kundabuffer*.[16] It takes on new significance when we consider the prospect of our own creation of artificial intelligences to serve our purposes. Maybe we should beware of the dangers of creating any kind of replication or "echo" of the human race! Every cosmos has its own kind of time and space, its own landscapes and history, and its own inhabitants, its creatures and intelligences. This may prove to be true of what is currently called cyberspace.[17]

Notes

1. This diagram is taken from unpublished papers of Solita Solanos, a onetime secretary to Gurdjieff.
2. See Rudney Collin, *The Theory of Eternal Life*.
3. From Marjorie von Harten, "Religion and Culture in the Ancient Americas," *Systematics* 1, no. 1. Heaven is represented as a spiral. As I will discuss in the final chapter, this means that another kind of action takes over after the steps.
4. Or, in computer terms, we have to have the software which can enable us to "open and read" the file of our destiny! In my interpretation, "being conscious" is a cognitive state which enables us to access otherwise hidden information.
5. This is the only place where I refer to the proper place of the second shock in the first octave. Strictly speaking, it is situated between points 8 and 9 if we take point 9 as the final do. In general, we merge the second shock into point 9.

6. See my discussion in chapter 10 of Gurdjieff's idea of the "inner body" that it is possible for a human to develop. The connection of each octave with just two of the points of the triangular figure is interpreted in terms of the will of the three bodies.

7. The last sentence of *Life is Real Only Then, When "I Am."*

8. William Pensinger, in his remarkable novel *The Moon of Boa Hinh*, uses the term *identity-transparency*, which expresses very well the meaning of point 9. In identity transparency, we have a concrete kind of individuality which is not simply singular. An identity-transparent individual can also experience the identities immanent in group experience.

9. Prince Yuri Lubovedsky in G. I. Gurdjieff, *Meetings with Remarkable Men.*

10. Bennett in his systematics gave the attribute of *integrative complementarity* to the ten-term system. This is extraordinarily apt for the discussion in this section. The transformation delineated by the enneagram is only fulfilled if it fits processes in a higher world or plays a specific and needed role in its functioning.

11. These are terms used in computing to designate a region between operations and memory.

12. J. G. Bennett, *The Dramatic Universe* vol. 3, pp. 170–73. Bennett was undoubtedly influenced by Gustav Fechner's (1801–1887) concept of the earth's "pool of memories." Cf. William James's essay on Fechner in *A Pluralistic Universe.*

13. A year before his death Bennett said that, although the concept of God might die away, we would always need some notion like that of the "communion of saints."

14. See J. G. Bennett, *Sacred Influences.*

15. See "Three Centred Being," in J. G. Bennett, *Deeper Man.*

16. See my explanation of *kundabuffer* on page 14.

17. *Cyberspace* is a term that was devised by the science fiction novelist William Gibson to designate the near-sentient world of electronic information processing. See his *Neuromancer.*

· 14 ·

Cosmic Interlude

"Real perpetual motion is a part of another perpetual motion and cannot be created apart from it. The enneagram is a schematic diagram of perpetual motion, that is, of a machine of eternal movement. But it is of course necessary to know how to read this diagram" (ISM, *p. 294*). *With these words, Gurdjieff introduced a thoroughgoing relativity into the question of immortality. In a simple sense, he is saying that everything is eternally real to the degree that it participates in God or the ultimate reality. As we explore his ideas, we will see that this participation is very close to "assimilation of the Word" and takes effect primarily in the world of impressions, the "third-being food" in the terminology of* Beelzebub's Tales.

As we look at the bigger picture, we discover (intimately near to us) the mystery of life. *Contemplation of the meaning of life is supremely important. We need to do this in tandem with the ultimate individual inquiry: "Who am I?" Gurdjieff's cosmic view is centered on the burning question of the significance of the arising of life, and it is this that leads into his assertion: "Life is real only then, when 'I Am.'"*

Contemplation entails holding the elements of our knowledge and experience together in a single view. Such a view is possible only through a certain light—equivalent, perhaps, to that of a laser beam. Ordinarily all the elements of our knowledge and experience are separated out or clumped together in bits and pieces. To bring the "everything" together into the "all" requires a higher energy of seeing.

Immortality and Finer Impressions

NEWTON SPECULATED that God must intervene in the dynamics of the solar system to maintain its stability, an idea we also find echoed in

Gurdjieff's *Beelzebub's Tales,* where he ascribes this role to mechanistically minded archangels.[1] Leibnitz, Newton's contemporary and critic, asked whether God was so lacking in foresight that he failed to endow his universe with a perpetual motion. Gurdjieff was aware of this problem and claimed he had the answer. Perpetual motion is provided by the enneagram, by the combination of the law of three and the law of seven. Of course, this is a relative perpetual motion, in that it is dependent on being fed and on feeding.

The perpetual motion of one cosmos is dependent on the perpetual motion of a higher cosmos; and the perpetual motion of the higher cosmos, in its turn, depends on the perpetual motion of an even higher cosmos, right up to the ultimate cosmos. Another way of talking about this is to say that if God is real, then everything is real, though in its own way. Reality is the whole chain of cosmoses and, by means of it, everything participates in God.

Immortality is actually realized in the midst of the cosmic flux of entropy. We can picture the cosmic flux as a stream descending down a hill and then think of the various organisms arising in this stream as wheels turning in the flux. In the turning, the circularity of process, something is also moved uphill against the stream. Generally what moves uphill serves as food for a higher circularity upstream. Within this two-way flow it is possible for a cosmos to assimilate substances from a higher level that have traveled down stream. This is Orage's poetical picture, which we came across in chapter 9. Though profoundly moving, Orage's picture suffers from its expression in terms of ancient atomism. It is important to grasp that the chemicals he speaks of have the *substance of impressions.* Gurdjieff says that man, as the evolving stem of the biosphere, is relatively unlimited in terms of his "third-being food": ". . . [man] can improve on his impressions to a very high degree and in this way introduce fine 'hydrogens' into the organism. It is precisely on this that the possibility of evolution is based. A man is not at all obliged to feed on the dull impressions of H48, he can have . . . H24, H12, and H6 and even H3. This changes the whole picture . . ." (ISM, p. 321).

To improve on your impressions is to *see.* What sees is not the eye but the "I." In Sufism it is called *ayn.* The different worlds are understood in terms of the seeing that belongs to them, not in terms of what they contain. A change in level of seeing is not a subjective enhancement. Gurdjieff made this point by speaking of levels of *objective reason.* The individual capable of seeing is capable of "knowing ever more and more about the laws of world creation and world maintenance.[2] He is not someone lost in mystic trances.

Deeper perceptions are reflected in the great recurrent myths, as Santillana brilliantly explored in *Hamlet's Mill.* Such myths form a bridge between the world of ordinary perception and the world of extraordinary perception. In doing this, they are forms of communication with higher intelligence. We feel this to be so and some of us have a great longing to reenter the worlds of perception which this ancient learning seems to embody. Gurdjieff may well be one of the few known individuals to have created a new mythology. His masterwork *Beelzebub's Tales,* though by no means accessible to everyone, has inspired thousands of people to awaken to the reality of higher worlds and to strive to enter them or, more accurately, to become part of them.

The ancient myths revolved around the cycles of the heavens, and they were cosmic visions. The ancient shamans, as well as "medicine men" of recent times, spoke of their function in terms of regulating the great forces of nature. To do this, they had to be able to see. We have to realize that this seeing did something for the whole of the planet. It is not a matter of some interior, hidden, and subjective state of mind. It is the core function of humankind, the part the human being should play in the evolution of the biosphere. The "mind" that everyone has and acknowledges is merely an apparatus for processing raw impressions and associations (H48).[3] There are other apparatuses for processing the higher hydrogens. According to Gurdjieff, these apparatuses only come into play with the arising of "I."

The Trouble Spots

The chance of individuality, of having an "I," is not universally distributed throughout the universe. It seems that it is only made possible at certain trouble spots. These are regions where the forces or tendencies coming from below and those coming from above meet, clash, and create uncertainty. We can picture this as a conflict between the upper and the lower dos of the cosmic octave.

To clarify the idea of a disorganizing force coming out of the lower do, we can look at the idea that the earth is being kept in quarantine, separated from contact with higher forces (higher alien intelligences, sanity, sinless beings, etc.). This intuition—which we can find in the writings of, for example, H. G. Wells, C. S. Lewis, Philip K. Dick, and Doris Lessing—is similar to Gurdjieff's. The Gnostics spoke of there being a false creation—the one in which we appear to live—in contrast with the real world of God.

The organizing force of the higher do can be understood in various ways. An interesting one is that the higher state of affairs lies in the future, but it is not accessible either by causality or by the usual run of intention. The reason for this is that there is a barrier between the world of the smaller present moment and the world of *progress*. This is the mi-fa interval. As Gurdjieff explained, nearly all human efforts fail at this interval. People do not recognize that an extra factor is needed, rather than more of the same. This factor appears as something artificial, but progress will not be made without this artificial help. The smaller present moment is not only smaller but, more important, less free. That is why nearly all our efforts result in going nowhere. In other words, time becomes just like Gurdjieff's "pouring of empty into void," or Locke's "perpetual perishing," because nothing real can be achieved.[4]

The introduction of special transformers into the trouble spots has the result of producing *autonomous existence:* entities that, relatively speaking, operate under their own laws. Such existence, produced by a subsidiary creative power, is autonomous within the scale of that creative power. Organic life is autonomous within the context of the sun. It is the means adopted by the sun to enable it to attain mastery over its domain.

The sun cannot have mastery over the earth through direct physical contact, because the planet would vaporize! In a more subtle world, however, the sun and the earth are not separate but brought into contact with each other through the action of organic life. They can communicate. The realm of communication is sometimes called the astral world (*astra* = star) and comes into play at the mi-fa interval.

The combination of physical and subtle actions, meeting and blending together in the interval as life, also creates conditions for the arising of individuality, a *third* kind of action. This third kind of action is intimately connected with the *second* si-do interval. The higher interval is, to use

Bohm's terminology, enfolded in the lower interval. It is unfolded only in the later stages of evolution.

Contemplation of the arising of life reveals deeper and deeper structures of meaning. The three actions meeting in the intervals exemplify the law of three integrating the seven steps of change. The enneagram is like a book that describes this integration. In this sense, it does contain the secret of life. Only, this secret cannot be read without the inner energy of contemplation.

Transmitting Influences

The ray of creation, or cosmic octave, has a twofold meaning. First, we have the creation of the various levels. Second, we have the prospect of a transmission down *through* them (ISM, p. 167). The transmission of influences requires something more than the bare creation of the various levels. At this point we can draw on our scheme of matter, energy, and information.[5] The first order of creation produces different levels of material organization by a progression of separation. There is another order concerned with the transmission of influences, or *information.* Information and matter are then linked in the general exchange of *energy.*

Gurdjieff's cosmic octave reaches from the Absolute down through various stages, or worlds or systems, such as galaxies and stars, including our own sun, to reach a state of blank inertia. Gurdjieff explains this chain of worlds as having certain critical transitions in its structure. The chain is not an unbroken continuum but exhibits structural discontinuities. In *Beelzebub's Tales,* this is explained as a change in the workings of the fundamental law of seven. Local features of the universe, such as our own solar system, also form their own chains and have their own critical points. In particular, there is an awkwardness in the connection to be made between the sun and the planets, on the one hand, and earth, on the other. The essence of the problem is how *higher influences* from the sun and planets can reach into the earth.[6]

The problem arises because of the fa-mi interface. We can imagine this interface as akin to a surface delimited, like a drop of water, by surface tension. It exists between two different states of matter. Both from above and from below, this surface will tend to act as a *mirror.* It is at this interface, which is none other than the surface of the earth, that something is needed to assist the transmission of higher influences into the body of the planet. In place of the surface mirror, we need something like a *lens*. This is provided, so Gurdjieff claims, by *organic life*.

Considering only one octave as spanning the whole range of possibility from the Absolute to Nothing lacks the detail required to show the place of planetary life. As shown in figure 14.1, Gurdjieff divides the primary octave of the ray of creation into three smaller octaves.[7] In the middle octave there is a place for organic life. We can picture the influences emanating from the sun being "refracted" by the various planets, though there is nothing established in physical science that substantiates such an idea.[8]

Gurdjieff's view of life is without any sentimentality. We should take account of the parallel views of Vernadsky, for whom the biosphere was a cosmic phenomena to be understood only within the context of the solar system as a whole. Vernadsky studied the effects of the biosphere on the matter composing the surface of the earth and formulated "biospheric laws" in completely materialistic terms.[9] Almost fifty years before James Lovelock was to publish his Gaia hypothesis—that the biosphere had actively shaped its environment upon the earth, even controlling the earth's climate and regulating the effect of increasing solar radiation—Vernadsky had the elements of such a theory. Life alters the physical nature of the

Ray of Creation		As Three Octaves	
ABSOLUTE	do	do	ABSOLUTE
ALL WORLDS	si		
		. . . . shock (unknown)	
ALL SUNS	la		
SUN	sol	do	SUN
ALL PLANETS	fa		
. . . . shock		. . . . shock (organic life)	
EARTH	mi	do	EARTH
		. . . . shock (unknown)	
MOON	re	do	MOON
ABSOLUTE	do		

14.1. Cosmic octaves.

earth's surface, which includes the atmosphere, hydrosphere, and lithosphere.

According to Russian scientists of the Vernadsky school, "there was a biosphere on earth before there was life."[10] The early "prebiotic" biosphere arose with the formation of the primitive atmosphere. This marked the arising of a circulation of matter and exchange of energy that is the foundation of the *biospheric cosmos*.

All three realms of the atmosphere, hydrosphere, and lithosphere (sometimes poetically evoked by the phrase "wind, waves, and rocks") are involved in the workings of the biosphere. However, the power of the biosphere is in producing a dance of atoms between them. An atom of carbon can have a very long and complex history in its migrations around the planet, not simply exchanging through the processes of photosynthesis and respiration. Carbon lost from the atmosphere or locked into the lithosphere is replenished by inputs from volcanoes. The total carbon cycle is not fully known, but interweaves through the three realms.

The three spheres are media of exchange. It is easy to see an analogy between these three and the "worlds" out of which the three foods of every living being come. In Gurdjieff's teachings, the atmosphere of the earth is associated with awareness on a planetary scale. He implied that it was the repository of ancient memories, rather like a collective unconscious.[11] In more material terms, it is the medium in which extraterrestrial material (in the form of meteors and cosmic dust) and intraterrestrial material (in the form of eruptions from volcanoes) mix. The amount of this material is relatively small at the present time, but in the early or hadean period of the earth it was a major factor. It also serves as a filter for ultraviolet radiation, necessary to preserve complex lifeforms. However, the main exchange of matter taking place through the atmosphere is due to *life*.

According to Gurdjieff, life arose from a "lateral octave," which fills the fa-mi interval in the octave between sun and moon and serves to connect the solar and terrestrial worlds. He ascribes its origin to the sun, acting in a quasi-independent way, as a subordinate type of creator (fig. 14.2). In this conception we find an anticipation of the enneagram. There is a transmission going through the sun. There is also a kind of secondary creation, beginning in the sun, that impinges upon this transmission and *enables it to penetrate into deeper levels*. Thus, we have a crossing-over of

Cosmic Octave					Life Octave
SUN	sol			do	SUN
PLANETS	fa			si	
(interval)	. . .	fa	sol	la	BIOSPHERE
EARTH	mi	mi			EARTH
MOON	re	re			MOON
ABSOLUTE	do	do			

14.2. Branching from the main octave.

octaves in which one produces an action upon the other. Using a metaphor from the physics of light: the universal ray from the Absolute combines with the specific ray from the sun, producing a pattern of interference. It is this pattern which is the origin of organic life. And: "organic life is an indispensable link in the chain of the worlds which cannot exist without it just as it cannot exist without them" (ISM, p. 305).

Organic life, a quasi-independent creation within the cosmic octave, is a center of self-organization, or *autonomic* existence. The term *autonomic* means having laws of its own. Organic life can be considered an echo of the creative power of the sun, while remaining constrained by the conditions occurring on the surface of the earth. In the context of the solar system, it represents the *evolving* aspect. Gurdjieff said that all the levels of the solar system are evolving, too, but their evolution is not possible without the stimulus or contribution of organic life. Here we can refer to Gurdjieff's well-known and shocking statement: "The moon at present *feeds* on organic life, on humanity" (ISM, p. 57). We can picture the whole solar system as autonomous and self-organizing, but this possibility must grow out of localized centers of evolution.[12] Different evolving centers may go in different directions. The harmony of the whole is not mechanically guaranteed.

Organic life on earth is a complex phenomenon in which the separate parts depend upon one another. General growth is possible only on condition that the "end of the branch" grows. Or, speaking more precisely, there are in organic life tissues which are evolving, and there are tissues which serve as food and medium for those which are evolving. Then there are evolving cells within the evolving tissues, and cells which serve as food and medium for those which are evolving. In each separate evolving cell there are evolving parts and there are parts which serve as food for those that are evolving. But always and in everything it must be remembered that evolution is never guaranteed, it is possible only and it can stop in any moment and in any place.

The evolving part of organic life is humanity. Humanity also has its evolving part but we will speak of this later; in the meantime we will take humanity as a whole. If humanity does not evolve it means that the evolution of organic life will stop and this in its turn will cause the growth of the ray of creation to stop. At the same time if humanity ceases to evolve it becomes useless from the point of view of the aims for which it was created and as such it may be destroyed. (ISM, p. 306).

Although Gurdjieff's picture remains one constrained within an hierarchical view, the single vertical column of the ray of creation is now extended sideways into various branches. The branches occur just where there are critical intervals in the vertical line between "the All and the Nothing." But, this sideways extension is not the end of the story: if we have a vertical dimension (of levels) and a horizontal one (of lateral branching), we can also have a dimension of depth. In the third dimension, the ensuing results of vertical and horizontal processes can be integrated; this is represented in the third phase of the enneagram, which we can call the region of "harmonious reconciliation" or, in Bennett's terms, the "flux and reflux of the spirit."[13]

Gurdjieff accommodates the octave of life within the part of the cosmic octave that extends from the sun to the moon. The sun is note sol in the cosmic octave (a curious coincidence!), but it is also the higher do of the octave of life. The lateral octave of life in a stepwise formation is shown in figure 14.2. The notes fa, sol, and la represent what we ordinarily recognize as "the biosphere." As we shall see later, this is tantamount to treating the life octave as starting up on the surface of the earth: the sequence shock, fa, sol, and la representing the *manifestation* of the evolution of life as we know it now. The Russian idea of a "prebiotic" biosphere refers to the do-re-mi precursor.

The structure of the lower part of the octave of life is more complex than it appears in Gurdjieff's diagram. Portraying the do-re-mi of life in terms of absolute-moon-earth is simply to draw a parallel. Just as, in the future, life may reach and colonize other planets of the solar system so, in the past, it may have originated from beneath the surface of the earth. The potential of life is inherent in the stages do-re-mi, but only *manifests* at fa.

The first three stages are not vanished into the past but still remain. They are both literally and symbolically "underground" and connect with our ideas of Hades. They are the nether regions. Gurdjieff also alludes to them as the realm under sway of the moon, the lifeless world. Another way of looking at them is that they are buried in the past. Hence the Russian scientist Lapo's idea of "traces of bygone biospheres."

The American scientist Thomas Gold has argued that there are biospheres throughout the solar system, based on chemosynthesis rather than photosynthesis and, therefore, liable to exist below the planetary surfaces. We can picture the lower do in terms of the energy sources *within the earth*. The interior of the earth is at a much higher temperature than its surface, due to radioactivity and gravitational sorting, and this gives rise to powerful chemical reactions. It may well be, then, that early life—or what is conceived of as the "prebiotic" biosphere—originated below the surface. In the last decade, newly discovered life-forms have been found around deep ocean vents, in effect deriving their energy from the *interior* of the earth.[14] The transition to photosynthesis may then be specifically related to the mi-fa transition. Our do-re-mi stages of the octave of life may include chemosynthetic bacteria, responsible for *cooling the earth* and paving the way for the ancestors of plants.[15]

According to this view, the lower do of the octave of life is to be associated with the energy sources *within the earth*, which are independent of the energy coming from the sun, the higher do. These energy sources largely derive from gravitational sorting. It is more than interesting to associate the lower do with gravitation and the higher do with radiation. The gravitational aspect of the lower do also reminds us of the role of the moon, possibly in relation to its tidal effects on the earth's surface. Influences from the two dos meet at the mi-fa interval which is located on the surface of the earth.

If there was no life on earth, then the ray of creation would be reflected back from the planet, which would act as an impenetrable surface or mirror. This is not so easy to understand, unless we suppose that the *earth* represents material existence and the *sun*, spiritual existence; that is, they are of opposing natures. It is only through the independent arising of life that the two natures can interpenetrate and be reconciled.

If we are to think in terms of evolution, then we must bring in a succession of events as well as a structure of levels. We picture the formation of the solar system from an accretion disk of various gases (possibly triggered to concentrate by a nearby supernova explosion). What becomes the sun derives from the concentration of gas at the center of the disk. The various planets and other bodies of the solar system condense out of the gas in orbit about the central mass. Once planets such as the earth have been formed as solid bodies and the sun has acquired enough energy from gravitational collapse to set off its nuclear reactions and begin to radiate energy, we can see that the earth will be receiving radiation from the sun but that this radiation will be simply re-radiated back into space. This is the physical equivalent to the earth as an impenetrable mirror. It means that the *power* of the sun is unable to penetrate into the earth. What enables this power to come into the earth is *organic life*. In a quite literal sense, organic life brings something of the power of the sun into the material of the surface of the earth.[16]

In the first or simply linear aspect of the ray of creation, all the various levels exist as *matter*. In the second, *energies* coming from a higher level are enabled to penetrate into the lower levels. Because of this interpenetration, *information* can pass between levels, specifically in the case of human beings and the "cosmic information" available to them.

We can therefore form a picture in which we see the emergence of the earth from the accretion disk and reaching a critical point at which the arising of organic life enables the sun and the earth to be coupled together in a new way (fig. 14.3). It was this coupling of sun and earth that Vernadsky considered to be the most important property of life. It is the outer form of the cosmic relation of earth and sun. In figure 14.3, the sequence from the accretion disk to the formation of the planet is represented by a curved line to anticipate the form of the enneagram. The straight line from the sun to the living earth is also anticipatory of what I call a line of command, which corresponds to a line in its triangular figure and is associated with the *logos*.[17]

Life enables the relatively high order of the sun's radiations to be captured and held on the surface of the earth. In evolving, the biosphere transforms the material surface of the planet. While the sun sends radia-

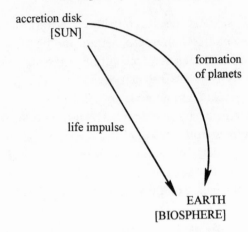

14.3. Life coupling Sun and Earth.

tion largely within the visible range, the earth radiates a lower-grade energy into space, and the high degree of organization represented by the biosphere derives from the difference between the two levels of order. Gurdjieff refers to organic life as an "organ of radiation" and says: "With the help of organic life each portion of the earth's surface occupying a given area sends every moment certain kinds of rays in the direction of the sun, the planets and the moon" (ISM, p. 148). The "rays" he speaks of should be considered more in terms of information than in terms of energy.

The most important role of life on earth is to serve as its *organ of perception*. It must not be supposed that Gurdjieff was entirely unique in addressing the question of how the forces of the earth and the forces of the sun were connected by living systems. It is important to mention the work of Rudolf Steiner (1861–1925), who branched off from the orthodoxy of Theosophy to form his own Anthroposophical movement. Perhaps because of the disparaging remarks about Steiner and his work in *Beelzebub's Tales,* few followers of Gurdjieff's ideas have ever attempted to pursue the many similarities between the two streams of thought. This is a great pity since many of Steiner's ideas provide ways of visualizing the interplay between the worlds that are treated in a more abstract way in Gurdjieff's exposition. Steiner's ideas also established some degree of connection with the mainstream of science, partly through his profound understanding of the methodology of Goethe.[18]

In Steiner's scheme, the "forces of the sun" are forces which act not from a localized center but from the "plane of infinity." These forces, therefore, are more like a suction or a pull than they are like a pressure or a push. In my approach, this means that the suction forces come from the *whole*, while the pushing forces come from the *part*. If we establish in ourselves the visualization of a pulling force, then we can begin to see how this must be intrinsically connected with perception. Steiner puts it this way: "This force of suction, even as it proceeds from the sun, works also in the human being, permeating his etheric body from above downward. In the human body therefore, two opposite entities are at work— solar and earthly. . . . If we perceive it clearly we may truly say that the polarity of sun and earth, into the midst of which the human being is placed, is really felt by us in every sense perception."[19]

The implicit idea in this description is that the "forces of the earth" are incapable of responding to the "forces of the sun": it is only when something embodied in earthly forces is capable of perception that the "force of suction" can produce an effect. The "force of suction" is a remarkable and useful way of visualizing what Gurdjieff meant by "higher influences." We are all too likely to regard any concept of influence as something that is coming from somewhere, a location, and therefore see it in the same way as we see the earthly forces, that is, the "force of pushing." The solar type of force is a structural pull which does not act upon matter but through perception. The higher worlds do not exert a pressure on the lower ones but a pull that is without any feature of localized force. This goes a long way to explain why it is that the important content of the ray of creation can never appear in any scientific study based exclusively on proximate causes. It also gives important substance to the idea that our perception harbors a kind of infinite potential.

What appears more strongly in Gurdjieff than in Steiner is the degree to which emphasis is laid upon uncertainty and hazard. At every stage, evolution is concentrated in small regions and is never guaranteed. He spoke of the historical evidence that humanity has reached a point at which it is moving in a circle so that every advance is at the expense of another retrogression. According to his theory of octaves, nothing can be done about this state of affairs except at one of the critical points of transition. Our task must be to recognize such a point if it occurs in our lifetime.

The Lateral Octave and the Solar System

Gurdjieff describes the lateral octave of the biosphere as being *initiated* by the sun and *starting* from the earth. The high do of the lateral octave of life is the sun. The middle notes fa-sol-la are organic life. This leaves the note si as that which Gurdjieff once called the heavenly host, life at the level of the solar system as a whole. This can be partially understood in terms of specific planetary patterns.

However, when it comes to the enneagram, an intervening octave is not presented in the same way but as a new *do* in the *mi-fa* interval of the main octave. Gurdjieff changed his presentation on different occasions. In the treatment of the ray of creation as three octaves, the main octave begins its ascent from the moon (see fig. 14.1). The moon is an independent center of gravity that attracts the material of the earth's surface. The material from which life arises is ascending away from the influence of the moon. In physical terms, it is indeed suspected that the arising of life on the earth is intimately connected with the contrasting effects of the sun and moon.[20]

The sun acts in the interval as an *energy*.[21] A critical step for the biosphere was the emergence of a means to capture the energy of the sun and bring it into itself, in place of the earlier mechanism of utilizing chemical potentials. If we count this step as the actual do of the octave of organic life, then we have to consider the further development of this new or additional octave. We have to find something that fills the mi-fa interval of *this* octave in its turn: we look for a further intervention (fig 14.4).

Gurdjieff, writing in *Beelzebub's Tales,* says that there was something in the evolution of life "unforeseen from Above." This may be a reference to the fact that the evolving octave of life needs its own kind of shock. The intervention that this requires is not of the same kind as the first. We may think of it as a *third-order* action. In terms of the evolution of life on this planet, it may be thought of in connection with the arising of man, or "three-brained beings," that is, beings capable of autonomous *individuality*. Such beings are capable of assimilating impressions on many levels. The three brains in combination with each other serve to provide an inherent *logos* or reason, capable of creative action in the face of uncer-

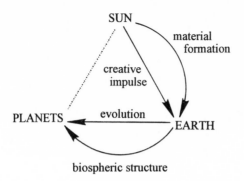

14.4. The requirement for further intervention.

tainty. The arising of three-brained beings is almost inevitable, given the requirement for life, but its consequences are unpredictable.

It is important to realize that any note within an octave can be taken as the do of another octave. In this sense, the first arising of life on this planet constitutes a do. If we now introduce the notion of a further shock (which we have called the third action) we can complete figure 14.4 into the form of a circle (fig. 14.5). When we do so, we have in mind point 9 as some kind of "solar destiny" which is the fulfillment of the sun and the realization of the whole solar system as an autonomous entity on a vast scale. To complete the picture, I have added the starry heavens and

THE STARRY HEAVENS

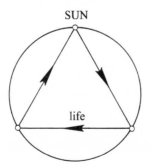

THE OUTER DARKNESS

14.5. Life in the solar system.

the outer darkness. The starry heavens is in the place of "point 10." In ancient times, the link with this realm was widely known as the Milky Way. This vast evolutionary process within the solar system is not only to do with the arising of life; it is also the *working out of a structure*. What this structure is appears to us as the present form of the solar system with its nine planets. The dynamic historical forces which shaped the drama of life on earth find themselves located and focused into the spectrum of planetary existence. What is historical becomes *synchronous*. We have the elements which appear in popular form as astrology.

Synchronous meanings cannot be explained by any causality, so they appear as if they cannot be explained at all or are simply arbitrary. It is nonetheless striking that if we range the planets around the enneagram as in figure 14.6—counting Mercury as point 1, Venus as point 2, and so on—then an interesting perspective emerges. Earth, with its single but massive Moon, appears at point 3. Mars is then point 4, and Jupiter is point 5. Between these two lies the asteroid belt, the chaotic region of the solar system. Point 6 is the place of Saturn. Uranus is point 7 and Neptune point 8. Between points 8 and 9 we find the small and desolate Pluto and its companion Charon, the Oort cloud, and the solar family of comets. The Sun appears as point 0 and, in its fulfillment as a member of a stellar community, as point 9.

The mystic Jacob Boehme called Saturn the "house of the sixfold spirit."[22] It has *three* main sets of rings around it. It is also known from antiquity as Chronos in the West—a lesser force than Kronos, the Greek

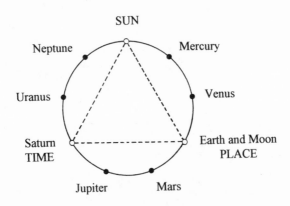

14.6. Planetary synchronicity.

equivalent of the Iranian Zurvan—and as *Kala,* or the Spirit of Time, in India. If Earth is "the place," then Saturn is "the time." Jupiter is the "imitation sun," massive enough to constitute another major force in the solar system. In certain interpretations it is the planet of consciousness, or the manifestation of power. (This is not the place to go into such fascinating lore, but the various correlations I have indicated will also appear in more empirical guise as we go on.) Remembrance of the asteroid belt between points 4 and 5, of the character of point 5 as Jupiter and of point 6 as Saturn or *Kala,* may prove to be useful metaphors.[23]

Notes

1. In the *Opticks,* Newton spoke of "inconsiderable Irregularities" in the solar system, arising through "the mutual Actions of Comets and Planets upon one another" which would occasionally demand a "Reformation" of the system. What is also interesting about this is that it is the very same scenario used by Gurdjieff to explain the action of archangels, who, to offset the irregularity introduced by a "madcap comet," were led to suppress human evolution.
2. This is one of Gurdjieff's five "strivings." See "Striving to Know Ever More and More." in chapter 16.
3. H48, or "hydrogen of density 48," is one of the hydrogens shown in Gurdjieff's diagram of the enneagram of the three foods of man. H48 marks the beginning of the octave of impressions.
4. I am now speaking of the cosmic octave as a vast present moment instead of a vast spatial architecture. In Bennett's model of the present moment, there is more than the dyad of past and future. Other features include the dyad of value and form and the tension of progress and retrogression. See chapter 19.
5. See "The Three" in chapter 6.
6. It is inevitable that our minds turn to astrology. If we go back to the time of Newton, evidence abounds of serious, advanced and experimental scientists—such as Newton himself and William Gilbert, famous for his studies of magnetism—being deeply concerned with this self-same problem. Most were believers in astrology. Gilbert's book *On the World* ends with a spirited attempt to provide a physical basis for it.
7. Fig. 14.1 combines material from two places in ISM, pp. 139–40 and 169.
8. The influence of the sun itself is another matter, but here physical science is concerned only with radiant energy and effects of the solar wind. Interestingly enough, the solar wind primarily affects our atmosphere and, through this, may affect organic life. Writing in the nineteenth century, Jevons proposed the idea that *cosmical variations,* including solar flares, had a great influence on human life, largely determining the cycles of economic behavior. W. S. Jevons, *Investiga-*

tions in Currency and Finance). Jevons's ideas are discussed in James Davidson and William Rees-Mogg, *The Great Reckoning,* p. 276. They also say that: "There is . . . established evidence of climatic fluctuations associated with the gravitational pull of the nearer planets on the earth's orbit." Rejected by the scientific community for more than a hundred years, such ideas are now taken more seriously. With recent discoveries in patterns of chaos, it is now easier to appreciate that small changes in parameters can have large-scale effects. However, there is one very important piece of physical evidence concerning the influence of the planets. It appears that the raw material of the earth's surface is particularly suited to the information of life. Now, some of this material came from outside the earth. In the early period of the planet, before the formation of the atmosphere, when the solar system had far more "debris" swirling around it than exists today, vast quantities of material impacted on the earth's surface, including material knocked off Mars. On the whole, the material was peculiarly favorable for the arising of a biosphere. See Christopher Chyba and Carl Sagan, "Endogenous production, exogenous delivery and impact-shock synthesis of organic molecules: an inventory for the origins of life," *Nature* 9 (January 1992).

9. See the appendix "Living Matter and the Evolution of Species" in Vladimir Vernadsky, *The Biosphere.*

10. See A. Lapo, *Traces of Bygone Biospheres.*

11. This is a fairly common idea, which can be found in the writings of Rudolf Steiner, for example. It relates to the intuition of a "pool of memory," or reservoir of experience, that I will discuss in the final chapter (as well as Jung's "collective unconscious"). Its association with the atmosphere or air is inevitable given the structure of the psychocosmology.

12. In a similar fashion, it is being suggested that the genetic material or organisms is dynamically self-organizing, irrespective of environmental factors, and that this dynamic arises from small regions within it. Cf. Stuart Kauffman, "Antichaos and Adaptation," *Scientific American* (August 1991).

13. See chapter 35 in J. G. Bennett, *The Dramatic Universe* vol. 2.

14. See *Proceedings of the National Academy of Science,* July 1992.

15. See D. Schwartzman et al. in "Did Surface Temperatures Constrain Microbial Evolution?" *Bioscience* 43, no. 6.

16. But only after photosynthesis has been attained.

17. See "The Logos" in chapter 6.

18. It is striking that some of the recent pioneers of the new science of chaotics have found a resonance with this methodology and even an appreciation of the work of some of Steiner's followers; cf. James Gleick, *Chaos.*

19. Quoted in George Adams, *Physical and Ethereal Spaces,* p. 61.

20. The moon "denies" the sun, in contrast to the earth which can be "receptive" to the sun.

21. In terms of our three basic categories of matter, energy, and information: the earth provides matter; the sun, energy; and the stars, information. That is why it

is sometimes said that we—that is, conscious individuals—come from the stars. Man is the animal that can find meaning in the stars. Philip K. Dick writes: "In creatures of all kinds there is a major instinct system that is termed 'homing.' An example is the return of the humpback salmon from the ocean back up the stream to the exact spot where they were spawned. By analogical reasoning, man can be said possibly to possess—even unknown to himself—a homing instinct. This world is not his home. His true home is in the region of the heavens that the ancient world called the pleroma. The term occurs in the N.T. but the meaning is obscure, since the exact meaning is 'a patch covering a hole.' In the N.T. it is applied to Christ, who is described as the 'fullness of God,' and to believers who attain that fullness through faith in Christ. In the Gnostic system, however, the term has more definite meaning. It is the supralunar region in the heavens from which comes the secret knowledge that brings salvation to man." *The Shifting Realities of Philip K. Dick,* p. 306.

22. Jacob Boehme, *How a Man May Find Himself and So Finding Come to All Mysteries, Even to the Ninth Number, Yet No Higher,* p. 12.

23. An important and useful text, which makes reference to the enneagram in this context, is *The Gnostic Circle,* by Patrizia Norelli-Bachelet. The arrangement of planets around the enneagram is often associated with astrology and, right from the time of Rodney Collin, the enneagram has been used as a system of astrological types. This was probably the precursor of the "enneagram of fixations" interpretation of Oscar Ichazo. However, this in no way detracts from the creative step that Ichazo made. What is more important is the fact that the enneagram came under the "attractor" of humans wanting to explain themselves and their limitations in relation to each other. This can be seen as a kind of "deviation" from the original vision in which the psychological and the cosmological were one whole. In general, the astrological approach is degenerate in this respect, because the cosmological aspect is reduced to the symbolic. The interesting, and possibly redeeming feature of the concern with typologies is that they are an intimation of the *synergic* idea, as expressed by Bennett. According to this intimation, the different types or elements can learn how to cooperate with each other to produce a coalescence in which a greater degree of wholeness may be realized. It is also true, though this would require a whole book to explain, that we humans can "play the role" of cosmic elements in their relations with each other. We have only to think of the roles of male and female, with which we are all familiar, to begin to feel the possibilities. The present sexual-linguistic conflict is just an episode in a long exploration by the human race of how it is possible for us to play these roles *consciously* and not be identified with them. As a far extension, we may think of combining the horizontal array of types with a vertical structure such as we find in Bennett's Ideal Human Society (*The Dramatic Universe,* vol. 3). The possibilities are legion, and the practical implications are profound.

· 15 ·

The Greater Present Moment

Gurdjieff says in Beelzebub's Tales *that it is highly probable that at no time will mankind have a common religion. This is quite a shattering statement. It suggests that all our usual ideas about world unity and common values are suspect. However, it is relatively easy to accept it as true as the twentieth century draws to a close, in a world more discordant than ever. New ideas emerge to take account of the facts which we cannot escape. This is an integral part of the teachings in Gurdjieff's book: free creative intelligence is always challenged to come up with ideas which neutralize the malevolent consequences of current assumptions. It is now incumbent on us to embrace in a single vision several, and sometimes mutually contradictory, views. It is a new vision of consciousness, an influx from the Creative Source into how we see.*

Enneagram of Worldviews

THE GREATER PRESENT MOMENT is an idea of Bennett's.[1] It is that our experience of now, even of our whole life, exists within a larger "now," corresponding to some higher order of intelligence. If we could enter the perception corresponding to the Greater Present Moment, then the whole sequence of an individual life, or even of successive generations, would appear as contemporary. We would then have a truly historical kind of consciousness. It would not be entirely retrospective but would include the *future*. It would extend beyond what has actually happened into the realms of meaning and purpose. What appears to us as past and fixed and what appears to us as open and yet to come would be so intimately connected that they could *exchange information* with each other.

In this chapter, I presume the form of such a historical consciousness, able to see how the Greater Present Moment is being shaped. The enneagram can be used as a model of a present moment on any given scale. The temporal span of the Greater Present Moment that concerns us includes the whole of the twentieth century and what might lie ahead in the twenty-first. However, this is not a matter of making predictions or seeing into the future. The future is still in process of being worked out, and what is significant is hardly predictable. We are going to look at the dominant attractors which may hold sway in the drama which enfolds us. These attractors will be described in terms of human visions. In some ways, what we are after is akin to the formation of a mirror from all the thoughts of mankind which might be capable of reflecting the deep knowledge.[2]

The human visions which concern us are the attitudes of mind which determine how the world of human experience and, consequently the external world, might be shaped. Our understanding of human nature depends on the world we are aware of. We live in a world partly already given, shaped, and ordered in various ways, and partly of our own making. We need to question the limits of our power over this world; indeed, people have been questioning this for centuries, perhaps for thousands of years (at least from the time of the Sumerians). Our power is not unlimited, partly because it is finite and partly because we do not *see* enough.

Gurdjieff points out that there is no single understanding of the word *world*. The world out there, the surface of our planet, is only one of many possibilities. The world defined by human experience, language, and history is yet another. Then there is the meaning of *world* in terms of many worlds, higher worlds, or even the whole world, or universe.[3] Hence, "world" in the enneagram is not invariant but corresponds to a way of seeing. The relation we have with the world is different in each of the three phases of the enneagram. In the first, the world is where we are and the place to which we belong. In the second, we find ourselves strangers in the world, alienated. In the third, we can transform the world as we transform ourselves. This means that what *world* signifies is different in each of the three phases.

On the right-hand side of the enneagram will be the tangible elements. On the left-hand side, the intangible ones. From this perspective, the pairs of terms *across* the enneagram are complementary to each other.

The drama of the Greater Present Moment is that of "making a new world."[4] We start from the premise that we are at a critical juncture, an idea I explored in chapter 12. We are moving from one epoch into another. The enneagram is polarized between two quite different interpretations of current history, stemming from the overlap of two different epochs. What I am offering may be no more than a plausible story, a myth of the times. This is, after all, an important aspect of our dilemma. The reason for saying this lies in our discussion of what *the world* means. For each of the attractors, *the given attitude is optimal for its corresponding world*. Each worldview determines what is rational or good; so it is not strictly correct to regard any attractor as superior to another.

We begin with the opening chord of the Greater Present Moment, characterized by confidence in our own powers and in the rationality of the universe—an inheritance from the proceeding thousand years of history. With the spread of democracy and the expansion and speeding up of world communications and technological innovation, a new phase of global awareness has been initiated. Humanity's view of the universe has been radically altered by discoveries in astronomy, geology, evolution, and the structure of matter.

The attractors specifying the emerging drama of the Greater Present Moment, represented as the nine points on the enneagram, can be summarized in the following way.

Point 1: The attractor of rationality and planning. The attitude here is that we find out what we need to know, and on the basis of this, we calculate what is to be done. All of the world's problems can be solved by reasoning, engineering, and management. A modern exponent of this attitude would be Buckminster Fuller. It is important to notice that these problems are all thought of in terms of the external world. Man can make the world into his own image. He does not have to change.

Of course, this attitude had its origins centuries before, but it has a certain poignancy when we consider the impact of the First World War, the rise of the totalitarian states, and the breakdown of classical science. Even without this impact, we have to remember that an overemphasis of this attitude was predominantly a Western phenomena. The more traditional Eastern view emphasized otherworldly values. Hence, we saw the influx of spiritual teachers from the East into the West, just when the West was losing its confidence. This points toward a different attractor, at point 2, concerned with the search for values.

Point 2: The attractor of belief and authority. The attitude here is that all knowledge and understanding of the world stems from underlying beliefs which ultimately cannot be reasoned out. It has its own rational basis in the fact that we tend to adopt a worldview on the basis of emotion first and then seek to justify it intellectually afterward. It is the realm of what ought to be instead of what actually is. Therefore, it is liable to be dogmatic. The attractor at point 2 is associated with the secular mysticism of the communist and fascist states and the reactionary religious fundamentalist movements, as well with the seekers who were to give birth to "New Age–ism." In general, this attractor has the character of mass movements or cults.

These first two points offer an overall perspective on the nature of the epoch. The rational element is progressive and deals in linear time, while the believing element tends toward a more static view. Both perspectives are validated by the present situation, in which we see not only radical advance and change but also much stagnation. In broad historical terms, we may also think of Toynbee's civilizations and their tendencies toward universal states (point 1) and universal religions (point 2). This is simply to point out that we can always find broader and broader interpretations of the points, depending on the scale of events that we have in mind.

Point 3: Here an important and new element comes into focus. It is no longer possible to anchor ourselves by means of rational knowledge or belief. *Reality itself is uncertain.* We have to make choices that put the value of our lives at risk. Bennett discussed this important new transition in terms of his master idea of hazard. The incursion of the idea that hazard is integral to reality opened a gateway in the human situation. However, what is a gateway to some is a barrier to others, as we shall also see in the case of point 6. A great number of people refused, and continue to refuse, to pass through this gateway into the birth of another kind of world. Instead, what we find in the unfolding of history is a backlash, a reversion to fundamentalism, nationalism, and other ideologies. This amounts to a *deviation in the octave.* A whole sector of humankind has gone off to live in the past.

Point 4: The attractor of the existential and contingent. The existentialists center on the fact that the act of choice is implicit in every moment and that there are no rules outside of this act to tell us what to do. We have to fill the void of uncertainty by our own actions. Neither reasoning (point 1) nor belief (point 2) can support us. Sartre says: "Man is condemned to be free." In parallel with this, in the domain of science itself, we have people such as Stephen Jay Gould who consider that biological evolution has no direction and is only an accumulation of contingent changes.[5] The historian H. A. L. Fisher sees European history as a series of contingencies having no pattern, no rhyme or reason.[6]

Part of the pull of this attractor is the feeling that we are on our own. It also pulls us into *action* and away from thought and feeling. It wakes us up to reality, to the here and now. We are what we do. The sense of anxiety this produces can lead us to look for personal power. This is a big issue in the context of the Greater Present Moment, because we witness the release of immense powers in the external world. Our vulnerability can be translated into a quest for power in ourselves. Here we meet up with the present times and its confusion. We look for the way out.

Point 5: The attractor in this case is liberation. In contrast with the existentialist, there is a type of "essentialist" who seeks escape from the world altogether. This individual seeks after a separate power in himself. This is the domain of sexuality and sorcery, of mind-enhancing drugs and revolt against the hold of society. In its most extreme forms, it regards the universe as hostile and alien. Castaneda's Don Juan wants to "dart past the Eagle," to escape the great force or entity that holds humankind in thrall. What is sought is freedom with substance. It is the attractor of creativity. This may pull us inward or outward.

The liberationist is set on divorcing himself from the world. He wants to be part of an elite. He is Colin Wilson's "outsider." The difficult point here is that only someone who has attained personal power has the strength to go further, and yet it is just this selfsame power that can hold him back. There is a need of cooperation among the liberationists, if they are to get anywhere. This is what they find most difficult to bring to realization. The possibility of such cooperation means that there must be a corresponding higher world order. People who would escape have to go somewhere. We find all kinds of beliefs about what this might entail, including the fairly common one that our world has been invaded by aliens. This carries the implication of a higher order of reality—maybe on another planet than our own—which already exists in some sense. In nearly all cases, the alternative "higher world" is *elsewhere.*

Point 6: What enters at point 6 should contrast with and complement what enters at point 3. The best term for this we can find is *providence.* It is the view that the world is providentially arranged to support, guide, and develop the potential evidenced in humans or, more generally, in life. There is a helping hand out of heaven or from some higher intelligence. There are higher influences, such as those Gurdjieff described as starting from outside of life. At point 6, the higher order can touch the lower order. A communication becomes possible. This is another gateway and also, at the same time, another barrier. The recoil from this point is back into the "cult" of humanity as it is, that identifies intelligence with its human and historical form.[7] This is the shadow side of the positive attitude that all mankind can share in higher values.

The next attractor is brought into play by an act of faith. Here, faith should be distinguished from belief, because it is effective as a connection with a higher order of events in a way that mere belief is not. What holds people back is the rejection of the world and elitism, properties of point 5. Expressed in religious terms, this amounts to failure to understand Saint Augustine's statement "Even sin serves." The world then appears as a place of horror and abomination, the work of the devil. The gnostic vision of the world as a "false creation" of the demiurge can be a cul-de-sac, in spite of its superior insight—if there is no faith in the power of what lies beyond.

Point 7 is the attractor of oneness and the cessation of separateness. It is unitive and usually associated with mysticism. However, this is not the vague and comfortable mysticism of the New Agers. It is the radical commitment to a change of being. Whereas the existentialist has to fill the present moment with his own act and the liberationist believes that the present moment is in fact empty, or "other," the true mystic *knows* that it is already full. The attraction is toward some final dissolution in a higher order. The mystic wants to drown in the ocean of God, to become one with the All. He is suffused with a sense of union. Its various forms include pantheism and the spirit cultures, including their recent information-technological manifestations.[8] The pull of this attractor is that of a "decreation" of the world, seeing past appearances to the Source (in earlier times, most beautifully expressed in the anonymous classic *The Cloud of Unknowing*). On the personal level, it may require a preliminary dissolution of the self, a "breaking apart" or inner death.

In Sufi tradition, there was an alternative to absorption into the Divine and the idea that God is everything. In this alternative, the individual retains his own reality but is integrated into the ongoing realization of truth.[9] In Gurdjieff's terms, this is the possibility of objective reason. Man retains his role as a processor of cosmic information. This brings us to the next attractor.

Point 8 is the attractor of the *supramental*. The term *supramental* was used by Sri Aurobindo to designate a higher form of intelligence in which the human could play an active role.[10] In this way, he or she can make a contribution to the world evolution, both physical and spiritual. The evolution of the individual and of the world are coupled together. This is associated with the traditional image of Masters of Wisdom in Sufi lore.[11] Such beings are supposed to maintain the world by their work and to correct for entropic trends by introducing new paths of transformation. Supermyths, such as that of the epochs used in this chapter, belong here. I will have more to say about the characteristic operation of the supramental later.

Point 9: The supramental attractor is under the sway of the synergic spirit at point 9, which it interprets in terms of master ideas. Synergy means "working together" (*syn* = together; *energeia* = working) and has been applied in modern times to technological development. Its original meaning was that of cooperation between the individual and God in humanity's salvation.[12] Bennett understands it in general as cooperation between different levels. It is at point 9 that we participate in higher intelligence, because we can "eat" cosmic information. Man and God enter into dialogue. The most astonishing feature of this view is the implication that even the higher level, God, *has to learn.*

If we now look solely at the points of the triangular figure, we can illustrate them in terms of physical science in the twentieth century. Point 3, of course, relates to the rise of quantum theory. Point 6 is only now finding expression in science—as insight into the deep structure (or "implicate order" in Bohm's phrase) of the universe.[13] Point 9 is even more radical, implying that the laws of the universe are themselves evolving.[14] As far as our picture of the human being is concerned, we can associate point 3 with the incursion of the idea of the unconscious—in other words, that consciousness is *plural*. This renders human motivation uncertain. In relation to this, point 6 can be associated with the rise of cultural relativism and its deeper ramifications in the prospect of a "transcultural personality"—while the final point 9 is being foreshadowed in the idea of "trans-specism," that the human being is but one element in a biospheric totality. The personal, social, and global forms of consciousness are in their revolutionary throes (see fig. 15.1).

Change of Epoch

The idea of epochs rests on the assumption that there is some overall orientation of mind among humankind and that this changes in definite intervals of time. These orientations seek to resolve some of the accumulated problems of the past, as well as point a way into the future. By their very nature, they persist for a long time, at least in human terms. Every change of epoch requires a breaking with the previous orientation and the taking up of something new.

The idea of epochs probably first arose several thousand years ago, when people first realized through their observations of the heavens that the patterns of the stars were subject to change. The "birth of time" must have been a shattering event.[15] Since that event (the precursor to our recent discovery of the Big Bang in which the universe came into existence), the epochs have been measured in time periods that are fractions of the Great Cycle in which the equinoxes make their precession, some twenty-five thousand years.

The belief that there is a correlation between terrestrial and cosmic events is an important one. It can be considered simply as a belief (point

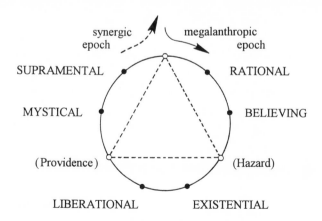

15.1. Making a new world.

2) or as an insight into the supramental (point 8). It offers the prospect of *aligning* ourselves with a tendency *inherent in the times* that will render our own efforts more effectual.

We can understand the content of the enneagram as a process of transforming the old epoch into the new, or of making a new world. According to Bennett, the synergic attractor is the call of the new age, the synergic epoch, bringing us out of the old age, the *megalanthropic* epoch. The last epoch was centered on individual human powers. Its residue is seen in our own time as emphasizing both the importance of genius and the tendency toward democracy. However, both these attitudes are being severely eroded as they mutually interfere with each other. The sources of human genius are being investigated in new ways that lessen man's unique claim to intelligence.[16] Democracy is no longer accepted as the only advanced form of government, partly because its implementation is proving so complex (as can be seen in Africa, the former Soviet Union, and even in the established Western democracies that are so bound up with rapid developments in the communication media).

It is too simplistic to associate the old age with point 0 and the new age with point 9. The old age recurs in the transition period. It has to be worked out and exhausted. That is why the kind of pattern we find in the enneagram is no simple ladder of advance but more akin to a *descent and new creation*. The new epoch cannot be built on the old, nor can the old be completely destroyed before the new arises. The friction between the two is the "energy of the time," associated with the bottom part of the enneagram.

Because of the time in which we live as individual people, coming up to the year 2000, the last pair of attractors (7 and 8) still appear to us in mystical terms. This is misleading. What appears to us as "mystical" belongs to the emotional imagery of point 2. To change terminology, what is really *spiritual* now will not appear as such. The nature of points 7 and 8 is not fixated on meditation and piety. These points really concern radical changes in the modes of perception and communication that people exercise. These changes are so radical that they can be said to amount to a change in human nature. We just do not know what is involved, only that there has to be some change. This will affect how human reality is to be seen—the relation between the individual and the collective, and the relation between internal human structure and outer communities.

If we think in terms of Gurdjieff's injunction to "strive to know ever more and more about the laws of world creation and world maintenance," we can understand the present situation as one in which humankind struggles to balance the forces of creativity and innovation with those of stability and conservation. Gurdjieff's myths concerning the role of angels, archangels, and sacred individuals in the drama of human life are also an expression of the deep forces working in the human consciousness. Bennett understood this as requiring a new understanding of "systems," or dynamic holistic structures. Hence his idea of synergy.

Interpretation of the apex point can take many forms. If, for example, we characterize the enneagram mainly in terms of the triangular figure or *logos,* then it appears different from descriptions stemming from the progression around the outer circle. We can picture, for example, the whole *logos* as a divine energy, or even in a personal way, as the intention of a new avatar. Sri Aurobindo himself laid claim to the role of Kalki, the new and final incarnation of Vishnu the Preserver. Others have prophesied the coming of a new messiah. In general, attention to the triangular figure leads us toward an interpretation in terms of revelation. This provides an important and necessary complement to any interpretation that stems from the standpoint of the progressive empiricism delineated in the outer circle. We can, for example, see the whole event in terms of a primary emanation from point 9, dividing into the two complementary modes of points 3 and 6, the "question" and the "answer."

The "old world" was impelled by a sense of increasing order in the world, an impulsion which culminated in the facile optimism and belief in progress that characterized much of the Western world in the nineteenth and early twentieth centuries. More recently, this has come to be seen as a chimera. It is more and more apparent that there is no progress in time at all, just as Gurdjieff said. This does not mean, however, that there is no progress.

We could fold the enneagram in half from left to right and refuse to acknowledge any advance, interpreting the higher forms of the left-hand side as simply imaginative versions of what we have on the right-hand side. This version would be a flat one, without any differences of level. Consequently, all advances would then be considered imaginary. We hardly begin to understand the contribution made by the mystic or the

seer to human history. Those who we presume have a higher consciousness are not sitting in governments!

We can see the circle of the enneagram in terms of descent and ascent.
The bottom part of the enneagram depicts a low point, a sphere of confusion in which the old values are lost and the new not yet attained. That is
why we find ourselves forced to couch the left-hand points in mystical
terms. This simply represents the fact that we have not as yet realized
what they mean in practice. This is not merely a lack of evidence in the
ordinary sense. We are not able to *see* the content of these attractors from
the perspective of the middle part of the enneagram. We would be able
to *see* points 7 and 8 only from the perspective of point 9, that is, from
the creative future. This order of perception would belong to the Greater
Present Moment. To attain this perception, we would have to detach
from that of our ordinary lives. I believe that this kind of perception does
come to people, only there is an enormous *communication gap*, indicated
in the enneagram by point 6 purely as an opening. As things stand, we
have no means of rational discourse on humanity's relationship with
higher intelligence.

Point 6 can appear to us as a mirror, in that all that has gone before is
reflected back as an image. In the more restricted view, the points beyond
6 are *merely* images. There is no higher intelligence, only ourselves. In the
less restricted view, what is reflected back only *appears* as ourselves. What
we see as an image of ourselves is more than ourselves: it is the Other
within our midst. We are fixed as humans with a specific nature only
within the range of our conscious minds.

The inner lines in the diagram represent the search for meaning that
we all undertake in some degree or other. Although my identification of
the different points is only provisional, we can begin to "read" the inner
lines. Take 1-4-2. The rationalist discovers that reality is basically uncertain (1-4). What is he to do? One thing he is likely to do is to revert to a
belief system (4-2). However, in doing so, he might take with him the
primary sense of uncertainty, which would change his beliefs. If, on the
other hand, he cannot make this integration, he will fall victim to what is
called the conversion syndrome. This happens a lot, even with intelligent
people. It happened to Sartre, who saw that there could be no effective
social structure or ethics on the basis of his existentialism and so became
a Marxist.

Whether the path 1-4-2 is degenerative or constructive depends on whether the further step is made, the linkage 2-8. The supramental (point 8) is not a dogma but rests entirely on the perception that there is some higher order of intelligence which is involved in the destiny of the world. Any creed or set of statements about this order is not what is essential. A critical point is that we have to take into account our "believing nature." Mastering this is very important. It offers the alternatives of imprisonment in dogma or a means of opening the mind to higher influences.

Points 1 and 8 complement or mirror each other. In the former, we have the world only as fact, as something to be studied, known, and dealt with. In the latter, we have the world as value, and as something to be created.[17]

Perhaps one of the central attitudes of point 8 is that any act of intelligence we perform has already been occasioned by an infusion from the supramental order. In the supramental operation, first the supramental descends, and then, we ascend into it. Without the first action, the second is not possible—or becomes a mere fantasy. When the descent of the supramental is taken in a subjective, personal way it is already degenerate, and the operation fails. There has to be a high degree of objectivity that includes impartiality toward one's own and others' experiences. Lack of this impartiality is evident in the fragmented, self-indulgent, and mutually exclusive movements sweeping the world, in which various "spiritual authorities" claim exclusive access to the truth. Anyone who strives to see the whole, to become impartial, is making an invaluable contribution to the welfare of the world.[18]

One of the striking forms of subjective response to the descent of the supramental is the world-rejection I have associated with point 5: the perception that what is most obvious is that the world is "wrong." This may even produce an incapacitating state of horror at the world, or the "Nero tendency" to fiddle while Rome burns. If the "eye of the heart"— what Gurdjieff calls the higher emotional center—is awakened, then the transition to the next point (point 7) is made. However, the mystic may be completely subjective and locked into his experiences. As a gnostic, he may evolve his own cosmology, but he has not yet made contact with what Gurdjieff calls the higher intellectual center. This means that he is still subject to belief, including belief in his own visions. In the early centuries of Christianity, there were a bewildering number of gnostic cosmologies, so many that the church was forced to suppress them all for the sake of establishing one set of beliefs that people could believe in. If we look at those events in the light of our enneagram, we can see that in doing this the church cast itself in the role of the supramental!

As with all these inner linkages, there are very great uncertainties in the triad 8-5-7. The content of point 7 is, it could be said, enlightenment. This is often taken to be a terminal point, an ending. However, in essence, it should serve as an *introduction* to unification with the supramental, or the "communion of saints" in Christian language (the true church infused with the Holy Ghost, or third force). Enlightenment gives the light by which *to see a higher world order*. Many great mystics have had profound influence on the conduct of human affairs. This is expressed, as we shall see in the next chapter, in the Beatitudes as the peacemakers. According to Gurdjieff, for example, two hundred conscious men and women could stop wars! They would do this not by holding peace conferences but by transforming energies.

Correlation with Centers

The attractor model of the ways of seeing may remind us of Gurdjieff's psychological scheme. In this scheme, the directives and characters of our actions and perceptions arise from the work of different centers. But Gurdjieff does not adhere to any one model: sometimes he speaks of three, sometimes of four or five or more such centers. The reason for this is that they are not *things* or objects but related to our *will* and *perception*. The structure and composition of the centers we distinguish depends on our view of the human being. It is usual to think of three centers—thinking, feeling, and moving—which seem to make obvious sense. However, on other occasions, he speaks of a sex center and, as I mentioned in earlier chapters, of a higher emotional and a higher intellectual center.

Our scheme of attractors can map into centers only with such qualifications in mind. As a first approximation, we can take the enneagram in layers and label them as shown in figure 15.2. I have called point 5 the higher moving center purely on analogy with how I have labeled points 7 and 8. There is no direct reference to such a center in any of Gurdjieff's writings or talks. It may well be, however, that his "instinctive center" belongs in this place. The instinctive center deals with the inner regula-

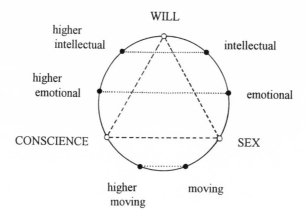

15.2. Enneagram as a diagram of centers.

tion of the body and is capable of prodigious feats of computation. It understands the mechanics of life. In one of his strange remarks, Gurdjieff says: "If you could become conscious in the instinctive center, you could talk with worms." It is also the seat of our *power,* and Gurdjieff sometimes alludes to a "big accumulator," accessing which is a momentous event in personal experience. Each of the higher centers gives access to a type of accumulator or power source. For point 7, the higher emotional center, this is the power of love. For point 8, the higher intellectual center, it is the power of cosmic information. In the case of point 5, the higher physical center, it is the power of life that Bennett called the Great Life Force. All three powers manifest in spiritual actions among humankind.

The layer shown in figure 15.2 by a dotted line between points 3 and 6 is intriguing. We would suspect these two points to correspond to *relational* kinds of centers since they govern critical transitions. Immediately, point 3 as the sex center springs to mind. The meeting of gametes is the basic hazard of human existence.[19] This leads us by association to consider point 6 as *conscience.* Gurdjieff calls conscience an organ and says that it is one of the few inner organs in us which has not completely atrophied. To see the line from 3 to 6 as spanning between the sex organs and conscience is quite startling. We should remember, however, that sex can allow a direct perception of the inner life of others.

To complete the triangular figure, we ascribe *will* to point 9. We must emphasize, however, that it is not to be confused with our ordinary ideas about willpower, which is not really will at all. What we mean can best be understood in terms of a compound concept of the "will to cooperate." The idea of such a will has hardly ever been considered, yet it is crucial for an understanding of our present predicament. It is similar to what the Greeks called *agape* and differs from the will of sex, or *eros.* Conscience is then yet another form of will, which we might understand as the will of submission that rightly governs our relationships with what is higher.

The points can also be described in terms of their dominant mode of *meaning.* To shorten our explanations, let us simply tabulate the points, including some possible correlations with Gurdjieff's centers:

0. *Survival.* Personality. Everyday life.
1. Rationality. Thinking center. Language.
2. Belief. Emotional center. Images.
3. *Hazard.* Sex center.
4. Existentialism. Moving Center. Action.
5. Liberationism. Higher moving (or instinctive) center. Energies.
6. *Providence.* Conscience.
7. Mergence. Higher emotional center. Love.
8. Supramental. Higher intellectual center. Truth.
9. *Synergy.* Cooperation.

The apex point (0/9) is not a center as such. I have included a reference to point 0 for completeness and to emphasize that all of the succeeding stages are significant advances.

Interpreting Progress

It should be made clear that the enneagram describes the domain of significant advance. It does not include the insignificant and shortsighted muddle in which we live for most of the time, merely surviving as personalities. Every one of the points of the enneagram, including point 1, is a positive realization. To enter the enneagram, we have to cross a threshold. This means that we have to have some aim relevant to the whole and also some experience of a significant part of it. We will then tend to gravitate toward one or the other of the nodal points.

To plan and calculate (point 1) or to believe in something higher (point 2) is not nothing, even when such attractors serve to blind us to the deeper possibilities.

I have attempted to show something of the *cumulative* character of the enneagram as we proceed from 0 to 9. In a simplistic sense, point 1 is associated with fact and point 2 with fiction. Both are important in human life, though even put together they are not enough. It may seem strange to depict the moving center and action as an advance on the previous stages, but this is an advance in terms of *concreteness*. We do more than we know and all the images we have of what we do are only partial and inadequate representations. Paying attention to what we *actually do* is a major breakthrough and changes everything. It is crucial for Gurdjieff's method.

When we pass from point 4 to point 5, the outer events of the world no longer appear real, and so we look behind the veil where we make contact with energies rather than behaviors. In the third phase of the enneagram, we enter the domain of wholeness and reconciliation. The will becomes important, and we can have a total experience. The mystic seeks to pierce the cloud of unknowing with the shaft of love. Finally, at point 8, the only issue is that of truth. This truth includes the harmony of fact and value.

It is difficult to discuss the various points because of our own tendency to evaluate them from the point of view of just one of them. The inner lines indicate how we should go in making a more objective evaluation, passing through each of the points but not as they appear around the circle. This enables us to take into account the primary interfaces that occur between the different phases or realms. For example, in the linkage 1-4-2, we study the implications of the incursion of the idea of hazard. In the linkage 8-5-7, we study the implications of providence. The link between 2 and 8 I have already mentioned. What of the link between 7 and 1? It is the recognition that, whatever our internal condition, the world remains—the world of doing, of shopping, of making money. Gurdjieff referred to it as the material question. Rational thought remains, after all. It was, for Steiner, the fundamental starting point. The point is that any higher attainment should include rational thought and not exclude it. We have always to live in the external world we have in common with every-one else. More than that, when this line is activited, it means that we have a "mysticism of the everyday" and the usual separation between inner experiences and outer knowledge no longer obtains.[20] This is absolutely crucial in the weaving of the *fabric of understanding.* It is this connection that ties the knot in the whole.

The middle realm between 4 and 5—representing the "fire of the age" or, to use Castaneda's term, the "energy of the times"—appears destruc-tive. That is why we feel our own age to be one of degeneracy and break-down. It is only when we can see beyond the veil of external events that this energy appears as creative and transforming. Alice Bailey, for exam-ple, saw the rise of the horrific totalitarian states of fascism and commu-nism as the visible side of the action of what she calls the first ray, the ray of willpower, which is the one informing our present age.[21] The interplay between points 4 and 5 is between where we have to do everything for ourselves (point 4) and where there is nothing to be done (point 5). We can see that the issue highlighted here is to find a way between ineffective fragmented action and defeatism.

If we were to contemplate world history from the standpoint of a con-cept of global control, then our first two points (1 and 2) would appear as *communism* and *fascism* respectively. Any shift of perspective alters what we see, and here we are adopting the believing outlook of point 2. From this vantage point, there is the supposition of rational or "scien-tific" global control at point 1 and a reversion to myth, as in the case of the Third Reich, at point 2 itself. However, surrounding point 2, we have only beliefs—whether Marxist, fascist, religious, or esoteric (the present cult of the New Age is just a belief system). The mid-twentieth-century world war then appears around point 3, in which we saw the collusion and conflict of communism and fascism. The *significance* of this war lay in the fact that both communism and fascism were *unreal:* both of them were at variance with the facts of life, with hazard. The Marxists were allied with a myth of historical necessity, while the Fascists were dedicated to bringing order into the "chaos that is Europe," also on quasi-historical grounds.

What appears to follow—in the aftermath of the Cold War, the dissolu-tion of the Soviet republics, and the emergence of the European Eco-nomic Community (in which Germany plays such a major part)—is the resurgence of an even more primitive era, that of the *nationalists*. What is at stake here is the search for roots.[22] The contrast—across the asteroid belt of chaos, where we even descend below nationalism to tribalism (as in the former Yugoslavia)—with point 5, is in the latter's *innovation*. We might think of point 5 in terms of the burgeoning experiments in cyberspace, vistas of virtual reality, and the like. In further contrast, then, what begins to manifest in the third phase of the enneagram concerns the new cultures emerging out of what is exemplified by the Internet, or global networking—which is the new mysticism of interconnectivity (and the *only* global culture that has ever been seen on this planet).[23] With an emergence of mankind into the third phase of this major transition, the issue of global control ceases to be in the context of military power, or even of power at all. The global intelligence implicit in computer networking is an *illumination*.[24] Significantly, it even appears to have played a significant role in the collapse of the Soviet system and provides challenging alternatives to the control systems of big business and governments.

As we go around an enneagram concerned with transformation, we should remember that that there is a *buildup* of processes and not simply a succession of stages. If we forget this, then what we see around the outer circle has the correct outer form but lacks the inner substance. It is only in the final stages (points 7 and 8) that we have all three processes blended together. The importance of the enneagram is in describing this blending, which produces the inner content for the outer form established in the early stages. The conditions for blending are set up by the inner lines. These, in their turn, derive from the *logos* (depicted in the triangle). At the heart of the enneagram, the threefold pattern is one whole. The further we get from this internal unity, the more fragmented and empty the enneagrammatic cycle becomes.

Returning to the historical perspective: the outer events of history, the events which are reported in the press and which make up the bulk of the content of history books, are an inversion of the inner events by which the human mind is changed. The general rule is to see all attempts at improvement crushed and turned back. In visible history, for example, what appears to have come into force at point 3 is not any general recognition of basic uncertainty but a rejection of it, in a reaction which has intensified rigid ideological passions. Human beings discovered uncertainty and then panicked!

As we imagine humanity approaching point 6, we should not think it likely that what is to come will appear as a sudden dawning of a perception of a higher order of intelligence. On the contrary, it is likely to appear as another expression of an accelerating disintegration. In part this is because the transition we face has nothing to do with retreat into monolithic systems but is an opening toward the real complexity of life. The general human perception of point 6 is likely to be associated with prophesies of doom and destruction—an intimation of the "death" involved, though misunderstood.

The transition associated with point 6 is dramatic because it combines two differently natured tendencies. The first of these must concern the preservation of the biosphere. In this respect, there is a difficult lesson to be learned: we live in a finite world with limited resources. Learning how to take care of the biosphere is now a necessity rather than a pious hope. However, to be able to do this, humankind must assume something of the role of the demiurgic or higher intelligences in whose hands the planet has been entrusted until now.[25] In contrast with this tendency, there is a crisis concerning human evolution. For the first time in human history, people are aware of the possibility of there being another step in the future of the species. At present, this is discussed in terms of three scenarios: that of spiritual technique, that of artificial intelligence, and that of genetics. Needless to say, all this is largely in the world of speculation. Its importance is to be measured in the power it exerts on the human imagination. We are facing the prospect of answering God's rhetorical question to Job—"Can you, by taking thought, add a cubit to your stature?"—with an affirmative.

This is one of the many reasons why an understanding of what evolution means is of critical and practical importance for our future. In this respect, we should also mention that the forces involved in human evolution *arise out of conflict and struggle*—an *increase* in hazard. The relative peace and stability, or *decrease* in hazard, required for our proper service to the biosphere is threatened by the urge to progress. The *subjective good* we seek for ourselves has to be reconciled with the *objective good* that has to be realized on this planet, for all life.

The various systems in operation on the earth—economic, military, political, cultural, religious, and so forth—are very closely coupled together. A global civilization has become inevitable. However, as I said before, this will come about through what appears to be its very opposite. We are already witnessing a widespread and powerful reaction against what is in progress. The fears of bureaucratic regimentation and the invasion of privacy by computer-aided information systems are real enough. But we can hardly begin to imagine the sort of regime that might win through. The usual ideas of world government and the creation of artificial intelligence are unappealing for very good reasons. We instinctively know what becomes of the dreams of technocrats and idealists!

As we lurch like some kind of deranged beast into a chaotic and unknown future, facile appeals to the reality of higher intelligence are likely to fall on deaf ears. Even if the idea is entertained, so long as it remains only an idea, it is, as with any kind of belief, no more than a psychologically comforting superstition. We can picture ourselves as reaching point 4 and then falling back away from the advent of chaos into the believing attitude of point 2. This century should have burned away facile belief, whether in God or in progress or in the goodness of man. But it only truly does this if we have a concrete historical *perception* and we are able to expand our present moment beyond the range it has in our daily concerns, our careers, and even our life spans. It seems that a true sense of higher intelligence can only come to those who realize, first that it is for real, and second and most important, that it is the higher intelligence itself that directs our understanding of it and not ourselves, as "creatures of mind." Mind itself is now the major global problem.

We then have to face the issue that what we call higher intelligence is not all of a kind but has its own diversity and structure. This is one of the fundamental insights of Gurdjieff's *Beelzebub's Tales*. The present widespread tendency to accept anything that comes through "channeling" as wise and good is a big mistake. Wisdom and goodness are relative to the purpose of the given agency!

The liberationist of point 5 is really the swan song of the old epoch. This is where the culmination of all that has come before is brought to a head. It cannot reach beyond except through losing itself. At point 5 we will also see people who are so detached from the world that none of its horrors can touch them. This kind of detachment will, in almost all cases, mean that they are pure spectators, possibly hooked on information technology like drug addicts. A number 5 attitude is "stoned."

Throughout all this, we can see that it is the movement along the inner lines that constitute will-intelligence, or intelligence connected with the creative future rather than with the mechanical consequences of the past. Every position in isolation will turn into something monstrous, or simply be a reaction against what has gone before. It is always necessary to return again and again to basic rationality and effective action (7-1). Then it is important to understand the essential limitations on our powers of control and prediction (1-4). From this stems the objective basis of ethics and of motivation (4-2), a connection that Bennett tried to draw attention to in the late 1960s with his talks on hazard. According to him, hazard was the real basis of the virtues and of intelligence in action. But, further than this, it was hazard that made sense of God (2-8) and enabled us to understand that the suffering of the world was an almost inevitable result of the reality of Love. Even though man missed the opportunities, there was a realm that restored them over and over again: in the sequence 8-5-7-1, we are restored to point 1 and can carry on once more, even if we fail to recognize the point of freedom opened at point 7. Bennett as a Christian could not but follow the injunction of Christ that we should lose ourselves so that we can find ourselves (5-7).

How is it possible that someone located at point 7 could be still not seeing the whole picture? The distinction to be made is that between fixity and participation. In Gurdjieff's early teaching, he made much of the staircase of the Way in which a movement by someone up to a higher step has to be supported by bringing someone else up to occupy the vacated place (ISM, p. 202). As a simplistic but meaningful image, we can picture the various points around the enneagram as a series of people at different places in the whole movement, holding hands, forming a chain, and moving in a dance. We remember Gurdjieff's movements and one of the essential messages or teachings they were designed to convey. It may well be that, for the sake of our proper understanding, we have to do all that we can to experience and move through each of the points on the enneagram.

Anyone who arrives at some point and then does nothing but consolidate his position acts as an obstruction (ISM, p. 202). This is the real danger of what Oscar Ichazo, Helen Palmer, and others have expressed as fixations.[26]

The inner lines are lines of Work. This kind of work can be defined as that which starts outside of the narrow present moment of ordinary life. It is intentional but requires our passage through changing orders of perception. The usual view is that this work is designed to take us from a lower level to a higher level, as if from step to step of a ladder. But this is not true. It is more like discovering the wholeness or totality of our humanity, through which we may come to see beyond the human.

Lines of Work

When we switch from the outer sequence of points around the circle to the inner lines, we are changing from a spectrum of states or views to a set of intelligent actions or communications. In every epoch the nature of the inner lines may be much the same. They represent the recurrent know-how of the Work, which is transmitted in a quite different way than external knowledge.[27]

Shortly before his death in 1974, Bennett outlined his cumulative understanding of the Work. For the last twenty years of his life, he was deeply concerned with correcting the prevailing unbalanced view of Gurdjieff's teaching, a view which held that only effort and suffering counted for anything. Bennett saw this as expecting to walk on only one foot. Together with the active struggle, there needed to be the opening of receptive channels. It was patently obvious to him that people who brought themselves to the point of making efforts often lacked the necessary understanding or insight, which would make their efforts effective—that is, bring them nearer to God or the truth.

From where can we derive the necessary guidance and insight to illuminate our struggles? Help comes from other people—from a teacher or someone "who knows something"—as well as from within. The two are not essentially in conflict but are complementary. Other factors are also relevant, such as the alternation between the line of service (Gurdjieff's "conscious labor") which engages us in the world and the line of interior ascent in which we are withdrawn from the world. In reflecting upon this and upon all his researches and investigations of spiritual systems over more than fifty years, Bennett saw that a more comprehensive account of the Work was needed.

It was evident that countless people had been subject to various teachings and influences but had never learned anything. This was a condition that Idries Shah also drew attention to, saying that it was necessary in the very beginning to "learn how to learn" and that very few seekers were even aware of the need for a line of work to enable them to assimilate what they had been taught or shown. Yet Gurdjieff had made so much of this throughout his own writings, speaking of the very "transubstantiation" of data in "my being" and the difference between "reason of knowing" in which our ideas remain fixed and "reason of understanding" in which our seeing can advance.

Bennett died before he could give full expression to his new synthesis, which promised to be a diagnostic tool of urgent relevance to anyone seeking a more constructive life. I speak of it here because it can be related to the enneagram of worldviews.

In the scheme of the sevenfold work, Bennett referred to three domains or worlds. The first is the world itself, the context of our experience. The second is that of our own selves, our inwardness. The third is that of the "community," in which the division between self and world can be reconciled. The seven lines of work divide between the active and the receptive sides of our nature. The active lines are:

1-4: *Assimilation*, making things one's own and finding out for oneself. What is theoretical has to be verified in the middle of life with its uncertainties.

4-2: *Struggle*, setting up in oneself the struggle between yes and no, which generates the raw material of the soul. This is really a testing and strengthening of the emotions.

2-8: *Service*, which is much the same as Gurdjieff's "conscious labor." The line of service is a connection with the future (much as parents serve the future in caring for their children). Service helps to neutralize the friction of struggle, relating the self to the world in a positive emotion.

The receptive lines are:

8-5: *Receptivity*, the ability to be helped. Where there is some contact with energies, it becomes possible to take into oneself energies from a higher level. Such energies are sometimes called *baraka* (in Sufism) or *shaktipat* (in the Hindu tradition). However, there is also an aspect of being able to take in superior *information,* or the ability to be taught.

5-7: *Submission* within, to what is higher in oneself. In the Christian tradition, this is associated with the guardian angel. It is tapping into what usually lies behind the veil of consciousness.

7-1: *Acceptance,* the purity which makes it possible for one to accept everything that happens to oneself as the will of God. The external world and the inner world are seen as two sides of the same coin, united in the Omniwill.

The seventh line is that of the Work manifesting itself directly. Thus, in this scheme, the Work itself is treated as an agency, seeking to penetrate into the mechanical blindness of the world. But we do not have to assume that it is an entity or spirit. In some respects, it corresponds to Gurdjieff's theme of how the higher influences enter into lower worlds. It is something in which care and transcendence are united.

If we look at figure 15.3 in relation to the scheme of the worldviews, we can see that the lines of work are concerned with how the various tendencies, associated with the various points, are balanced and reconciled through the inner lines. The seventh line of work, which is represented by the triangular figure itself, then appears as the threefold form of hazard, providence, and synergy. It is crucial to realize that the Work is not the product of human effort but something that can *inform* human

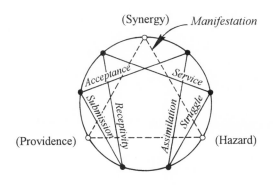

15.3. Lines of work.

effort. Rumi spoke of this when he said that the seeker needs to find a lodestone which can point him in the right direction, a metaphor that Gurdjieff developed in his idea of the magnetic center. The usual condition of the uninformed seeker is diagnosed as "making efforts to avoid efforts." People can do the most extraordinary and even dangerous things, but it is another thing to be connected with the Source, with the Great Work. As popular wisdom has it: "God does not ask us to do anything which we cannot do"; however, we fail to do the very things which we can and should, and try instead to do other things which we cannot and which have little value.

It is plausible to regard the outer guide, or teacher, as standing for us in the place of point 3. This has enormous implications, because it is concerned with how hazard and its consequences are dealt with. This is usually spoken about in terms of *obedience* on the part of the student which links him with a greater vision than he possesses. Equally, we may well regard the inner guide or *conscience*, that which alone can tell us what to do and reveal our own destiny, as standing in the place of point 6.

There is much to be said about the implications of the scheme of the seven lines of work, but here it is only proper to mention a few of them here. First of all, they do not fall into a sequence: the inner lines concern the regulation and harmonization of the disturbances brought in by an intentional connection with the world, self, and community. Secondly, their function is to *enable the Work itself to manifest*, and in this we suppose that, although man should not be mechanical or passive, his efforts are only effective if they come under the pattern of the Work itself. Thirdly, in this respect, the lines of work can be thought of as tunings of the human instrument.

The question of service in the world (the line 2-8 in the enneagram) is a very big one. There can be no formula by which we can know what benefits the whole. But it is only in the connection with what serves the whole that our own struggles can find their purpose, and it is this, in turn, which gives us the inner serenity by which we can accept all that comes to us as "God's will" (the line 7-1 in the enneagram).

Overview

A final comment is needed on the considerations that led me to formulate the various attractors as I did.

Each of the succeeding stages (clockwise) is driven as a reaction to the one before. The preceding stage is seen as incomplete, and the succeeding stage seeks to compensate for what it lacks. At the same time, each stage is an anticipation or interpretation of the stage that succeeds it. It is pulled, as it were, from what lies ahead.

From the point of view of the reactive sequence, we have something like Hegel's dialectic of thesis-antithesis followed by synthesis. Only, there is something more. From the standpoint of the left-hand side of the enneagram, the succeeding stages integrate into themselves what has gone before. They are not derived by reaction but from integration. The tendency, then, of the enneagram in the reverse direction (counterclockwise) is truly synthetic. Using the language of the triad, we can say that impulses deriving from the third phase of the enneagram have the character of the third force or reconciling principle. The third force has an influence on the reactional interplay initiated in the first phase of the enneagram process. And just as we need the energy provided by our reactions, so does the world process of realization.

We suppose that the world process of realization has to come up with something like human beings, beings capable of consciousness yet tied into space and time. Our reactions and general turmoil arise from a kind of friction between the nature of consciousness and the nature of life. It is not really anybody's fault!

If the kind of coherent and creative synthetic overview of the Greater Present Moment we have discussed is a reality, this does not mean that is capable of taking over and directing the energies of the countless human minds which it contains. At best, we have the prospect of higher influences seeking to enter the human situation. This cannot of itself overcome the fragmentations and limitations to which mankind is subject. At one time religions may have served as an apparatus for connecting humankind with higher influences. A radically new solution in a more synergic form needs to be found.

Notes

1. J. G. Bennett *The Dramatic Universe,* vol. 4, pp. 56–62.
2. Idries Shah, *Tales of the Dervishes:* "The Three Dervishes."
3. See BT pp. 1214–47, where he uses the word *world* to discuss the lack of objective meanings in ordinary discourse.

4. This phrase appeared in the title of Bennett's book on Gurdjieff, *Gurdjieff: Making a New World*.

5. Stephen Jay Gould, *Wonderful Life*.

6. H. A. L. Fisher, *A History of Europe*, p. v.

7. Here I refer to my opening discussion of intelligence in the Introduction.

8. The spirit cultures, such as those of Asia, have the attitude that the divine intelligence pervades everything. This has a resonance in contemporary information networks and the science of neural nets. Later in this chapter, I refer to these scientific and technological phenomena.

9. There is the distinction between "northern" and "southern" Sufism, the latter being the more devotional and merging. See J. G. Bennett, *Masters of Wisdom*, pp. 118–19.

10. Sri Aurobindo, *The Synthesis of Yoga*.

11. See Bennett, *Masters of Wisdom*.

12. Originating with Duns Scotus.

13. David Bohm, *Wholeness and the Implicate Order*.

14. The extraordinary American philosopher Charles Sanders Peirce anticipated this a hundred years ago.

15. I am indebted to William Sullivan for conducting research in South America to verify this astonishing hypothesis, first put forward by Giorgio Santillana and his wife Hertha von Dechend in their masterful *Hamlet's Mill*. Sullivan's own book, *The Secret of the Incas*, is an important contribution to our understanding of the momentous feats of intelligence brought about by ancient man.

16. Edward Matchett's unpublished study of the arising of genius, made for the Science Research Council, led to his realization that it is intimately connected with tapping into a quasi-infinite source of information, constantly available, that he calls *media*.

17. See chapter 17.

18. In the last years of his life, Bennett strove to create a sacred image of *nature*. He said that we should learn to love nature; only, he also insisted we should first realize that nature loves us. Without this first step, our love will be a false projection. Similarly, we should not try to love children without first realizing that they are love. These ideas convey something of the attitude of the supramental attractor. It requires a resolute abandonment of any megalanthropic idea we have of our powers as extending into higher realms. Our task is to *learn how to cooperate* with higher intelligence.

19. I am indebted to Chris Thompson for pointing this salient fact out to me, though he should not be blamed for any excesses in my interpretation.

20. This attitude is beautifully expressed in the classic *Sacrament of the Present Moment* by the eighteenth-century Jesuit Jean-Pierre de Caussade.

21. See Alice Bailey, *The Externalisation of the Hierarchy*.

22. The great Czech statesman Vaclav Havel argued in 1994 that below the global technocivilisation, more primitive and tribal feelings are growing.

23. This is strictly true only in regard to mass culture. There could well have been a global high culture thousands of years ago among an elite.

24. The term *illumination* is often found in spiritual literature. Bennett defined it as the coalescence of unitive and creative energies. In Alice Bailey it is the second ray of Love-Wisdom. Bennett often remarked to us that perhaps the computer is the most *spiritual* manifestation of our age!

25. This is a major thesis of Bennett's. The overall idea begins with a spiritual view of creation and proceeds through the unfolding of life by demiurgic action to the present stage at which we come into responsibility for our own condition. An active visualization of this sequence has a very real effect on our participation in the direct creative action which lies at the heart of nature and which is capable of revealing our own nature.

26. It is important to grasp that the fixations are "negatives." The worldviews I have described are all "positive." Putting the two sets of terms side by side is mutually illuminating; for example, to see the mystical attitude as the counterpart to the butterfly tendencies of type 7, or providence as the counterpart to the "ego-cow," the groupie. What I have to point out is that, by making the terms of the triad part of the circle of types, there is tremendous loss of depth. This self-same loss of depth is exactly what is described according to the fixations. So, to *translate* the Gurdjieff system into the Ichazo one, we have to make a kind of "inversion" of the terms and collapse the triad back into the place of the circle. Once this has been grasped, the two interpretations can enhance each other.

27. The interplay between the logic of the outer circle and the logic of the inner periodic figure is supremely important. This is taken up in later chapters. See especially chapters 18 and 19.

· 16 ·

The Great Amen

One of the most important and yet enigmatic early pronouncements of Gurdjieff was that true prayer is assured of an answer. Prayer puts us face to face with the realities which make us what we are. If we cannot pray—that is, communicate with the source of our being—then we are lost. As cognitive beings, our task is to acknowledge how it is. When we say "Amen," we mean "So be it." The intelligence handed down to us by our forebears of the ways of God is more than life itself. In prayer, we make a return to our origins. The act, from the outside, is nothing but a set of words accompanied by an emotional posture. From the inside, however, it is the core of truth. May all our prayers be absolute!

Praying in Three Worlds

MEDITATIONS on the Gospels have occupied Ouspensky, Maurice Nicoll, and Rodney Collin as well as Bennett. Some of these writers have found that the enneagram provides a key to understanding sacred texts in general and Christian texts in particular. The feeling has always prevailed that the writing of the Gospels was done with superior knowledge—and even that the drama of Christ itself was played out with a deep understanding of the relations between the different worlds that impinge on human life. The Gospels were designed to show these relationships to all those who could enter into the events of the life of Christ.

It may seem absurd that religious texts could be deliberately constructed according to principles which can be analyzed. In chapter 11, I discuss studies which have been made showing a strict cyclical structure in many ancient texts, religious or mythical. This is allied to accuracy of transmission as well as ease of memory and coherence of vision. There are many interpretations of the texts, and we could not claim to have found the "true" one. However, one thing is almost certain: all spiritual people have come to understand not only that we live in different worlds but that the primary pattern of all reality is the *bringing together of three worlds*. It is this near certainty which allows us to assert that all the great texts are articulations of this realization and it is the same realization which constitutes the *logos* of the enneagram.

The archetypal, recurrent story is that of a journey—or progression through, or integration of three worlds. In most traditions, these worlds are usually conceived as earth, heaven, and man—or some analogue of them, such as the dead, the gods, and the living. It is a mistake to picture these worlds in any linear relation, such as the human being placed between heaven and earth. A far better understanding can be gleaned from figure 16.1, *Opus B* by Oscar Reutersvaard (first shown in chapter 7 and repeated here).

Let me say a little more about this "impossible" relation. Usually, if we think of different worlds, we think of them in a linear hierarchy, one above the other. This would make the highest of a set of three worlds farther away from the lowest than the middle one. If we looked at these worlds in terms of body, mind, and spirit, we would expect mind to be closer to the spirit than to the body. Sometimes, however, we feel that

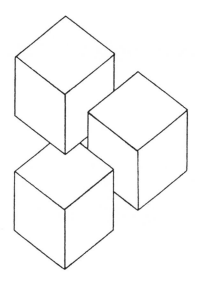

16.1. The "impossible" relation between the three worlds.

this is not true, and we suspect that the body is much closer to the spirit—perhaps because we recognize that the mind is just like a dream. If we give some credence to this suspicion, it throws some light on the structure of the worlds implied in the enneagram. After all, if there were just a linear hierarchy, then we would be just a piece of some larger chain of worlds. Somehow, the three worlds are joined together in a close-knit way (as I intimated when I talked about cosmoses). It is this that enables us to be a being.

Sometimes we find in actual experience that linear order is replaced by circular order. Take the example: A loves B; B loves C; C loves A. The hardest "eternal triangle"! Maybe A does not love C; or B, A. Similarly in the case of the worlds. The relation which exists between adjacent worlds does not carry over into the next. So although we can link the worlds in pairs, this linkage does not operate between the *three*. Hence the relevance of the picture of the "impossible" relation.

Regarding the picture of body, mind, and spirit, we can say that the mind is higher than the body and the spirit higher than the mind, but we cannot then conclude that the spirit is higher (in the same sense) than the body. Maybe the spirit and the body coincide at some point that cannot even be imagined. Reverting to one of the early representations of the three worlds—the dead, the living, and the gods—we might bring to mind the extraordinary concept of Christ descending into Hades.[1]

Putting aside the associations we have with the idea of three worlds, we can look at them from the perspective of the law of three itself. As I have intimated, the idea of threeness as significant has arisen in every culture (independently or not) and takes a variety of forms. What is important for our approach is the kind of *order* in which the three are taken into the understanding. The most primitive, or linear, is that in which the three form a chain: A acts on B; B then acts on C. The relation has one direction, and it reminds us of the order of time. However, since we have a unity of threeness, this can also be looked at as a kind of circulation: A-B-C-A, and so on. This may remind us of Gurdjieff's portrayal of the initial sequence of steps in the octave turning into a circle and blocking progress. If we revert for a moment to old images, the kind of circulation we have described is very similar to pictures of hell. The beings in this world go round and round, not getting anywhere. *No Exit*, Sartre's drama portraying three people locked in to each other, his vision of hell, is savagely acute.

In the next domain or world, the order of the three elements is something different. I referred to this order in my earlier discussion of the triad (chapter 6), where it was shown in figure 6.2: A acts on B, as it were, but it also acts on B *through C.* There are two effects and, because of this, there is some uncertainty and newness—in other words, life. In this domain, we have more than a linear order, and we have to picture it in two dimensions. The indirect or mediated action is not strictly within linear time, and so we can think of it in terms of eternity. I hasten to add that this is not as mystical as it sounds. This kind of order is to be found in quantum phenomena. Say we have a particle going from A to B (this would exemplify the action I spoke about). Then, we will find that the waveform of this particle can travel through C. The character of C—for example, a magnetic field—can affect the outcome at B. In more familiar terms, we can think of person A speaking to person B, telling them something; when, at the same time, the sheer *presence* of a third person C modifies what this means to B.

Now, of course, the tristinctive characters of the three terms can be regarded as homologous throughout the worlds. So A always maintains a certain A-ness and so on. This may remind us of the enneagram. The three elements of the triangular figure are reflected into the operations taking place in each of the three main sectors or phases. What we are now exploring are the differences in type of order that occur between them in the different phases.

In the third phase, or world, the three elements have immediate mutuality. This is figured in the Holy Trinity of Christianity. To allow for the full independence of each of the terms, we need to picture this order in three-dimensional space. A mathematical form we can use represents each of the three as vectors which can operate on each other, producing each other. These kinds of operations can be taken to symbolize a kind of anti-time. It is not "mere" eternity. It is active and creative—*changing so fast it is ahead of change.* In this guise, it is no mere recurrence of the original kind of stagnation in a now-lofty guise. If we refer to this as heaven, then we hope that this word no longer signifies a place of repose. Here we part company with the ancients who attached this idea to the perfect circulation of the empyrean—though we must remember the magnitude of the effect of the ancient discovery of the major shifts in the order of the heavens, associated with the precession of the equinoxes.[2]

If we can keep in mind our picture of the three worlds, their "impossible relation," and the different orders of relationship they entail, this may aid our understanding of what prayer signifies.

The Traditional Forms

For the moment, I will concentrate on the two great statements of the Gospels: the Lord's Prayer and the Beatitudes. Toward the end of his life, Bennett paid great attention to these. He had felt the immense significance of the New Testament nearly all his life and had made the appearance of Christ a cornerstone of his last book *The Masters of Wisdom.*

My treatment of the Lord's Prayer will differ from his in one very important respect. In his account, the sequence of the prayer proceeds according to the clockwise direction around the enneagram. In my version, it proceeds in the converse way, because value proceeds from 9 to 0 while fact proceeds from 0 to 9. A prayer is the invocation of value. It is the invoking of a higher power into our lives and begins from God.[3] In the tradition from which the Gospels were written, the format of a sacred text usually took the form of a ring in which one half of the text was echoed by the other, though in a reversed way.[4]

We take God as "Our Father" to be the apex point 9 of the enneagram. The prayer then proceeds from the world of God or heaven to the bringing of this world into the earth. It ends with the needs we have. The first half of the prayer is an affirmation of faith, while the second half is petitional.

9. Our Father,
8. Who art in Heaven,
7. Hallowed be Thy Name.
6. Thy Kingdom come,
5. Thy Will be done, on earth as it is in Heaven.
4. Give us this day our daily bread.
3. And forgive us our trespasses as we forgive those that trespass against us.
2. Lead us not into temptation,

1. But deliver us from the evil one.
0. For Thine is the Kingdom, the Power, and the Glory (for ever and ever), Amen.

The Beatitudes then show how all this is to be realized. The realization of any of the nine points is a beatitude. The sequence, now in the clockwise direction, is:

0. And he opened his mouth and taught them saying:
1. Blessed are the poor in spirit, for theirs is the kingdom of heaven.
2. Blessed are they that mourn, for they shall be comforted.
3. Blessed are the meek, for they shall inherit the earth.
4. Blessed are they who hunger and thirst after righteousness, for they shall be filled.
5. Blessed are the merciful, for they shall obtain mercy.
6. Blessed are the pure in heart, for they shall see God.
7. Blessed are the peacemakers, for they shall be called the children of God.
8. Blessed are they which are persecuted for righteousness' sake, for theirs is the kingdom of heaven.
   Blessed are ye when men shall revile you and persecute you and shall say all manner of evil against you falsely for my sake.
   Rejoice and be exceeding glad. . . .
9. Ye are the salt of the earth. . . .
   Let your light so shine before men, that they may see your good works and glorify your Father who is in heaven.

With point 9, we have the absolute demand to manifest the will of God. Here we find the source of the Lord's Prayer. Point 8, which is always a reflection or image of point 9, is the beatitude in which "they" turn into "ye."

Again, the enneagram shows its two sides. From 0 to 4, Jesus speaks of those who realize what they lack. From 5 to 9, he speaks of those who realize a virtue.

We would expect points 3 and 6 to have a special significance, since they reflect the primary *logos* as well as marking the key transitions between different worlds. Point 9 depicts those who can manifest the "Father who is in Heaven"; point 6, the "pure in heart" who will "see God"; and point 3, the "meek" who will "inherit the earth." In the prayer, these are "Our Father," "Thy Kingdom come," and "Forgive us our trespasses as we forgive," respectively. Looking at this, we can begin to see that the first phase of the enneagram concerns the *underworld* and not the earth. To inherit the earth is a major step. Thus, we generally do not really live in the biosphere, but live in an artificial world of our own making, which is a *lesser reality*. We have to feel and experience our privation, which Gurdjieff expressed as "realizing one's nothingness and helplessness." Only then are we able to reach the earth at point 3.

The whole of the first phase of the Beatitudes refers to our waking up to our situation and the realization that we are not in control. In the second phase, we are filled with something, which is a higher substance. Instead of the ephemeral energies of the psyche, there are the energies of the soul. This is the possible significance of the line 9-3, which relates these first two phases together. The filling with righteousness is the mirror of our asking for daily bread. It is striking that, in this stark vision, the energies of the soul are not even ours but have to be given "every day." They will only come if we expunge the psyche. This is a very strong feature of Gurdjieff's teachings, which assert that *we live a shadow life without substance*. This shadow life exists in the world of culture and external media which we have to see as nonexistent.[5]

With point 6, we come under the laws of the kingdom of heaven. However, this is no release from the sufferings of life but even an intensification of them. It is the realm of "intentional suffering" in Gurdjieff's terminology. At point 6, we can "see God," but according to Gurdjieff, this is *purgatory:* we see, and yet we are not united. This is the meaning of the line 6-9. However, along the circle, the issue is now the kingdom of heaven manifest on earth, as in the "peacemakers." The line 3-6 designates the realm between heaven and earth. Heaven and earth are not united; this is the realm of disjunction. The alternation between righteousness and mercy is, for example, a dominant theme in Semitic religion.

There is a profound *internal discourse* or teaching which can be elicited through contemplation of the inner lines. It was deliberate that I did not draw a diagram of the enneagram with the phrases of the religious text placed around it. If there is any benefit to be reached from our considerations, it is by way of an *internal* contemplation that takes place "against" the *external* order or sequence. We may bring to mind the pattern of the inner lines if we wish. We contemplate the relation on the right-hand side. An action begins in us, perhaps. We begin to see, for example, that a connection between the poverty of spirit of point 1 and the comforting of point 2 is by way of being given "our daily bread," point 4 of the prayer. Similarly, the connection between the peacemakers and those who are persecuted is, perhaps, to be found in that most universal and "impossible" assertion: "Thy will be done."

The Lord's Prayer is the New Testament's answer to the Ten Commandments. Jesus said that all the law and the prophets were to be found in the two injunctions to love God and love our neighbor. It is easy to see this *logos* in both the Lord's Prayer and the Beatitudes. When we draw out the parallels between the Lord's Prayer and the Ten Commandments, the contrasts are very striking. Since the Commandments were brought down from the mountain (the "same" mountain as Jesus ascended to speak to his disciples), again we have the enneagram in reverse order.

9. Thou shalt have no other gods before me.
8. Thou shalt not make unto thee any graven image.
7. Thou shalt not take the name of the Lord thy God in vain.
6. Remember the Sabbath day, to keep it holy.
5. Honor thy father and thy mother.
4. Thou shalt not kill.
3. Thou shalt not commit adultery.
2. Thou shalt not steal.
1. Thou shalt not bear false witness against thy neighbor.
0. Thou shalt not covet thy neighbor's house, nor thy neighbor's wife, nor anything that is thy neighbor's.

We notice that the first three commandments are all negations. This is in contrast with the Lord's Prayer, where these same three ideas are presented as positive affirmations. The second half of the commandments are all in the form "thou shalt not." The placing of the injunction against adultery at point 3 looks strange until we remember the Gospel story of the woman taken in adultery ("Let he who is without sin cast the first stone"). In the Lord's Prayer, we have at the same place that we should be forgiven as we forgive others. Point 2, "lead us not into temptation," is an obvious parallel; and so is point 1, "deliver us from the evil one," or false witness. Point 0 in the Lord's Prayer is again an affirmation, "Thine is the kingdom," whereas it is negative in the commandments, "thou shalt not covet." Both refer to the question of who *owns*.

The same pattern that we see in the Ten Commandments and in the Lord's Prayer is found in the opening declaration of the Qur'an, marking an unbroken continuity between the three great monotheistic religions of the Middle East. Thus:

9. In the name of Allah, the Compassionate, the Merciful.

8. Praise be to Allah, Lord of Creation,

7. The Compassionate, the Merciful,

6. King of Judgment Day.

5. You alone we worship,

4. and to You alone we pray for help.

3. Guide us to the straight path, the path of those You have favored,

2. Not of those who have incurred Your wrath,

1. Nor of those who have gone astray.

In reading these parallels there is an extraordinary sense of a single revelation that embraces the three religions. Scholars, however, regard this as a mere property of inheriting a common literary and social tradition (a tradition which, however, reaches back into early Mesopotamia, the favorite culture of Gurdjieff!).

Gurdjieff sometimes spoke of his teaching as an esoteric Christianity and said that he was concerned with helping people to be able to be Christians. Therefore, it is not surprising that we can find in his teaching a reflection of the Beatitudes and other of Christ's teachings. Here are some obvious parallels:

1. *Blessed are the poor in spirit.* This is to realize that all the power and glory is God's and that we have nothing of our own. It is Gurdjieff's "realization of one's own nothingness," which is the only true beginning point of the Work.

2. *Blessed are they that mourn.* This is the realization that we need to be saved from temptation and evil. It is Gurdjieff's "realization of one's helplessness in the face of everything around one." These first two realizations are the practical foundation for entering into the Work.

3. *Blessed are the meek.* Meekness means to forgive those that trespass against one. This was very important in Gurdjieff's teaching: "Learn to bear the unpleasant manifestations of people toward you."

4. *Blessed are they that hunger and thirst after righteousness.* They will receive their daily bread. In Gurdjieff we find this as the prayer to "transubstantiate in me for my being." "Bread" is *being*-food, whatever that is.

5. *Blessed are the merciful.* This is only through the working of the will of God on earth as in heaven. It is this which lies behind Gurdjieff's doctrine of the "law of the reciprocal maintenance of everything existing." Gurdjieff himself exhorted his pupils to honor their father and mother and respect the religion of every person. He also said: "One must do everything one *can* and then say 'Lord have Mercy!' "

6. *Blessed are the pure in heart.* The kingdom of God is in the pure heart. This is the state of those who live on the planet Purgatory as described in *Beelzebub's Tales,* who are blessed with the appearance of God to them, which only serves to intensify their self-perfecting.

7. *Blessed are the peacemakers.* This is in the Name of God. According to Gurdjieff, there are "individuals sent from Above" whom we can regard as "children of God." Once, he said that "two hundred conscious men and women could stop war on earth."

8. *Blessed are they which are persecuted for righteousness' sake. Blessed are ye when men shall revile you . . . for my sake.* Our Father is in heaven. Gurdjieff said that the inevitable result of impartiality in a time of troubles is to become the target of hatred by the surrounding sleeping people (those who have not gone up a mountain).

9. *Let your light so shine before men. . . .* This is the hardest of all to explain and to understand. In the context of Gurdjieff's teachings, it is to manifest the Work or, rather, to let the Work manifest through us. Beyond the scope of ideas and persuasion, it is people who most influence people. We can touch the Work in another person, because it is in a person. But this is very different from any public display, or any cult of personality.

Striving to Know Ever More and More

Gurdjieff's own five commandments, the *obligolnian strivings,* can be taken as a new interpretation of the Beatitudes (BT, p. 386). He says that

those in the time of Ashiata Shiemash who followed these commandments automatically became the leaders of those around them, much as
Jesus says: "Let your light so shine before men, that they may see your
good works and glorify your Father which is in heaven." However, Gurdjieff's third striving is quite unique in a traditional context: "the conscious striving to know ever more and more concerning the laws of world
creation and world maintenance." This appeal to knowledge and understanding is a feature of changes in human possibility over the last two
thousand years. It is important to realize that Gurdjieff spoke to any
individual capable of finding his or her own reality. Such a call makes
sense only in the context of the modern world. Knowing more and more
about the laws of world creation and world maintenance is not synonymous with science. It belongs to the character of the synergic epoch,
which I spoke of in the last chapter.

The present escalation in human population and technology is a feature of this epoch. It has created the conditions for a merging of intelligence of different orders—including the artificial, organic, human, and
demiurgic—but only those in contact with the creative future can witness
its realization. The conscious participation in the birth of a new epoch is
very different from simply being swept up in its external manifestations.
One of the most important features of this conscious participation is in
the realization of new modes of cognition. I said that knowing more and
more about the laws was not exclusively a matter of science and that it is
accessible to anyone who is able to find his or her own reality, or individuality. This cannot make sense in terms of the previous epoch. It can only
make sense in the context of an epoch in which tracking the way back
into ourselves utilizes the same media as enlarging our perception of the
cosmos. This means that the cognitive atmosphere of the planet is undergoing radical changes.

In the last chapter, I discussed the coming about of a new age through
the mediation of two insertions into world history: first, a realization that
hazard and uncertainty is intrinsic to reality; and second, that a providence or higher level of information informs the world. *To accept uncertainty is to open a doorway of perception.* By entering into the realm of
new perceptions, we can then come to another door, in which both ourselves and our world are revealed in a totally new light. This door opens
to the realm of angels, as they have been called: the messengers. *We need*

to learn to cooperate with higher intelligence. We need not regard the angels as providing solutions to our problems. Their important role, as they arise within us and between us, is to restore something of the original connection between will and perception that was sundered long ago.[6]

The present change of epoch may be a major episode in the drama of our restoration to sanity. According to Bennett's theory of epochs, these changed in a cycle of two to two and a half thousand years; but there was also a great cycle of about twenty-five thousand years. This gives us a tremendously different perspective. If we ascribe the first great cycle of human existence (as *Homo sapiens sapiens*) to the first phase of an ennea-gram on this larger scale, then we are now in the midst of the second. This second great cycle began with agriculture and the move toward set-tlement, cities, and civilization. Perhaps the cycle of great revelations of two thousand years ago constituted point 4, and we have now entered into the chaotic transition toward point 5, an unthinkable apocalypse, in which the whole meaning of good and evil is liable to be transformed (as Gurdjieff suggested). We are like a planet veering towards a vast cloud of unknowing. What is totally unthinkable for us is the third great cycle, beginning some ten thousand years from now, a point 6 of unimaginable content and significance.

With the notion of three great cycles of human history, we return to the conception of three interlocking worlds with which we began.

Notes

1. There is an apocryphal story attributed to Gurdjieff in which Christ is pictured in a Hell full of piles of shit everywhere. The people there spend all their time trying to walk around the edges and not sink into it. When Christ arrives, he chooses the biggest pile of shit and jumps right into the middle of it!
2. This was the master idea of Giorgio de Santillana and Hertha van Dechend's *Hamlet's Mill*. It is brilliantly discussed in William Sullivan's *Secret of the Incas: Myth, Astronomy, and the War Against Time*.
3. This was first pointed out to me by Ted Matchett.
4. See chapter 17.
5. Contemporary scientists and philosophers are recognizing that our so-called con-sciousness is a product or effect of language and culture, but they fail to see, of course, that this information-based nothingness can give way to a genuine

transorganic and substantial consciousness. The externally based, culture-bound fictitious consciousness is what Gurdjieff calls personality. The seed of a genuine consciousness in us, he calls essence.

6. See "Beelzebub's Story" in the Introduction.

· 17 ·
The Tescooano

Once, when I had occasion to work closely with an industrial scientist, I was able to find out what he actually did in solving the technical problems he tackled. Much to my initial surprise, he told me that his first step was always to find out what the material in question felt like. It was only much later, when the problem had been effectively solved, that he wrote up his investigation in an approved form. Such anecdotes are, in fact, legion. What effectiveness scientists and engineers actually do involves a far more intense or deeper kind of perception than the ordinary. Benjamin Lee Whorf, a master of language, earned his living as a chemical engineer, and he was able to see the problem he was called into solve almost instantaneously. A friend of mine who worked for Du Pont was able to distinguish whole ranges of color where I would only see a single one.

Depth in perception is a neglected aspect of cognitive science. The enigma is why it has been neglected. Part of the reason is that such perception is linked with being, and some kind of drastic decision has been taken in Western culture to ignore the reality of being in order to advance in functional mastery.

How Deep Is Reality?

W E   H A V E no way of knowing how universal is the kind of experience we have. It may be that there are forms of experience in which the sense of self and world are very different from our own. What we suspect and feel of the experience of other species such as dogs, whales, and birds is still vaguely familiar. In regard to whole planets and stars, we do not know whether there is anything remotely like "experience."[1]

Within our experience there is an important sense of what is *real*. We are able to distinguish between the real and the *appearance* of the real.

What is real has a *depth* to it. This is in contrast with the images of things that we might produce, for example, on TV screens. If we come closer to a real object, then we see more and more detail inherent in that object. But, if we come closer to the image on a screen, the object dissolves into pixels that are a property not of the object itself but of the system of image production. What is real has a structure in depth and does not merely lie on the surface of our perception. This points to something fundamental to our experience.

Machines can show a kind of intrinsic detail but in a different sense than natural objects do. For example, we can look at a motorcar not only in terms of its visible parts, such as crankshaft and pistons, but also in terms of its invisible ones. These include its chemistry (in relation to its use of fuel) and its information processing (in relation to its electrical systems). But this detail is very different from the straightforward wealth of observable detail found in natural objects on different scales.

Art is somewhat in-between. On the whole, however, a painting has a detail which belongs to what it shows as a whole. The palette knife strokes of a Van Gogh are an integral part of what the painting is and are not merely there to produce an effect at a certain distance in the eye of the spectator. That is why we have to see it "in the flesh." It is possible to look at a painting from far or near and still *see the same* painting, even though it may *look* very different.

James Gleick, the author of *Chaos,* says of the mathematician Benoit Mandelbrot: "To Mandlebrot, art that satisfies lacks scale, in the sense that it contains important elements in all sizes. 'With Ruysdael and Turner, if you look at the way they construct complicated water, it is clearly done in an iterative way. There's some level of stuff, and then stuff painted on top of that, and then corrections to that.' "[2]

Mandlebrot's insight is important. It says that the sense of a real vital phenomenon comes from the copresence of different levels. Interestingly enough for our study of the enneagram, he speaks specifically of *three* levels of execution. It is more than likely that all natural phenomena—and also "art that satisfies"—have at least a three-level structure. If this is lacking, then we sense that something is wrong, that we are merely in front of an image. There is a remarkable scene in the movie *Iceman:* A man unfrozen from the Antarctic ice is placed in an artificial biosphere replicating the climate of the region tens of thousands of years ago. During the course of his explorations, while he is fishing in a stream, he comes across a power cable. Puzzled, he follows the cable back to its source, which is in a control tower where contemporary observers are keeping watch. The illusion is broken.

The pioneers in chaotics have opened up the study of ordinary, everyday phenomena—such as dripping taps, the clouds in the sky, our awareness of color, and so on. Everything that is interesting and natural in our perception has a depth of detail. Take something even as simple as looking at a single human hair. From a distance, it is merely a line, in one dimension. As we come closer, the line of the hair acquires a breadth, in two dimensions. Then, very rapidly, we move into a three-dimensional perception of the hair. It looks like a cylinder. As we come closer still, using a magnifying glass or microscope, we begin to see a surface, a two-dimensional appearance once again (just as we live on a two-dimensional surface on the earth as perceived on our scale). A further degree of approach begins to reveal that this surface is not simple but develops toward three dimensions yet again. If we move any closer, we lose all sense of the hair as a whole.

It is possible to understand such a sequence in terms of the enneagram. The two periods of two-dimensionality indicate the onset of the critical points. The critical points are nonintegral dimensionality—that is, they are *in between* two and three dimensions. In the first phase of the enneagram we move from one to two dimensions. In the second, from three to two dimensions, and in the third, from three to one again (this time, in terms of subcomponents of the hair). It is the weaving together of these different orders of perception that convince us that we are seeing something real:

1. as a line
2. as having a thickness
3. in-between
4. as fully three-dimensional
5. as a surface
6. in-between
7. surface depth
8. component structure

0 and 9. the hair as "invisible"

Similar considerations apply in audition. We tend to assume that if there is a conversation going on, this is something definite. However, what this conversation is depends on where we are. Imagine a group of people chatting together on a lawn. If we are part of the group, we will be listening to just one or two speakers. The rest is filtered out into background noise. Now, if we separate from the group and wander around the outside of it, we can become aware of the conversations in total. Maybe we do not hear any definite piece of conversation at all. However, what we hear is still recognizable as conversation. If we move farther off, there is a point at which the conversation simply becomes a kind of buzz, unrelated to language. Moving still farther, we cannot detect the sound at all.

We experience this kind of thing all the time, and yet, in our thinking, we tend to neglect its phenomenological richness. It is because we can experience the conversation in various orders of detail that we see it as something really going on. In the cinema, we are unable to do this. However, a skillful cinematographer will often introduce different sound perspectives on what we suppose to be the same scene and hence build up a conviction of reality.

The overlapping of different layers of perception is rooted in our experience of the real world. It should not be surprising that the enneagram is constructed according to our experience. It deals not in idealized, abstract objects but in the depth of phenomena. I must add that the three orders or levels are not simply arranged in a hierarchy but are *enfolded*—to use Bohm's terminology—together into the whole. According to our perspective, one or other of them is unfolded into our perception. Similarly, in a structured transmission of knowledge, such as a sacred text, there will be three layers of strata of information, which are enfolded in each other. Gurdjieff referred to this as legominism.[3]

Apparatus of Perception

Gurdjieff offered the enneagram as an apparatus which could serve to amplify and refine our understanding. It does not, in itself, provide the knowledge which has to be obtained by empirical means and hard experience. What it can do is enable us to utilize, to greater effect, all the knowledge and experience we have.

In Gurdjieff's *Beelzebub's Tales,* a *tescooano* is a device that amplifies perception. This leads us to suppose that the enneagram will correspond very closely to the working of such instruments as telescopes and microscopes.[4] This correspondence was closely investigated by Ken Pledge, one of Bennett's students. He showed that the form and operation of a spectroscope followed precisely the indications of Gurdjieff's enneagram.[5]

Some of the principles of the tescooano can be discussed by considering a simple compound microscope. It is an instrument for the eye. The eye takes, as subordinate aspects of itself, two artificial lenses. One of these is called the objective and, the other, the eyepiece. The human eye is point 9; the object lens, point 3; and the eyepiece lens, point 6. The eye is at the apex point, while the lenses occupy the base of the triangle. The imperative of the microscope is to see (as, in the case of the restaurant, it is to eat.) This forms into a *logos,* because of the three openings which occur at points 3, 6, and 9.

If we lay out the basic form of the microscope, as shown in figure 17.1, we notice that nothing is happening, because there is *nothing to be seen.* It is a state of pure possibility.

Next, we consider what the microscope *does.* It brings very small objects within the sphere of our perception. It brings about a change in scale, which is signified by the power of the microscope and calculated as a product of the magnifications of the eyepiece and the objective. For this product to take effect, there must be something to look at, an object that is illuminated. The objective and the eyepiece must be the right distance apart, so that the image formed by the objective can serve as the object for the eyepiece. Finally, the eye must see something, and what it sees is the virtual image created by the eyepiece. There are three main component stages in producing the change of scale: first, the illuminated object;

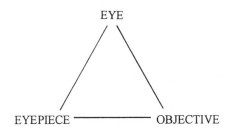

17.1. Basic form of a microscope.

second, the image produced by the objective; third, the image of the image produced by the eyepiece.

These, in their turn, can be matched with three differently natured *processes*. The first process consists of the light rays coming from (or through) the object. These rays are selectively focused by the objective lens inside the body of the microscope. Rays coming from this image pass, in their turn, through the eyepiece lens and into the eye. The second process consists of the formation of images, rather than the pathways of light. First, the object lens forms a real image of the object (a real image is one that can be projected onto a screen). Second, the eyepiece forms a virtual image of the objective's real image. It is this virtual image that can be seen by the eye itself. The octave of images is akin to air in the realm of foods. However, it is also important to see that these images are, in a very strict sense, *artificial*.

We do not really see the images; *we see the object*. The real image arising inside the body of the microscope cannot be seen without some further operation. We could interpose a screen on which the real image would fall, making it visible by reflected light. However, this would not provide sufficient magnification. Reflection would constitute a deviation in the octave: the critical transition would not be made.

Instead of a screen we have an eyepiece which draws the process further on. The virtual image produced by this second lens, in its turn, cannot be realized without the seeing eye. This brings us to the third process: the eye is looking for what is *meaningful*. Without the discerning eye, the whole fails. It takes some training to learn how to look.[6] The extraordinary microscopist Anton von Leeuwenhoek (1632–1723) was able to see things through his primitive instruments that others could not see until a century or more after him. The untrained eye will not be able to see very much, no matter the degree of technical sophistication of the apparatus.

Before we arrive at the enneagram, we need to move from a description of the microscope as three components to a description in terms of six components. In figure 17.2, we have a picture of two overlapping triangles. One of them—eye, objective, and eyepiece—is concerned with what *sees*, while the other—object, real image, and virtual image—is concerned with *the seen*. As yet, we do not show how they interpenetrate each other.

I have labeled the six components with the numbers they will have when we come to the enneagram. The components are shown in their

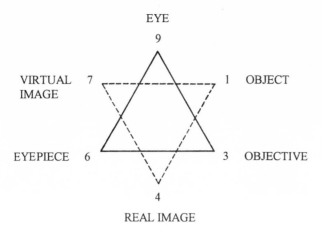

17.2. The active structure of a microscope.

relationships and not in their spatial configuration, although the real image does lie between the objective and the eyepiece. Obviously, the object is not between the eye and the objective lens. The virtual image is not between the eyepiece and the eye but, roughly, in the plane of the object.

When we turn our attention to the primary octave of light transmission, we can make finer distinctions than before. For example, the light coming through or from the object is selectively focused by the objective. Not all the information carried by the light passes through the instrument. This means that we have both the originating light through the object (point 1) and that bundle of rays which is brought into focus, or selected, by the objective (point 2). In place of the one object we have two distinguishable components. Similarly, there is the real image (point 4) formed by the objective, and the rays issuing from it (point 5), which are brought into focus by the eyepiece lens. And, in the final phase, there is the virtual image (point 7), formed by the eyepiece and the light rays (point 8) as they enter into the eye. The bundles of rays in each phase are then represented by the dynamic "emergent" points 2, 5, and 8. In each case, these bundles correspond to the next optical apparatus.[7] Recalling our earlier discussion of hydrogens, we can see that this means that the bundle, in each case, is of the same density or character as the do of the next octave. This is simply because they have been selected by the lens.

The light that enters the eye is *intentionally selected by the eye.* In the language of octaves, we can put it in another way: the presence of the higher do encompasses the note si and the critical interval between them. This is the point 8. *The seeing of the eye comes out of the eye into the apparatus.* We now have the completed form of the enneagram.

The main difference between the structure of six points shown in figure 17.2 and the complete enneagram shown in figure 17.3 is that, in the latter, we can take into account the selection of a particular level of detail and structure from the possibilities of the object. The specific features are selected by (a) movement of the specimen under the objective, (b) selection of objective lens, and (c) focusing. As the selection ensues, the light rays coming from the object are processed: in the first phase, they are *selected* as relevant; in the second they are *composed* into images; and, in the third, they are *seen* as meaningful.

Any one objective lens can be a complex combination of lenses, designed to compensate for the aberrations produced by a single lens. A compound microscope usually has three or more objectives of different strengths. The eyepiece has two component lenses and is fixed. The body of the microscope extends between points 3 and 6, between the objective and the eyepiece. Interestingly enough, the main focus wheel is mounted about halfway along the body. So, while the eye, the seeing intelligence, is at point 9, directly beneath it—between points 4 and 5—is the hand, the doing intelligence.

In the inner sequence of lines 1-4-2, we have the functional power of

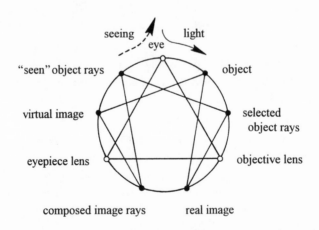

17.3. Enneagram of a microscope.

the objective lens. The focus knob controls this linkage by altering the distance between the object and the lens. Point 7 is the point of focus in the third octave. The sequence 8-5-7 stems from the eyepiece lens. It is controlled by the eye itself in that it has to conform to what the eye can bring into focus. The two linkages connect up by the lines 2-8 and 7-1, which are two identities. The connection 2-8 means that the rays selected at point 2 are the same as those delivered at point 8. The connection 7-1 means that the virtual image is formed roughly at the plane of the object (and not inside the body of the microscope, for example).

The inner lines, being cyclic, have no starting point. In the abstract calculations, based on $\frac{1}{7}$, the sequence can start from any of the six points.[8] If we take the first fraction, $\frac{1}{7}$, or the sequence 1-4-2-8-5-7, we can read it as follows: First is the alignment of the light source illuminating the object (1), then the adjustment of focus (4), which selects a specific feature of the object (2), presenting it to the inquiring gaze (8). This gaze asks a question or proposes a hypothesis which is answered by what is found (5), that may then be studied (7). The "end" of the line 1-4-2 is united with the "beginning" of the line 8-5-7; and the "end" of the line 8-5-7 is united with the "beginning" of the line 1-4-2. We can imagine the action as a shuttle going back and forth, weaving a fabric. The fabric is perception.

The hexadic cycle is a dialogue between intelligence and mechanicality by way of illumination, focus, and judgment. It proceeds through three worlds of different natures. In the first, the object is aligned in the field of light to provide the needed quantity of illumination. The nature of this world is one-dimensional and quantitative. In the second, it is brought into focus as an image. The nature of this world is two-dimensional and qualitative. In the third, the meaning of the object is realized. The nature of this world is three-dimensional and structural.

There is an interesting way of representing the cyclicity of the inner lines of the enneagram. This is as an Oruboro spiral, as shown in figure 17.4, which vividly conveys the sense of an organic flux, a weaving of processes. It is possible to feel this pattern as a dance. The critical points 3 and 6 appear as centers of gravity, around which the flux is organized. Points 0 and 9 appear below and above, to emphasize the structural extension of the whole, the integration between levels.

In the case of the microscope, the two centers of gravity correspond to

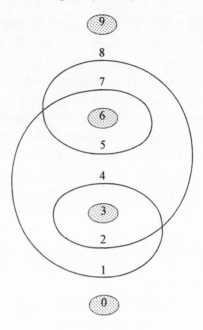

17.4. Oruboro spiral.

the sphere of operations (point 3, positioning the object, changing focus) and the sphere of perception (point 6, selecting the feature, "reading" its meaning). Both 0 and 9 correspond to the primary intention: to see. We should remember the simple case of pouring a glass of water (discussed in chapter 7). In its crudest rendition, the two centers of gravity correspond to body and mind, as they might be experienced in ourselves.

If what is seen is represented by the triplet 1, 4, 7—the object, the real image, and the virtual image—then the seeing is represented by way of the triplet 2, 5, 8—the selected, composed, and seen rays. In this formulation, that which sees is given by our original triplet 3, 6, 9. The way in which these relations interpenetrate and *lead to a progression* is represented in the inner lines. Thus, of course, we do not end up simply registering the object in our eye, but we come to recognize it, to discern its important features, and grasp their significance.[9] What can be seen has a *depth* to it.

We have not accounted for how the illumination of the object is produced, nor how the eye forms an image on the retina. These should be briefly explained to make a more complete picture. The illumination is a result of another organized process or a series of processes. There will be a source of illumination, a mirror to reflect the light onto or through the object, and a condenser lens to produce more brightness. In octave language, the final do of this previous process becomes the new do of the first octave for our microscope. Looking at the other side altogether, the formation of an image inside the eye belongs to the second process of the enneagram of the microscope: it is the completion of this second octave. Of course, the eye is also an intelligence and, in the third octave completes itself within the brain, that is, in the mind.

All that is revealed in this description is the interweaving of intentionality with mechanism. The eye is intentional, while the issuing of the light rays is mechanical. There is a way in which this can be represented in purely physical terms. *Behind* the eye is the *brain,* and in this brain a construction is made that is located, not inside the brain, but in the objective world. This can be pictured as information (of a certain kind) coming *out of the eye toward and into coincidence with the object.* The brain image and the object are matched where the object is. This has recently been called the theory of quantum touching, because, quite literally, the brain reaches *out* to touch the object. In the physical theory of light, there are two solutions to the equations which describe how light behaves. In the one, light is as we usually think of it, traveling from here to there forward in time. In the other, it is the reverse, and light travels from the future to the past. The latter, called advanced waves, can be pictured as coming out of eyes toward the objects we see.[10]

It is very important to realize that, if we think of the structure of perception from an external and static point of view, the enneagram becomes irrelevant and we have only the outer shell. In fact, it is quite common to describe apparatuses only in this way, so that it becomes necessary to receive instruction on their operation and how they are used for a purpose. The usual description does not contain any freedom; and, therefore, there is no involution or evolution, and nothing is really happening. Freedom would only come into view if intention were brought into the apparatus itself, which would make it a true experiment or act of perception.

In real science, the scientist as will or intention is *immanent* in the experiment: he then both sets up the experiment and sees the result. Setting up the experiment relates to the sequence starting in 0 and ending in 9. Seeing the result relates to the sequence starting in 9 and ending in 0. He enters into the experiment by way of the gates represented by the points 3 and 6. In the case of the compound microscope, he can adjust the objective (point 3) while he looks through the eyepiece (point 6). It is enough to say that the scientist descends, as it were, from point 9 into point 8 and that this then enables the whole of the movement to be initiated—in which case, a transition can be made from simple existence to meaning. Then an apparatus is "filled with the Holy Ghost" and has its own triangle (just as Gurdjieff said that certain plants, like the opium poppy, have). If we picture an apparatus such as a microscope in use, then we can see all the nine lines of the enneagram at work. If, on the other hand, we picture it as an object, the enneagram is only latent.

The left-hand side of the enneagram is centered on purpose and value, while the right-hand side is centered on mechanism and fact. I have described the object (point 1) and the light entering the eye (point 8) in the compound microscope in these terms. Light comes out of the object mechanically but enters the eye purposefully. Similarly, the two critical points 3 and 6 are sometimes called the mechanical and the intentional ways-in, respectively. In speaking of the will of the scientist entering into the apparatus, I mean to say that purpose is an integral part of the whole process and that, without the element of purpose, the process is not complete.

In the right-hand side of the enneagram, the initial material (in this case, made of light) is broken down into various parts. In the left-hand side, these parts are reassembled into a new unity.[11] The process coming from point 0 develops toward increasing complexity, whereas the process as it goes toward point 9 develops toward increasing unity. The unity at point 0 may be called extensive and the unity at point 9, intensive. In much the same way, all the other pairs of points can be interpreted (see fig. 17.5).

Vision

The idea that all *dynamic and transforming organizations* devolve into three aspects can appear very abstract and far from our immediate experience. In fact, this is not true. It stares us in the face every time we look at the world.

We have two eyes which, in operation together, reveal a world in depth. The perception of a world in depth is the very essence of the idea of our

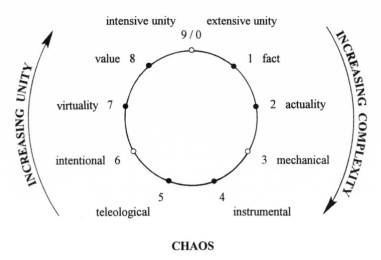

17.5. *Enneagram as fact and value.*

being in the midst of the world. Each of the two eyes has a power of estimating distance, but the actual experience of depth is something more. The synergy of the two eyes is extraordinary. We may believe that three-dimensional experience is automatically guaranteed, but a little attention to visual experience will soon show that "depth has depth." The experience of depth can be vivid and startling. There is an immediate new sense of the body being here; consequently, that "I am here." It is self-revealing. That this type of experience of the so-called external world has such power in revealing ourselves to ourselves conforms to the principles of self-organization.

The two eyes are the outer forms of the internal organization. That is why traditional metaphysicians such as Rudolf Steiner have distinguished the two eyes as having different natures.[12] This is especially the case when we are dealing with something that is strongly connected with us. Modern studies are suggesting that we are coupled with our environment in such a way that this coupling produces or shapes both ourselves and the environment. If we are to deepen our perception, we must become aware of the coupling itself.[13]

An interesting possibility suggested by the enneagram is that this coupling takes two forms, which are then harmonized together. In the one, the coupling takes place by an actual exchange of material or energy. In the second, it is by way of the mutual generation of information. Put in simpler, everyday terms, this refers to "eating" and "experiencing." They are represented by the two critical points 3 and 6. In their guise as gateways, point 3 is the way out and point 6 the way in. The first creates a world out there, and the second, a world in here.

This is the practical and concrete realization of the triad. The triad cannot be observed, only realized through an active participation. Each of the three terms of a triad is active in its own way. Ordinarily, the third term, the reconciling, is seen only as a neutral background. What brings us into the triadic reality is when this third term is seen as active—a state from which a new degree of freedom arises.

This is particularly apposite when we think of the still-current vogue for considering the two sides of the brain as representing two different kinds of mind.[14] However, even those who have explored the idea sympathetically have, on the whole, failed to see that the main significance is in looking toward the primary or third form of mind, in which the two sides are reconciled. This would then be "mind in depth." It is an important experience to become aware of alternative forms of mind—and to become aware of how these might have shifted in relative prominence in historical times; but it is another major step to go through the tension of the two main alternative forms of the right and the left brain and find their reconciliation.[15]

It must be a task for anyone in any period to grasp this essential fact. Whether one lives in the ego-striving era of modern times or in the "dreamtime" of the aboriginal, one needs to find the more central mode of mentation and experience which is in operation in any time and in any culture. This applies today when, still, the basic cultures of the West are left-brained and the basic cultures of the East are right-brained. It is only through the third or primary brain that Gurdjieff's "real information" can be transmitted from generation to generation.

Therefore, seeing in depth is not only a matter of visual perception but also applies to the perception of reality. One of the Idries Shah's teaching stories presents an allegory of a dervish who has to find a magic mirror. Through diligence and grace, he finds it suspended by a thread in a well, but because it is made out of the thoughts of men, it is only a fragment. Nevertheless, it is enough to show the dervish the "Deep Knowledge."[16]

The domains of experience that we call perception and mind are begin-

ning to be studied in cognitive science. However, this study remains confined to the level of H48, to use Gurdjieff's terminology. There is almost
no attention paid to the depth of either perception or mind, only to their
operation at the usual, most automatic level. When I speak of "depth," I
mean that there are higher levels of experience of perception or mind, so
evident from the cultures of all ages that only the most deliberately obtuse
could fail to notice. The intense sense of depth in visual perception, again
to use Gurdjieff's terminology, belongs with H24. At a deeper level still,
there is the experience of H12, which, when it comes, amounts to a satori,
a moment of insight into experience itself. An artist worthy of the name
cannot do without H24, which is his or her basic raw material of work,
or "food." However, according to Gurdjieff, this only gives what he calls
subjective art. Objective art uses the materials of H12 and H6 as food.
And so does objective science.

Gurdjieff's objective science is an extraordinary conception. It can in-
furiate anyone who has an appreciation of the immense amount of work
that goes into making any scientific advance and, sometimes, appears as
mere charlatanism in its apparent claims of possessing superior knowledge. As I have implied, Gurdjieff knew next to nothing of the advances
taking place in twentieth-century science and did not appear to care
about them at all. He left all that to pupils such as Ouspensky and Bennett. His concern was with the seeing of what lies within our own experience, the deeper kinds of perception which are possible for us—including
the possibilities opened up by H12 and H6, which are the energies of
objective perception. It is only through these energies that we can see the
greater possibilities of science or, for that matter, the greater possibilities
of art. As we go up through the hydrogens, our grasp of the way in which
we are coupled with our environment changes in very important ways.

There is a thread that goes through the octave of perception, the third
partial octave of the enneagram, that is a special kind of language. This
kind of language is exemplified in the enneagram itself. It is also to be
found in other traditions, and both the Kabbalah and the *I Ching* are
major examples.[17] The point of these languages is not what is first apparent. They are not some kind of occult speculation or dogma about the
workings of the world or human beings, in terms so vague that they can
be made to fit anything. They are constructed to facilitate a translation
between the different levels of experience. Their structures emulate the

structure of perception; but, that this can really be so, only begins to appear to us through the workings in us of H24. Hence the emphasis placed in Gurdjieff's system on basic inner work involving attention and intention.

What is at stake is a perception of the real situation of the human being on earth. We can see this perception as a return into the form of the whole. Whatever the empirical and theoretical data we acquire from science, it will only constitute the first octave and give nothing in depth. Without an awakening of our inner powers, a true perception is not possible. Even this is not enough: we need the mirror formed from the totality of human thoughts, that is capable of reflecting the deep knowledge of the third octave.

Notes

1. Though science fiction writers such as Olaf Stapledon (in *Starmaker*) and Frank Herbert (in *Dosadi Experiment*) have imagined that there is. We should remember D. E. Harding's astonishing definition of the planet as "consciously dead."
2. In James Gleick, *Chaos*.
3. See chapter 11 for another description of legominism.
4. In the chapter on *heptaparaparshinokh*, the law of seven, in *Beelzebub's Tales*, Gurdjieff writes at some length on the mythological Chinese apparatus for comparing vibrations.
5. "Structured Process in Scientific Experiment," in J. G. Bennett, *Enneagram Studies*. This is one of the most brilliant expositions of the enneagram as applied to an apparatus. Its detail and precision are astonishing. Pledge is always at pains to point out that it is only by a thorough and practical immersion in setting up and using an apparatus that we can even begin to understand what the enneagram shows us. He offers a salutary correction to the superficiality of approach that is prevalent. The well-known saying "God is in the details" applies here. He has been a trenchant critic of my approach and extremely valuable in bringing me to task.
6. See Mary Abercrombie, *The Anatomy of Judgement*, a classical study of scientific education.
7. In the previous chapter, I discussed the fact that there are three parts of the apparatus.
8. See chapter 1.
9. See "Learning to See," in Abercrombie, *The Anatomy of Judgement*.
10. I am indebted to Peter Marcer of the British Computing Society for discussions of these ideas. Marcer has long been an advocate of a new view of computation

based on the concept of the "quantum computer." This concept is a radical alternative to the way in which computer science has gone since the end of the Second World War and offers a much more realistic model of the way in which the brain works.

11. I will refer to the same idea again in chapter 18, where I discuss the structure of ancient texts.

12. Rudolf Steiner, *Speech and Drama.*

13. See Francisco Varela, Evan Thompson, and Eleanor Rosch, *The Embodied Mind.* This book discusses this issue from the standpoint of cognitive science and Buddhist psychology.

14. And the two sexes as differing in the connectivity of the two hemispheres. This has a bearing on my discussion of sex in chapter 10.

15. See Julian Jaynes, *The Origin of Consciousness and the Bicameral Mind.*

16. "The Three Dervishes," in Idries Shah, *Tales of the Dervishes;* this also relates to Bennett's suggestion that the higher intelligence is embodied in ideas.

17. In chapter 19, I show a possible correlation between the hexagrams of the *I Ching* and the inner lines of the enneagram.

· 18 ·
Recurrent Meaning

When I once asked J. G. Bennett what he considered to be the most important novel, he chose James Joyce's Ulysses because, he said, it faithfully depicts the inner life of an ordinary man. After a constant immersion in the belief that only Gurdjieff and his followers have anything significant to say about man, I found this response a relief. In fact, the life of the "ordinary man" is extraordinary, once we have begun to see it. We all share in a human nature that is full of wonder. It has always been too easy to turn away from humanity in the name of the ideals of the Work and forget that we have a common source and a shared experience. The nature of our experience is fathomless. All of us are concerned in finding out its meaning and stretching further into unknown worlds as best we can.

We are awed by experts and authorities, among them the artists, priests, and scientists who seem to go so much further than the average, as well as spiritual teachers, such as Gurdjieff, who live a life of the inexplicable. Because of the sway of authorities of all persuasions, we tend to neglect our shared nature. We imagine that science is done only by people with degrees, working in laboratories. This cannot be right. All that matters is our intent and our integrity. If we want to understand how things work, than we shall learn. It is all there, in the very structure of our experience. We just have to find out how to bring intent into what is natural.

Joyce's Ulysses is a masterpiece that uncovers the recurrent structure of experience. As Leopold Bloom passes through Dublin during one day, he passes through the history of the human race. This day is the same as every other until the end of time. By being the same, it becomes unique and imperishable. It is terror. It is liberation.

The Paths of Experience

EXPERIENCE GENERALLY follows the course of events in the external world, governed by a sequential order that we call time. Yet there are other aspects of experience which are not structured by time at all. They are just "in the now," with no before and after, and appear timeless. These are such features as the consciousness within us and the energy of a rock poised on a hill outside us. What is in time and what is in the timeless must be connected. In the next chapter I will be discussing this connection in more detail, but for the moment let us postulate it as a third aspect of experience. It is through this kind of experience that we are able to act intelligently in the world: being in the timeless moment without the coercion of time is to dream, while lacking any sense of the timeless is to be only a machine.

We learn about the type of experience that is both in and out of time through *recurrent events*. These are not events which repeat in exactly the same way. If a scientist repeats a series of experiments of identical design, for example, the results are not exactly the same. It is, in fact, the liability to variation which makes such events real. If we find the experiments coming up always with the same result, too precisely, we begin to suspect the scientist of fraud! So it is with all of our experience of intelligent action.

Through recurrent events, we see the same thing happening but in different ways and in different circumstances. As this penetrates our experience, we begin to see a *configuration of action* which signals attainment in the given kind of task. We begin to understand the why and how of what works. We become able to generate the action out of ourselves, or by invoking what is needed, to produce something exactly corresponding to the configuration of events we have found in all successes.

What enables us to recognize an event as one of a type, as the same thing, is the space of possibilities defined by the triad of commands from which it is created.[1] The totality of combinations of the three commands is contained in this space. It is from this plenum that we derive the various initiatives needed to begin and control action. The strong intersections of the commands that appear at points 3, 6, and 9 are responsible for the initiation of the three transformative processes (fig. 18.1). If we fail to treat any of the three as independent, something in its own right, then we go badly wrong. To come to understand how we may combine together the three in a coherent totality, we need recurrent experience through which we can learn how to harmonize them. Simply going through the same kind of thing, over and over again, will not be enough.

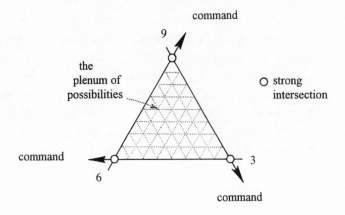

18.1. The possibilities of transformation.

We need to be able to measure—or to assess, or to feel and sense—the degree of coherence of our transits through the critical points. We need to be able to adjust the relative strengths of the three processes, as if we were learning how to perfect a culinary recipe that uses three main ingredients. Recall that Gurdjieff speaks about the need to adjust the proportions of the three "foods" entering into an action, by "strengthening or weakening different parts of the process."

The triangle, or *logos,* that sets the boundaries of possibility, defines the situation only a qualitative sense. It says nothing about how much of anything is needed, or how long it should last. In contrast, the circular sequence connotes a definition in a quantitative sense. The two realms of quality and quantity need to be coalesced, as is represented by the recurrent sixfold figure. This figure is associated with intelligence. As we shall see in the next chapter, we can take the different lines of the inner figure as similar to the lines of command and even consider them independently of each other. For the moment, let us confine ourselves to dividing the inner lines into two sets of linkages, 1-4-2 and 8-5-7. These two say something about the way in which the two critical transitions are made.

The first critical transition, in the region of point 3 of the enneagram, can be thought of in terms of experiment. This means that we find out what works by trying things out. We bring concepts and action into a unity by adjusting them to each other. To do this, we must separate what we do from what we see; otherwise, we can never learn but only repeat the same patterns. We have to take some risks, but not in the sense of a naive gambler hoping that eventually something will pay off. What we are after is what seems to work fairly consistently within a given range of circumstances.

The second critical transition is more a matter of understanding. If we say that in the first transition we are adjusting what we do, then in the second, here we are adjusting how we see. This we cannot learn by doing. What is required of us is to "stand under" something of a higher order. It is a matter of nondoing. In this realm, timing becomes all important. Consider, for example, something as simple as taking a rest—if we take the rest too soon, or too late, it is hardly beneficial. In a similar vein, in the work of creative thinking, it is necessary to let go at a certain point—too soon, and all we have is daydreaming; too late, and we are restricted by old ideas. People recognize the reality of propitious times, and that is why they turn to divination.[2]

An alternative interpretation of the two kinds of critical transitions is cybernetic. In the first transition, our concern is with maintaining direction toward the goal. We need to monitor what is actually happening and compare this against what we have intended, for only then can we make the necessary corrections to keep on course. In the second transition, we do not remain tied to the original goal we set ourselves, *because something superior has begun to show itself.* Strictly speaking, this is something creative which must, to be authentic, go beyond our intentions. The cybernetic interpretation has the value of distinguishing the two halves of the enneagram. On the right-hand side, the side of the first critical transition, we have control and the known. On the left-hand side, where we have the second critical transition, we have letting go and the unknown.

The adjustments we can make around the critical transitions are represented in the enneagram by the inner or periodic lines. We can begin to sketch out what they might mean for us. In the part of the inner sequence 1-4-2, we have the adjustments or learning which are, as I said, experimental in character. Imagine that we stand at point 1. From there, we look along the inner line to point 4 and anticipate what will happen when we arrive there. Out of this anticipation, we prepare ourselves for the transition (through point 3) and this brings us forward to point 2. After the transition, when we actually arrive at point 4, we can compare our memories and anticipations with the reality. However, we will not learn anything unless we first notice the transition (point 3). What we learn concerns the *relation* between points 1, 2, and 4 (fig. 18.2).

In the left-hand part of the inner sequence, 8-5-7, we have a different kind of story (see fig. 18.3). Imagine that we stand at point 5: we have to receive some indication, some intelligence, from point 8. Without that indication, what we do is lacking in direction or is merely a result of the accumulated momentum of the process. In psychological terms, we need to be given the confidence to step into the unknown. This confidence stems from the *relation* between points 8, 5, and 7 which is such that, at point 5, there is a *waiting* that is active. Simone Weil most wonderfully expressed this in her writings as "waiting on God" which, as she ex-

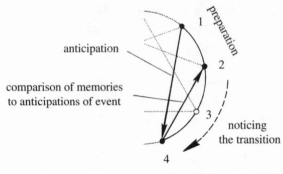

18.2. 1-4-2: Experiment.

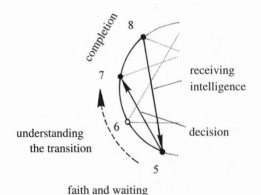

18.3. 8-5-7: Understanding.

plained, should obtain in everything, even school studies.[3] At point 5, the receiving from point 8 leads into the movement toward point 7. Again, we cannot learn of this dynamic relation unless first we notice and acknowledge the critical transition at point 6. It requires something like an act of faith: faith that what is God can reach us, faith that there is a hand out of heaven.

Another informative pattern divides the sequence into 2-8-5 and 7-1-4 (fig. 18.4). Each of these triplets has a foot in each phase of the enneagram. They represent two ways in which the three octaves combine. In the first, we have the essential character of evolution. As Rumi puts it: "Evolution comes from necessity. Increase, then, your necessity!" The relation 2-8-5 arises out of a sense of need. This need is not answered in a way that reaches our experience until point 5. On the other hand, the relation 7-1-4 is more in the nature of an accumulated know-how or expertise. Successful anticipation of point 4 is the attainment of the professional.

It is highly likely that Gurdjieff's conception of the "way given by God for man's self-perfecting" also illuminates what is represented in these inner lines. He said that this way consists of conscious labor and intentional suffering. It is fairly clear that the first belongs to the right half and the second to the left half of the total process depicted in the enneagram. Putting it crudely, in the first we do, while in the second we are "done unto." It is only in the "crux" of these two that transformation is possible.

We can picture the three main parts of the enneagram to ourselves in simple but telling ways: If the outer circle represents our diary, then the

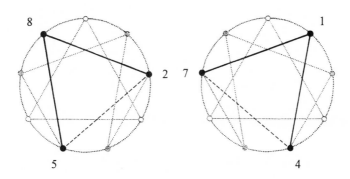

18.4. 2-8-5: Wisdom; and 7-1-4: Know-how.

inner sequence represents our notebooks, and the triangle, our creed. If the outer circle represents our daily lives, then the inner sequence is that of our *sadhana,* or spiritual practice, and the triangle is our faith. If the outer circle is sequence of time, then the inner periodic figure is synchronicity, and the triangle is timelessness.

Even simply to know that there can be different orders of life within the same life can mean a great deal.

Structure of the Week

In chapter 11 I discussed the inherent structuring of ancient texts. These texts are archetypes of the texts we can write for ourselves. It is interesting, however, to look further back beyond the ancient texts to an earlier epoch still, the wisdom of which we find embedded in the constructions and settings of megalithic culture. The framework and structures of myth across the globe undoubtedly arose from these earlier forms, the intellectual history of which we have little knowledge. What we do know, if we are not determined to deny this like most scholars, is that they were based on technically proficient and extensive astronomical knowledge. Knowledge was woven into patterns, and the remnants of these patterns have been perpetuated in such things as the days of the week. As is widely known, the days are named after or in relation to the Sun, Moon, and known planets of early times: Mercury, Mars, Venus, Jupiter, and Saturn. The weekly order is Sun, Moon, Mars, Mercury, Jupiter, Venus, and Saturn. But why are they in this order, which appears to bear no relation to their observable characteristics?

I am indebted to Robin Heath for pointing out the most probable explanation, which has a bearing on our notion of an internal order, in contrast to an external order.[4] Heath argues that in the early cosmological tradition, extensive use was made of symmetrical cyclic figures. If we arrange the seven planets around a circle in order of their apparent angular velocity, and then form the symmetrical cyclic sevenfold figure inside the circle, we find what is shown in figure 18.5.[5]

Starting with the day of the Sun and following the lines of the inner figure, the days of the week unfold as they have been handed down in various traditions. Ouspensky, in attempting to understand the ennea-

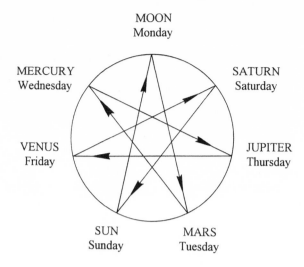

MOON
Monday

MERCURY
Wednesday

SATURN
Saturday

VENUS
Friday

JUPITER
Thursday

SUN
Sunday

MARS
Tuesday

18.5. Days of the week.

gram, himself arranged the days of the week around a circle but failed to grasp the essential point (ISM, p. 378). The direction of internal flow is contrary to that of the outer order.[6] Heath suggests that the heptagram star evolved out of the use of the pentagram, in the sense that the Sun and Moon can be seen as additions. The fascinating thing is that the Sun-Moon line then occurs in association with the position of Gurdjieff's shocks in the octave. The Sun-Moon line divides the circle in the ratio of 2 to 3, corresponding to the *dominant* in music. Following the order around the circle, as shown in Heath's diagram, mi-fa takes us onto this line and also si-do. These are the two extra or critical transitions.

I have adduced a brief sketch of this material just at this point, not only to highlight the significance of the contrast between the inner and the outer sequence but also to acknowledge that Gurdjieff himself knew a great deal about the tradition of which we have been speaking. Taking his reduced companions out of Russia in the throes of revolution, he was able to predict exactly the location of certain dolmens.[7] It is highly probable that this prediction was based on a kind of mentation which belongs to the early cosmological tradition and which has been summarized, or encapsulated, in the enneagram itself.

Intentional Method

After our excursion into the ancient world and the structural organization of texts, we turn to the modern world and the scientific method. Method or know-how is connected with the inner lines of the enneagram.

The inner lines designate the way of intention. They ensure that something is achieved or learned. They should, then, apply to the activity of science. In the course of the development of science, various theories or paradigms began to emerge concerning the structure and logic of the true scientific method. One of the earliest of these was the inductive model of Francis Bacon. Enraptured by the emergence of experimental science and the various discoveries that were being made by explorers reaching to the four quarters of the globe, he took his stand against the intellectualizing of the scholastics, the remnants of the Middle Ages, who spouted all kinds of notions and explanations that had no foundation in fact. He said that the proper scientific method was simply to observe the phenomena (either occurring naturally or generated by experiment), gather information, and inductively reach the principles which lay behind them. Bacon's idea was that science should proceed in a bottom-up mode, starting from the multitude of phenomena and reaching toward the underlying principles or axioms.

Unfortunately, there is no way of proceeding from the phenomena to the principles by any logical or procedural step. Instead, we have come to realize that the scientist *always looks at phenomena through the eye of theory.* What matters in experimental science is to make an experiment which puts some theory to the test. Without the "eye of theory" the scientist would have to proceed almost at random. He or she would have no criterion for doing one experiment rather than another and would spend his or her time collecting data that would, in fact, be meaningless.

Science is really a kind of seeing. We have discovered that even our physical sight is theory-rich in that it proceeds from some idea about what is being seen and then checks this out, making improvements over the initial hypothesis in the process. We always start from some idea about what is out there in the world.

The inductive, bottom-up method corresponds, in terms of the enneagram, to plodding around the outer circle without much hope of ever making a significant step. For the purposes of talking about experimental science, we can picture the first phase of the enneagram in terms of apparatus. The second phase, then, concerns the phenomena being "put through" the apparatus, to constitute an experiment, or to show what is hidden. The third phase concerns the meaning of the results and hence theory.

The constitution and design of apparatus is a critical factor in the development of science. The development of special instruments can reveal to our senses the presence of phenomena usually out of their range. The inductive scientist would have to gather the pieces of his apparatus and put it together without any ultimate sense of what it was going to reveal! In the second phase, phenomena of some sort would occur, but the inductive scientist would have no idea what particular feature of the phenomena to measure. In the third phase, such a scientist would gather together whatever results had been obtained but would not know how to treat them (for example, what mathematics to use) because of the lack of guiding theory. Any general conclusion he came to regarding the phenomena would have to be mere guesswork.[8]

In contrast, the actual working method of scientists proceeds differently. (See fig. 18.6) To a surprising degree, this way of working is precisely spelled out by the sequence of the inner lines of the enneagram. The first realization is that the design of a particular piece of apparatus is related to the specific phenomena the scientist wants to study or measure. The usual starting point is some kind of apparatus that already exists

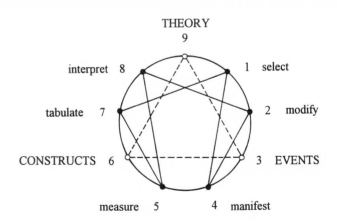

18.6. A sketch of the scientific method.

(point 1) but needs to be modified and improved (point 2) in order to isolate just the phenomenon of interest. In nearly all cases, there are various other phenomena which can mask the effect of the particular phenomenon of interest. The design of the apparatus must take account of this (or such masking effects must be separately measured and accounted for). Hence, the setting up of the experiment follows the linkage 1-4-2, where 4 refers to the particular phenomenon of interest. However, experiments enter into relatively new fields, and scientists can never be completely sure they have got it right. Some degree of hazard and uncertainty remains.

The new octave that comes in at point 3 starts with events, actual occasions on which something happens. The purpose of the apparatus is to enable the scientists to make manifest definite phenomena from these events, in order to disentangle their various components. This is the basis for measurement (point 5). The new octave that comes in at point 6 starts with constructs, that is, ways of interpreting the results of experiments. These enable the scientist to assess what is significant information (point 7) and produce an intelligible interpretation of what has been measured (point 8).

The design of the apparatus (point 2) is related to the hypothesis (point 8). It is this that makes it significant. Experiment for its own sake is a waste of time. Some important feature of theory has to be tested, because without this the experiment has no focus (point 5). Now, how is the theory to be tested? It is by comparing predictions which can be derived from the theory with what actually happens (the line 8-5). Therefore, at point 5 we have to make a specific set of measurements.

What is involved here corresponds to what is called the hypothetico-deductive method, first spelled out by William Whewell in the early part of the nineteenth century.[9] He argued that somehow the scientist came up with some idea about how the world was made—it could be by pure imagination or abstract calculation or sheer guesswork—but what made this idea a scientific one, and not merely a speculation, was that it was of such a nature that it could be put to the test. From the theory (point 8) predictions had to be made that could be tested (point 5). By finding discrepancies between what we should expect from the theory and what we find in practice, we have a way of improving on our theories.

The further steps in the method involve taking the results of the experiment and processing them (point 7) so that they can be significant for the theory. For those without experience of scientific method, this may seem obscure. Just think of it as having a lot of numbers and then having to make sense of them. They have to be tabulated, put into graphs; errors have to be calculated, and so on. In this way, we have the sequence 8-5-7.

What happens next? Well, in science it is not enough for one scientist to do a critical experiment. It must be repeatable. So the process has to be done all over again by different people or repeated with some modifications. This is the line 7-1, in which the published results (point 7) from one laboratory lead to another laboratory (point 1) working to verify them.

All of this can be spelled out in even more detail in terms of the three processes, in which the first runs all the way around the circle. We then have to consider that the running of the experiment (point 4), the measurements (point 5), the calculations (point 7), and the conclusion (point 8) are all part of the "process of the apparatus." Certainly measurement and calculation are.

Then we consider the phenomena. These impact at point 3 and seem to leave the story at point 6. However, point 6 (in terms of the second process) constitutes a transition point to a deeper level. We go from the measurable properties to the underlying forces and processes. For example, we may have measured the magnetic moment of a proton, but we are then supposing that this is due to a property called spin. We have not measured or observed the spin, but we believe it to be there, and so it is incorporated into the domain of theory. So points 7 and 8 in the second octave deal with the underlying phenomena relating back to the basic laws. We have the mathematical model which enables us to relate spin to magnetic moment (point 7) and then the physical model which enables us to give some meaning to the idea of spin in the first place (point 8). The supreme point 9 represents the integral acceptance of the theory evolving from point 8 into the general corpus of the scientific worldview.

Even though the experiment has its outer order, governed by a sequence in time, its actual organization is quite different. This dichotomy was brought out by the biologist Peter Medewar in a classic radio talk, later published, called "Is the Scientific Paper a Fraud?" Speaking in our terms, he says that what the scientist essentially does is to work according to the inner lines; however, what he says about what he does in his scientific paper follows the outer circle.[10]

We also have an interesting illustration of the forward and backward movement of the enneagram. Theory and practice operate in the enneagram in opposite directions. We may think of Einstein, who began his work on relativity with *Gedanken* (thought experiments, point 8), proceeded to mathematical models (tensor calculus, point 7), from which critical measurements could be conceived (point 5), which identified new phenomena (point 4), and eventually entered into the design of apparatus (points 2 and 1), such as in particle accelerators, which have to take account of relativistic effects. This stream was balanced in the counter direction by the work of such experimentalists as Michelson and Morley, who were testing out the hypothesis that the earth moved in relation to an ether.

We can also see that there are crucial facts, which we can associate with point 5. For example: the discovery of cosmic background radiation (at temperature 3 degrees Kelvin) was critical for the general acceptance of the Big Bang theory of cosmology; the failure of classical theory to account for the energy-distribution of black-body radiation was crucial for the discovery of quantum mechanics; and so on. Gurdjieff gives the name *harnelaoot* to this place in a process, and it represents the maximum tension between its outer and inner aspects (in this case between experiment and observation, on the one hand, and theory and calculation, on the other). In the philosophy of science, it is the possibility of *falsification* that is central to Karl Popper's understanding of scientific method.[11]

I should emphasize that having an intentional method in no way guarantees us from making mistakes. In the case of scientific experiment, we may fail to take account of certain masking phenomena—because we do not know enough at that stage—and we may make wrong assumptions in putting our theory to the test. It is finding out about these things that can constitute some of the most important contributions of experimental science. In a sense, whatever the result of a well-designed experiment, there is a gain. The negative result of the Michelson-Morley experiment to measure the movement of the earth through the "ether" was crucial for relativity theory.

The three types of processes involved in the enneagram of scientific work can be expressed in the following terms:

1. What we can do—the technology and know-how of experiment
2. The world as phenomena—what can be made part of our experience
3. What we can think—the meaning of our knowledge

We might think back to the paradigm of the restaurant and picture the enterprise of science in corresponding terms. The various mental images we can conjure up serve as useful metaphors—once we have put the work in to make them meaningful. Another useful metaphor is that of an engine: (1) apparatus, (2) working substance, (3) application. A steam engine (apparatus) uses steam (working substance) to drive a machine (application). Similarly, in a restaurant a kitchen (apparatus) uses food (working substance) to satisfy customers (application). In science, experimental laboratories (apparatus) use phenomena (working substance) to empower theory (application).

The roles of apparatus, substance, and application are relative to the first octave. The second octave becomes a kind of apparatus in its own right, and then the third octave takes the role of its working substance.

In the case of science, the third process has the power to be something sufficient unto itself. Leonardo da Vinci said: "There is no result in nature without a cause; understand the cause and you will have no need of the experiment."[12] Many mathematical physicists have said that the very beauty and elegance of their theories is an adequate criterion of their truthfulness. James Maxwell introduced a fourth equation into his summation of electromagnetic theory purely on aesthetic grounds—and laid the foundation of the modern theory of light and the practical developments of radio communication. Paul Dirac concluded that there must be "antimatter" twenty years or so before any such thing was found. However, we should also appreciate the extent to which prejudice and the inability to think in new ways have delayed scientific advance—for example, Alfred Wegener's (1880–1930) theory of continental drift was ignored for decades, not on empirical grounds but because it was "unthinkable" for his generation.

We can have a science in which only the linkage 8-5-7 is significant. This is the case with cosmology where it is not possible to do experiments—although one can develop apparatus and make measurements (point 5), as we saw with background radiation. Here, technological developments—such as those connected with space travel and infrared imaging, and so forth—introduce different domains of measurement. There is little doubt that the development of new equipment serves to enlarge the range of phenomena which can be studied; just as the development of theory makes it possible for new classes of phenomena to be considered as part of scientific study. This has been the case recently in such diverse fields as chaotics and biospherics. Thus, the range, complexity, and interconnectedness of phenomena are enriched both by theory and by technical progress. It works both ways.

The design of experiments, which transform technical know-how into a means of access to phenomena is the intelligence apparatus that arises around point 3. Its equivalent at point 6 appears more abstract and concerns mathematical methods and modeling (in the contemporary world, computers play an important part in this).

A final comment, this time about point 10 (the implicit whole). Here stands the human organism (including mind, of course) as it has evolved within the biosphere. Konrad Lorenz, in his major book *Behind the Mirror,* points out that the human organism with its knowledge and power has evolved out of the total experience of life on the earth. Given the way that the human organism has evolved, it should not be surprising that its powers of abstract thought should afford insight into the workings of the physical world.

Backward and Forward

It is interesting to look at the natural counterpart or complement of science, which is technology. We call it the counterpart for the following reason: in science, we go from artificial operations on the world into the world of ideas, whereas in technology, we go from the world of ideas into the world of artificial operations. The world of nature, or phenomena, is common to them both. Reducing it to its very simplest, we have two directions of flow, as shown in figure 18.7.

When we consider a technologist of genius such as Nikola Tesla (1857–1943), we can see that what he does is to get an idea *to work in practice.* Thus, for example, we read that "as early as 1882 . . . he began serious and continued efforts to embody the rotating field principle in operative apparatus." And, later: "Even Mr. Tesla himself did not, until after pro-

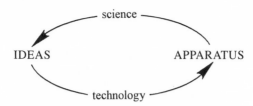

18.7. Science and technology as complementary.

tracted effort and experimentation, learn how to construct alternating current apparatus of fair efficiency."[13] Getting an idea to work is one of the most exacting and difficult things to achieve. There are barriers between the world of ideas and the world of apparatus. It is hard to get something that works at all, and then it is a problem to make something that works well or efficiently. Incarnation is not easy.

The technologist who turns an idea into an apparatus brings higher influences into lower worlds. We can picture to ourselves what this might mean if we take the example of something that does not yet exist, such as a machine based on the *electroweak force* for generating electricity. The electroweak force is still something largely theoretical and is not a factor in the technosphere. As the technosphere enlarges, through the progressive incarnation of ideas, what is possible in experimental science also enlarges. The technosphere constitutes a kind of pool or reservoir of "apparatus stuff" on which scientific investigation can draw.

So we begin to have a picture in which the work of the technologist could, perhaps, be represented as an enneagram in reverse. The Manhattan Project started with the recognition that mass could be converted into energy. It took intensive years, thousands of people, and billions of dollars to get it to work in a bomb. One of the most significant sticking points was how to achieve a critical mass of fissionable material by explosive compression. The solution to this problem came by way of the leading explosive technology of the time. Here we meet again the significance of point 3 on the enneagram, but from the other direction. At point 5 we have a design, but we do not know how to build it so it works. At point 4, we are trying various approaches. At the other side of the critical transition, at point 2, we have one device that actually works. Even this needs refinement and standardization, which is represented by point 1. At point 0, we enter the sphere of manufacture, which belongs to another domain.

There is the question of point 6. In the usual enneagram, this is a critical transition, similar to point 3. Does it have this role in the backward direction? After all, here we are dealing with a *descending octave.* Starting at point 9, or do, we have the recognition of the practical significance of mass being converted to energy. At si, or point 8, this is converted into the decision to make it a bomb. At la, or point 7, this steps down to a specification of fissionable material and the mechanism of attaining critical mass. Then, at sol, or point 5, there is a design.

Now, in one sense, this sequence just follows naturally from the beginning. However, in another sense, something is required to enter into the process: the *conviction that it can be done.* This infuses the total system. It involves a judgment about the state of parallel or connected technologies. It is interesting to note that this need not appear at point 6, between points 7 and 5, but is required right from the start. In moving from point 9 to point 8, a decision is made that rests on this judgment.

When Leonardo worked on the design of flying machines, he had no contemporary technology which could support their realization—no adequate power sources, no alloys, and so on. There comes, in the history of invention, a time when certain things are possible, but it will require the utmost to achieve it. There was a time when the computer became practicable, not simply possible, or when the atom bomb became practicable—or a journey to the moon.[14] To put these things into the actual world of things required much expenditure of effort and creativity, but their time had come. What matters, from the perspective of the archetypal technologist at point 9 is to see what is evolving. Imagine him looking down into the actual world of things: he sees new developments and tendencies in techniques and materials that can be extrapolated toward the assembly of a critical mass.[15] He then descends to meet the emergent situation and exploit it. Interestingly enough, the region of point 6 is very much to do with *timing,* as was suggested earlier on.

The technologist has to have a sense of the whole state of the technosphere. When he incarnates an idea into a machine, he does this in the context of a complex total system, with which he needs to be in tune. This tells him that the time may be ripe for the new invention, and it also indicates where the new techniques and materials may be found. He is like the character in the Sufi story who goes into a shop and asks the proprietor, "Do you have leather? Do you have needle and thread?"

When the man in the shop agrees, he is asked, "Then why don't you make shoes?" The perception on one level sees the unity of what are separate things on a lower level.

We may conclude that there is a case for saying that technology is the counterflow of science. Certainly, science has the aim of unification, while technology has the aim of proliferation. Equally clearly, the two cross over one another, support each other, and exploit each other. The experimental side of science is not possible without a supporting technology, and technology does not develop fast unless it draws on fundamental theory.

There is another perspective still, in which we conceive of an enneagram which encompasses both science and technology by having the former on the left-hand side and the latter on the right-hand side. However, these would then appear in the guise of the inner lines: science in the linkage 8-5-7 and technology in the linkage 1-4-2. They are like the two "brains" of modern technoculture which cross-fertilize or stimulate each other.

It is important to stretch our minds in this way, because we have to make sense of what we do. Even if we are simply making up a story to satisfy a subjective need for meaning, this has objective ramifications. In this case, there is an urgent need to make sense of the advent of science and technology on this planet and to understand where they might lead us. We speak of them as "they," as if they were independent powers—and, in some sense, that is what they are. Each has or "is" a partial intelligence. It is most important that we see how they may work together, because this implies a higher intelligence than either. If we think of science and technology as, for example, the two halves of the inner lines of the enneagram, we are beginning to conceive of a superbrain and put ourselves in the place of an intelligence which sees through both eyes. As Leonardo pointed out: "Science, knowledge of the things that are possible, present and past; prescience, knowledge of the things which may come to pass."[16]

From time to time, we have mentioned a higher or "demiurgic" intelligence. This is higher intelligence in the *technological* sense; one of the jobs of which was to establish life on this planet: the *theory* had already been developed during previous generations of research in previous star formations! The conviction that pervades this action has been revealed to us as one of love and compassion; the practical step by which it was accomplished being the use of surfaces.

Notes

1. See "The Logos," in chapter 6.
2. The art of divination rests on the idea that, in some way, everything is in connection with everything else. Because of this, local regions contain information which is global. The kind of problems we face in living are very much bound up in the uncertain relation between the locality of our concern, where we can experience and do things, and the Greater Present Moment, the structure of which is going to determine whether we succeed or fail or the way in which things work out. If we are able to tune into the hidden information which is only implicate in our situation, then we can act more wisely or see things with greater wisdom. The tuning that is required needs to relate to patterns, rather than to discrete bits and pieces. In some ways, the rituals of divination are in themselves the key, rather than in any system which might be used of interpretation. In the case of the *I Ching*, the preparation already produces an intuitive state. The forms and symbols of the techniques used serve to reflect the hidden information which is coming *from within*. They do not constitute the information themselves.
3. See "Reflections on the Right Use of School Studies with a View to the Love of God," in Simone Weil, *Waiting on God*. The practical technique is in the discarding of the inadequate and faith in the availability of what is right. We call this tuning. See also "Two Principles of Living," in Bennett, *The Way to Be Free*.
4. See Robin Heath, *A Key to Stonehenge*, p. 67.
5. Ibid., fig. 31.
6. Ichazo mistakenly takes this direction as signifying the negative import of the internal sequence 1-4-2-8-5-7. The idea that there are bad versions of a structure is strangely archaic. Perhaps he is trying to fit in the idea of the negative laws of world 96 which appear in the Gurdjieff-Bennett system.
7. This is mentioned in Thomas and Olga de Hartmann, *Our Life with Mr. Gurdjieff*.
8. However, statistical studies can show correlations between different phenomena, such as between lung cancer and smoking, before the underlying mechanism is discovered. Such correlations relate to the right-hand understanding of the enneagram, as I discussed earlier in this chapter.
9. See R. E. Butts, ed., *Theory of Scientific Method*.
10. The relation between the inner and the outer sequence remains one of the most fascinating features of the enneagram. In one of the most remarkable and original papers published on the enneagram, "Structured Process in Scientific Experiment," Ken Pledge shows that the setting-up of a piece of scientific apparatus must follow the inner lines, while its functioning follows the outer sequence.

11. Karl Popper, *The Logic of Scientific Discovery.*

12. See Leonardo da Vinci, *The Notebooks of Leonardo da Vinci,* p. 61.

13. *Inventions, Researches and Writings of Nikola Tesla,* p. 4.

14. Of course, we do have intriguing anomalies, such as Charles Babbage constructing a computer in the nineteenth century, which become the stuff of alternative histories, as in the science fiction novel *The Difference Engine* by William Gibson and Bruce Sterling.

15. This was one of the most important characteristics of Buckminster Fuller. See the first chapter of his posthumous *Cosmography.* Fuller offers a wonderful example of adopting the attitude of being a global citizen, a person able to act in terms of a hundred-year time span, or Greater Present Moment. This is not arrogance at all! It is inherent in the nature of intelligence.

16. *The Notebooks of Leonardo da Vinci,* p. 65.

· 19 ·
Remember to Remember

If we have reached some creative insight or some deeper perception, we find it difficult to remember how it came about. It is for that reason that we consider the creative step to be spontaneous, unconscious, and generally out of our control. We do not know how to make it happen again. As T. S. Eliot says: "We had the experience but missed the meaning. . . ." What we have to do is build a bridge of remembrance, a way of recapitulation that can reengineer the same event again. This then is true mastery. The completion of understanding is to be able to recreate an insight at will. Progress takes place within the present moment as we integrate our experience in and out of time.

The Transformational Present

WHILE THE OUTER sequence of points in the circle of the enneagram is simply a circulation, the periodic form of the inner lines of the enneagram suggests recurrence. The difference between the two is very important. If we imagine ourselves going round the circle we may have the appearance of getting somewhere; but we come to the end only to start all over again. In the inner lines, starting again is intentional. In the psychological scheme of Castaneda's school, for example, this is related to the practice of *recapitulation*. As we consciously remember, what we remember does not remain the same. There is a transformation.

The inner lines suggest that there is an action that is constantly *entering into itself*.[1] This allows for the whole to wax stronger or weaker—or to become more or less integrated—as it recurs in the triple flux of the octaves. It would then seem reasonable to look at our own present moment to exemplify what these lines mean.

Everything that we can do, everything that we can reach, all our realizations, have to be accomplished in and through the present moment. I have used this idea frequently. Now is the time to affirm that this is not any psychological or emotional feeling of "now" but the way in which we can be said to exist. The feeling of now is certainly part of the present moment, as is the sense of time passing; but it has a shape, a meaning, and a purpose that is more than temporal. That is why the heading of this section refers not merely to the "present moment" but to the "transformational present."

I will use the model proposed by Bennett in his *Dramatic Universe*, but with some differences.[2] I have already mentioned the obvious temporal aspect, and it will come as no surprise to learn that we should include past and future in our representation of the present moment. We function in time and space. The question "Well, just how long is 'now'?" depends for its answer on how "now" is construed. If we are imagining an abstract line of time then the "now" becomes an ungraspable fiction. Time is somehow "thick" and is more than a line.[3] The word *present* is sometimes used to designate this. The present has shape, coherence, and direction.

From whence does its shape come? The answer is twofold. First, there is shape because there are shapes! Very simply, there are forms of all kinds, around us and in us, forms which persist and against which we experience the flux of time. This can be thought of as the fullness of space, in contrast with the space dimension, which is characterized by separation. The fullness of space is topological, and everything is a part of everything else in terms of *presence*.[4] Second, there is something of a very different nature: *values*. Values do not persist; they draw us on. They give meaning and purpose to what we are doing. Without values, the present collapses into the workings of a machine.[5]

Values give the present moment a direction. We can imagine this in existential terms as something like a set of fields. For example, when people are gathered together in a dialogue, their "common presence" is informed by their collective *information field*.[6] Each of the people will have a value-structured force in the field, which can lead to both conflict and cocreation.[7]

The realm of forms and values cannot be entirely described in terms of function. It also has to do with being. It is in terms of being that we can think of degrees of inner togetherness, and it is through the inner lines that we explore the togetherness of ourselves.

The flux and the shape of the present are not the whole story. There remains to answer the most important question: Through what do we have a hold or influence on existence? This is from our will. Again there are two aspects to this. On the one hand, we are committed to a pattern of living that will recur throughout our lives. This is in part due to what is generally called character and includes choices made perhaps long ago in early childhood. (Some would argue for the relevance of things done in previous lives or the general cosmic configuration at the time of birth.) This pattern tells us who we are and gives us the sense that "this is my life." There is also a freedom of decision. It is decision that creates a new future beyond recurrence. It is decision that embraces the unknown and the unforeseeable. Here decision is not making up our mind, but intentional creativity. If the recurrent pattern signifies *fate*, then the realm of free decision must signify *destiny*.

We must be careful to distinguish this kind of decision-making from what is familiar in business. Kierkegaard's "leap into faith" is an excellent paradigm.[8] Freedom of decision comes at point 8 in the enneagram model, and, without this, the inner lines do not fully come into operation. It is the way out of having to repeat the patterns instilled in us.

Putting these factors around the enneagram highlights something that has been implicit all along: that this symbol describes the transformational present, that it is a diagram of what Bennett calls the war with time.[9]

The three terms *function, being,* and *will,* used in figure 19.1, are descriptive of the three octaves. Function is *what* we do; being is *how* we are; and will is *why* we act.[10] The transformational present is a region of movement and change, of feeling and the changeless, and of knowing and creation. We need to recognize that these combine not in a sequence but in an integration of the three that can progress.

The sequence of the inner lines represents progress within the present moment.

1–4: anticipation
4–2: selection of actualization
2–8: freedom from locality
8–5: commitment in faith
5–7: action in conscience
7–1: recapitulation in consciousness

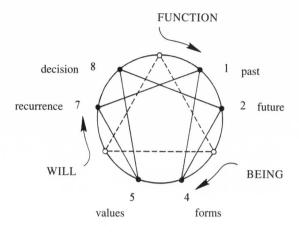

19.1. Enneagram of the transformational present.

The six aspects of the present moment, which appear to come to us from different directions, are brought together by the inner lines. They are able to fuse together, and, as they do so, a new kind of wholeness emerges: a *soul.* We have to make what happens to us our own. We have to make what comes to us externally and extensively into something arising from within, intensively. Either we eat the world, or the world eats us.

Among other features, the inner lines represent the operations of *intelligence.* It may be useful to attempt to spell out in general terms the characteristic contribution of each of the six terms, showing the inner and outer aspects:

inner figure	*outer circle*
the *integrative action* is:	*present-moment characteristics:*
created by 8	decision
regulated by 7	recurrence
focused by 5	values
modulated by 4	forms
selected by 2	future
started by 1	past

The intervals between the points around the enneagram represent types of operation. In the context of the transformational present, these are:

1-2: flux
2-3: uncertainty
3-4: formation
4-5: chaos
5-6: development
6-7: transformation
7-8: creation[11]

The intervals between points 1, 8, and 9 are of a different order (see below). Point 9 always stands in strongest contrast to the interval 4-5. In the transformational present, point 9 is an "I"-ness that links with the dimensionless, spiritual reality of point 10. We use the term *individuality* for this. The 4-5 region which we have associated with turbulence, fire, and chaos represents all those influences upon us which, in their myriad of forms, inform every fleeting moment with the background noise of the universe. A point I am continually stressing is that the enneagram does not, and should not, prescribe any doctrinal interpretation of human reality. My definition of point 9 is as abstract as I can make it and is not intended to refer merely to a person who is "good." The interpretation any one of us might make depends upon our worldview (largely determined in the sector 3 to 6 of the enneagram).[12] Just by way of example, we might consider the following to be true—

8–9: liberation
9–1: incarnation

—and to represent the way of Mahayana Buddhism, in which the Buddha incarnates out of compassion, without compulsion. The 7-8 operation would then have to be interpreted as decreation rather than creation, to fit Buddhist doctrine. The elements in the outer circle represent the sources of suffering (*dukkha*) and the inner lines, the way out of suffering. The enneagram is indifferent to which interpretations we believe, but it reminds us of their consequences.

The recurrent and integrative nature of the transformational present means that "I" permeates in some way throughout the whole— throughout the seven or nine operations; throughout the steps of integration; and throughout the whole process. How can we picture this? Some people carelessly position the "I" in the center of the enneagram, but there is *no central point* in the enneagram, and similarly there is no central "I" in us either.

Jung's concept of *individuation* is pertinent here. It gives us a new perspective on the inner lines. We have begun to see that the character of these lines can be expressed by a different perception or understanding of the points that are connected by them. In the case of Jung's understanding, point 7 would appear as the "shadow," point 8 as the "archetype of individuation," and point 5 as the "ego." It is the inner communication 8-5-7 that can restore the wholeness of the individual.

Each of us may be tempted by some particular metaphor for the guiding principle of the whole. It is an issue that is also culturally biased. It is important to recognize the enigma of the guiding intelligence. We do not see point 9 on the enneagram. What we can see is point 8. Gurdjieff himself elaborated this metaphor in terms of the master (point 9) and real steward (point 8) (ISM, p. 60). If we think of an orchestra, then the conductor is not at point 9 but at point 8. When Ernest Ansermet conducted, he did so on behalf of God. In the case of an orchestra making a performance, we will find that point 9 is as much in the audience as in the performers.

In the outer circle we have the sequence of action, stage by stage. This is set in motion by a desire and assisted almost to completion by the mechanical shock at point 3. All the stages have to be recovered and integrated together for the octave to be fully completed (reaching point 9, or do). The return transforms what was driven into what is freely chosen. Desire sets the outer process in motion, but, in the recollecting of the return, only the love inspired by reconciliation serves.

All that is set in motion by desire and mechanism has to be regained by love and free intelligence.

The Inner Lines

An alternation between the outer flow around the circle and the inner recurrent oscillation always appears. There is a mutual impact of the two tendencies. The tension between the outer and the inner forces works in various ways. At point 2, for instance, the forward tendency is toward point 4, while the inner line attractor is toward point 8. This is the split between doing and seeing that makes the critical transition at point 3 meaningful. Only at point 5 do we have the two tendencies in concert. This we understand as accepting the reconciling force that enters at point 6.[13]

The language that I am inviting into our discussion is deliberate. It is homomorphic with the dialectic that Gurdjieff engaged in in his early teaching, when he attempted to go from the cold and desolate infinitudes of the ray of creation to an evolutionary and increasingly living universe of compassionate communication. The mythic dimensions of this dialectic are immense. All the various cultures of the world may be seen (in their conflicts and complementarities) as inevitable reflections of a cosmic truth which must find expression somehow in human minds.

The interplay between the inner and the outer lines is not a struggle of opposites. Only, the dominance of an inner line can shape or influence the connections between the different stages. The inner lines are strengthened through understanding. Through repetition alone, the whole system acquires a set of biases. If we have a situation in which there are many people working as a team, then each of them will have a particular bias, a particular emphasis on one or other of the inner lines. This does not distinguish them as different "types": it only points to their different dispositions. Often we need changes of personnel to achieve the balance of forces. A leader who does not understand about the inner lines, who is completely task-orientated, will tend to fail because the inner periodic figure is allowed to be fragmentary or misshapen. The task-orientated manager tends to neglect the inner work and resort to crude ideas of motivation. ("Motivation" corresponds to the drive of the Terminator).

The inner lines now appear to us as a subtle art concerning the use of experience—or of people, too. For our own selves, we can come to recognize the way in which we avoid certain requirements of the whole, something that has to be cured before the whole can come to birth in us.[14]

If the outer circle delineates the operations we enter into, then the inner lines depict the meanings of qualities that inform us and are akin to *feelings*. Using this idea to guide us, we can divide the lines as right and left and picture them in the following terms to provide a different illustration than we had before:

1-4:	want	
4-2:	can	the inner feelings
2-8:	wish	

. . . .

8-5:	faith	
5-7:	hope	the "theological" virtues
7-1:	charity	

This interpretation corresponds to the scheme of *latifas* or "subtleties" that can be found in Sufism, though in different terminology. Every individual or group or tradition that ventures into the inner lines evolves its own terminology and even its own phenomenological manifestations. The recurrent theme throughout is that there is an inner work or set of powers by which we are able to enter fully into the present moment.

It is important to emphasize that entering into the inner lines is to proceed otherwise to the more mechanical sequence around the circle. There is a tendency for any state or action to lead automatically to another, almost as a reaction.[15] The emotions follow definite sequential patterns. It is an important step to be able to break this sequence by adopting the different sequence of the inner lines. This is the art of life: it is only by proceeding otherwise that we can learn and change.

The theme of the "transformational present" can be associated with the characterizations of the present moment that are found in the *I Ching*. In this divinatory text, the emphasis is on the pattern of the moment, which is expressed in terms of a six-line figure or hexagram. The lines can be broken (*yin*) or unbroken (*yang*), and so there are sixty-four possibilities. It is highly probable that the six inner lines of the enneagram and the hexagram structure of the *I Ching* have a similar purpose and meaning.[16] To illustrate the idea, I will show how we might show on the enneagram a specific hexagram: Unsettled (number 64), ䷿.

This hexagram maps into the inner lines as in figure 19.2

The three terms *earth, man,* and *heaven* indicate the Chinese trinity. Sometimes, these are applied to the lines of the hexagram, and this enables us to offer a possible correlation with the inner lines of the enneagram (there are other possibilities):

MAN

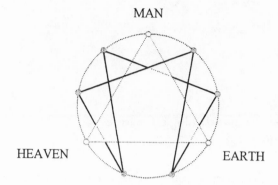

HEAVEN   EARTH

19.2. Enneagrammatic representation of a hexagram.

line	trinity	inner lines
6	heaven	8–5
5	heaven	5–7
4	man	7–1
3	man	2–8
2	earth	4–2
1	earth	1–4

In using the *I Ching* itself, there are many interpretations of the *yin-yang* distinction, far more subtle than differentiating the weak and the strong, or the feminine and the masculine. We would expect to find a similar subtlety in regard to the inner lines of the enneagram.

These inner lines represent "self-observation" and "self-knowledge," but divorced from their personalistic associations. The idea that when we observe ourselves, there is some kind of person looking at some other kind of person is rather sick. It is a mere reflection of our social cruelty and exploitation, and it tends to foster alienation from ourselves. The inner lines are "self-observation" without any artificial "self" invented for the job. What threads through and informs the nexus of selves is not a self but *intelligence*.

Edwin Wolfe tells a story of asking Gurdjieff about self-observation:

"We feel that there may be something wrong in the way we are doing self-observation. Are we wrong, Mr. Gurdjieff?"

"Never you do self-observation," he said forcefully. "You do mind observation. Mind observation you do can even make psychopath."[17]

Remembering

As complex and multilayered beings, we pass through many different kinds of experiences or states during our lives, or even during a single day. We might think of a whole hierarchy of states and imagine them arrayed around the symbol of the enneagram in the outer circle. While it may be true that we pass through all these experiences, it is not true that we automatically *remember* them. Indeed, memory itself is different for different levels of experience. The experiences associated with the second phase of the enneagram and, hence, the second octave are marked by an inner intensity that mere memory of "what happened" cannot carry. On one day we hear a piece of music, and we are in rapture. The next, we find the same piece banal. Something—in the second octave—is missing. If we try to bring it back, we find we have only the form and not the content. The inner intensity we once had has gone out of sight into the unconscious, and we do not know how to bring it back at will.

It is even harder to remember an insight into meaning or purpose. Just suppose that there is a sense of objective purpose we can access, a sense that links us with our destiny. In the course of events, this comes and goes. It may come and go very quickly indeed, dwelling in us for a matter of seconds or even less. We might call to mind Gurdjieff's theme of the burning question which, he said, it was necessary to have if we are to go forward in our quest for reality. For how long can we sustain such a question in us? A scientist or artist is able, in some measure, to "maintain" in this region. In doing so, he or she has what Ouspensky called long thoughts capable of transforming their understanding. In this region, what matters is not so much inner intensity as quality of seeing.

In the course of events—that is, as we go through the outer cycle—our presence in the higher regions is the more and more fleeting the higher we go—until, at the end, we are hardly there at all before we "fall asleep" once more.

To "remember to remember" is to be able to bring back and enhance what is meaningful in our experience. It demands a deliberate and subtle practice. In place of the "pouring of empty in void" that Gurdjieff rightly criticizes, we build an understanding of who we are and what we should be doing. This is possible through the inner lines.

The inner lines, in their turn, need to be directed by the triangle, the *logos* in us. In general, this is the triunity of active intelligence, love, and will. Ultimately, we have to learn to *let will have us*. We do not "have" will!

The inner lines constitute what Edward Matchett has called the inner life activity. It is a constant reentering of ourselves into ourselves. It is a dialogue we are having with ourselves. If the inner lines are active, then we are never at a loss. Whenever we engage in a process, we can have the confidence that we have an intimate connection with all its stages, at every moment. We understand that we must consciously assimilate everything that happens to us, or it will be forgotten and lurk unsuspected in the unconscious, influencing us in ways we are not aware of.

The pattern of the inner lines has its origin with point 8. This point is the "representative of the creator" where the "creator" is point 9. Point 8 arises out of point 9. In Sufi terminology, if 9 is the sun, then 8 is the moon. It is what Sri Aurobindo calls the descent of the supramental, and we need to allow it into ourselves. In Western parlance, it is the destiny that shapes our ends. The line 8-5 represents the pull of destiny on our egoism, the inner challenge of ourselves with which we were conceived. It then follows that the line 5-7 represents what follows from our agreement: "Be it done to me according to Thy Word." Why, then, should we have to return again, as indicated along the line 7-1? The reason for this is to make a true beginning. In ordinary life, we are constantly seeking to build on what we have achieved; only, this will not support us on the path of transformation, and is to build upon sand as in the Gospel parable.

The inner lines 1-4-2 concern what we have to "do by day," while the others concern what we must "do by night"—that is, in the regions beyond our usual consciousness.

Every Day

Just as the enneagram divides between right and left, between day and night, so does it articulate the layers of our experience (in the vertical direction). In an earlier chapter, I referred to the celestial analogues of the empyrean and the sublunar region. These reflect into the range of our own experience (fig. 19.3).

There is a tide wafting us into and out of the world. It is only when the different layers of experience begin to interconnect that we begin to understand what our life *is*. Until then, we pass from one layer to the other in a condition of forgetfulness. When we begin to remember that we live and die every day, then another order comes to life in us. In a strange way, all of us, whatever our beliefs and experiences, realize this. As we become adult, we establish a pattern of meaning that makes sense of having to wake up in the morning and go to sleep at night. Take point 2. For one person it will mean simply a cup of coffee and a cigarette. For another it will mean at least an hour of inner attention. Similarly, point 7 might mean to one a nightcap of whisky and a rigorous recapitulation of the day's events to another.

In a banal sense, point 3 is leaving the house in the morning, and point 6 is returning in the evening. For an intentional life, they represent the focus of a decision and a remembering. For a man or woman who practices inner work, morning and evening are marked by particular intentional work. In the Gurdjieff-Bennett tradition, point 2 is the morning exercise, characterized by conscious, elaborate, and specific attention.

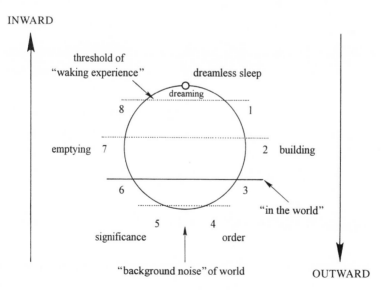

19.3. Enneagram as levels of experience.

Point 7 is the meditation or review of the day (in which events are viewed in reverse order). The cognition that we will fall asleep is very significant. How we deal with that reveals us to ourselves.

Similarly, sexual relations usually take place either on waking or before sleeping. We speak of a man and woman "sleeping together." This signifies the deeper level at which the real action of sex occurs. Sex is in essence spontaneous and contrasts with the deliberate and focused nature of external work. It accords with the essential character of inner work, in spite of tendencies to make the work within as mechanical as the work without.

We lose ourselves in the world in a complementary way to that in which we lose ourselves in sleep. This lends our usual "waking" state a certain ambiguity. We are contextual creatures, constantly striving for optimum meaning of our purposes through a variety of contexts. The "whole man" is identified, alert, asleep, focused, spontaneous, engaged, and detached in several measures. The inner circuitry represented by the periodic lines designates the growing intelligence of the whole.

Reading the Enneagram

The enneagram is a message. It can inform our lives. To find this message, we have to unpeel the layers just as we might unpeel the layers of an onion. The enneagram even tells us how to do this unpeeling.

I will begin with the movement around the enneagram in a circle.

The Circle

The first process goes in a circle and then repeats (fig 19.4). This is Ouspensky's picture of eternal recurrence, in which we do the same thing over and over again. In his novel on the subject, *Strange Life of Ivan Osokin,* the hero is powerless to change this endless repetition even when he has access to the knowledge that this is happening. It is not enough to be aware of recurrence; we have to be *able to do* something about it. Osokin says: "It is hard to believe that I can actually do nothing at all. But, at the same time, what have I done so far? I have only spoiled everything."[18]

We can think of our daily lives. We wake, rise, and go about our business and our play and then sleep once more. The sleep we have at night is the "sleep" we have in passing from point 8 to point 1 again. We are

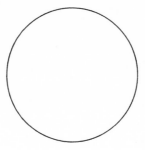

19.4. The circle.

not aware of point 9 at all. In the Hindu tradition, for example, point 9 exists only in dreamless sleep, and the transition from 8 to 1 is made in dreaming sleep. We have no idea how our "consciousness" is reconstituted at the break of day. "Who" informs our organism to have the sense of "I"?

The First Octave

To get around to the starting point again, there have to be the interventions Gurdjieff called shocks. In the first octave of the process (fig.19.5) around the circle, the first intervention is provided mechanically (there would not be any repeated processes otherwise). The right-hand side of the enneagram is the mechanical complement of the spiritual, left-hand side. Gurdjieff gave the example of our transformation of food, that will continue to cycle round and round as long as we breathe.[19] This cycle

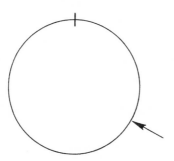

19.5. The first octave.

goes from food in the stomach to spermatogenesis, from 1 to 8, over and over again, and this is what life is about.

Any "yoga" we do will operate from the external and give only external results. We are just in personality. We can meditate forever, but we remain outside ourselves. We are in what the Chinese call guest position, not in host position.

The second intervention has to be conscious. In the first octave, this must take place in the region between point 8 and point 9. But that is where *we are asleep.* The transformation does not go beyond sex to self-creation (called by Gurdjieff *resulzarion*) because we "are not there."[20] Maybe *something else* is there?

The Second Octave

According to Gurdjieff, we have to use up the stuff of dreams, or we can no longer function in the waking state and are not able to sleep properly—and so we require the intervention of artificial stimulation, such as entertainment.[21] This gives a pseudoshock at point 6 in contrast with the genuine article that comes from within.

The second octave (fig. 19.6) has to start because it provides the intervention in the first octave that keeps the first going in the right direction. In its turn, the second will not develop very far unless the third octave intervenes. This cannot come about mechanically; it has to arise consciously. Gurdjieff spoke about the third octave as "impressions," but

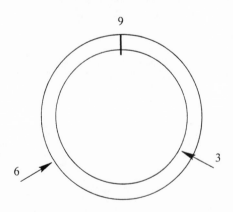

19.6. The second octave.

these are conscious impressions and not reactions to stimuli. To receive and be aware of impressions in a conscious way is linked to a type of perception that was talked about by Gurdjieff as self-remembering, which, however, refers to conscience more than it does to any state.[22]

When the second octave is enabled to develop, it becomes the means of feeding or manufacturing the second being-body, or *kesdjan* body. This body is not like the etheric double, beloved of occultists, but has specific properties and structure of its own unlike those of the physical body. It is unlikely that conscience can play a strong role in life unless there is enough inner substance through which it can make itself felt. The "blood" of the kesdjan body is an active inner life.[23] This is made out of a material similar to dreaming but acts in an opposite way. We become aware of recurrence and can begin to do something about it. We are growing from essence—the state in which we were born and not the state which has accumulated through external impacts. The main characteristic of essence is that it does not rely on memory or calculation but deals with things as they are without images or explanations.

The Inner Lines

The inner lines (fig. 19.7) develop (rather in the sense that a photograph develops when placed in the right chemicals) when the second octave is stimulated by the third octave. If we eschew this talk of inner bodies, we can still identify the inner lines with what in Hindu terminology is called *sadhana,* or spiritual practice. Sadhana is what we do inten-

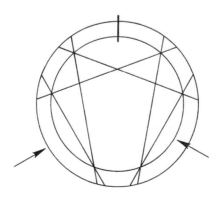

19.7. The inner lines.

tionally with our inner lives apart from our involvement in the world. Our daily round goes about the circle, while our inner lives develop in the inner lines. As we have seen, these may develop in unbalanced ways, because of our emotional or cultural preferences.[24]

The purpose of sadhana is to make the internal connections through which the transformative process can be monitored and guided. It is another kind of repetition. It may have all kinds of external forms and be described in all kinds of terminology, but it amounts to what Gurdjieff calls work on oneself. By this, recurrence is changed.

If we eschew all reference to spirituality, we can still think of the requirement for a business organization, for instance, to go on learning and to cultivate a state of learning in a way that is not immediately linked to economic advantage. This is to take the psyche of the organization as of primary value. The inner lines are signs of psychic health. This realm has to be dealt with on its own terms. Some kind of inner life will always come about in time, but it may well be diabolical or deranged and deeply destructive of purposeful endeavor. Things going wrong in this realm are far more damaging than things going wrong in external operations.

To some degree the inner lines are self-reflexive. They are the key to integrity in life. This means that they concern our communication with ourselves, or the communication of an organization with itself. In the case of an organization, dialogue is needed, in which values and attitudes are brought into the light of consciousness. With this in place, the organization can have a "virtual" identity not dependent on place and function.[25]

With the arising of the second octave, we can become aware of the different order in events and we can master dreaming. "Yoga" comes from within. We begin to grasp that what we have called the unconscious is, in fact, the true consciousness. In Castaneda's scheme, it is to be centered in the "second attention."

The Third Octave

The third octave (Fig. 19.8) requires that we *know what we are doing.* It is intentional creativity. The inner lines made it possible for us to always find the connections that work. What goes further is the *return to the source*, which needs the second conscious intervention, or conscious

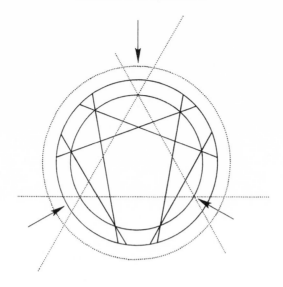

19.8. The third octave.

shock, between points 8 and 9. It is this that enables us to "be" at point 9 and "know the place for the first time," in Eliot's phrase.

The Triangle of the Logos

In Gurdjieff's psychocosmology the further development of the third octave feeds the third being-body, or body of the soul. It is now that the three points of the triangular figure become "filled with the holy ghost," and the power of the reconciling force begins to manifest.[26]

For a person, this means to become entirely spontaneous. For an orga-

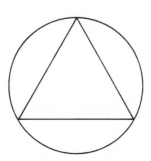

19.9. The triangle of the logos.

nization, the prospects are intriguing. Beyond the virtual organization, there is the *free organization*. It consists of pure information able to create organizations anywhere at any time.[27] It is similar to an autocatalytic enzyme.

Gurdjieff's three series of writings exemplify the progression from outer circle to inner lines and to the triangle:

first octave:	*Beelzebub's Tales*	outer circle
second octave:	*Meetings with Remarkable Men*	inner lines
third octave	*Life Is Real Only Then, When "I Am"*	triangle

The "yoga" that is possible here takes us through death. It is the *Bardo Thodol*, the Tibetan Book of the Dead.

The Final Shock

In the Gurdjieff lore, the final or "second conscious" shock (fig. 19.10) is associated with the transformation of negative emotions (ISM, pp. 190–93). This, the most important factor in the whole enneagram, is hardly ever discussed. There are good reasons for this. The idea of transforming negative emotions suggests a very powerful mode of tantra.[28] Certainly, we must have the transformation of the negative into the positive, because here we go beyond the opposites. Even more seriously, it is here that we are concerned with overcoming evil and sin. It is salvation. It is

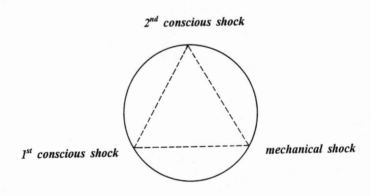

19.10. *The three shocks.*

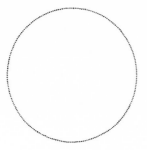

19.11. Emptiness.

the core of the "esoteric Christianity" that Gurdjieff said lay behind his Work (ISM, p. 109).

Recurrence is ended. With this, we leave the enneagram.

Notes

1. The description here corresponds to what we might find in such diverse areas as hermeneutics and the autopoeisis of Varela. It also ties in with some of the recent discussions about the nature of consciousness which emphasize its self-referential nature. In general, such interpretations are aligned with being rather than with function or will.

2. J. G. Bennett, *The Dramatic Universe,* vol. 4, pp. 13–7.

3. See the extended discussion of this point in my book, *A Seminar on Time.*

4. I had some interesting discussions with David Bohm about his ontological concepts of space. In his view, everything is somewhat included in everything else (which later led to his ideas of "implicate order"). Imagine a set of regions which overlap each other: There is something of *a* in *b*, of *b* in *c* and of *c* in *d*; therefore, there is something of *a* in *d* even though they appear separate.

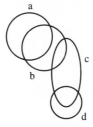

5. The connection between external form, or the world, and internal form, or values, is the topic of the four-term system, or *tetrad,* that is the "task" of the interval between points 3 and 6. In essence, their connection is through the

intersection of doing and seeing, or various other kinds of complementarities. The enneagram is a structure of structures, an immensely compressed encoding of strings of complex tasks.

6. This is a term used by David Bohm, particularly in respect to the dialogue process. It derives from his last work on the ontological interpretation of quantum mechanics. Whenever a group of people sit down to talk with each other, they share in a common information field. This defines their collective possibilities.

7. Participants in a dialogue operate on the same information field but tend to want the field to be structured according to their own view of things. This leads to conflict. I am indebted to Hashim Abu Sido for pointing out to me that "the more people believe in the same thing, the more they are likely to come to want to kill each other." If people can become aware of this tendency and learn to bear conflict within themselves and not simply project it out upon others, then they can become capable of cocreation, a new kind of group creativity. See my *Structures of Meaning*.

8. "Without risk there is no faith. Faith is precisely the contradiction between the infinite passion of the individual's inwardness and the objective uncertainty." Kierkegaard, *Concluding Unscientific Postscript*, p. 182.

9. See chapter 42 in Bennett, *The Dramatic Universe*, vol. 4.

10. See Bennett, *Deeper Man*, pp. 13–24 for a discussion of these terms. In Bennett's schema, they also correspond to three kinds of time: linear, horizontal, or ordinary time; hierarchical, vertical time, or eternity; and heterarchical, deep time, or hyparxis.

11. These terms are partly derived from those that Bennett uses in "The Operations of History," in *The Dramatic Universe*, vol. 4, pp. 76–79.

12. Ordinary speech contains a lot of wisdom. We talk of minding as caring about, concern with, taking as real, and so forth, and we could well call the 3-6 region the *region of minding*.

13. In chapter 15 I called the inner line of work *submission*.

14. See "Lines of Work," in chapter 15.

15. We came across this idea before in "Overview," in chapter 15.

16. I owe this insight to Simon Coxon who is currently working on the structure of the *I Ching*. He personally favors another correlation than the one I have used, taking the lines in the sequence they appear in the enneagram.

17. Edwin Wolfe, *Episodes with Gurdjieff*, p. 11.

18. Father Giovanni, when asked by Prof. Skridlov why he did not return to his native Italy and bring faith to his own people, tells him that faith comes from understanding, and understanding arises only from "true knowledge of past events" and "experiences personally experienced." See Gurdjieff, "Father Giovanni," in *Meetings with Remarkable Men*.

19. Ouspensky, *Strange Life of Ivan Osokin*, p. 208.

20. Gurdjieff, *Beelzebub's Tales*, p. 761. This is the only place where this substance is mentioned.

21. "And why these contemporary theatres of theirs with their contemporary actors have become useful of improving the quality of their sleep was due to the following circumstances" (BT, p. 506).

22. See "Correlations with Centers" in chapter 5.

23. Gurdjieff calls this substance *hanbledzoin* and says that it derives from the planets and sun. Bennett explains it in terms of the strength of essence in contrast with the strength of personality: see J. G. Bennett, *The Way to Be Free*, pp. 65–70.

24. A complete sadhana should encompass the human totality, including body, mind, and heart. Mostly, however, people cultivate only some part of the totality. I looked at this earlier when I discussed Bennett's seven lines of work in chapter 15.

25. There are now virtual organizations that have no premises and next to no permanent staff.

26. In Bennett's system it is called the body of the will, and will correlates with the triad.

27. This is the claim made for Sufism by Idries Shah. See Shah, *The Sufis*.

28. Tantra is sometimes called the left-hand path because it works with the negative principle.

Afterword

THE BEGINNING OF DIALOGUE

GURDJIEFF'S story of two strangers meeting in the desert and sharing their understanding through scratching enneagrams in the sand should be remembered. The enneagram is to be used to enable us to communicate in understanding. The main drawback of a book such as this one is that it comes across as some kind of insular and authoritative statement. In spite of numerous references to the work of other people, there are no voices here except my own, and this can lead to misunderstanding.

It is in the flow of meaning between people—or "dia-logue," in Bohm's term—that the enneagram comes to life. Maybe it can also help us tell better stories; but no good story comes out of rigid adherence to a formula. We must value the uncertainties, the ambiguities, and the range of alternatives that the enneagram throws up. We must be able to enter into the world of the enneagram and then leave it aside, its contribution having been assimilated. So, after their dialogue, the two strangers leave their enneagrams to be wiped out by the wind.

The enneagram is not some kind of ultimate truth. It is a way of contemplating everything we know about something all at once. Just as with a computer, if we put garbage in, then we will get garbage out. I believe that the enneagram points the way to a whole range of symbolic forms, or structures of meaning. All that is essential is some superimposition of two or more forms of understanding and the ability to bring these together into a new synthesis; just as the two eyes combine to produce the sensation of depth and two people coming together in real dialogue can generate a new understanding.

In one of the last chapters of *Beelzebub's Tales* ("Beelzebub Explains to His Grandson the Significance of the Form and Sequence Which He

Chose for Expounding the Information Concerning Man"), Beelzebub describes how new impressions have to be brought together with corresponding ones already in us. This constitutes the essence of understanding. It is nothing like thinking in the ordinary sense. It is the ability to read experience. So we have to remember that the enneagram is written in the language of experience. We need to feel and sense ideas entering into definite locations in us according to their intrinsic nature.

Draw the circle of your life and mark some points of meaning. Draw some connections between them. Make what you draw substantial in terms of what is really in you and not just words. Start to listen to what the diagram says. Find the centers of gravity that come from real experience, and feel and sense how they combine into a definite direction that you can take. Walk through the world with fresh eyes. Learn to think directly in terms of what is.

GLOSSARY

Terms in italics are used as in Gurdjieff's writings and talks.

absolute   The ultimate condition, not to be confused with a being or entity.

action   Technically, energy multiplied by time; the existence of a complete event.

air   The substance or content of the second octave in an enneagram, the intermediary phase associated with cyclicity; energy; memory and learning; hence "remembrance" in Sufism.

autonomy   Living under its own rule.

apparatus   A construction that bridges a critical interval; something that combines uncertainty and mechanism.

biomes   Specific forms of the biosphere on a terrestrial scale, such as the rainforest.

biosphere   The autonomous link between sun and earth, the dynamic transforming power on the surface of the earth; an almost closed cycling of matter which feeds on and generates information.

center   A type of will and perception operating in man—as used in BT and ISM.

coalescence   The fusion of two substances which maintains their independent character.

command   Information in its will-aspect; a rule.

communication   The exchange of information made possible by consciousness.

communion   The stage beyond communication of immediate, nonlocalized, mutual relevance.

community   The togetherness of individuals; the stage beyond the enneagram.

computation   Information in process; everything that exists computes; computation may outstrip actuality, and then we have "mind."

computer   Device for processing coded information.

conscience   The communication link between the lesser and the Greater Present Moment.

conscious shock   Impact of active information; direct perception.

consciousness Used by Bennett in an unusual sense as the unattached side of awareness, which opens the way to cosmic information.

contemplation The way of direct access to the realm of cosmic information—by way of unfolding the implicate order of experience.

cosmic information the cognitive content of the higher energies; traditionally associated with the heavenly bodies.

cosmos A relative whole; a world unto itself—thought of as unifying three worlds in a unique way.

critical transition Where a process changes its nature.

djartklom The instantaneous separation of the three forces of the triad.

drama Where uncertainty and choice meet; complement of *apparatus.*

dyad The power of opposites; the principle of universal uncertainty; the axiom of choice.

earthly Having the character of operating from a location in space and time.

energy The power of action, but also the substance of perception.

enfoldment Idea of Bohm's that structures are folded into each other so that they do not appear but contain the meaning of what happens.

evolution Going from a lower to a higher level of operation.

explicate Term used by Bohm—meaning what is apparent, visible, in time and space.

food The basic stuff of an octave; what is needed to sustain a cosmos; the material of transformation.

freedom An operation of the triad in which something is liberated to enter into new creations on a higher level.

God Any version of ultimate wholeness or source, beyond any form of distinction.

harnelaoot The entrance to the dramatic; the critical moment.

harnelmiatznel Blending of the lower with the higher to actualize the middle.

hazard The intelligent form of sacrifice; what evolution feeds on; "nothing ventured, nothing gained."

hydrogen The density of matter, or the level of existence; used in a special sense in ISM.

implicate order Term used by Bohm to signify the unmanifest levels from which action springs.

impressions Information as food; there are gradations of impressions on different levels which the human can assimilate.

individuality A realization of will as a unity.

information The third category of existence; the regulative principle between matter and energy.

informing Literally, "putting the form in"; the action of bringing in higher information.

intelligence Creation in recurrence; the stable form of newness in the universe; arises wherever the third force of a triad is independent of the other two forces; as an energy, a coalescence of creativity and consciousness. Higher intelligence is not restricted by the properties of a mind based on an organic body.

intentionality The complement of mechanicality.

interval The breath or mark of a movement between levels.

involution Going from a higher to a lower level of operation.

kesdjan **body** Second body; spirit body.

kundabuffer An organ implanted by higher intelligence to distort human perception of reality; as used in BT.

law A cognized pattern of meaning; a meaning that informs cognition.

legominism A means of encoding and transmitting insight; an artifact constructed "not according to law but otherwise"; as used in BT.

level Distinct order of relation, or energy, symbolized by the series of integers.

logos A discrete triad of commands that unfolds from will.

logosphere The sphere of meanings; a reservoir.

matter What is residual; the reference for any action; inertia.

mdnel-in A portal or opening in the processing of events which allows new influences to enter.

meaning Meaning defines itself; the unity of intent and discovery; active information.

mechanism That which repeats almost identically.

mechanicality Where the third force is not independent.

monad A potential cosmos.

noosphere The sphere of mind, proposed reconciliation of the conflict between technology and ecology on earth. It is assumed that this sphere has to develop out of terrestrial memories and is associated with the earth's atmosphere, or subtle body.

obligolnian strivings Categorical imperatives of contact with being; duty inherent in becoming conscious.

octave Scale from a lower do to a higher do (from eight); a span of the "same."

okidanokh   The basic stuff of will (from "soul-carrier"); used in BT.

organic life   The flora, fauna, and foscalia of the earth; used in a technical sense in ISM.

pentad   Five-term system representing dramatic uncertainty.

perception   Information pulled by will.

perfecting   The essential contrast with mere repetition.

phase   A third of an enneagram, such as the points 0, 1, and 2 taken together.

present moment   The basis of perception; a fusion of space and time; through which a will can see; the lesser present moment is mind, the greater present moment is higher intelligence.

ray of creation   The *octave* of the universe spanning all levels within the *absolute*.

reservoir   A buffer-store of "material" which is not structured by any specific function but is freely available to sustain a set of transformations.

second conscious shock   Transformation of negative forces; enters at point 9.

seeing   Where will infuses information.

sensitivity   The ordinary stuff of awareness, in which all life participates.

shock   The means of switching between two different modes of operation.

solar   Has the character of operating from the "plane of infinity" without process.

soolionensius   Period of planetary tension, stimulating new perceptions.

soul   In Gurdjieff's language, the third body, the body of the will.

spirit   The infusion of higher influences; the presence of superior information; usually associated with breath.

synergy   Term used by Bennett to characterize the emergent epoch, in the sense of cooperation between different levels.

technics   Systems utilizing information to control energy and matter.

technosphere   The artificial part of the biosphere.

tetrad   Four-term system in which opposites exchange roles to sustain creation.

third force   The unifying term of the triad, associated with the category of information.

triad   Three-term system; the dynamic heart of meaningful change; the unfoldment of will.

truth   The realization beyond separation and identity.

unfoldment   In Bohm's terminology, the bringing out of what is enfolded into manifestation.

unitive energy   Term used by Bennett to designate integration, or love, the synergic energy.

will   Self-command; the enfoldment of the triad.

word   Traditional form of the concept of the third force as infusing the will of God; connected with information.

world   A totality of conditions corresponding to a certain content of existence.

References

Source Material

Gurdjieff, G. I. *Beelzebub's Tales to His Grandson. All and Everything:* First Series. The original (and best) translation into English is available only from Two Rivers Press, Aurora, Ore.

————. *Life Is Only Real Then, When "I Am," Meetings with Remarkable Men,* and *Views from the Real World* are published by Routledge and Kegan Paul in the United Kingdom and Dutton in the United States.

————, and Thomas de Hartmann. *Complete Piano Music of George I. Gurdjieff and Thomas de Hartmann.* Performed by Cecil Lytle. Tuscon, Ariz: Celestial Harmonies, 1993. CD includes the music for thirty-seven of the movements. The movements themselves are recorded on film and video by the Gurdjieff Foundation but unavailable to the public. However, some of them may be glimpsed in the film made of *Meetings with Remarkable Men,* directed by Peter Brook.

Ouspensky, P. D. *In Search of the Miraculous.* New York: Harcourt, Brace and Co., 1949.

————. *Strange Life of Ivan Osokin.* London: Faber and Faber, 1948.

Bennett, J. G. *Deeper Man.* Santa Fe: Bennett Books, 1994.

————. *The Dramatic Universe.* 4 vols. London: Hodden and Stoughton, 1956, 1961, 1966.

————. *Enneagram Studies.* New York: Samuel Weiser, 1983.

————. *Gurdjieff: Making a New World.* Santa Fe: Bennett Books, 1992.

————. *Hazard: The Risk of Realisation.* Santa Fe: Bennett Books, 1991.

————. *Sacred Influences.* Santa Fe: Bennett Books, 1990.

————. *Sevenfold Work,* London: Coombe Springs Press, 1979.

————. *Sex.* York Beach, Me.: Samuel Weiser, 1981.

————. *Talks on Beelzebub's Tales.* York Beach, Me.: Samuel Weiser, 1988.

————. *The Way to Be Free.* York Beach, Me.: Samuel Weiser, 1992.

————. *Witness.* London: Hodder and Stoughton, 1962.

Enneagram-related Books

Various writings concerning the enneagram, not published in books, are in circulation. There are, for example, applications of the enneagram in businesses, and material on a possible Armenian Zoroastrian source for the enneagram has been available through e-mail. Among various books containing material on some version of the enneagram, I can mention the following, in illustration of the variety.

Bakhtiar, Laleh. *Traditional Psychoethics and Personality Paradigm*. Chicago: Kazi Publications, 1993. The author claims the enneagram (she does not use that term) for Islamic thought (see below). Her diagrams are more complex than in the standard version, but no explanation is given of their derivation, nor is Gurdjieff mentioned.

Blake, A. G. E., ed. *Enneagram Studies*. New York: Samuel Weiser, 1983. A collection of all the material available from the writings of J. G. Bennett and his pupils. See also the general bibliography under A. G. E. Blake (page 369).

Jung, C. G. *Psychology and Alchemy*. Princeton, N.J.: Princeton University Press, 1970. Not explicitly dealing with the enneagram, it nevertheless contains material that directly illuminates the principles and is an invaluable resource.

Kabbani, Shaykh Muhammad Hisham. *The Naqshbandi Sufi Way: History and Guidebook of the Saints of the Golden Chain*. Chicago: Kazi Publications, 1995. The chapter "A Meeting with Gurdjieff" contains an obscure, and evocative, reference to the "knowledge of the nine points": "Each one of the nine points is represented by one of nine saints who are at the highest level in the Divine Presence."

Naranjo, Claudio. *Character and Neurosis: An Integrative View*. Nevada City: Gateways/IDDHB, 1994. The most substantial of the numerous books on Ichazo's enneagram of personality types, backed by academically sound psychological concepts.

Nicoll, Maurice. *Psychological Commentaries on the Teaching of Gurdjieff and Ouspensky*, vol. 2. London: Vincent Stewart, 1952; York Beach, Me.: Samuel Weiser, 1996. This volume contains the basic teaching about the enneagram as given through Ouspensky.

Norelli-Bachelet, Patricia. *The Gnostic Circle*. New York: Weiser, 1978. An interesting study, from an Aurobindean point of view, of the enneagram and the zodiac. The author has the fascinating idea that the enneagram represents Shakti, the Divine Mother.

Palmer, Helen. *The Pocket Enneagram*. San Francisco: Harper, 1995. This is the most accessible and brief version of the "fixationist" scheme. It includes material on interpreting the inner lines in terms of work on oneself.

Smith, Russell. *Gurdjieff: Cosmic Secrets*. Sanger, Tex.: The Dog, 1993. An enthusiastic attempt to sort out the numbers introduced in Gurdjieff's teaching of the octave, with numerous diagrams and calculations. The author attempts to incorporate the structure of DNA, only he uses an incorrect form.

General Bibliography

Abercrombie, Margaret. *The Anatomy of Judgement*. London: Free Association Books, 1989

Adams, Douglas. *The Restaurant at the End of the Universe*. London: Pan Books, 1989.

Adams, George. *Physical and Ethereal Spaces*. London: Rudolf Steiner Press, 1978.

Albert, David. "Bohm's Alternative to Quantum Mechanics," in *Scientific American*, May 1994.

Allen, John. *Biosphere 2: A Human Experiment*. Edited by A. G. E. Blake. New York: Penguin Viking, 1993.

Aristotle, *Poetics*. Translated by John Warrington. London: Dent and Sons, 1963.

Anirvan, Sri, and Lizelle Reymond. *To Live Within*. Masham: Coombe Springs Press, 1984.

Aurobindo, Sri. *The Synthesis of Yoga*. Pondicherry, 1970.

Bailey, Alice. *The Externalisation of the Hierarchy*. New York: Lucis Press, 1981.

Bauval, Robert, and Adrian Gilbert. *The Orion Mystery*. London: Heinemann, 1994.

Bennett, Elizabeth. *Idiots in Paris*. Daglingworth: Coombe Springs Press, 1980.

Berger, John. *A Fortunate Man*. New York: Pantheon, 1982.

Blake, A. G. E. *Intelligence Now*. Sherborne: Coombe Springs Press, 1975. Hypertext version, Blake and Co. 1995.

———. *A Seminar on Time*. Charles Town, W. Va.: Claymont Communications, 1989.

———. *An Index to "In Search of the Miraculous."* Charles Town, W. Va.: Claymont Communications, 1992.

———. "Artificial Worlds: The Enneagram of Closed Engineered Ecological Systems" in *Impressions* (Journal of the Claymont Society, Charles Town, W. Va.) 8, no. 1 (1994).

———. "Business as Transformation," in *Future Management*, no. 2 (1995) (Centre for Management Creativity, Seattle).

———. *The Triad*. Bridgewater: Duversity Special Publication, 1995.

———. *Structures of Meaning*. Bridgewater: Duversity Publications, 1996.

———. "The Three Levels of Learning in Self-Organisation; Beyond Survival in the Twenty-first Century." *CMC Newsletter*, July 1996.

Blake, Anthony (ed.). *Enneagram Studies*. New York: Samuel Weiser, 1983.

Blake, William. *Complete Writings*. Oxford: Oxford University Press, 1969.

Boehme, Jacob. Translated by John Sparrow. *Concerning the Three Principles of the Divine Essence, the Eternal Dark Light and the Temporary World*. London: John Watkins, 1910.

———. *How a Man May Find Himself and So Finding Come to All the Mysteries, Even to the Ninth Number, Yet No Higher*. Edmonds: Sure Fire Press, 1990.

Bohm, David. *Causality and Chance in Modern Physics*. London: Routledge and Kegan Paul, 1959.

———. *Unfolding Meaning*. Mickelton, Gloucestershire: Foundation House, 1985.

———. *Wholeness and the Implicate Order*. London: Routledge and Kegan Paul, 1980.

———. *On Dialogue*. Ojai, Calif.: David Bohm Seminars, 1990.

———. *Thought as a System.* London: Routledge and Kegan Paul, 1994.

Bohm, David, and B. J. Hiley. *The Undivided Universe.* London: Routledge and Kegan Paul, 1993.

Botkin, Daniel. *Discordant Harmonies.* Oxford: Oxford University Press, 1990.

Brenan, Martin. *The Boyne Valley Vision.* Portlaoise: Dolmen Press, 1980.

Butts, R. E., ed. *Theory of Scientific Method.* Indianapolis: Hackett Publishing Co., 1989.

Castaneda, Carlos. *The Eagle's Gift.* New York: Simon and Schuster, 1981.

Caussade, Jean-Pierre de. *The Sacrament of the Present Moment.* London: Harper-Collins, 1989.

Chomsky, Noam. *Reflections on Language.* London: Fontana, 1978.

Chyba, Christopher, and Carl Sagan. "Endogenous Production, Exogenous Delivery and Impact-Shock Synthesis of Organic Molecules: an Inventory for the Origins of Life," in *Nature,* 9 January 1992.

Climacus, Johannus. *Ladder of Divine Ascent.* New York: Paulist Press, 1982.

Club of Rome. *Limits to Growth.* London: Earth Island, 1972.

Collin, Rodney. *The Theory of Eternal Life.* Cape Town: Stourton Press, 1960.

———. *The Theory of Celestial Influence.* London: Vincent Stuart, 1954.

———. *The Christian Mystery.* Mexico: Ediciones de Sol, 1954.

Crawford, H. J., and C. H. Greiner. "The Search for Strange Matter," in *Scientific American,* January 1994.

Crombie, A. C. *Science, Optics and Music in Medieval and Early Modern Thought.* London: Hambledon Press, 1990.

Dante. *Divine Comedy.* 3 vols. London: Penguin Books, 1990.

Daumal, Réne. *Mount Analogue.* London: Penguin, 1974.

Davidson, James, and William Rees-Mogg. *The Great Reckoning.* London: Pan, 1993.

Davies, Paul. "Why is the Physical World So Comprehensible?," in *Complexity, Entropy and the Physics of Information.* Edited by W. H. Zurek. Santa Fe Institute, 1991.

Dawkins, Richard. *The Blind Watchmaker.* London: Penguin Books, 1990.

Dick, Philip K. *In Pursuit of Valis.* Edited by Sutton. Calif.: Underwood-Miller, 1991.

———. *The Divine Invasion.* New York: Vintage Books, 1991.

———. *Valis.* New York: Vintage Books, 1991.

———. *The Shifting Realities of Philip K. Dick.* New York: Pantheon, 1995.

Douglas, Mary. *In the Wilderness, the Doctrine of Defilement in the Book of Numbers.* Sheffield: University of Sheffield Academic Press, 1993.

Eliade, Mircea. *The Myth of Eternal Return: or, Cosmos and History.* Princeton: Princeton University Press, 1991.

Eliot, T. S. *Four Quartets.* London: Faber and Faber, 1955.

Engels, F. *Ludwig Fuerbach and the Outcome of Classical German Philosophy.* Lawrence and Wishart, 1941.

Ernst, Bruno. *The Eye Beguiled.* Cologne: Benedikt Taschen, 1992.

Evola, Julius. *The Metaphysics of Sex.* London: East-West Publications, 1983.

Feyerabend, Paul. *Against Method.* London: Verso, London, 1978.

Feynman, Richard. *QED: The Strange Theory of Light and Matter.* Princeton, N.J.: Princeton University Press, 1985.

Fisher, Hal. *A History of Europe.* London: Eyre and Spottiswoode, 1935.

Fort, Charles. *Book of the Damned.* Ace Books, 1941.

Foster, David. *The Philosophical Scientists.* C. Hurst and Co., 1985.

———. *The Intelligent Universe: A Cybernetic Philosophy.* New York: Putnam, 1975.

Foster, David, and Pamela Tudor-Craig. *The Secret Life of Paintings.* London: Boydell Press, 1986.

Frankl, Viktor. *Man's Search for Meaning.* London: Hodder and Stoughton, 1964.

Fuller, Buckminster. *Cosmography.* New York: Macmillan, 1992.

Gebser, Jean. *The Ever-Present Origin.* Athens, Ohio: Ohio University Press, 1991.

Gibson, William. *Neuromancer.* London: HarperCollins, 1995.

Gibson, William and Bruce Sterling. *The Difference Engine.* London: Gollanz, 1992.

Gleick, James. *Chaos.* London: Sphere Books, 1987.

Gold, T. "The Deep, Hot Biosphere," in *Proceedings of the National Academy of Science,* July 1992.

Gould, Stephen Jay. *Wonderful Life.* New York: Norton, 1989.

Guénon, René. *Lord of the World.* London: Coombe Springs Press, 1983.

Harding, Douglas Edison. *The Hierarchy of Heaven and Earth: A New Diagram of Man in the Universe.* London: Faber & Faber, 1952.

Harten, Marjorie von. "Religion and Culture in the Ancient Americas," in *Systematics* 1, no. 1.

de Hartmann, Thomas and Olga. *Our Life with Mr. Gurdjieff.* New York: Harper and Row, 1964.

Havel, Vaclav. Quoted in *Newsweek,* 18 July 1994.

Heath, Richard. "Some Possible Achievements for Megalithic Astronomy, from Harmonies of the Sky." Unpublished paper.

Heath, Robin. *A Key to Stonehenge.* St. Dogmaels: Bluestone Press, 1993.

Heinlein, Robert. *The Puppet Masters.* London: New English Library, 1981.

Herbert, Frank. *Dosadi Experiment.* Berkeley: Berkeley Publications, 1984.

Hodges, Andrew. *The Enigma of Intelligence.* London: Unwin, 1983.

Ibsen, Henrik. *Peer Gynt.* London: Penguin Books, 1970.

———. *Hedda Gabbler.* London: Penguin Books, 1971.

Jacques, Elliott with R. O. Gibson, and D. J. Isaac. *Levels of Abstraction in Logic and Human Action.* London: Heinemann, 1978.

James, William. *A Pluralistic Universe.* London: Longmans, 1909.

Jaynes, Julian. *The Origin of Consciousness in the Breakdown of the Bicameral Mind.* Boston: Houghton-Mifflin, 1976.

Jonas, Hans. *The Gnostic Religion.* Boston: Beacon Press, 1963.

Jung, C. G. *Psychology and Alchemy.* Princeton, N.J.: Princeton University Press, 1970.

Kaufman, Stuart. "Antichaos and Adaption." in *Scientific American,* August 1991.

Kirk. G. S., and J. E. Raven. *The Presocratic Philosophers.* CUP, 1957.

Klee, Paul. *Notebooks.* Vol. 1, *The Thinking Eye.* Ed. Jurg Spiller. London: Lund Humphries, 1961.

Knedler, John, ed. *Masterworks of Science.* New York: McGraw-Hill, 1973.

Knuth, D. E. *Surreal Numbers.* London: Addison-Wesley, 1974.

Krishnamurti, J., and David Bohm. *The Ending of Time.* London: Gollanz, 1985.

Lapo, A. *Traces of Bygone Biospheres.* Moscow: Mir Publishers, 1982.

Lawrence, D. H. *The Rainbow.* London: Penguin Books, 1969.

Lem, Stanislaw. *One Human Minute.* London: Mandarin, Andre Deutsch, 1991.

————. *Microworlds.* Harcourt Brace Jovanovich, 1986.

Leonardo da Vinci. *The Notebooks of Leonardo da Vinci.* Translated by E. MacCurdy. London: Jonathon Cape, 1956.

Lessing, Doris. *Shikasta.* New York: Knopf, 1979.

————. *The Making of the Representative for Planet Eight.* New York: Knopf, 1982.

Levy, Steven. *Artificial Life.* London: Jonathon Cape, 1992.

Lewis, C. S. *Out of the Silent Planet.* London: Allen Lane, 1938.

————. *That Hideous Strength.* London: Allen Lane, 1945.

————. *The Great Divorce.* London: Geoffrey Bles, 1946.

Lindsay, David. *Voyage to Arcturus.* London: Macmillan, 1963.

Lorenz, Konrad. *Behind the Mirror.* London: Methuen, 1977.

Lovelock, James. *The Ages of Gaia.* New York: Norton, 1988.

Margulis, Lynn, and Dorian Sagan. *Microcosmos.* New York: Summit Books, 1986.

Marshack, Alexander. *The Roots of Civilisation.* London: Weidenfield and Nicholson, 1972.

Martin, Thomas Commerford. *The Inventions, Researches and Writings of Nikola Tesla.* Hollywood: Angriff Press, 1981.

Matchett, Edward. *Journeys of Nothing in the Land of Everything.* London: Turnstone Press, 1975.

Medewar, Peter. "Is the Scientific Paper a Fraud?" In *Experiment (A Series of Case Histories).* British Broadcasting System, 1964.

Miller, Henry. *Tropic of Capricorn.* London: Flamingo, 1993.

Monod, Jacques. *Chance and Necessity.* New York: Random House, 1972.

Moore, James. *Gurdjieff: The Anatomy of a Myth.* Shaftesbury: Element, 1993.

————. "The Enneagram: A Developmental Study," In *Religion Today* 5, no. 3.

Mourelatos, A. P. D., ed. *The Pre-Socratics.* New York: Doubleday, 1974.

Mumford, Lewis. *Technics and Civilisation.* London: Routledge and Kegan Paul, 1946.

Nagel, Ernest, and James Newman. *Gödel's Proof.* New York: New York University Press, 1974.

Naranjo, Claudio. *Character and Neurosis: An Integrative View.* Nevada City: Gateways/IDHHB, 1994.

Needham, Joseph. *Science and Civilisation in China.* Cambridge: Cambridge University Press, 1954.

Negroponte, Nicholas. "Less Is More: Interface Agents as Digital Butlers," in *Wired,* June 1994.

Nicolescu, Basarab. *Science, Meaning and Evolution.* New York: Parabola Books, 1991.

Nicoll, Maurice. *Psychological Commentaries on the Teaching of G. I. Gurdjieff and P. D. Ouspensky.* London: Vincent Stuart, 1952. York Beach, Me.: Samuel Weiser, 1996.

Nietzsche, Freiderich. *Thus Spake Zarathustra.* London: Penguin Books, 1961.

Norelli-Bachelet, Patrizia. *The Gnostic Circle.* New York: Samuel Weiser, 1978.

Odum, E. P. *Ecology and Our Endangered Life-Support Systems.* Sunderland, Mass.: Sinauer Associates, 1989.

Orage, Alfred Richard. *On Love, with Some Aphorisms and Other Essays.* London: Janus Press, 1957.

Palmer, Helen. *The Enneagram.* San Francisco: HarperSanFrancisco, 1991.

Pascal, Blaise. *Pensees.* Oxford: Oxford University Press, 1995.

Peirce, Charles Sanders. *Essential Peirce.* Vol. 1. (1867–1893). Edited by Nathan Houser and Christian Klösel. Bloomington: Indiana University Press, 1992.

Penrose, Roger. *The Emperor's New Mind.* Oxford: Oxford University Press, 1990.

Pensinger, William, and Cong Huyen Yon Nu Nha Trang. *The Moon of Hoa Bingh: A Novel.* Phra Singh, Thailand: Autopoy, 1995.

Pledge, Ken. "Structured Process in Scientific Experiment," in J. G. Bennett, *Enneagram Studies.*

Pogson, Beryl. *In the East My Pleasure Lies: and Other Esoteric Interpretations of Plays by William Shakespeare.* York: Quacks Books, 1994.

Popper, Karl. *The Logic of Scientific Discovery.* London: Routledge, 1992.

Popper, Karl, and John Eccles. *The Self and Its Brain.* London: Routledge, 1990.

Priestly, J. B. *Man and Time.* New York: Dell Publishing, 1968.

Reage, Pauline [Dominique Aury, pseud.]. *The Story of O.* London: Corgi Books, 1972.

Renfern, Colin. "World Linguistic Diversity," in *Scientific American,* January 1994.

Rilke, Rainer Maria. *Duino Elegies.* Translated by Leishman and Spender. London: Hogarth Press, 1963.

Robinson, Kim Stanley. *Red Mars.* London: HarperCollins, 1993.

———. *Green Mars.* London: HarperCollins, 1993.

———. *Blue Mars.* London: HarperCollins, 1993.

Rucker, Rudy. *Mind Tools: The Five Levels of Mathematical Reality.* London: Penguin, 1987.

Russell, Bertrand. *Principles of Mathematics.* London: Allen and Unwin, 1951.

Sagan, Dorian. *Biospheres: Metamorphosis of Planet Earth.* London: Arkana, 1990.

de Santillana, Giorgio, and Hertha von Dechend. *Hamlet's Mill: An Essay on Myth and the Frame of Time.* Cambridge: Gambit, 1969.

Sartre, Jean-Paul. *Being and Nothingness.* Translated by Hazel Barnes. London: Methuen, 1957.

Schwartzman, D., M. McMenamin, and T. Volk, "Did Surface Temperatures Constrain Microbial Evolution?" in *Bioscience* 43, no. 6.

Senge, Peter. *The Fifth Discipline.* London: Century Business, 1990.

References

Shah, Idries. *Tales of the Dervishes.* London: Jonathan Cape, 1969.

Sherrard, Philip. *The Greek East and the Latin West.* Oxford: Oxford University Press, 1959.

Spengler, Oswald. *Man and Technics.* London: Allen and Unwin, 1932.

Stapledon, Olaf. *Starmaker.* London: Penguin, 1979.

Steiner, Rudolf. *Speech and Drama.* Anthroposophical Publishing Company, 1960.

Subuh, Pak. *Susila Budhi Dharma.* Subud Brotherhood, 1959.

Sullivan, William. *Secret of the Incas: Myth, Astronomy, and the War with Time.* Crown, 1996.

Tudor-Craig, Pamela, and Richard Foster. *The Secret Life of Paintings.* Boydell Press, 1986.

Varela, Francisco. *Principles of Biological Autonomy.* New York: North Holland, 1979.

Varela, Francisco, Thompson, Evan and Rosch, Eleanor. *The Embodied Mind.* Cambridge: MIT, 1991.

Vernadsky, Vladimir. *The Biosphere.* Tucson: Biosphere Press, 1986.

Vizinczey, Stephen. *The Rules of Chaos.* London: Macmillan, 1969.

Waddington, C. H. *The Ethical Animal.* London: Allen and Unwin, 1960.

Walker, Kenneth. *A Study of Gurdjieff's Teaching.* London: Jonathon Cape, 1957.

Webb, James. *The Harmonious Circle.* London: Thames and Hudson, 1980.

Weil, Simone. *Intimations of Christianity Amongst the Greeks.* London: Routledge and Kegan Paul, 1957.

———. *Waiting on God.* London: Routledge and Kegan Paul, 1952.

———. *Selected Essays, 1934–43.* Oxford: Oxford University Press, 1962.

———. *Formative Writings 1929–1941.* London: Routledge and Kegan Paul, 1987.

Weightman, Simon. "Symmetry and Symbolism in Shaikh Manjhan's *Madhumalti.*" In *The Indian Narrative: Perspectives and Patterns.* Edited by C. Shackle and R. Snell. Wiesbaden: O. H. 1992.

Wells, H. G. *Mind at the End of its Tether.* London: William Heinemann, 1945.

———. *The Shape of Things to Come.* London: Everyman, 1993.

Wilson, Edward O. *Biophilia.* Cambridge: Harvard University Press, 1984.

———. *On Human Nature.* Cambridge: Harvard University Press, 1978.

Wolfe, Edwin. *Episodes with Gurdjieff.* San Francisco: Far West Press, 1980.

Yates, Frances. *The Art of Memory.* London: Penguin Books, 1966.

Young, Arthur. *The Reflexive Universe.* New York: Robert Briggs, 1984.

Zaehner, R. C. *Zurvan: a Zoroastrian Dilemma.* Oxford: Oxford University Press, 1955.

Zureck, W. H., ed. *Complexity, Entropy, and the Physics of Information.* Redwood City: Santa Fe Institute, Addison-Wesley, 1990.

Relevant Movies

Babette's Feast, directed by Gabriel Axel, 1987.

Bladerunner, directed by Ridley Scott, 1982.

Demon Seed, directed by Donald Cammell, 1977.

Iceman, directed by Fred Schepisi, 1971.

The Kitchen, directed by James Hill, 1961.

Meetings with Remarkable Men, directed by Peter Brook, 1977.

Orlando, directed by Sally Porter, 1992.

Solaris, directed by Andrei Tarkovsky, 1972.

The Terminator, directed by James Cameron. 1984.

Terminator 2, directed by James Cameron, 1991.

Things to Come, directed by William C. Menzies, 1936.

Total Recall, directed by Paul Verheoven, 1990.

Tron, directed by Stephen Lisberger, 1982.

Until the End of the World, directed by Wim Wenders, 1991.

The Wife, the Cook and the Lover, directed by Peter Greenway, 1989.

Index

This is by no means a comprehensive index, only a starting point for recapitulating points of interest. Included are significant references given in notes. The words in italics are non-English words, Gurdjieffian terms, or titles, given with approximate translations where necessary. A separate index of proper names follows this one.

Index of Proper Names

The names Gurdjieff, Bennett, and Ouspensky are not included in this listing, since they appear so frequently.